MASH FAQ

MASH FAQ

Everything Left to Know About the Best Care Anywhere

Dale Sherman

APPLAUSE
THEATRE & CINEMA BOOKS
An Imprint of Hal Leonard Corporation

Copyright © 2016 by Dale Sherman

Published in 2016 by Applause Books
An Imprint of Hal Leonard Corporation
7777 West Bluemound Road
Milwaukee, WI 53213

Trade Book Division Editorial Offices
33 Plymouth St., Montclair, NJ 07042

All images are from the author's collection unless otherwise noted.

The FAQ series was conceived by Robert Rodriguez and developed with Stuart Shea.

Printed in the United States of America

Book design by Snow Creative Services

Library of Congress Cataloging-in-Publication Data

Names: Sherman, Dale.
Title: M. A. S. H. FAQ : everything left to know about the best care anywhere
 / Dale Sherman.
Other titles: MASH FAQ
Description: Milwaukee, WI : Applause Theatre & Cinema Books, 2016. |
 Includes bibliographical references and index.
Identifiers: LCCN 2015042244 | ISBN 9781480355897 (pbk.)
Subjects: LCSH: Hooker, Richard. MASH. | Korean War, 1950-1953—Literature
 and the war. | MASH (Motion picture) | M*A*S*H (Television program)
Classification: LCC PS3558.O55 M3755 2016 | DDC 791.45/72--dc23
LC record available at http://lccn.loc.gov/2015042244

www.applausebooks.com

Dedicated to my brother Lowell, who watched often with me as we grew up, and can still do the "only two endings to every episode of *MASH*"

Contents

Acknowledgments

T hanks to Brian Schnau and Mike DeGeorge, who as always tried to give me editing suggestions early on, and I apologize to them for not getting them more involved this time around. Thanks to RJ at the MASH4077tv.com website for his enthusiasm and assistance, especially in the "Running of the Nurses" chapter. Thanks to Ed Barreveld at Storyline Entertainment for his assistance with a photo question, and both Lori Martin and Joel Woodard with additional photo opportunities related to *MASH* products. Thanks to JoAnne Hudock for allowing me to use her photos of the action figures for the toy chapter. I also greatly appreciate Willie Hornberger allowing me to use the picture of his father in this book, and for his correspondences—I only wish we could have talked more.

Thanks to everyone at Applause Books for their patience and hard work with the editing of this volume in the FAQ series. Thanks to my family for their patience as I worked on the manuscript. Most of all, thanks to H. Richard Hornberger, Robert Altman, Larry Gelbart, Alan Alda, and all others involved with the creation of *MASH* in all its various forms over the year. Some may have disagreed with other visions, but all took a hand in creating a fictional world that reverberated in reality since the late 1960s.

Introduction

And Then There Was Korea

MASH is no more.

That statement is certainly self-evident when discussing the television series known as MASH that ran on the CBS network for eleven years—nearly four times longer than the conflict it used as its basis. The last original episode of the series, "Goodbye, Farewell and Amen," aired on the CBS network on February 28, 1983. The finale became the most-watched program ever to have aired on American television, keeping that distinction for twenty-seven years; while the previous seasons of the program had already gone into syndication, with repeats of the various episodes already airing at multiple times of day around the U.S. and the world. In the end, the television series would jump-start the careers of many of the actors, writers, producers, and directors of the program during the course of the production history of the show and beyond. Yet, even with that history cemented for all to see—and even with brief nods to the past in the years to come (through documentaries, interviews, and even commercials)—there would be no more new MASH episodes; no more antics of Hawkeye, Houlihan, and the rest; no more studies into the nature of people—or, rather, Americans—struggling to stay human in the Korean War. MASH was gone.

Of course, MASH would not have been possible without the success of the 1970 film of the same name (with or without asterisks, but I'll get back to that annoyance in a few paragraphs). The movie solidified Robert Altman's career as a movie director after years of television work and a couple of low-budget films. Without the popularity of the movie, the series never would have *happened*, and a number of actors from the movie found themselves propelled into fame and fortune just like those from the later television series. The film would go on to win an Oscar for Best Screenplay and is listed by the Library of Congress as being "culturally significant," and subsequently released on a number of formats, from 8mm film to videotape, to laserdisc, to DVD and Blu-ray. Yet, although deemed a classic, it lives even further back in the minds of the general public—some of whom may even be big fans of the television series, but had never seen the movie that helped get the long-running series started. A situation that may help explain the divide between fans of the movie and fans of the series as to which is better; a shift that included the director of the film as well.

And if the movie is forgotten, there is definitely something to be said as to the interest the public has about the original novel, *MASH: A Novel About Three Army Doctors*. The book was released in 1968 after numerous attempts to get it published, which led to the film and the series that followed, as well as all the mass merchandising and memories of fans worldwide. Yet how many have read the novel? Or know that the author would attempt to establish a literary franchise that went on for years once it was clear that the characters of the first novel had a life of their own? Sure, some may have finally gotten around to reading the original novel, but what about the two sequels done by Richard Hooker (aka H. Richard Hornberger) after that? Or the twelve-book series of satirical novels concocted by William E Butterworth, a writer mainly known for his military action novels? Some don't even realize how different the novel is from the movie based on it, not to mention that there is another, alternate history to these characters from the movie and television series thanks to the various literary sequels.

Nevertheless, even with all this expansion of the *MASH* mythology from 1968 through 1983, after the television series there have been no new aspects of this universe. From an entertainment standpoint, *MASH*—or *M*A*S*H*, or all other variations of how the name looks—certainly was done and has been done for decades.

And is it *MASH*? *M*A*S*H*? *M-A-S-H*? Sure, it's all pronounced the same, but from a purely visual look, how should the title appear? It may sound silly, but it is a debate in fan circles that has gone on for years. When the military established the mobile army surgical hospital, it made sense to call it MASH (there would soon be variations of this naming, but the title of MASH for such units continued for many years even after they were no longer officially called such). When the Richard Hooker novel was released, the established naming remained, with the novel being called *MASH*. Then comes the movie, and the studio, 20th Century-Fox, decided that the title needed to be stated in some fashion to make sure people knew it was not

A rare promotional Christmas photo of the cast from the last years of the television series.

just a "mash" of things. Thus came the asterisks between each letter, making the title *M*A*S*H*. Then the series came along, and the movie titling stuck as well, although some official items related to the program would revert to simply *MASH* (Arlene and Alan Alda's book *The Last Days of MASH* is a good example of this). With this in mind, while switching back and forth between the various ways of titling the movie, show, and book could be done, after a while it may seem a bit confusing (not to mention a good chance of the author goofing up and using the wrong style in reference to one or the other). Thus, for the sake of sanity, anything related to the real *MASH* and subsequent fictional *MASH*s will be referred to without the asterisks.

Beyond the field of entertainment, stopping for good is also what happened to the very thing that *MASH*—in all of its various creative forms—was based on. In 2006, the last mobile army surgical hospital (MASH) of the U.S. Army—the 212th—was closed in Pakistan, due to the changeover to the larger, more effective combat support hospital (CSH) created in the 1970s. The speed and efficiency of transporting wounded soldiers and others from the field to a place of safety to receive complete hospital care through the CSH made the use of the older MASH less effective, if not obsolete in many cases. Progress had pushed the old concept of the MASH unit out of the way.

And thus, all that remains now of this fascinating spark of life in this vast crazed hell of war is what we have seen in a theater, watched on television, or read in a book. And it has remained popular through the years, telling us stories that humanize the military and the doctors not only of the war it is based on, but of any war. And although the series has had its fair share of criticism over the years—from suggestions of "political correctness" to accusations of racism and certainly signs of misogyny in all its various forms—the image of what we've seen in *MASH* is what we know today as the Korean War.

Which in some ways is a disservice to both *MASH* in all its various incarnations in both fiction and reality. No doubt, there are many reading this due to their interest in the series (which can be broken down further into periods that fans like or dislike more than others). For many, the concerns in this book should be on what was done there instead of what happened elsewhere. Yet, to really understand the program and the reaction of the characters, as well as our own reactions to them, we need to go further in-depth. Beyond the series, the movie, the books, and even the war itself. Somehow, what started as just another military comedy based on a semifantastical remembrance of one man's wartime stay shaped movies, television, and our perceptions of war and politics in the 1970s that still reverberates today.

In other words, in order to really understand what *MASH* is all about, we have to understand the reality that gave birth to the fiction, and a fiction that helped shaped our reality.

It Was in All the Papers for a While

A Brief History of Korea and the Forgotten War

When Larry Gelbart, the man who helped "develop" *MASH* for television, passed away, Alan Alda paid tribute to the man in an article for the *Los Angeles Times*. Amongst the memories mentioned was one of Gelbart telling Alda about the ending the writer had envisioned for the program: "At the very end, the camera would pull back and reveal the fake set with its lights and crew, even the snack stand and its coffee pot and peanut butter jar—as if to say, we know this was just a show, the real people in this story really hurt and died." It would have been a fascinating way to end the long-running series, but in a way it would have also been a repeat of a message already given in the program in the first season many years before.

In "Yankee Doodle Doctor," a first-season episode of the television series written by Laurence Marks, both Hawkeye and Trapper John get annoyed with a documentary being filmed at the 4077th about the doctors' work on soldiers; in particular with Frank Burns' script for the film that makes them all out to be "saints in surgical garb." The pair sabotage the filming and later the film itself by turning it into a comedy that mocks Frank's narratives. However, the comedy comes to an end in the final scene of the movie, as Hawkeye is shown sitting in front of a wounded soldier. Talking directly to the camera, Hawkeye explains the fifty-fifty chances of a soldier making it through being wounded in a battle and how the doctors can only do so much to save them. He ends his speech by saying that war is not a movie. Gelbart's imagined concluding shock of the series had already been stated within weeks of the show's premiere: The fantasy of fiction, even when it is close to the facts, can only remain a fiction.

There is no doubt that *MASH*—in all of its forms—has assisted in keeping the Korean War in the memory of the American public decades after its end in 1953. Perhaps even more so than some of the other wars that occurred before and—unfortunately—since. With so much history to remember, even World War II has become a bit of a fuzzy memory for many Americans; at least those who did not have parents of age that lived through the war firsthand. Going further back, ask anyone what the Spanish-American War was about and you'd be lucky to get a hesitant "Teddy Roosevelt fought in that one, didn't he?" Yet anyone who has seen an episode or two of *MASH* can at least say that it was a war fought somewhere in the middle of the twentieth century and involved Americans trying to help the South Koreans against the North Koreans and/or the Chinese.

At the same time, *MASH* has been a hindrance to many people's understanding of the war and even Korea itself; a program that helps perpetuate iconoclastic images that do not fit into the reality it is based on. Beyond the obvious time differences of a three-year war being fought for more than eleven years on television, there are other clear indications that things are not quite clear anymore to viewers and readers as to what the war was about. Even the film gets details wrong for various reasons—some of which were intentional and will be mentioned further on. Because of this, fans can walk away from the series believing certain things happened before, during, and after the war that are not correct. People forget that the Korean War was not a little dustup that was "won" by anyone in particular; nor that our involvement came about after years of concern toward another country's well-being. Or even that it was about "fighting the communists." Americans stirred that pot with many others to create the climate leading to the war, and the results were not as pleasant as the series had no choice but to portray for a network television program of the 1970s.

Plainly, the series had a tendency to skirt over major hunks of the history that is the Korean War. We know that there were battles and the line between the two sides would change, but little else. General Douglas MacArthur gets a lot of mention because he would become bitterly entangled with the memories of that war, and his successor, General Matthew Ridgway, is mentioned often (sometimes not even in the correct chronological order of events), but General Mark Clark, who was there to see the war end, is unimportant in the television series. Kim Il Sung—the leader of the North Koreans and instigator of the attacks that started the war—is rarely mentioned; the same with his counterpart, Syngman Rhee, in the south.

Truman, Eisenhower, Mao, and Stalin—all major individuals involved in the war—are simply punch lines to jokes. You hear of Seoul and Tokyo, but American towns and cities (even fictional ones) got more airplay on the series than important locations in the war such as Pyongyang, Pohang, and Inchon. Pork Chop Hill—a pivotal, bloody, and ultimately senseless battle that has been the subject of theatrical movies, and which would have made for a strong episode of the series—is mentioned offhandedly near the end of the show as if not important.

These and many other topics should be examined to compare the reality of the Korean War and the fiction of *MASH*. As much as we can praise the series for allowing us to remember this moment in our collective world history, as Hawkeye said early in the program, war isn't a movie. In some cases, what really happened sounds more like a movie than what we see in theaters anyway.

Where Is Korea?

The whole of Korea is a peninsula that mainly borders China in a northeastern segment of the continent of Asia, extending east and southward of the mainland. For Americans, think of how part of Florida dips southward in the U.S., but then take that tail and attached it to Long Island and you'll have a good idea of how Korea fits adjacent to China. The uppermost northeastern tip of the country borders Russia. The border that separates Korea from China and Russia is made up of two rivers—the Yalu (referred to as the Amrok in Korea) and the Tumen—with the Paektu Mountains, containing an active volcano, in-between the rivers. The entirety of Korea covers 85,232 square miles, with North Korea containing a little over 46,540 square miles and South Korea at a bit over 38,691 square miles.

Korea is also very close to Japan, with the distance between the Tsushima Island, Japan, and Geoje, South Korea, being only 60 miles, and only 342 miles between Kosong, North Korea, and Matsue, Japan. Such a short distance certainly has added a reason for why Japan and North Korea have built up a war of words and sometimes firepower over the years (although there is a longer history there for such animosity, as described further on); not to mention why the Japanese repeatedly looked to Korea to conquer in the early part of the twentieth century.

After World War II, Korea was sliced into two countries—North and South Korea, with a border that stretches 148 miles inland from the Yellow Sea in the West and the Sea of Japan in the East. The border includes the

Central Intelligence Agency map of North and South Korea from 1983.

Courtesy of the Library of Congress, Geography and Map Division

Korean Demilitarized Zone (DMZ) with a width of approximately 2.5 miles. It is there to protect or deter (depending on which side one asks) civilians on both sides from considering the possibilities of making a race to the other. Not that it has kept several from trying and some succeeding (typically, and ironically, by crossing over into China in order to avoid the border between North and South). Although commonly thought of as being a straight line following the path of the 38th parallel, the border between North and South actually begins to the southwest of the parallel and crosses over to end in the northeast of the same.

The capital of South Korea is Seoul, which is the Korean city most commonly mentioned in the television series. The city, located 35 miles south of the DMZ, is the largest in both North and South Korea, with a metropolitan population of over 25 million. Located by the Han River and within a mountain range, Seoul went through various name changes through the years—depending on who was occupying it at the time—and would be established as a capital in Korea beginning in 1392 by the Yi dynasty. Because of its history and location, Seoul would become a key target during the Korean War and the first for the North Koreans in the outbreak of the war in June 1950, changing hands four times through the three-year conflict.

The capital of North Korea is Pyongyang, which has been a major city in northern Korea since nearly as long as Seoul and is the oldest and largest in North Korea. Again, like Seoul, the city has gone through a number of name changes and been established as a capital off and on; in the case of Pyongyang, since the seventh century and for over four hundred years during the Koryo dynasty. Roughly eighty-five miles north of the DMZ, the city became the capital of North Korea on September 9, 1948. After the North Koreans took Seoul in the war, Pyongyang became a prominent target for the South Koreans and UN troops during the war, and was occupied for several weeks in late 1950, leading some to believe that the war was nearly over and also marking the emergence of the Chinese into the war in December 1950. It has remained the capital of North Korea ever since.

Korea Before the War

Charles K. Armstrong begins a short history of Korea for the Asia Society website, "Korean History and Political Geography," with a Korean proverb: "When whales fight, the shrimp's back is broken." This is a good description of the plight of the Korean people over many centuries, with several countries fighting over a unique, albeit small, section of land in Eastern Asia. It also hints at why such a country would want to isolate itself against the world, not to mention how those living there would want to prove to the world that they can't be knocked down by outside influences.

The Korean Peninsula had inhabitants at least as far back as 8000 B.C., but feuding between various factions within and outside of the country led to continuing changes in its political and social order until the first century B.C. and the creation of what is known as the Three Kingdoms. The kingdoms were made up of Goguryeo, Baekje, and Silla and lasted until 668 A.D., when Silla defeated Goguryeo, after having conquered Baekje in 660 A.D. This was done by Silla with military assistance from the Tang Dynasty of China. Silla eventually drove the Tang Dynasty out of the country in 679, thus solidifying a love/hate relationship between China and Korea that has morphed over the centuries, but still remains to the present day.

Silla was split into two separate states—Balhae and Unified Silla—during what is commonly referred to as the North South States Period, which lasted from 698 A.D. to 926 A.D. During this time, unrest in Unified Silla led to the breakup of the state into what is referred to as the Later Three Kingdoms of Korea (so called owing to heirs from the original Three Kingdoms having established claims to portions of Unified Silla), from 892 A.D. to 936 A.D. Due to years of internal conflict, Silla would eventually surrender to one of the other kingdoms, Goryeo (establish in 918) in 936. The Goryeo dynasty, also known as the Koryo dynasty, would give birth to the name of the country as it is remembered today—Korea (or Corea)—and continued until 1392 when it was replaced by the Joseon dynasty (Choson dynasty).

It is with the Joseon dynasty—which lasted until 1910, although losing much of its power by 1897—that the country would establish Seoul as a capital for the country. The five-hundred-year period also saw the development of many of the elements of Korean culture, such as advancements in language. It also saw a number of attempts to overthrow the country by Japan (1592–1598), and two Manchurian attempts (1627 and 1635)—the major seeds that led to the Korean people wishing to be left alone and eyeing outsiders with suspicion. Such an isolationist agenda is why Korea became known as a "hermit kingdom" during this period. Not that it helped to want to keep to itself, however—the second Manchu war found Korea having to submit to the Qing dynasty, a fate that lasted until Japan ventured another go at Korea in 1876.

With Japanese warships heading toward Korea, the Joseon dynasty—still in control, although with the Qing dynasty holding most of the cards—decided to sign the Treaty of Ganghwa (sometimes listed as the Treaty of Kanghwa) in 1876. The treaty was to help open ports to Japan and set up the free exchange of trade between the two countries, but it was pretty much an open secret that it was heavily in the Japanese favor and the Joseon dynasty was slowly handing control of Korea over to the Japanese.

It was at this point that America came into the picture, although not without a struggle beforehand.

America's Relationship with Korea Before the War

It is common knowledge through history that one thing those in the West wanted was trade with the East, whether by travel through Europe and Asia to get to India, China, and Japan for trade, or by finding an alternate route across the ocean(s) to such areas. However this goal was achieved, the idea was to get rare items from such lands to sell in Europe and later America.

Established as a free nation in the late eighteenth century and after plenty of years of fighting with European powers, America was still working itself up to become a major power in the mid-nineteenth century as many European countries were beginning to gobble up ports and other routes in Asia (if they hadn't already). Dealing with countries like Britain, Germany, and others as "middlemen" to get goods instead of going directly to the sources in Asia was certainly no way to set the United States up as a world power. Especially with European countries that may not have been on the best diplomatic terms with the United States anyway. Thus, the U.S. had to find their own way to venture into Asian trade.

It was 1844 when the United States signed a treaty with China for commercial import/export, which led directly to an attempt to do the same with other Eastern markets like Japan and Korea. Commodore Matthew C. Perry's trade agreement with Japan in 1854 helped advance this objective, but with Japan and China secured for trade, interest in Korea dried up. After all, "the hermit kingdom" was known in the West as a country that really wanted to keep to itself (and with good reasons), and Korea's public policy maintained that trade with outsiders beyond those already established was something simply not to be done. If any other country wanted something from Korea, they went through China, Russia, or Japan, who had plenty to offer anyway, so there was no need to aggressively pursue relations with the country.

On the flip side, there was nothing to be said for not extending a hand to help any foreigners who found themselves needing help in the Korean peninsula. No need to create trouble with those who did not want to cause any, after all. The proof of such a "thanks, but no thanks" policy toward trade had been plenty, with reports of ships having come into Korea from foreign powers that were provided food, equipment, and in the case of those unable to return under their own power, means to get back home through China, yet no willingness to trade. The U.S. itself bears witness to stories of Americans who had found themselves in the good graces of the Korean people upon arrival before being sent away. Perhaps not to the point of wanting to change the course of Korean political history by suddenly wanting to trade goods, but at least nothing that led to hostilities. Thus, the overall attitude of the U.S. was, "if they want to be left alone, leave them alone."

Then the General Sherman incident of 1866 would become the linchpin to Korea having to wake up to the "new world" kicking and screaming.

In late summer 1866, a schooner that was originally the USS *Princess Royal* but then renamed the SS *General Sherman*, and chartered by a British company called Meadows and Co. but bearing the United States flag, sailed into Korea to establish a trade agreement. Bearing cotton, tin, and glass, it also came with cannons and guns, ready to fight off attackers. It was a hostile representation of power (or possibly even fear) that helped set a

tone of concern, which was only agitated when the crew of the schooner moved up the Taedong River toward Pyongyang after being warned to turn back. A second warning at the following stop, this time given by a representative of the Pyongyang governor, Yi Hyon-lk, led to Yi and those with him to be detained by the *General Sherman* crew for undisclosed reasons. (Some suggest that Yi was held ransom in hopes of forcing a trade deal, while others have suggested that Yi had attempted to stop the crew from going to shore, which led the crew to detain him.)

North Korean stamp celebrating the destruction of the British-staffed, American commercial ship, the SS *General Sherman* in 1866. It would be the spark that would draw Korea into the eyes of the world.

Yi was able to escape, but whether by design as a show of force or in defense against attackers, the *General Sherman* began shooting at people on shore as it continued on its way, killing soldiers and civilians. It then for some reason turned back, only to run ashore. Leaving the schooner open to attacks, the Korean soldiers and civilians were more than happy to partake. After four days of fighting, the General Sherman was set on fire, with the crew either dying from burns or being beaten to death by Koreans upon reaching the shore.

The lack of forthcoming information about the incident to the U.S.—as well as the attempts to rebuild the ship for Korea's own use after the attack (it would later be returned to the U.S. and used as a cargo ship until it was destroyed in a storm in 1874)—led to the United States taking serious notice of Korea for the first time. It was exactly the opposite of what Korea wanted, but assurances were made to those in power that the United States was a small colonial country that would not dare try to bother Korea again. Thus, inquiries by the U.S. to obtain more information about the General Sherman were ignored. (To be fair, Americans saw Korea as a small, subservient country that did whatever the countries around them told them to, so neither party involved was really seeing the other as a threat.)

An attempt by the U.S. government in 1870 to establish a diplomatic relationship with Korea was botched so badly by both sides that U.S. vessels were sent in 1871 in demand a response. After five Korean forts were destroyed and more than two hundred Koreans were killed in the fighting, the United States decided nothing good could come of the destruction and left in order to cool things down (a withdrawal that only reinforced to Koreans that Americans had no stomach for war). Besides, for the moment the United States had closer-to-home worries to deal with than Korea, although there was still thought about pursuing some type of deal with the country in the future.

Of course, once you had nations in the West nudging at the sleeping nation in the East, everyone began to take notice. This is one reason Japan was eager to gain control over Korea, thus leading directly to the Treaty of Ganghwa in 1876 discussed in a previous chapter. Korea, as had been the fashion in earlier times, went to China for help. Yet China had enough problems with the Japanese—a conflict of interest over the Ryukyu Islands came to a head in the 1870s—and didn't need the additional headache of throwing Korea into that mix. Instead, and logically, it was suggested that Korea look to the U.S. as a means to (as stated in several sources, in particular Max Hastings' *The Korean War*) "check the poison with an antidote." Establishing trade and diplomacy with the United States—a country that seemed only interested in trade, and had basically strong-armed an agreement with Japan several years before with Perry's trade agreement of 1854—would box Japan into a corner (at least for a time). After all, if the Treaty of Ganghwa were to make Korean independent, then it certainly would not help to have Japan try to enforce restrictions to such "independence." With the United States signing the Treaty of Chemulp'o with Korea in 1882, many countries in Europe and even Russia would sign similar treaties with the nation.

It was a safety net for Korea that China wholeheartedly supported. With this support, however, Korea had no choice but to go public. Worse, it only momentarily slowed down the Japanese and still drew China into the situation. Disputes between Japan and Korean citizens led to the Joseon dynasty—which was still in control in Korea, at least on paper—requesting help from the Qing dynasty to shut down the fighting in order to maintain peace with the Japanese. It was a plan that backfired badly, with the Japanese feeling threatened by the number of troops sent by the Qing dynasty to assist. This led to the First Sino-Japanese War of 1894–1895, which was fought between the Qing dynasty and Japan in Korea, with the Korean populace getting caught in the crossfire between two countries they didn't want there anyway.

The defeat of the Qing dynasty led to the Treaty of Shimonoseki in 1895 and Korea becoming independent from Chinese rule. This was not celebrated in Korea, as it really meant that the Japanese had an even firmer grip on the nation. An attempt to get additional assistance from Russia only led to Russia eyeing Korea for itself, which escalated into the Russo-Japanese War of 1904–1905, with Japan victorious (one begins to see why Japan walked into World War II feeling indestructible, after knocking off both China and Russia just a few decades before). Unfortunately from a Korean standpoint, this changeover meant little to the West, as most countries already had trade and diplomatic agreements with Japan anyway. When the citizens tried to take matters into their own hands, Japan annexed Korea in 1910 and the Joseon dynasty was no more. Korea still existed, but Japan was making the rules and would begin a campaign to eliminate Korean culture and history over the next three and a half decades. During those years, there were protests from Korean immigrants and Christian missionaries in America, but America and most other countries in the West were too concerned about actions in Europe in the days of World War I and after to worry about Korea.

Then came Pearl Harbor on December 7, 1941, and America's jump into World War II.

Suddenly Korea was important again, especially as the United States could see in the closing days of the war that Russia was looking to finally get Korea after so many past failed attempts. With enemy forces being wiped out by the Allies in 1945, an agreement was reached between U.S. president Harry S Truman and Soviet leader Joseph Stalin that the Russians would purge Korea down to the 38th parallel of the enemy, while the U.S. forces would do the same up to the 38th parallel—hence, the reason why we have all this business about the 38th parallel in the first place. The idea would then be to let Korea become an independent country once again, after a five year "trusteeship" of the country by the U.S., Russia, Britain, and China. And what did Koreans think of this? Well, no one was really asking them. Even with no battles in the streets, Koreans were once again seeing other countries tell them what to do—this time through politics alone. The whales were fighting and the shrimps were getting their backs broken, as history had shown them.

Meanwhile, the bigger powers were having their own issues—the U.S. and Russia ended World War II as allies with the feeling that the knives would soon be out, and other countries standing around the perimeter of their schoolyard fight were egging the two on. It would quickly become known as the Cold War, and would last for decades (in some ways, it still prevails to the present day). Korea would be one of the testing grounds of the new games of "push me, shove you" going on in the world, as the Soviets were just as concerned that the U.S. would try to expand their political goals in Korea just as the U.S. assumed the Soviets were looking to take over the country.

By 1948, the U.S. had managed to get an agreement set to either see the country unified as an independent state or, if Russia was unwilling, to have an election held for South Korea, with America agreeing to militarily help the new nation until the new country's own forces could take over (and, yes, this sounds very much like what America would do in both Iraq and Afghanistan in more recent times; which just goes to show that the U.S. never listens to history when we think we have clever ideas). With the Soviet Union little interested in giving up on Korea—just as the United States had assumed would be the case—an election was held and Syngman Rhee, a strong anticommunist (who had little love for the U.S.), was elected president. Meanwhile, the Soviets had already established a new capital for the northern portion of Korea in Pyongyang and set up Kim Il Sung as the leader of the other new nation.

Syngman Rhee, the South Korean leader, shown here greeting Douglas MacArthur.
Courtesy of the Library of Congress

This was all well and good, but behind the scenes those in power in the U.S. were getting mixed signals as to the effectiveness of the South Korean army (soon to be known as the Republic of Korea Army, or ROK). It had been estimated that in all probability South Korea would easily be taken over by North Korea (especially with help from the Soviets, who shared a border and were not an ocean away like the U.S.). There were even estimations that if the ROK got so much as a mere "bloody nose," South Korea would fold. Further, if the U.S. were to follow through with bringing their troops home after the agreed-upon five-year trusteeship, the country would soon be unified under a communist rule if the Soviets told North Korea to do so. However, it was also assumed that the Soviets would have too many fingers in other pies—especially the increasing pressures facing them in East Germany—to bother with such an invasion, so it was hoped that there would be some breathing space before anything of the sort would occur.

Thus, the strategy for the U.S. became one of "best to get out before such a takeover occurred so it didn't happen under the United States' watch, which it shouldn't anyway." With complaints in Congress about spending money on this foreign land while there were bigger troubles in Europe to worry about when it came to the Soviets, the final U.S. troops left Korea in June 1949.

South Korea knew it was in trouble, although perhaps not as much as the U.S. predictions were suggesting. With the U.S. forces gone, it was clear that North Korea would attack at some point and probably soon. Yet, any request for help from the U.S. was given little thought by Korea's former partner, and even a new American policy to stop the Soviets' expansion of communism in the Pacific showed more concern about Japan than Korea. Further, Koreans under UN rule were less than happy to see many of their countrymen who had helped the Japanese during the war, and were thus considered traitors, remaining in the country in leadership roles. To them it seemed like madness; but to America—which was trying to build up a strong relationship with Japan—it was the way to appease their former enemy by not pushing for punishing those connected to Japanese involvement during the war. Nevertheless, all these elements combined to leave many Koreans cold to the idea of the U.S. being associated with the country in any fashion.

In the spring of 1950, it was becoming increasingly clear that the U.S. was moving on from Korea, and—worst of all—word was leaking out to the world at large that they had little to no concerns over the nation. The worst stroke came in January 1950 when U.S. secretary of state Dean Acheson told the National Press Club that the Asian Defense Perimeter—an area that the U.S. would defend if the Soviets ever tried to attack it, containing Japan, Okinawa, and the Philippines—did not include South Korea. To the Soviets, China, and North Korea, this was pretty much an invitation to take South Korea.

In the fall of 1949, Kim Il Sung went to Moscow to convince Stalin that such an attack would cause an uprising in the south that would overtake the government put into place there and quickly unify the country. Stalin was less than impressed by the plan, while the Chinese held back judgment. Kim Il Sung was convinced, however, that such an uprising would be seen as an internal conflict instead of one supported by outside forces, thereby forcing America and the recently established United Nations to stand back. The North Koreans predicted that without such assistance, the war would be over within three weeks and the entire country would be under communist rule. The Soviets, still with some misgivings, agreed for North Korea go ahead with the invasion.

It was to begin three years of bewildering embarrassments for all involved.

The War Itself

As Dong-Choon Kim states in his book *The Unending Korean War: A Social History*, the Korea War would become known in the Democratic People's Republic of Korea (aka North Korea) as the "Fatherland Liberation War." In the Republic of Korea (South Korea), it had a simpler and better-known name—the June 25 Incident. As Dong-Choon Kim goes on to explain, "This disparity indicates that the North regards the war as a war to drive America from the peninsula and to achieve unification, whereas the South sees it as an incident in which Soviet-backed North Korean communists illegally invaded the South on June 25, 1950, plunging the entire Korean population into chaos." In other words, it was, and is remembered as, a war about outsiders, which was typical in the history of Korean.

Yet the North Korean name projects not only an image of inaccurate ideals (after all, the Americans were already out of the country and had little concern for Korea until North Korea invaded) but also an incorrect conclusion (as the war merely reinforced America's involvement in Korea rather than drove them away). The South Korean name, albeit—as Dong-Choon Kim points out in his book—an attempt to dismiss the war as a trifling "incident," at least has a strong grain of truth in it: the Korean War started on June 25, 1950.

In the early morning of June 25, 1950, North Korean forces crossed the 38th parallel, claiming that the ROK had invaded North Korea and thus they were merely involved in a counterattack to protect themselves. Yet it was clear within hours that the invasion was happening in various spots further south than the border and thus this was no mere one-off fight—it was war. Before the day was out, the United Nations voted to condemn the attack, demanding that North Korea withdraw from the South. With the Soviet Union not present—due to a boycott that had been in effect since January over the UN refusing to recognize China under communist rule (this is briefly hinted at in the season three episode of the *MASH* series, "Bulletin Board," where Frank Burns discusses the reason for the war and mentioned Chiang Kai-Shek as the president of the Republic of China in 1949)—and with evidence that the attack had been started by the North without justification, the vote was unanimous.

In Washington, it was clear that the previous year's attempts to distance the U.S. from Korea were tragically backfiring. The Americans had set up a fight that involved a country they supported, and while perhaps not citing them in recent public discussions, the U.S. had never completely broken away either. Plus, with South Korea being overrun by a country under communist rule—not to mention one also known to be in strong union with the Soviets—to do nothing now would give the United States an even bigger black eye than they already had. North Korea had suddenly forced America to actively return to Korea and fight—a measure that had not been anticipated by North Korea, the Soviets, or the Chinese. Further, by June 27, it was decided that other forces from countries that were part of the UN would assist the South Koreans as well. It was a shocking blow to the Soviets and North Korea: everything was supposed to be swiftly resolved, and now—thanks to Kim Il Sung's impulsive actions—it looked like a real fight was on their hands. One that would be impossible to back down from.

On the American front, another issue arose: it was after the UN resolution that a reporter asked President Truman if the fight to come could be considered a "police action," a term used previously to mean that any fighting was to be limited and presumably quickly ended. Truman agreed with the terminology, and it would haunt him from that point forward. There were good reasons from Truman's standpoint to use this term: to call it a war could have kept Americans feeling positive about the battles and deaths occurring in Korea in the long run, but Truman was facing the ramifications of looking too eager to stage such a conflict. Police action sounded more like what was hoped for—a mopping up of discontent and righting simple wrongs for the South Koreans that, hopefully, would be over quickly and with few casualties. In hindsight, it was not a term appreciated by those who would fight in the war—and is thus mentioned in the *MASH* television series in a sarcastic manner, as it was by many who fought there. After all, when the fighting continues for years and there are friends dying around you in battle, such a term as "police action" appears quaint instead of as the horror it actually was.

While the UN worked on what to do, the North Korean army was continuing with their assault on the South, capturing Seoul on June 29. On June 30, Truman ordered U.S. ground forces into Korea, along with air support from the U.S. Air Force. This presented another issue—Congress had cut funding to the military after World War II, and most of the experienced soldiers of that war had moved on to new careers and lives. There was the draft to help feed bodies into the military system, but there was no way those versed in the ways of warfare were going to come back to fight in a "police action" for a country that the U.S. had been ignoring for years. It was also a different type of warfare that many were not used to, with guerrilla tactics being the norm. There was also issues with America's fighting power—although America could stand strong on the amount of firepower it had, most of it was built for European occupation, where land was typically flat and solid. Korea's terrain was mountainous and full of vegetation one minute, swamps the next, and everything in between. Essentially, America was about to go into a fight with a military that was ill equipped, ill trained, and in some ways, ill advised. The first U.S. troops to see action, on July 4, 1950, were pushed back. By July 14, the UN agreed to allow the U.S. to decide who would take command over the multinational troops being sent to fight in Korea, and General Douglas MacArthur was picked for the role.

MacArthur had played a pivotal role in U.S. fight through the Pacific during World War II, leading to him becoming the Supreme Commander for the Allied Powers (SCAP) in Japan after the fighting ended in 1945. This was mainly to help organize the rebuilding of Japan and set up a democratic government until President Truman agreed to transfer back power in 1949. Even so, MacArthur stayed on in Japan as SCAP, which naturally put him in a good position to take on the role of commander of the forces to fight in the Korean War.

It was a losing war at first, with UN forces attempting to slow down the North Korean forces long enough to get more troops and equipment in place to counter them. By August the South Korean and UN forces had a perimeter of roughly 140 miles around the port of Pusan, in the far southeastern corner of Korea, with North Korea having taken over the rest of the country. Although North Korean forces continued to fight, they eventually pulled back in early September, showing that MacArthur's troops were at least getting a chance to catch their breath after multiple defeats earlier in the war. By that point, most of the troops from around the world had been put into place, with South Korean and American soldiers heavily outnumbering those fighting under the umbrella of the United Nations Command. Additional soldiers were from the United Kingdom, Canada, Australia, Ethiopia, Turkey, Thailand, the Philippines, New Zealand, Greece, France, Colombia, Belgium, the Netherlands, South Africa, and even a handful from Luxembourg.

With things in place, MacArthur pulled off a master plan that was to be his crowning achievement in the war—the Battle of Inchon. On September 15, an amphibious attack occurred at Inchon, far from the Pusan Perimeter,

Douglas MacArthur in Suwon, Korea with Courtney Whitney, Matthew B. Ridgway, and William B. Kean, and thus contradicting the long-standing rumor that MacArthur never set foot in the country during the war.   *Courtesy of the Library of Congress*

in the northwest corner of what was South Korea (and bordering the capital city of Seoul). It was a bold move that worried the UN command as too big a risk, but which caught the North Korean forces completely off guard. Before the end of September, Seoul had been taken back, and North Korean forces stuck between Seoul and Pusan were in hasty retreat or surrounded. Those forces pulled back from the 38th parallel, and there were signs that the war would soon be over with North Korea in humiliating defeat.

Yet MacArthur was determined to press on. To be clear, he was not alone, and any further objectives he pushed toward were agreed upon by others in the chain of command, as long as there was no presence of Chinese or Russian military forces. After all, what was to stop North Korea from pulling the same stunt once the UN forces were gone? Nevertheless, a war that was looking to be over before the end of 1950 if the UN forces had stayed with the original objective of forcing the North Koreans back over the 38th parallel would suddenly take on a new life as it was decided that the eradication of the communist influence in all of Korea was needed, pushing South Korean and UN forces onward to the border between Korea and China.

This was a dilemma for the Soviets and the Chinese. Russia was already beginning to send signals to the UN that they would like to see things resolved before it got any more embarrassing for the new communist nation. Meanwhile, seeing that Kim Il Sung had now brought the Americans and UN forces straight at them, the Chinese knew they had to step in to clean up North Korea's mess. In early October, the Chinese began supplying military assistance to North Korea to fight back the UN forces. Once again, it was a secret that was pretty open on both sides, although American and UN intelligence suggested it was not as large as the hundreds of thousands of soldiers the Chinese would soon ship in to help. Even so, UN Forces overtook Pyongyang before the end of October, and MacArthur began asserting the view that continuing into China would be next.

It was not something China wanted to hear—Truman and many others on the other side of the war were less than thrilled with MacArthur's goals as well. Righting a wrong in South Korea was one thing; perhaps even trying to push out more of the communists in North Korea could be defended in the eyes of the world, but invading China—even though it was clear that China was helping the North Koreans—would not help anyone. Worse, the war had started with MacArthur and others (including Truman) suggesting that atomic weapons could come into play at some point. With American men being slaughtered in a country no one really wanted to fight for except to save perceived notions about communist agendas that were characterized as subhuman, the idea of dropping nuclear weapons on the enemy grew more enticing over time. By the end of 1950, MacArthur was considering how the war would be wrapped up within a matter of days if he could just get the okay to drop thirty-four atomic bombs on strategic locations around Korea and China. And making clear his plans to enter China in defiance of President Truman showed the world that MacArthur was knowingly being insubordinate. Worse yet, in the early days of the war, MacArthur had been granted power over the use of such bombs in the Korean theatre. Compounding all this was the fact that not only were MacArthur's further plans for assaults against North Korean and Chinese forces failing, with Seoul once again retaken by the North Koreans (only to be taken back in March 1951), but many attacks proposed were quickly determined to be incapable of even getting off the drawing board. Further, the foot soldiers were also becoming surly toward the general, especially in light of rumors

President Harry Truman would find himself politically crippled by the Korean War, with his assessment that it was a "police action" haunting him for the rest of his time as president.

Courtesy of the Library of Congress

that he rarely left Tokyo, and possibly never set foot in Korea, thus fighting the war from the safety of another country while men were dying left and right for his own agenda, if not amusement. (The third-season episode "Big Mac" parodies this resentment, as the 4077th prepares for a visit by MacArthur, only for him to whiz through in his escorted jeep with no acknowledgment beyond a brief salute.)

Truman knew MacArthur had become a liability in the war. On April 11, 1951, he relieved the general of his command and brought him back to America, ironically as a war hero who received the praise of Washington and the country. He would die in April 1964, with many wishing to remember him as the hero of the Pacific theatre in World War II, rather than the man who nearly started World War III in Korea.

MacArthur's replacement was essentially his second in command, General Matthew Ridgway (who occasionally received some mention in *MASH* episodes). He would stay on until May 1952, when he was reassigned to command NATO forces in Europe (after a general by the name of Eisenhower had to leave to take another office, but more about him in a bit). Ridgway was replaced by General Mark Clark, who continued in that role through the end of the war. From there, the fighting would continue, settling along the 38th parallel. Over time, talk of armistice would begin over and over again, only to usually be halted by the Chinese for assumed violations that rarely could be substantiated, including rumors of UN forces using gas warfare that incited the press but proved to be untrue. ("The Incubator" episode from the second season of *MASH* shows Hawkeye and Trapper inadvertently suggesting to the press that U.S. forces were using gas warfare, an action that in reality would probably have gotten the two more than a simple slap on the wrist, what with China's accusations already flooding the press.)

Meanwhile, fighting would continue, and continue, and continue, with the war becoming one similar to World War I, where small patches of land were fought over, won, and lost within days (see the season one episode "The Ringbanger" for a discussion of this topic). This can be seen in the various histories of the war—the last two years of the three-year war typically take up a mere third of each history or less, as skirmishes became more and more routine and pointless, with the only thing new being who died next. Which points out a major element that soon was realized by all: the American and UN forces had the weapons and the know-how to fight, but the Chinese had one thing that even the North Koreans did not—the bodies. The Chinese could and did send many men to die in Korea; more than could be overcome with just advanced weapons and military intelligence.

It became a stalemate, with all involved starting to see that the only thing being accomplished was killing. It was an age-old story for Korea—other countries had come in to fight, leaving a lot of cities destroyed, civilians killed, and nothing resolved. The difference was that Korea—on both sides—brought in these countries that had been continuously nudging at the "hermit kingdom," only this time to have their men die for Korea. In some ways, one could call it Korea's sting after their hive had been swatted too many times by those around them.

By the third year of the war, even with the endless sending of men to die in Korea, China was beginning to see it as much as a lost cause as the UN forces. Then with Stalin's death in March 1953, there wasn't anyone left for Kim Il Sung to impress. It has been suggested in more than one source that General Mark Clark's offer to exchange sick and wounded prisoners of war in February 1953 helped solidify efforts to begin ending the war. On July 27, 1953, the armistice was signed and the Korean War was over.

Although there were still ramifications to come.

After the War

America's enthusiasm for the war—or, rather, "fighting the commies"—was strong at first, but when the fighting continued longer than anyone assumed a "police action" would take, dissatisfaction and disinterest grabbed hold. The war's biggest profiteers in America were individuals like Senator Joseph McCarthy who used the war as a means to tear at the Truman administration and the Democratic Party, claiming them to be helping the communists in the Korean War, which further diminished chances of the administration to bring the war to a halt (as China, the Soviet Union, and North Korea took such a stance as a sign that America would soon give up on the war in order to save face with the American public). Blasted by both the Democrats and the Republicans for trying to keep a steady balance in a war that could easily escalate into a nuclear war between China and America, Truman would see the closure of his career coming and decided not to run in 1952 for reelection. (He claimed that no president should be seated for more than two terms, but many believed it was due to his dismal chances of being reelected and his reasoning being an excuse to avoid embarrassment.)

Besides, the Republicans had someone else ready to take the presidential office in the '52 election who was a military hero. And not Douglas MacArthur (although MacArthur would attempt to run, only to do miserably at the Republican convention, with 10 votes out of a possible 1,206). That man was Dwight D. Eisenhower (1890–1969), who had risen to Supreme Allied Commander in the European theatre during World War II (much as MacArthur had in the Pacific). He had also been appointed governor of the U.S. Occupation Zone, establishing a strong stake for the Allied forces in Germany after the war that would help preserve the peace and avoid the type of conflict that had developed in Korea.

The Republicans had gone after Eisenhower in 1948, but it was only in 1952 that he was heavily sought after to the point he relented to run.

The Republicans had been building up a campaign that would be fixated on someone going in and winning the war in Korea—something Truman had been unable to accomplish. As it stood, the strongest vote in the campaign up to that point was that of Robert A. Taft, a senator from Ohio who believed in a form of isolationism that meant nonintervention in other countries unless there was an immediate threat to the U.S. It also meant pulling out of the Korean War, and possibly NATO (with which Eisenhower was involved), and Eisenhower agreed to the presidential run in order to avoid setting up an administration that he saw as abetting the Soviet Union in the Cold War, rather than avoiding them.

The campaign was heavily influenced by a variety of factors, with the idea of stopping the war with a mighty swing of American—or rather Republican—military power being just one element. Still, Eisenhower would campaign on the concept that Truman and the Democrats had set up the war to occur after diminishing military power and interest in South Korea, neglecting to mention that he was one of the members of the Chiefs of Staff that suggesting doing so in the late 1940s (he would go on record after his presidency warning against excessive military spending as well). Off the campaign trail, Eisenhower was not so sure about what could be done in the war, however, and although he would famously proclaim, "I will go to Korea" (a quote found at the beginning of the fourth season of the *MASH* television series), in order to end the war, he was rapidly coming to similar conclusions as Truman that the war was a deadly stalemate that had little chance for any winners. Nevertheless, his election, which came about thanks to the war, saw Eisenhower in the forefront of advancements for the nation, including the creation of NASA, the Interstate Highway System, as well as an early adaptor to desegregation. He also helped boost the career of a Republican by the name of Richard M. Nixon, who would go on to battle a different war many years later as president.

But all this political maneuvering held only so much interest to the public, as the dragging out of the fighting led to many Americans simply turning a blind eye to a war on the other side of the planet that was not a pleasant one to cover in the press. More importantly, it was a war that came to a conclusion that seemed to not really settle anything other than what was there to begin with—a North and South Korea, one communist and the other not. Even the borders of the country appeared to be the same.

The war would eventually become known as "the forgotten war," for many in America, especially those who fought in it, had friends die in it; and those who returned found a United States that was indifferent to their sacrifice. Soldiers returned to families and friends who thought they had merely been away for a while—some would even come back to accusations that they had been in prison somewhere, rather than a war in another country. Meanwhile, these young men had left a country going through rapid changes that saw the quiet, respectful, orderly world of happy main streets and picket fences becoming one more turbulent, with teenagers full of angst, strange music filtering through the radios, and other adults who showed them little of the respect returning military men got after World War II. On the military side, the subsequent Vietnam War of the 1960s and 1970s would prove to many that America didn't learn much from fighting in Korea. Far too many military experts came away from Korea suspecting that America could win any conflict with China as long as the bullets kept flying, forgetting that most of the firepower used in Korea was not adequate for the climate (and even worse in the hotter, damp, southern region of Vietnam). China also had more bodies to throw at a war and better propaganda methods than the U.S., which meant that the longer the conflict continued, the more corroded support became with the American public. Essentially, China knew that if they just stuck it out, they would eventually be able to drive other forces off.

Yet all this is about the other countries. What of Korea itself? As is commonly known, the war amounted to little in the way of progress. In fact, due to its ending in an armistice, many see the war as not having ended. North Korea still looks to one day unite with South Korea under one communist rule, while South Korea hopes to one day see the public overthrow the Northern political region and join them. Meanwhile, North Korea continues with the propaganda that Americans are out to destroy them, while South Korea bristles at the possibilities of what North Korea's supporters may one day do. It was clear even in the days of the war that the splitting of the country created a civil war that has never been unified or even stabilized. Instead, everyone plays into a game that involves one country trying to impress upon the world that they are the big boys on the block, followed by the other, and everyone else in the world stepping back as far as they can in hopes that they don't get caught in the crossfire.

One lingering factor that did come out of it, however, was the creation and execution of the mobile army surgical hospital.

2

He Was Drafted

How the Mobile Army Surgical Hospital Became a Reality

A s discussed in the first chapter, the Korean War brought about a lot of changes for the U.S. military. After coming off the glow of helping to win the Second World War, America was discovering in the warzone of Korea that things could not stay status quo; the methods of fighting, weaponry, and strategic planning had to change with the times. As the old saying goes, necessity is the mother of invention, and the Korean War would ignite some much-needed changes—for the bad as well as the good.

One of those that would make a positive impact was a fairly new concept in servicing the wounded during the war. At least it was a fairly new concept from an American point of view. And, as it turns out, it was given a chance to succeed mainly because necessity demanded it.

Treating the wounded in wartimes had always been a problem, not only due to the difficulty for armies to carry the equipment and personnel with them, but also due to the lack of cleanliness required for saving lives. Even when one could perform surgery to save a life, the lack of an antiseptic place to operate out in the fields—even with available tents and equipment—made many surgeries dealing with wounds ineffective. Particularly with wounds in the torso. A shot to the arms, legs, and even some areas of the head could be treatable; maybe to the point of amputation of an arm or leg, but still survivable. A shot to the gut was almost always a guaranteed death sentence, however. As Sanders Marble points out in an article in the *Journal of the History of Medicine* up through the Second Anglo-Boer War (1899–1902), abdominal wounds were 87 percent fatal, and a shot to the small bowel would mean no chance of survival. (Even a shot to the chest had better odds, at 62 percent.) By the turn of the century, surgeons were attempting to perform surgery to save such wounded soldiers, but at a 100 percent mortality rate. Oddly enough, the Russians discovered in the

Russo-Japanese War of 1904–5 (as discussed in the previous chapter) that setting up stations for the wounded near combat helped saved lives that routinely would have been lost while attempting to transport the wounded to the rear where the hospitals were, but such information was not shared with other countries.

Thus, it was not until the First World War that a method was chosen to create aid stations—areas established near the fighting where a handful of medics and surgeons could stabilize the wounded for movement to other safer locations—and field hospitals—farther back from the fighting, where the wounded could be treated with more care before either being released to their units or sent further back for more treatments. Which the French adopted, not the Americans. Up to that point, most wounded who could make it (and many who didn't, but tried anyway) were evacuated from fighting to the rear of the fighting or even farther back if doctors and surgeons were there. But that form of treatment was rapidly losing any meaning when World War I saw anyone transporting the wounded under heavy fire quickly enough to save them as impossible.

The French, and soon after the British, realized that they were not only losing men to wounds that were treatable, but losing men who had been trained. With their deaths came the need to replace them, usually with men without the hands-on training necessary to win battles and with additional expense of transport, training, and so on. On the other hand, an experienced soldier who is wounded could be patched up near the field of combat and sent back out to fight. Efficiency of cost and logistics ruled the thinking, and while it was great to actually save lives as well with new ideas for bringing treatment closer to the wounded, humanitarian gestures were not exactly the prime mover in setting up medical—and in particular surgical—stations closer to the action.

While the British mainly went with building hospitals closer to the fighting, the French came up with the idea of the ambulance chirurgical automobile (which translates into English as the automobile surgical hospital). These, as listed in Marble's article, were usually within "four to twelve miles behind the front." This actually was not a completely new idea at the time either, as the concept of having surgeons available nearer the front line (e.g., forward surgery) goes back to the Napoleonic Wars and Baron Dominque Jean Larrey (1766–1842). Larrey, typically considered the pioneer of forward surgery in the battlefield, would also help create the concept of the ambulance and was the originator of triage, which is the determination of who gets treated first based on the seriousness of wounds and injuries. This was a fresh topic in the eighteenth century, where it was not unusual for the wounded to be treated based on rank first (watch every fifth episode of the series with Frank Burns to see him trying to go back to the "old-fashioned" way of doing things). By the time of the First World War, the French began using the term triage so much that it became part of the common terminology for pre-op across the board and into the future.

The auto-chirs, as everyone at the time called the Ambulance Chirurgical Automobile, could be moved to where needed in the fighting. However, to help with the speed of such moves, the auto-chirs rarely had any bedding or even some supplies that would be needed. Thus, these moved from one field hospital to the next and usually as a means to help with demand for services at such stations, with the auto-chirs handling surgical cases, while the field hospitals would deal with minor injuries, mental fatigue, and the numerous gassings that took place during the war. This may seem limiting, but the consensus was that the auto-chirs needed the flexibility to move when and where required, and if they were set up independently from the field hospitals with their own bedding, etc., they could easily be stuck in a tight spot with patients they couldn't move. The *MASH* series would use such a concern with the spinal patient in the "Bug-Out" episode (season five, episode one), which saw Hawkeye, Houlihan, and Radar stuck at the abandoned 4077th location because they couldn't move the patient after the surgery. This was the type of situation the auto-chirs wanted to avoid, and while they were mobile and involved surgery, there was much room for improvement into what was to come.

Even with such limitations, by June 1918, the U.S. Army was convinced the idea was a good one and set up their first such unit, which was called a mobile hospital (MH). Such MHs carried—as Marble states—a traditional "twelve officers, eighty enlisted men, and twenty-two nurses," although this could change over time depending on necessity. The focus was on surgery, with the emphasis on moving patients to hospitals in the rear of the fighting or to adjacent field hospitals (if available) as quickly as could be done. The units could be moved, and did frequently during the final months of the war, albeit with more effort and trucks needed than originally planned. Even so, and with some other ideas tossed around for similar types of medical units, the Mobile Hospitals proved to be fairly successful.

After World War I, progress was made on paper as to how to make the units—now referred to as surgical hospitals (SH) rather than mobile hospitals—more efficient; yet that's what it remained for years: progress on paper. It was only once the U.S. entered World War II that the chance came to see if any of the ideas worked in practice. This came with the okay to create portable surgical hospitals (PSHs), which Marble points out in his article had only three surgeons, one anesthetist, thirty enlisted men, and—if lucky—a handful of nurses (but most probably not). Oddly, this is quite similar to the number of personnel we became used to seeing on *MASH*, with the O.R. (operating room) being occupied by less than a handful of surgeons, a few nurses, and what appeared to be only a couple dozen servicemen doing chores, even though this was not the reality of the MASH units during the Korean War (but certainly the reality of putting together a television show with limited cash).

The reason the PSHs came into play was that the fighting in the Pacific demanded treatment of the wounded in terrain that made it impossible to transport casualties in an easy and safe manner, as well as wanting to keep the units small for easier movement. The PSHs first appeared in October 1942 in New Guinea, and then later in Burma in 1943; setting up sometimes within a mile of the fighting, with the idea that they could treat the soldiers and be able to keep them alive until they could be transported to better facilities. In Burma, a PSH was assigned to each regiment or division, including those of the Nationalist Chinese Army forces (hence, giving the Chinese a good understanding of the work the later MASH units would

A look at the 45th Surgical Hospital in 1953. It had previously been known as the 8076th MASH from July 1950 through January 1953 before MASH units were converted into the more "updated" (but essentially the same) surgical hospitals.
Courtesy of the Office of Medical History

do in Korea). Unfortunately, hiccups in a system that was new and in areas where supervision was not easy (thus creating disciplinary issues) led to the PSHs being deemed too unreliable, especially in light of the fact that they were rarely as mobile as planned. More importantly, although they were saving lives, the PSHs were not producing soldiers who could return to battle, thus making one of the main points of such forward surgeries moot.

Better success was happening with the SHs in Europe, mainly through watching how the British were advancing on the concept, albeit more in line with previous auto-chirs that attached themselves to field hospitals. Such SHs were called auxiliary surgery groups (ASGs). The four ASGs in the European theatre—consisting of only two surgeons, an anesthesiologist, a nurse, and two enlisted men—would support troops in North Africa, Sicily, and Italy. In both the cases of the ASGs and the PSHs there was one consistency—air transport of supplies and the removal of the injured to rear hospitals once stabilized clearly were shown to save lives. From that point on, air support would be the backbone of the medical units, especially for the MASHs in Korea. Interestingly, although the movie and television series of *MASH* would show us images of helicopters in their opening credits—due to them being a common element of what we saw of battle footage from the Vietnam War (mainly of soldiers jumping from and heading to helicopters during battles)—they also reinforced one major element of what made the MASH units work in the first place, the ability to transport the wounded quickly and save lives.

By the time the war was over, the results told the story and the ASGs were deemed successful enough to lead to the development of the mobile army surgical hospital. In their article "The Mobile Army Surgical Hospital (MASH): A Military and Surgical Legacy," Major Booker King and Colonel Ismail Jatoi show statistics that demonstrate mortality due to battle wounds dropping from 8.5 percent in World War I to 4.0 percent in World War II; and the Korean War, with the MASH units in place, dropping the mortality rate down further to 2.5 percent (characters in the *MASH* series could say they saved lives 98 percent of the time because it was a true statement of the times, and not just a stance to make the 4077th look like the holy grail of MASH units, as could be suggested by the boasting manner). Thus, in 1948, the army decided to use the blueprint of the ASGs from the Europe campaign and create a new unit to be called MASH. Yet again this was on paper only, and it would be another two years before the concept would be put into practice.

Although some in the military were still skeptical of the idea, including MacArthur (who would later become a big supporter), there was one advantage of the new MASH unit over that of more conventional methods to use in the Korean War: its small size. The reason this was important was that medical officers were finding themselves with the same problem discussed in chapter 1 by other branches of the military—a lack of personnel that could immediately jump into the war in the summer of 1950. On July 1, 1950, the first MASH unit—the 8055th, which is important to remember for the narrative of what is to follow—was organized for the war, and it consisted of "ten medical officers, ninety-five enlisted men, and twelve nurses." This was solely because that was the most that could be assembled as quickly as needed. The unit would be moved to Korea after a brief organizational period in Yokohama by July 6, whereupon an abandoned schoolhouse was found in Taejon, near the Kum River to establish its base along with a clearing station for the 24th Infantry. Later in July came the 8063rd MASH, along with the 1st Cavalry Division, and quickly followed by the 8076th MASH in Pusan.

As mentioned in the first chapter, the first few months of the war were essentially a game of waiting out the North Koreans until more UN troops could arrive. Because of this, the war was going badly, and the surgeons and nurses at the new MASH units were finding themselves trying to save lives while dealing with dysentery (amongst other diseases; in fact, disease was the number one reason for treatment at MASH units, even over wounds), lack of personnel, and soldiers who were not ready for combat. Further, although the Geneva Convention forbad shooting at medics in the field (doctors, etc. were considered noncombatants, and to kill one was considered a war crime), North Korean soldiers had no concerns about such and found shooting at defenseless surgeons and nurses a good sport, which led to medics and those at the MASH units being issued weapons to protect themselves. This attitude would change once the Chinese stepped into the picture, as they knew killing medical personnel and the wounded was not good public relations, and if anything, they understood that the best defense in the fighting was to make it a propaganda war as much as a military one. Trapper's reasoning in the "Rainbow Bridge" episode of *MASH* was not that far off—the Chinese may have not been the kindest with prisoners of war, but they at least treated the wounded and medical staff with some respect. As for the North Korean soldiers, when fighting got too intense at aid stations, it was not uncommon for the medical staff to have to leave the wounded behind to face execution by the enemy; stories of whole staffs at aid stations being wiped out, execution-style, by the North Koreans in the early days of the war were not unusual either. Another reason that medics and medical officers were given weapons to protect themselves: it was essential in an environment where the rules may have been there but certainly were not respected by the enemy. (Although the series makes it appear that the doctors rarely had weapons—besides Potter and the clumsy, paranoid Frank Burns—the reality is that guns were issued to the doctors, and in the novel Hornberger even has Hawkeye and Duke shooting at a departing jeep.)

The physical layout of the MASH unit was similar to, but not quite the same as, that in the series. First off, the mobility of the MASH units was much needed in the early days of the war, so having buildings built was not likely when the need to move quickly was critical. Instead, locations with preexisting buildings were good to have if possible (Col. Potter searching for a location that had an abandoned schoolhouse on it in "Bug-Out" from season five is a good example of this), but otherwise, everything was pretty much in tents, including the O.R. It was only in later periods of the war that building would occur, as the need to immediately move became less.

Further, the movie and series gave us a much more sanitized concept of the MASH setup than in reality, most probably to not upset viewers who may have been turned off by some of the drastic measures the surgeons had to use. *MASH* gave us plumbing, where faucets are used to help scrub up before surgery, while it was not uncommon in reality for doctors to shove their hands in drums of water and then rinse off in another drum in order to be ready. Nor was it likely in the early days to see operating tables and gurneys. Most setups were comprised of boards with sawhorses in place underneath in order to make due for operations. O.R.s were crowded—something that one can see in the *MASH* film—with not much room to move around, unlike the spacious feel of the O.R. in the series. And while we get a good idea that the colonel's office was in the same place as the O.R., post-op, and the x-ray room, most MASH units also contain had an indoor pre-op (the series made it look as if everyone just stayed in the hall or outside until surgery was needed), nurses station, and other functions of the area.

At first the estimate was that the MASH units would need sixty beds, but due to the rush of wounded and the sick that came to the units at more than a thousand a month in the first couple of years of the war, the number quickly swelled to two hundred beds per unit. This would diminish as the war progressed, especially in the last few months of the war, but it was not unusual for surgeons to arrive at a MASH unit in the first two years of the war only to go directly to work in the O.R. for possibly sixty to eighty hours with little more than a few minutes to relax. Men were dying at a rapid pace, and surgeons were desperately needed in the newly formed units.

Sleeping was done in tents, with nurses usually bunked together in one large tent, just as the enlisted did. Officers may get something fancier, but not by much. Besides, with the way time was spent either working in the O.R. or trying to escape anything related to surgery, not much time was spent in the sleeping quarters beyond sleeping. Contrary to what may be remembered from the series, while sleeping bags were evident, the bedding was mattress-like bedding with linen rather than foldable bunks. Heat was tough to get in the winter as well as too prevalent in the summer, and it was not uncommon to find the O.R. stifling hot—especially in such locations where the O.R. was merely a tent (instead of the nice wooden structure seen in the television series). Lighting, plumbing, all other utilities that seem to be somewhat normal in the movie and series were limited and difficult to keep functioning, if available at all. It is obvious that those in control of the series and film looked at the primitive conditions of the real units and realized that audiences would have a hard time believing it, even just twenty years later. So such things were given more of the look of the MASH units of the last days of the war—when things were stabilized to the point that building could be built and plumbing, lights, and so on were more readily available—rather than what would have been much more common in the early days of the war in 1950–1951 (a period in which much of the early seasons of the program took place).

As with the army, the biggest issue was finding people to go to Korea. Worse, experienced doctors who had returned from World War II were not about to leave their cushy practices at home in the U.S. to fight in the Korean War. At least, not unless they were pushed into it. And certainly not any that had connections with politicians, etc. who could keep them out of the war (Major Winchester's plea to his family to use their connections to get him out of the 4077th was more typical than one might think). This is when the Doctors Draft Act came into swing, which was passed by Congress on September 1, 1950, and required doctors aged fifty and under to register to go to Korea. The setup appeared to "level the field," but was rather a brilliant method to let those who were the politicians' friends not even have to break a sweat over the possibilities of going. The first to go were those who had used the Navy Specialized Training Program (known as V-12) or the Army Specialized Training Program (ASTP) in order to get student tuition to go to medical school. Next were doctors that had no military record. The last in line were any doctors who had already served since September 1940.

What this meant was that everyone who had come back from WWII could sit back and not worry about going. It also meant that anyone who had war experience wasn't going; nor were they helping with training these men in their twenties, fresh out of school, and forced to go. Thus, the doctors being drafted to go to Korea were those who had little experience in the real world of medicine, much less medicine in war conditions. Worse yet, there was no one to guide them as to what to expect when they arrived in Korea or even obtaining proper military training. This explains in some ways why protocol was so lax at the MASH units and why those who saw the movie and later television series usually felt that the attitude of the doctors toward the military was one of the things *MASH* really did get spot-on. Those who went were rarely shown that there was a need to respect the military beyond rank and privileges. Meanwhile, those with military training did give the doctors and nurses the room to go their own way, as long as it was not dipping into insubordination or diverting war efforts. No one was blind to how the war was setting up new standards for fighting that had not been there in WWII, and thus there were bound to be areas where a little leeway had to be given—in particular with people without a military history like the young men and women being thrown into the MASH units. Serious infractions, however, were not tolerated. Some stunts pulled in the movie and series—such as Houlihan's exposure in the shower from the film—would have caused more ripples than what appeared. Yet, for example, tickets sold to allow the enlisted to look through holes in the women's showers were considered harmless and ignored by the officers (albeit, in hindsight, would be considered a step too far in this day and age).

Which naturally leads to a question that cropped up often in the movie and the series—sex. Again, infractions could get one in serious trouble, and for many, the type of work often made it tough to even think straight, much less carry on with someone else in hiding. Still, it was not completely out of the question for there to be some mutually agreed-upon liaisons here and there, as well as reports of men and women who met at such units and eventually married once they returned to "the real world." Even so, discretion was the key—certainly not the openness seen in the series. Then again, if such things were reflected in a proper way, Burns and Houlihan's affair would have been cut down on Day One (or certainly any chance for them to try to impose their will on others would have been quickly shut down with threats of exposure that would have ruined both of their careers and lives).

Most doctors were assigned for a year, with the first several weeks being training in Japan, followed by nine to ten months in a MASH unit in Korea. At the end of their service period, doctors could request to stay for another few months, but rarely more than three to four months, although some stayed a big longer (but certainly not the length of time Hawkeye was there, which he established as early as the fifth season as having been more than two years). After that, you went home. Also, contrary to what was stated in the series (in the early seasons of the program and specifically in the second episode of season eight, "Peace on Us"), there was no points system that could affect when someone was sent home. Such a system was used previously, but by the Korean War, it was long gone, and those who went usually had a good idea of when they would be able to leave (unless they decided to extend their stay, which a surprising number did agree to do). The reason for this was a determination that there was a limit to how long a doctor or nurse could last in the field before they became a deterrent due to fatigue (and what occurred to Hawkeye in the series would certainly suggest this to be the case). It held true for other roles in the unit as well, with nurses usually lasting less than six months and the enlisted less than eight months. While this was all well and good for the members of the unit to know that they would not have to stay terribly long , it also meant that just as the individuals were really learning their roles, they were being replaced by raw recruits.

If you had the stomach for it, you usually stayed with a MASH unit for your duration. Those who left early typically did so due to personal circumstances. Affairs at home, disease, and injury could sideline you to the point of going home, and signs of mental instability—which could easily happen under the circumstances—would get you sent off as well. Incompetence was also easily spotted and dealt with (and one reason why the character of Frank Burns had to be altered for the series, as will be discussed later). Otherwise, as long as you did your job and did it well, there was no reason to ship you anywhere else unless you were needed.

The number of standard personnel was a bit higher than seen in the program—there were usually anywhere from fifteen to seventeen doctors assigned to a MASH unit, although the rotation was so crazy it was not uncommon for some doctors to rarely bump into each other during their time at the unit. (Thus, the first-season episode "Tuttle," where Hawkeye makes up an officer that everyone comes to believe is real although they've never actually met him, is feasible in such an environment where you could go through the war never meeting someone in the next tent.) Additional officers who did administrative work were attached as well, while the number of nurses was around fifteen to twenty. Enlisted to help with the unit, including some who could perform minor medical duties, numbered around one hundred twenty instead of what looked to be six or eight seen in the series. There was also an auto pool, which was necessary for a unit that had to be ready to pick up and leave at a moment's notice, with a fleet of jeeps and trucks, but which we rarely saw much of in the series itself.

A majority of those who passed through MASH units were not the injured but the diseased—with a variety of ailments leading to time in bed before being sent back out to their units in the field more convenient than sending them to a hospital farther back from the fighting. Nature itself was more of a combatant at times than the enemy, and it was not uncommon for a number of diseases to strike down soldiers, as well as being the main reason that MASH units had water trucks for drinking and washing rather than risk any of the streams nearby. Concerns about possible biological and/or chemical attacks from the enemy also sent some soldiers to the MASH units. Tapeworms were also a major concern, and it was not uncommon to spend time when working on stomach wounds picking out these parasites one by one and dropping them into buckets by the operating tables before proceeding with surgeries.

The MASH units moved frequently in the first year of the war in order to keep up with the constant changes in the battle lines. Cowdry in his article states that the 8055th moved twenty-seven times within the first year of the war, leading to doctors and nurses rarely being able to keep track of the days. After that, things began to calm down with the stabilizing of the battle line around the 38th parallel, and units began to move less frequently. By the final months of the war, it was possible to find personnel at a MASH unit that had never even had to move. This was not only due to the lack of need, but because it created such chaos that it was detrimental to the units. The 8055th lost all its bedding and linen in one such move because someone got careless with a cigarette in the truck carrying all of those items, thus having to go without for several weeks. One documentary on the *MASH* (movie) Blu-ray has a doctor mentioning that his unit attempted a practice move late in the war that went so badly it was decided simply never to do one again instead of trying to work out the kinks.

With the units finding themselves more secured in their locations, the mobile aspect of the MASH became less of a concern than having the heavy equipment that would have been impossible for a unit on the move but could save more lives. Thus, an incident in the first-season episode "The

The front of the Battalion Aid Station for the 9th Infantry Regiment. Such aid stations were seen often in the television series and were much closer to the action and more dangerous than anything the officers back at the MASH units had to deal with.

Courtesy of the Office of Medical History

Incubator" could actually have been right out of the real-life stories of doctors in the MASH units.

By the end of the war, the MASH units had proven their success, although variations of the same were being used in other ways, as Otto F. and Pat Apel in the excellent book *MASH: An Army Surgeon in Korea* points out: "During the war surgical sections were assigned to units throughout the theater, ranging in size from battalion aid stations to regimental combat teams to evacuation hospital. Many were referred to in the common vernacular as MASH."

The progression for those injured in battle in the Korean War typically went as followed:

- As Otto Apel makes clear in his book, the first to see you would be "Medics (army) or corpsmen (navy and Marine Corps), enlisted personnel who were trained in first aid [and] attached to combat units down to the company level." A good example of this in the *MASH* series is the fourth-season opener, "Welcome to Korea," where Radar and Hawkeye are taking BJ back to the 4077th. On the way they meet a group of soldiers on the road who are then attacked. While BJ and Hawkeye help, there are medics who are part of the troop that are patching up soldiers hit as well, while also calling in transport to get the wounded out of there.

- Depending on the severity of the wounds, you would either be sent directly to a MASH unit if closer and time was of the essence, or to an aid station. As mentioned previously, aid stations would commonly be closer to the fighting than any MASH unit, and a good example of one in the series appears in the third-season episode "Aid Station," where Hawkeye, Houlihan, and Klinger go to assist at one. At such stations, triage would be done to determine if the wounded could be fixed up there, sent to a MASH unit, or even pushed back to a hospital in the rear (possibly even Japan, which was less than an hour away by air). The most extreme cases went by helicopter, usually the Bel H-13, known as a medevac (medical evacuation). Otherwise, you went by anything else that could quickly get you to where you needed to go. The objective of such stations was much like that of the medics out in the field—patch up the wounded well enough to get them to the next place without them dying on the way.

- Arriving at the MASH unit, triage would once again rear its head as part of pre-op. Pre-op (pre-operation), as commonly seen in the *MASH* series, usually involved Hawkeye running around and judging the order of who to operate on first due to severity of wounds. The episode "The Court Martial of Hawkeye Pierce" brilliantly parodied this simplification of the procedure by showing Frank Burns in essentially a dream sequence merely glancing at the wounded in pre-op and deciding who he would work on first (it also showed what really occurred, with Hawkeye and BJ refusing to work on patients who were not properly prepped by Burns in pre-op). In the real war, pre-op would be supervised by a nurse to judge the order, as the doctors were usually too busying getting ready to start surgery to do it (if the run was slow, a doctor would assist). The seventh-season episode "Hot Lips Is Back in Town," where Houlihan motivates her nursing staff to run triage—as if it were a revolutionary new concept—was actually pretty routine during the war itself.

- Surgery could be just about anything, with the emphasis on saving lives or functions. If a wounded man was best to have a limb amputated, that was pretty much the end of discussion if it meant the quickest way to save a life. The idea, as established numerous times on the program, was to perform "meatball surgery," and in relation to *MASH*, it is first mentioned in the novel that the film and series were based on. The objective

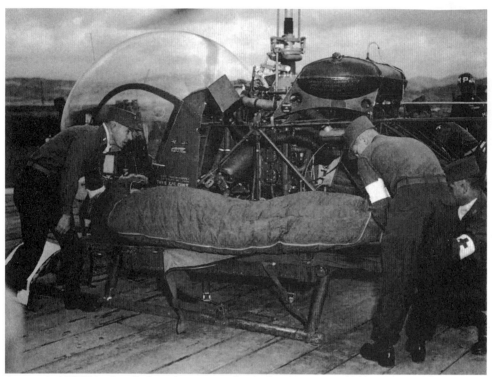

A wounded POW is placed aboard an evacuation helicopter in April 1953.

Courtesy of the Office of Medical History

was to get things done quickly enough to save a life, move the wounded out of O.R., and start on the next wounded person. Nothing more, but more importantly, nothing less.

• Once a wounded person had been stabilized, the objective was to get the patient out of the MASH unit as quickly as possible. This usually meant going to a clearing station to be evaluated as to your next destination, which could be going back to the fighting after recovering from wounds, back to a hospital farther from the fighting (such as Japan), or even back to the States for good. Someone with a particular type of wound might be sent to a different MASH unit that specialized in that injury before going on to a clearing station (as Apel explains, the 8055th specialized in head wounds, and after being stabilized, a patient would be shipped to the 8055th; the 8063rd dealt with hemorrhagic fever, a disease that was a basis of an episode in season four, "Soldier of the Month"; and so on).

The MASH units would perform their duties well, but as the war began drawing to a close, the units changed in their structure once again. With the need to move no longer an important part of their mission, the name was changed to that of surgical hospitals (mobile army), although commonly referred to as MASH units anyway. They became settled, with more equipment—in other words, just another field hospital. Stories swirled in the last months that the discipline of such units was eroding as fast as the number of patients they were seeing (from more than a thousand in the first two years of the war to sometimes less than a hundred in the last year). But, overall, the MASH units proved to be effective, and their usefulness would continue for years to come and would be renascent in every new medical unit created for war efforts today.

One of the units from that war, the 8055th, would spark a resurgence of interest in the MASH units in a whole new way years later. True, the 8055th was not only the first unit in Korea during the war, it had built a reputation as one of the best and busiest of the units in the theater. Yet perhaps in a greater historical context these days, the 8055th stood as the foundation of the mystical 4077th unit of the television series, the movie, and—of course, its birthplace—the novel of *MASH*.

3

An Extra Gallbladder a Week

H. Richard Hornberger and the Creation of a Novel . . . and Fourteen Others

On February 1, 1924, Hiester Richard Hornberger was born in Trenton, New Jersey. Sharing the same name as his father, Hornberger quickly began using his middle name of Richard, rendering his first name with simply an initial instead. Going by the name of H. Richard Hornberger became so ingrained that it would be common for him to never be referred to in biographical material as anything other than H. Richard; nor would there be much effort to list his name in any other fashion in most reports about his life and career. Close friends from college onward called him "Horny," however.

Raised for a time in New Jersey, Hornberger eventually moved to Bremen, Maine, where his mother's side of the family lived. He attended Bowdoin College in Brunswick, Maine, a place Hornberger later remembered to *TV Guide* in 1973 ("It Pays Me an Extra Gall Bladder a Week" by Neil Hickey, March 24–30, 1973) as not exactly motivational, "I had the lowest marks of any pre-med student in the class." Even so, he managed to get into Cornell Medical School, after a chemistry teacher stated in his application that Hornberger was "peculiar, but worth taking a chance on." It was in college that Hornberger became the editor of the college's paper, the *Bowdoin Orient*, which he also wrote for.

Once out of college, he began his internship when he was caught up in the Doctors Draft Act of 1950 and sent to Korea in the late fall of 1951 as a surgeon. He quickly settled down in the community of the 8055th MASH unit, while sharing with other doctors a tent that was referred to by those who were stationed at the unit as "the Swamp." A photo of Hornberger standing outside of the tent even shows the same insignia on the door that would be found on "the Swamp" where Hawkeye and the others lived in both

H. Richard Hornberger, left, the creator of *MASH*, standing outside the original Swamp in Korea. Note the symbol on the door, which will reappear on the door of the Swamp in the film and television series as well. Hornberger would later voice his appreciation for the film, but found little use for the television series.   *Courtesy of Willy Hornberger*

the movie and series. The symbol is one seen on a number of book covers by author W. Somerset Maugham (*The Razor's Edge, Of Human Bondage*), who used what is thought to be an ancient Moorish symbol to ward off the "evil eye" as a good luck charm, which certainly would be fitting for a group of young doctors out in the middle of a war.

As mentioned in the previous chapter, 1952 saw the war stabilizing in a way that made it easier and safer for the doctors, nurses, and enlisted working at the various MASH units to do their job than for those who came before them. That is not to say that it was easy work per se—the war was still ongoing and some of the bloodiest battles were yet to come in its last year—but the desperation of the early months in trying to stay ahead of the enemy and the horrors of trying to save lives too near to the fighting were mostly in the past. The 8055th by this point was located in Uijongbu (sometimes listed as Uijeongbu), a city that was a major battle site within the first few days of the war in 1950, but by 1952 was safely ten to fifteen miles behind the lines (depending on where the line of scrimmage was that week). Naturally, that was still too close to the fighting, and the personnel saw too many of the dying and the dead, but it was a step up from what came before. The doctors and nurses also had a little more free time between shifts, leading to more laxness in the rules than when the stress of war was more intense.

Hornberger would spend a total of eighteen months overseas, a majority of that time working with others at the 8055th. By that point, the philosophy was, as Hornberger put it himself, "Do the job well, and after that—do as you please. We were out there in the middle of nowhere. What could they do, fire us?" This attitude would be reflected in his letters home—one of which appears in Andrew Carroll's book *War Letters: Extraordinary Correspondences from American Wars*—in which Hornberger would explain more about the drinking and partying he and others at the unit did than about any of the more depressing elements of the work. (Although, as Carroll mentions in his book, Hornberger at one point in his letters discusses the irony in seeing more men come in with wounds due to friendly fire and accidents than from enemy fire, which feeds into the "war is crazy" attitude found in all the various versions of *MASH* as well as showing that raw soldiers were the backbone of the battle zone.)

After leaving the war, Hornberger worked for the Veterans Administration and then returned to Bremen, Maine. He settled in Broad Cove (erroneously called Crabapple Cove, the home of Hawkeye Pierce, in many biographies, thanks to a whimsical reference to the fictional location in the 1973 *TV Guide* article amongst other reporting over the years) and eventually built a home for his wife and their family just a short distance from his mother's house. Once back home, he began working six to seven days a week as a thoracic surgeon (just as Hawkeye would become in the novel) for Thayer Hospital in Waterville, Maine, where he specialized in gallbladder, hernia, and lung operations until his retirement. He passed away on November 4, 1997, from leukemia, survived by his wife, two sons, and two daughters. He is buried in Bremen, Maine, where his tombstone lists him as H. Richard Hornberger.

Starting on *MASH*, the Novel

In 1956, Hornberger began work on a novel that would reflect on his time in the Korea War and at the 8055th. Admittedly, it also greatly fictionalized his time there in a comical fashion, with the character of Benjamin Franklin Pierce (named after a family member named Franklin Pierce) being a stand-in for himself. Or, rather, a stand-in for what he would have liked to have been while in Korea, as he told *TV Guide* in 1973: "Hawkeye does a lot of the things I'd like to do." The manuscript would be completed around 1959 and consist of a number of stories dealing with various events that happened to the main characters of Duke, Hawkeye, and their associates while working as surgeons at the 4077th. Although Hornberger himself, in interviews, would consistently play himself off as "an amateur and a dabbler," it was clear from his work in college and other sources that he had a strong interest in writing, and had even stated that "only World War II stopped him from becoming a professional sportswriter." Because of this, he felt strongly enough in the results to think it stood a chance of being published. Hiring an agent, Malcolm Reiss, Hornberger sent the manuscript to publisher after publisher with no positive results; each time refining it a tad before sending it off again.

By the mid-1960s, Hornberger was beginning to wonder if anything was ever going to happen to his manuscript. It was during this period that a mutual doctor friend of his introduced him to an acquaintance who would help shape the manuscript into the novel it was to become, W. C. Heinz.

W. C. Heinz and the Creation of Richard Hooker

W. C. Heinz was born January 11, 1915, in Mount Vernon, New York. A newspaper man who wrote about World War II while on assignment in Europe, he returned to the U.S. to become one of the best-remembered sportswriters of the twentieth century referred to by *Sports Illustrated* as the "Heavyweight Champion" when it came to writing about sports. In the late 1950s, he began writing fiction as well in various magazines, producing the boxing novel *The Professional* in 1958, which gained him a telegraph from Ernest Hemingway who proclaimed it "the only good novel I've read about a fighter. . . ." He followed that with the semi-autobiographical book *Run to Daylight*, focusing on a week with Vince Lombardi as he coached the Green Bay Packers. He continued to write fiction and nonfiction for many years; entering the Hall of Fame for the National Association of Sportscasters and Sportswriters, as well as the one for International Boxing. He passed away in February 2008.

Although Heinz had made his career in sports writing, he was intrigued by other subjects as well and in 1961 wrote a cover story for *LIFE* magazine about "a day in the life" of a surgeon preparing to do a lung operation. Assisting Heinz with that article was a surgeon by the name of J. Maxwell Chamberlain, who would go on to help Heinz with background material for his 1963 medical novel *The Surgeon*. Hornberger was a friend of

Chamberlain, and when he discovered that his fellow surgeon knew Heinz, he asked if Heinz would look at his manuscript for *MASH* to see what could be done to improve it.

Heinz and his wife read the manuscript and enjoyed it, but Heinz immediately saw where there were problems. As he told Nathan Ward in *American Heritage*, "It was funny—within the realm of decency, once I cleaned it up, since it was full of those jokes that doctors like to make about the body." The two collaborated on changes needed for close to a year, with the pair trying to pull the various episodes in the manuscript into a coherent format. "There isn't a hell of a story line in *MASH*," Heinz told *American Heritage*, "just a succession of operations and techniques and humor. The only thing that holds it together is the characters and the familiarity that the reader comes to have with them." Heinz was also instrumental in putting together the chapter dealing with the football game, which made sense with his sports—especially that of football—background.

Due to the amount of work Heinz contributed, along with some concerns about a doctor writing a novel about being a doctor (some may have interpreted it as showing a lack of discretion, which could hurt a surgeon's career), the pair agreed to come up with a pseudonym for the author's name. With a nod to golfing, Hornberger decided that Hooker would make a good last name for the fictional writer, and thus Richard Hooker became the writer of the book called *MASH: A Novel About Three Army Doctors*.

With the improvements, the manuscript finally got a bite after being rejected by seventeen publishers (a couple of sources make this number much larger—anywhere from thirty-four to forty-two, and Heinz once stated twenty—but nearly all interviews with Hornberger and others confirm seventeen). The publisher was William Morrow and Co., which was founded in 1926 and known for publishing general audience fiction, mostly in paperback, including titles by Ray Bradbury and the *Perry Mason* series by Erle Stanley Gardner. The writers' agent was offered $5,000 for the rights, which was gladly accepted after so many years of trying to even get a publisher to consider looking at it. In preparation for its release, the galleys for the book were sent to writer Ring Lardner Jr., either to get a blurb to use for the cover, as Lardner states in his book *I'd Hate Myself in the Morning*, or to review for the *New York Times* as Lardner's agent, George Litto, states in the book *Robert Altman*.

Regardless of why he had it, Lardner liked the galleys he read, and over time began thinking about how the novel would look if brought to the big screen. This would, of course, lead to the production of *MASH* as a major motion picture, which is covered in detail in a subsequent chapter of this book. For the moment, however, the novel was released in hardcover by William Morrow & Co. in 1968, with a subsequent paperback edition picked up by Pocket Books, a division of Simon & Schuster, in 1969. Thanks to the release of the film in early 1970, the book continued to sell in paperback for much longer than normally seen for a first-time novel, and suddenly Hornberger was being asked to do a sequel.

This led to Hornberger starting on a sequel that dealt with the adventures of a handful of the characters from the first novel in Crabapple Cove and Spruce Harbor, Maine. The novel, *MASH Goes to Maine*, was released in 1972 and went through multiple editions over the years, while 20th Century-Fox immediately picked up the movie rights. For a couple of years, Fox took a serious interest in turning the sequel into a film (although discussion about a possible television series appears to be merely the hyperbole of a *TV Guide* writer), but eventually passed, feeling that the television series had by that point become the definitive presentation of *MASH*.

William Edmund Butterworth III and the Pocket Books Series

That didn't stop Hornberger, however. Or at least Pocket Books, who saw the popularity of the television series begin to blossom and knew they were sitting on a goldmine. Back in the 1970s and before, it was not uncommon for publishers to take movie and television characters and have authors throw together quick little 150–190 page novels to sell to fans. Some of these—such as the early James Blish *Star Trek* books—would be based on actual episodes of the series from which it was taken, but a good majority of them were brand new adventures for the characters. For the most part, none of them were very good, but occasionally a gem or two would pop up out of the slew of tie-in novels, and they usually sold well. *MASH* easily fell into this money-maker concept, with Hornberger agreeing to have the series begin. However, he was making good money as a surgeon by then, going on to be one of the innovators of gastric bypass surgery, which he would write about for the *American Journal of Surgery* in April 1976. Because of that, he didn't really want to spend the time to write the novels.

Thus enters another writer into the literary world of *MASH*, this time an author by the name of William Edmund Butterworth III. Butterworth was born on November 10, 1929, and established a career as a military man after joining the army in 1946. He eventually saw the Korea War as a correspondent and later an officer dealing with public relations pertaining to the war, and it was there that he would see MASH units in operation. After the war, he continued to work for the military in connection with publications, but soon his itch to write went beyond that of the military and into the public world of fiction. By the late 1950s he hooked up with the same literary agent Hornberger had (in fact, Butterworth would see one of the first submission copies of the *MASH* manuscript thanks to his connection to his agent), and began writing novels under his real name. With an ability to write fast and well, Butterworth was soon branching out into writing books under a number of pen names, such as Walker E. Blake, Eden Hughes, Webb Beech, and Edmund O. Scholefield.

As Butterworth told the Police Chiefs Association in a speech from January 2003, the publisher kept demanding another *MASH* sequel, which Hornberger felt he did not have in him due to his career as a surgeon. Finally, they reached the offer of $100,000 if Hornberger would let someone else ghostwrite a sequel. He finally agreed, but only if he could pick the writer to do the job and then okay what he had written; if he turned it down, he still got to keep the $100,000, and no book would be published. The publisher agreed and began sending a series of authors to meet with Hornberger, only to have the doctor reject all the "long-haired liberals," as Butterworth stated Hornberger called them. His agent, knowing Butterworth's own experience in the war as well as his politics being similar to Hornberger, contacted the surgeon to see what he thought. According to Butterworth, Hornberger okayed the deal, figuring, "since he would get $100,000 either way, and they were going to pay the ghost, he thought it was better to have a fellow fascist get money than some long-haired liberal. So it didn't matter that the fellow fascist had never before written one humorous word on purpose. We Korean War vets have to stick together." (It should be noted that Butterworth was being cheeky here, as the term "fascist" was obviously an in-joke between the writer and his audience.)

Butterworth was surprised that his manuscript, *MASH Goes to New Orleans*—written in three weeks—was not only accepted but would sell a million copies. After that, the publisher wanted more, and the pair worked out a deal where Hornberger would approve the manuscripts and Butterworth would do the writing—with the two splitting proceeds fifty-fifty. Butterworth would only write one other book in the series that year, but by 1977 had written ten more for a total of twelve before dwindling sales ended the run. It was a relief to the coauthor of the original novel, W. C. Heinz, who shared in the byline of "Richard Hooker" but considered the Hornberger/Butterworth series to be "trashy" and "crap" and thus detrimental to the pen name. (Oddly enough, although the cover of each paperback states

"Richard Hooker" as one of the writers, the copyright information inside would always say "Richard Hornberger.")

As for Butterworth, he would go on to write a series of military action novels under the name of W. E. B. Griffin—a name that, according to his son, was picked to make sure that no one going into a new novel by Butterworth would expect a satire like the *MASH* sequels.

Hornberger Goes It Alone in the End

This was not the end for Hornberger when it came to writing, however. In 1977, he returned to write one more novel starring the characters of his first book. The book, *MASH Mania*, would be a return to the characters in the present day, ignoring all the stories done in the Butterworth series as if they did not exist. Nor would Hornberger present anything in the novel that would tie into the television series—a program that outlasted anyone's expectations and hung his characters, particularly Hawkeye, with liberal and antiwar sentiments that he did not agree with. When the series started, Hornberger (according to the 1973 *TV Guide* interview) was making $300 an episode as it aired. At the time, he was happy with the amount and felt uneasy in stating his true feelings about the program, going so far to say, "I'm not going to knock anything that pays me an extra gallbladder a week for no work."

Over time, that changed. By the later 1970s, Hornberger wrote a letter to *TV Guide* distancing himself and his version of the characters from the television series. Producer Burt Metcalfe in the book *They'll Never Put That on the*

<Metcalfe,>

" 'M·A·S·H' IS THE BEST AMERICAN WAR COMEDY SINCE SOUND CAME IN."
—Pauline Kael, New Yorker

" 'M*A*S*H' is what the new freedom of the screen is all about."
—Richard Schickel, Life

" 'M*A*S*H' is a cockeyed masterpiece—see it twice."
—Joseph Morgenstern, Newsweek

" 'M*A*S*H is a fascinating film... full of style, emotion, reason and intelligence that define the work of a living art."
—Vincent Canby, New York Times

" 'M*A*S*H' begins where other anti-war films end!"
—Time Magazine

20th Century-Fox presents An Ingo Preminger Production
Starring DONALD SUTHERLAND · ELLIOTT GOULD · TOM SKERRITT
Co-Starring SALLY KELLERMAN · ROBERT DUVALL · JO ANN PFLUG · RENE AUBERJONOIS
Produced by INGO PREMINGER Directed by ROBERT ALTMAN Screenplay by RING LARDNER, Jr.
From a novel by RICHARD HOOKER Music by JOHNNY MANDEL Color by DE LUXE® PANAVISION®
ORIGINAL SOUNDTRACK RECORDING ON COLUMBIA RECORDS

R RESTRICTED

The movie poster with the "peace sign on legs" symbol that will become synonymous with the book series—both the Hornberger trilogy and the *Mash Goes to . . .* series.

Air, states that Hornberger wrote to the network several times complaining about the series. For him, the movie was fine, as it stayed close to the plot and nature of Hawkeye and the others as found in the novel. Yet the Hawkeye of the movie may have had no patience for military bureaucracy, but thought the war was needed; Hawkeye of the series would weekly state his disgust at the brutality of the war. It was a transformation that put Hornberger—the man on whom Hawkeye was based—on edge. "I think we should have been [in Korea]," he told UPI soon before the end of the series ("*MASH* Isn't Funny to the Original Hawkeye"). "If you're going to start a war, you might as well play to win. No one in their right mind would be pro-war, but I operated on a thousand or so wounded kids, and I know more about war than a bunch of under-educated actors who go around blithering those sanctimonious self-righteous noises." It also did not help that the series was being remembered more than his novels; nor that he had signed the contract allowing the use of his novel for the series thinking it would run a few weeks and then disappear. As it was, even though he was getting $500 an episode by the end of the television series' run, the money dried up after that, as he was not paid for repeats or syndication of the series. Meanwhile, 20th Century-Fox and others involved would continue to profit on reruns and other various sales.

This left Hornberger bitter over what was done to his characters. John Baxter in his book *A Pound of Paper: Confessions of a Book Addict* states that Hornberger became so frustrated by the 1980s that he refused to sign copies of his novels, even the first one. When asked by Larry Gelbart, the writer who helped develop the novel for its television version, his thoughts on the series, Hornberger snarked, "I like the theme song; after that it gets kind of dull." Hornberger's final appraisal to UPI as the series was ending in 1983 pretty much put it on the line: "My wife and I were in a hotel room in New Zealand one time and had the choice of watching *The Dukes of Hazzard*, *MASH*, or an educational program on the artificial insemination of cows. I chose to watch the cow show."

Hornberger would sometimes speak of writing more novels, and a manuscript for a fourth novel—involving Trapper John becoming president of the United States—was written, but MASH Mania in 1977 was to be his last. By the time of his death in 1997, the series he had little patience for beyond a paycheck had superseded any other image of the characters found in the film or in any of the novels. No doubt, it was an irritation to the original writer that even getting paid a gallbladder a week did little to calm.

4

Not Missing the Last Page

H. Richard Hornberger's *MASH* Trilogy

One thing that must be clear to *MASH* fans who have seen only the television series, the novel, or the film—none of the plots or characters really quite jibe with their alternates in the other versions. There are some drastic changes, in fact. Fans of the series would be shocked by the boorish nature of the Swamp men in the film, and subsequent fans of the series and the film would be amazed at what the characters get away with in the novel. Because of the changes between the various formats—from printed page, to movie screen, to television—the only way for fans to really wrap their heads around each is to ignore the others. Thus, we have to think of each existing in its own creative universe, with nothing quite matching between each of them.

But it goes further than that. The coauthor of the first novel, W. C. Heinz, disowned the dozen books later ghostwritten by William E. Butterworth III, and ignored the two subsequent sequels written by Hornberger. Hornberger also ignored the Butterworth series in his two sequels (to be fair, one was written before Butterworth was even involved). Thus, characters do things in the original novel that don't quite match what they would do in the Butterworth series, nor in the "Hornberger alone" sequels, *MASH in Maine* and *MASH Mania*. And just as we can look at the resolution to the television series and conclude that it would not be the logical end for the same characters in the movie, we can do the same thing with the characters from the Butterworth novels versus the Hornberger-penned ones.

It is only fair then that if the movie and television series are to be dissected within these pages, then the various novels should be as well. First, naturally, a look at the novel that started it all.

MASH: A Novel About Three Army Doctors

- Written by H. Richard Hornberger and W. C. Heinz under the pseudonym of Richard Hooker.
- Release Date: October 1968 by William Morrow & Co.
- Pocket Books paperback edition released in November 1969 (multiple reissues with variants of the cover since that time).

The first edition shows a comical drawing of the three doctors of the novel—Hawkeye, Trapper, and Duke—under one helmet. They are holding martini glasses, cards, a football, a hockey stick, and a baseball bat. Subsequent paperback editions around the time of the film's release in 1970 and for many later reissues switched to the iconic "Peace Sign on Legs" image (a hand giving a peace sign and standing on two female legs in heels).

Plot

It is mid-November 1951 at the 4077th Mobile Army Surgical Hospital ("the double natural," as it is referred to in this and many of the Butterworth novels), located near the 38th parallel in Korea. Corp. Radar O'Reilly is playing poker with the dentist of the unit, Painless Pole, when he overhears

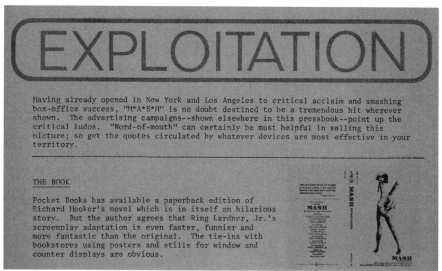

Promotional tie-in to the novel from the film's pressbook, showing the cover and suggesting—in a backhanded way—that even the book's author thought the film was better than the novel.

their commander, Lt. Col. Henry Blake, screaming over the phone to Brig. Gen. Hamilton Hammond, demanding two new "cutters." Neither O'Reilly nor Painless is excited beyond the possibility of finding two new suckers to play poker.

Traveling in a jeep assigned to them from the 325th Evacuation Hospital, the two new "cutters," Duke and Hawkeye, stop along the way for drinks and discuss their new positions. Knowing that the 4077th commander is desperate for their services, they assume that if they perform well they'll be able to get away with anything. They arrive at the MASH unit and enter the mess tent, where they are spotted by Blake, who assigns them to Major Hobson's tent and tells them to report at 9:00 that night to start work.

Their stay with Hobson doesn't last long, as Hawkeye and Duke take an immediate dislike to the man due to his loud praying at all hours of the day and night and his insistence on protocol that leads to Duke tackling him in anger. Hobson is finally sent home by Blake after he begins praying loudly in the mess tent before every meal, leaving the 4077th one doctor short.

Soon after a new surgeon arrives, with Duke and Hawkeye happy that they've now got a "chest-cutter" (a doctor who is expert at surgery of the chest, as can be guessed by the nickname). However, everyone but Duke and Hawkeye is unnerved by the new man, and the only things known about him—besides being a good surgeon—are that he's thin, doesn't talk much, carries olives around for his martinis, and rarely is out of his parka. Hawkeye is positive he has seen the man before, but it is not until he is reminded of a college football game that he remembers the man as the quarterback of the other team whose pass he intercepted, "Trapper" John McIntyre.

Hawkeye, Trapper, and Duke all live in a tent called "The Swamp," and many are invited for drinks on a regular basis, including the Catholic Chaplain, Father "Dago Red" Mulcahy. They detest, however, the Protestant Chaplain, who goes by the nickname of Shaking Sammy (due to his tendency to glad-hand anyone and everyone) and has the habit of writing letters to soldiers' families to let them know all is well, without knowing if the soldier is still alive. One such letter intercepted before mailing angers Hawkeye and Duke, who shoot out the tires on Sammy's jeep as he attempts to drive away. The Swamp men then kidnap Sammy and tie him to a cross surrounded by flammable material and make it appear they are going to burn him to death. Blake is ready to court-martial them, but a warning of heavy casualties leads to Blake having to admit defeat; he needs them and drops the charges.

Painless Pole is beloved by the outfit for his dental office that includes a never-ending poker game, a pool table, beer, and a record player, besides the dental chair he uses for his patients. He's also known for being well endowed, and people come from miles around to see him in the shower just to take a look at what they had heard about in rumors. The one negative thing about Painless Pole is that he goes through a monthly depression for one to three days, and in the latest such emotional state he has mentioned to Hawkeye that he is impotent. After telling them he plans to commit suicide, Hawkeye and the others convince him to take a "black capsule" for the deed. This turns out to be a ruse to help cheer him up, which involves having him parachuted out of a helicopter with a gold medal on his penis. The prank does the trick, and Painless is soon back to his normal self.

Nearly a quarter of the way into the book, the reader is finally introduced to Capt. Frank Burns, a man who hates Hawkeye. It's a mutual feeling, and it isn't helped when Hawkeye tells Frank that he's going to have one of his six brothers burn down Frank's home back in the States. With his tendency to claim "God's will" or someone else at fault for his own mistakes, an incident in the O.R. where Burns blamed a clueless private over the death of a patient causes Duke to break Frank's nose, bust his lip, and do damage to one of his knees. A reckless surgery on another patient that nearly kills the man leads to Trapper decking Frank as well.

Meanwhile, Maj. Margaret Houlihan arrives to take over as the chief nurse. She sees Burns as a stellar doctor, little realizing that Blake has Trapper fixing all of Burns' mistakes in the O.R. and in post-op in secret (another reason why Trapper detests Frank). She also takes an instant dislike to Hawkeye, who points out not only how bad a surgeon Frank is, but that she is a "regular army clown." When Trapper is made chief surgeon (mainly due to his covering up Frank's mistakes) and insults Houlihan, she teams up with Burns to write a letter to General Hammond that takes much longer in her tent than it should. Although no one knows the details, Trapper begins referring to Houlihan the next morning as "Hot Lips," and Hawkeye makes one too many suggestive comments to Burns in the mess tent, resulting in Burns throwing a coffee urn at Hawkeye and then punching him repeatedly just as Blake enters. Blake sends Burns home, but tears into the men in the Swamp for setting Frank up. The men are not heartbroken, with Duke saying that if he gets "into Hot Lips" and decks Hawkeye, perhaps he can be sent home as well.

Ho-Jon, the Korean boy who helps attend to the needs of the Swamp men, is drafted into the Korean army and returns soon after as one of the wounded. Hawkeye decides to get Ho-Jon into his alma mater and has Trapper grow out his beard in order to sell pictures of Trapper as Jesus Christ. They go on a personal appearance tour with Trapper as Jesus to other units in order to raise cash and make enough to successfully send Ho-Jon to the U.S.

A congressman's son is wounded in a training exercise in Japan, and General Hammond sends for Trapper to take care of the young man. Trapper takes Hawkeye with him for the trip in hopes of catching some rounds of golf, knowing from the x-rays that the chest wound is not as serious as the doctors in Kokura suspect. Arriving at the hospital and making a mockery of the hierarchy, they are introduced to the anesthesiologist while performing the operation, and it turns out to be an old friend of Hawkeye, Capt. Ezekiel Bradbury Marston, V (also known as Me Lay). Me Lay invites them to Dr. Yamamoto's Finest Kind Pediatric Hospital and Whorehouse, where Me Lay does some medical work with the kids as well as inspects the women working there. After dressing down Colonel Merrill for bringing them there on a case that could have easily been done by someone there, the pair con some British officers into a game of golf before going to Yamamoto's place.

Me Lay tells them about a newborn that may need surgery, leading to Trapper and Hawkeye arranging to have the baby taken to the military hospital. The nurses are willing to help, while Colonel Merrill is driven to Yamamoto's place and photographed with one of the prostitutes in order to keep his silence. Afterwards, an attempt to enter a golf tournament goes sour, but Hawkeye and Trapper are happier with the results of their surgeries, and Me Lay agrees to adopt the baby.

Hearing of coming wounded, the pair arrive back at the 4077th to face a flood of casualties that leave them and anyone handy—including Father Mulcahy—in the O.R. for days. Still, the Swamp men manage to survive along with their patients. However, a near-miss in surgery by Hawkeye, along with Duke and Trapper having lost a patient over what should have been a routine procedure, has them all depressed. Blake, looking to help, brings in other men who are known to be even more out of control than the Swamp men in order to get their spirits back up, and it works. However, it also leads to the name-calling of Houlihan getting out of hand. Houlihan threatens to resign her commission, and Blake dares her to do so, leading to Houlihan calling General Hammond about the situation with the Swamp men. When the Swamp men find out that Blake is in trouble, they go to bat for him by talking to Hammond. Hammond, impressed by the men, sees

Blake in a new light and ignores Houlihan's request. Houlihan disappears from the novel at this point.

Blake, with Hammond in his corner now, is sent to hold temporary duty at a hospital in Tokyo, leaving the 4077th in the hands of a regular army surgeon, Col. Horace Delong. Delong immediately gets on Hawkeye's bad side by questioning his surgical techniques and is then questioning the sanity of the men when they begin to make a "mermaid trap"—mainly as a means to pass the boredom, but subsequently to confuse Delong (it is noted that Blake deliberately did not warn Delong about the Swamp men). Delong arranges for the trio to be taken to the 325th Evacuation Hospital for evaluation, and Hawkeye nearly is sent back to the U.S. for observation when Blake appears and cancels the whole thing, knowing it for the gag it is.

The men decide to put together a football team and bring in a ringer by the name of Oliver Wendell Jones, aka Spearchucker Jones. Jones was a fullback in the pros before becoming a neurosurgeon, and Hawkeye thinks that if they get him moved to the 4077th, they could put together a team that will beat the 325th Evacuation Hospital, who consider themselves the champion football team in Korea. Blake goes for the idea, and they work out a bet with General Hammond over the game, not realizing that Hammond

A scene from the film adaptation of *MASH* of the football game. Of these characters, Hawkeye, Duke, Spearchucker, and Trapper will return for both of the *MASH* sequels written by Hornberger, while Duke and Spearchucker will eventually be written out of the *MASH Goes to . . .* series after only a couple of books.

has multiple ringers on his team. Risking a lot of money, the 4077th goes on to win the game and the bet with some deceptive plays.

As the weeks close in for Hawkeye and Duke to leave, the two begin to drift off from the 4077th to do other things when times are slow. Two new captains are brought in to learn the ropes, and Blake has the pair work with them to teach "meatball surgery" to the new doctors who are taking too long in the O.R. This goes well until one learns that his wife has lost her mind without him, forcing his return to the States. The Swamp men then mail letters to their wives, asking that they do the same to get them home quicker.

It is February 1953 (just a few months before the end of the war). Duke and Hawkeye are told they are being sent home. The pair has a going-away party with many of the regulars of the camp and salute Blake in his office before leaving. They continue with disrespecting the military on their way home, but realize as they get closer to their destinations that they are rapidly turning back into normal men again rather than the animals known as being part of the Swamp. Hawkeye's plane lands, and he arrives to see his wife and his two boys. They greet him with open arms.

In Review

The most interesting thing about *MASH*—and probably a good reason for why so many publishers turned it down—is that there is no arc to the characters or the plot. An arc is a fundamental element in writing a novel—showing the rise of a character, a crisis for the character to resolve, and then a resolution. To see characters whiz through a story—even better, a war novel—without any ramifications for what they had seen or done makes the manuscript look like it is missing chapters and a conclusion.

Yet sometimes the "amateur" (as Hornberger called himself) can bring something fresh to writing, and it works for Hornberger to break the mold. His story is one of various episodes that these characters experience over the many months that Hawkeye and Duke are in Korea. That has functioned in serialized fiction before *MASH*, but rarely as one for a linear storyline about characters. Usually in novels, such episodes lead up to a big event that changes the hearts of at least one character, if not many. That's not the case in *MASH*, however. They come, they conquer . . . and they leave. That's *MASH*.

The movie will have the same structural issues upon release with reviewers as well—nothing really happens even though everything does in a sense.

Yet that is the novel. And the same with the life of many who were involved in the war that kept their sanity the best they could by "disconnecting" in the way that the Swamp Men do while at the 4077th. They are sincere in wanting to save lives; everything else is irrelevant to that task. Social mores and military procedures mean nothing to them and are ignored, because such things merely block out their ability to function. Thus, the structure of what a novel should be also can easily be erased for the necessity of the characters and the good of the novel. To conform to what is expected in the structure of storytelling would hurt the validity of the text.

Even so, it is easy to see the material that Heinz brought to the manuscript once he began working with Hornberger. The doctor was known for his interest in golf, so the golf game may have come from his pen, but the nuances of the golf scam in Japan sound much like they came from a sportswriter. More specifically, football is a sport that was close to Heinz (he wrote Vince Lombardi's autobiography, after all), and the long passages dealing with plays and the elements of the gambling involved must surely have been a strong contribution by him to the novel. Oddly enough, it is usually the football game in both the film and novel that fans knock as being the dullest part of the story.

Perhaps the most fascinating thing in the novel is how truly menacing Hawkeye, Duke, and the others can be. Trapper and Hawkeye of the series would not last a day with the same characters from the novel (perhaps the film, but definitely not the novel), which is not only a sign that things had to be scrubbed first for the film and then later the series, but also that audiences' tastes—at least at the time—in viewing television and film demanded so. It is one thing to read in a novel about men who perform a fake crucifixion, but another if it's on the big screen. It certainly would not have worked on the small screen, and it remains somewhat easier to look at Hawkeye being a single man going after numerous women (and often failing) than the one who is married and messing around with Lt. Dish in the film (or doing more with various business girls in the novel). Also, it is made clear early on that Hawkeye, Trapper, and Duke know they can get away with everything because they are so good. A little humility goes a long way and was used in the series to make plain that the doctors saw themselves as merely doing what anyone humanly could, rather than being hotshots who blew off anyone trying to talk them down a little as in the novel (the movie doesn't bother addressing the issue, moving at too fast a pace for us to really consider the idea). For this reason, it is possible to come out of *MASH* disturbed with the main characters, especially as you wait for something to happen to them that will allow them to be knocked down a peg and then bring themselves back up, as would be expected in normal plotting of a story. Hornberger and Heinz attempt to bring a bit of this into the storyline with the cases that depress the Swamp men two-thirds of the way through the novel, but it is ultimately a setup for Houlihan going to Hamilton and an excuse to write her out of the book. Because of the results, the plot point never quite emerges as a "game changer" for the characters.

Even so, the book was a success and a sequel demanded. But what can you do with a war-based comedy when there's no war to fight?

MASH Goes to Maine

- Written by H. Richard Hornberger under the pseudonym of Richard Hooker. There has been no indication that any other writers were involved in the development of this novel, unlike the first novel or the subsequent Butterworth series.
- Release Date: February 1972 by William Morrow & Co. Pocket Books paperback edition released in January 1973 (multiple reissues with variants of the cover since that time).

With the iconic "Peace Sign on Legs" image from the film becoming synonymous with the franchise, it was only natural for the sequel novel to use a variation on that theme, this time with a lobster replacing the hand.

The Sphere edition out of Britain used a similar concept, but boosted the lobster up a tad so that the model's entire posterior can be seen.

Chapter 11 from the novel was reprinted in the January 1972 issue of *Playboy* magazine in order to help promote the novel and was given the title of "Who Stuck the Flag in Rev. Titcomb?"

The sequel was optioned as a possible movie by 20th Century-Fox, but once the television series began to take off—and with the remote chance of obtaining the services of the actors from the first film—the idea of a film adaptation fell through by 1972.

The book is dedicated to Bill Heinz, the cowriter of the original novel in the series.

Plot

Summer 1955. Hawkeye had come back from Korea to work at a VA hospital in Spruce Harbor, Maine, until he can pass his surgical boards. After being forced out of that hospital, and with a year at another, Hawkeye ends up joining Trapper John to work at Saint Lombard's Hospital in New York City. The objective is that if he can get a year's more work in thoracic surgery, he'll be able to go back to Maine with the ability to write his own ticket as a surgeon.

In April 1956, Hawkeye and Trapper run into Me Lay, who tells them about two surgeons: Ramsey Coffin, a surgeon their age who is stuck on himself, and Wiley Morgan, an older surgeon who is past his prime. Thanks to working with two practitioners at the hospital, a Brit named Tony Holcombe and old-timer Doggy Moore, Hawkeye begins seeing a steady stream of patients and decides to open up a clinic with Holcombe to be called the Finestkind Clinic and Fishmarket. Hawkeye's first decision is to contact Duke Forrest who is happy to join up, and a deviant con allows Spearchucker Jones to sign on in the small Maine town without raising any racial issues.

Trapper is reluctant to join them, and it takes a complicated con on both him and an investor that involves a golf game, the receptionist who wants to marry Trapper, and another "black capsule" to get Trapper John to agree. In doing so, Trapper gets the girl, but decides to live in a tent with her on a nearby island, where their shenanigans in the bushes leads to a frequent fly-by from a commercial flight going to Spruce Harbor (and the introduction of Wrong-Way Napolitano, who will appear in many of the Butterworth novels).

The rest of the book deals with antics of the locals, including a reverend and his wife whose "love thy neighbor" policy is a bit too literal. This isn't unusual for the area, as it seems nearly everyone in town is on the chase with each other, leading to Hawkeye forcing Ramsey Coffin to flee the city by having him contract "the clap" and pass it on to a number of married women in town. There is also the story about Moose Lord, whom Hawkeye treats for esophagus cancer in an age when the only hope was drastic surgery. As surmised early on, Moose eventually passes away, but lives long enough to give himself and his family closure, which is all Hawkeye can do.

The book ends in the early 1960s, with Kennedy as president and town-favorite Doctor Doggy Moore accidentally shot in the heart. Through each of their specialties the former MASH men save Doggy's life, showing them that in a few short years and with the advancements in technology, they are much better surgeons than ever before.

In Review

Some reviews at the time of release thought *MASH Goes to Maine* an even better, funnier novel than *MASH*. Yet in reading it more than forty years later, the seams are more evident. It was one thing when Hawkeye and the others were fighting the military, as everyone, from the top on down and from inside or out, could tell you that the military—like any government function—sometimes needs to be taken down a few notches. When it comes to characters trying to live their lives in their small town only to deal with doctors who keep interfering because they can . . . it seems more invasive to some readers. There isn't much of that in the sequel, but it is there, and the choppy style of multiple stories that don't really lead anywhere begins to drag a bit by the time it gets to the final chapters.

Race also plays a bigger part in the second book, as Jones' decision to move to the town is played out as a chance for Hornberger to use hidden racism as a means to con the townspeople into letting Jones stay. Hornberger is willing to play with the idea a bit, but won't go whole hog on his views about such matters until his final book in the series, *MASH Mania*. The amount of sex in the novel is also surprising in that the original novel did not feature so strongly that everyone was doing pretty much everyone else as it does in the second novel with the town of Spruce Harbor. This factor may have helped get chapter 11 (about the sex-crazed Rev. Titcomb and his wife) into the pages of *Playboy*, although the strongest chapter in the novel is chapter 8 ("The Sound of the Moose"), dealing with Moose's struggle with cancer and certainly one that could have worked as a short story on its own.

Readers at least get to meet the wives of the various Swamp men, although they do not do much more than tut-tut the antics of the husbands. Other characters such as Doctor Doggy Moore, Jocko Allcock, and Wooden Leg Wilcox are introduced, and will return in the final novel, but namely work on the same level as incidental characters from the first novel. They are there to be eccentrics, have odd stories told of each, and then pop up once in a while to throw in occasional gag lines and not much else.

Even so, this time around, Hornberger does have an arc in mind—the novel ends with the principals coming together and learning a bit about themselves in the process. They have grown. Maybe not emotionally in their behavior toward others, but at least on the level of seeing that they have learned more about their professions. It shows the growth of Hornberger as a writer as well. Once you hit the limelight with the first novel, even when you try to go back home again (which the structure of *MASH Goes to Maine* does in many ways), ultimately you have to prove your worth instead of just repeating everything. As mentioned in the previous chapter, however, two novels had been enough for Hornberger, and he was ready to let the stories about Hawkeye, Trapper, Duke, and Spearchucker end with the second novel as he went back to concentrate on his first passion of medicine.

Pocket Books refused to take no for an answer, however, and so soon came the *MASH Goes to . . .* series that were listed as being written by "Richard Hooker" but were actually ghostwritten by William E. Butterworth III. Thus, although *MASH Goes to Maine* did not sell as well as the first novel, it sold enough to publish the books ghostwritten by William E. Butterworth over the next three years, as well as one final novel from Hornberger himself.

MASH Mania

- Release Date: December 1977 by Dodd, Mead & Co. in hardback.
- Written by: Listed as by Richard Hooker. The copyright states H. Richard Hornberger.

The cover art—showing Halfaman frightening one of the prostitutes with the bird costume—was designed by Tim Gaydos. Of interest is that the book lists nine of the Butterworth novels; the three released in 1977 are missing from the list.

The book would later be reissued in paperback by Pocket Books with a return of the "peace sign on legs" image, and with the army helmet on the forefinger like in the original version of the image.

Sphere's cover shows the "peace sign on legs" with bandages wrapping the forefinger and middle finger, while clutching a $100 bill.

Plot

The novel takes place between 1971 and 1975, with flashbacks to earlier times. It is partially written in the first person by "Richard Hooker," who is the administrator of the Spruce Harbor Medical Center, but it is not unusual for the narrative to slip back into the third person when needed to advance the story.

Hooker introduces the novel by describing what Hawkeye Pierce is like; specifically how Hawkeye considers liberals to be patronizing morons and how much he hates the psychologists that have moved into the medical center but do little to help anyone. This leads into a story about Hawkeye having no issues with racial name calling as such words "under certain circumstances establish a bond of understanding and even affection." It also lands him in trouble after calling Dr. Jones an "unconscious nigger bastard" during a televised golf game. After much protesting by others, Hawkeye remedies the situation by chasing Jones down the hall with a cracking whip in front of the committee who were sent to hear Hawkeye's apology. They then take off together on a vacation with their angry wives.

Sometime later, Jones runs into issues when a rare bird, the black-headed grosbeak, attracts the attention of visitors to his home. The gang—Hawkeye, Spearchucker, Duke, and Trapper—chase off the onlookers by dressing up a man, known as Halfaman, in a bird costume similar in color to the rare bird. This causes Jones' wife, Evelyn, to send him packing before finally forgiving him.

In 1971, Trapper locates a heart surgeon to join them by the name of Walter "Boom Boom" Benner, not realizing that he is essentially a foster son to Hawkeye, and that the man may be extremely intelligent, but tends to use the term "boom boom" to describe everything when not spouting odd phrases in order to confuse people. The assistant Wood Leg Wilcox helps "Boom Boom" get out of working the emergency room after it is clear that he works best in surgery, but not one-on-one with patients coming in with minor ills and injuries.

Bored, the gang picks a nonsensical fight with Goofus MacDuff, the medical director, and Dr. Ferenc Ovari (nicknamed "Rex Eatapuss" by Hawkeye). This leads to the doctors being considered insane and sent before a judge to rule if they need to go to the "funny farm," but the judge sees through the silliness and ignores the complaints against them.

At Christmas, a litter of puppies has Jones blackmailing most of the town in order to raise money for the underprivileged, while also giving the puppies away to deserving kids. The following July, Meanstreak Morse, Hawkeye's brother-in-law, returns to town after becoming a neurosurgeon. The chapter deals with his many struggles to go to college and become a surgeon in his thirties, including happily beating up liberals at the university and converting to Judaism in order to get into medical school.

Elsewhere, Duke finds that an Asian woman who married a drunkard named Laurier Castonguay is living in squalor with her kids. Forcing the family to move into town and start things anew, Duke manages to turn their lives around, while Amiko, the wife, becomes the operating room supervisor at Spruce Harbor Medical Center. Hawkeye also hires a new surgeon to take some of his load of work, Dr. D'Artagnan Maguire, who is hesitant due to his "being black." Hawkeye makes plain that he doesn't care and has

Maguire bring his family to live in his house with his kids while Hawkeye takes his wife on vacation. The doctor accepts.

The final third of the novel deals with the gang's growing discontent with the psychologists and psychoanalysts in the medical center, especially when they are required to be examined by the mental health practitioners. This is colored by the view that such individuals are paid a lot of money to not do anything but send the troubled people right back to the doctors for advice if anything else happens, making their purpose meaningless. The introduction of a rape counselor is the last straw for the doctors, who first taunt the woman by asking her advice on how to rape a woman and then later set up the prostitutes in town to accuse the elderly Dr. Doggy Moore and what turns out to be a toothless old bear of rape, thus making her and the whole mental health clinic look silly. The novel ends with all the psychologists and psychoanalysts being forced out of town, but Dr. Ovari becomes the manager of the Finestkind Seafood Restaurant because any psychologist is a "born thief and a con man" and would do well in such a role.

Returning Characters

Hawkeye, Trapper John, Duke Forrest, Oliver Wendell Jones, Mary Pierce, Lucinda McIntyre, Me Lay Marston (mention), Evelyn Jones, Wrong Way Napolitano, Ho-Jon, Goofus MacDuff, Dr. Doggy Moore.

Character Development

- Although most of the information would have been relevant to the second Hornberger novel, it turns out that Hawkeye and his wife essentially adopted a young man and helped get him become a surgeon. We also learn that in the 1950s Meanstreak Morse got Hawkeye's sister pregnant when she was fifteen and thus had to marry her.
- Jones' wife's name is revealed for the first time, and readers find out that he has a son named Olly.
- Henry Blake is now a major general. No other information is given as to where he is located these days.

Inconsistencies

The Finestkind Fishmarket and Clinic is referred to as the Finestkind Clinic and Fish Market in *MASH Mania*.

In Review

It's a rough final ride into the literary sunset of *MASH* with H. Richard Hornberger's *MASH Mania*. The first novel shows us a group of men trying to stay sane within the madness of the military and the war. The second expresses how the oddness of small-town life could be both a blessing and a curse, and demonstrates a progression in Hornberger's ability to wrap a series of misadventures into a nice package by the final page. As discussed in the subsequent chapter, William E. Butterworth's twelve novels are silly satirical fantasies that just happen to feature our regular cast of characters from the first novel. They're fun on a different level and even at its most biting, don't mean to offend. At least they can be ignored.

MASH Mania, however, expresses a high level of anger that Hornberger had about the system, about people, about politics, about race, and about *MASH*, the television series, that hasn't been seen before in his novels. Further, it is a product of its time that may not rest as well with readers today as it did when published in the 1970s. A good example is one of the main plots in the novel: Hornberger clearly has issues with the use of psychoanalysis—a very popular subject of the 1970s—and has Hawkeye rant early in the novel about psychology in order to frame his argument that expensive services being rendered by individuals in the field rarely help. Hawkeye will do so again later in the novel, repeating some of what was already said earlier and thus looking as if the author, rather than the character, is blowing off steam. The conclusion of the storyline is also choppier than expected. A prank dealing with having an elderly doctor and a bear accused of raping women in the town, and the surprise reappearance of Henry Blake, along with a bunch of tents brought in to deal with those needing assistance, supposedly drives out the entire mental health care system from the city, but it's never quite explained why this would occur. Yes, we do see again how Hawkeye and his friends can tear down false idols and make everything right, but the process doesn't seem to fall into place in a way that makes it appear to be a logical conclusion from their antics.

Further, there are two elements in particular that have become more pronounced in the years since the book was first released that have tainted the novel: race and sexual abuse. In the previous novels, Hawkeye avoided racial slurs beyond those applied to Asians, and that was minimal and made sense in relation to the time (it was the Korean War, and it would have been easy to fall into calling the enemy "gooks" without any intention of meaning it for all Asians). In addition, Hawkeye's relationship with Spearchucker is drawn to demonstrate that he doesn't care about color as much as about the person inside the skin. Yet *MASH Mania* has Hawkeye defending his need to use the N-word, stating that he means it as an endearment when saying it to Spearchucker and anyone else, including a prospective young doctor who agrees to live in Hawkeye's house. He's not alone in doing this either; Duke, Trapper, and even Spearchucker himself throw the word around.

No doubt Hornberger is trying to say that friends don't let words bother them—that they don't mean anything in context. Yet, because Spearchucker seems to take it so easily,it could be questioned if he is really not bothered, or if he feels he can't say anything about it, which of course is far from what the author's intention. Still, if Hornberger really wanted to deal with the concept of racial slurs and how they are used, he could have addressed it from Jones' perspective. Instead, it's all set up for Hawkeye cracking a whip at Spearchucker as a punch line to a limp joke.

Secondly, there's no way of getting around the rape jokes in the final third of the novel. Admittedly, such humor has only recently become passé, and even then not completely (for example, prison-related "don't drop the soap" jokes still are used to the present date without much criticism), while in the 1970s it could still lead to punch lines in films and television, even on a show that has been so often charged with being "politically correct" as *MASH*. The punch line to "House Arrest" in the third season is that of an officer accusing Frank of rape (with both Hawkeye and Trapper making fun of the concept), while the same season's episode "Rainbow Bridge" uses rape as a setup for a punch line mid-episode. Still, in such cases, rape remains a concept that has no ultimate meaning; in both cases it is clearly hysterical grandstanding. In *MASH Mania*, Hornberger has the MASH men cornering the female rape counselor and ganging up on her as they describe ways that they are interested in raping a woman, forcing her to flee in fear. They then have prostitutes in town falsely claim rape in order to make the counselor and others look foolish. The worst effect is that Hornberger takes a character written as a cantankerous but ultimately kind soul, Dr. Doggy Moore, and transforms him as being in on the prank and acting lewd toward women after admitting to the false rape—an image that doesn't jibe with the second novel's portrayal of the character (having him accused and him destroying everyone with how idiotic it was to think so would have been fitting, but as it is here, it seems completely out of character).

It's shocking, but not in the way intended. Shaking Sammy on the cross in *M ASH* was shocking, but he was deserving of the prank because of his insensitivity to the soldiers who were dying. The shower prank in the *MASH* film is unsettling, but the women of the MASH unit are shown to be in on

Alan Alda as Hawkeye from the television series. Hawkeye had been created as a character that Hornberger saw as "doing things I wish I could." Changes in the character in the television series that Hornberger felt did not reflect his vision—especially politically—would be a major disappointment to the author.

the prank, and it becomes one of a person who needs to be taken down a notch. We let it go, because there's still a general sense of silliness and that no one ultimately is being hurt. It's different in *MASH Mania*, however. The rape counselor is just a person trying to do her job (and is shown doing so), but we're supposed to side with Hawkeye and the others simply . . . well, simply because it was Hawkeye and the others. In "House Arrest" it only works because it is clear that no one believes the charges, but the person will have to go through the bureaucracy of an investigation anyway. In *MASH Mania*, Hawkeye and the men are threatening rape because they think it's funny. We've gone from men trying to keep their sanity in a crazy world, as in *MASH*, to a group of powerful bullies who happily hurt people who haven't done anything to be targeted by them.

No doubt Hornberger felt he had to make a stand. It is clear from the rare interviews Hornberger did that he was not happy with what he saw as the "liberal direction" of the television series. More specifically, how Hawkeye was changed to fit into what Hornberger saw as a "liberal," which bothered him. As mentioned before, Hornberger over the years made clear that Hawkeye was not just his main character in the novel, but a romanticized version of how Hornberger saw himself. He wanted this character to be what he wished he had been (if not saw himself as being while there). Hawkeye is Hornberger.

Which makes clearer why he eventually became vocal about his hatred for the series. Hawkeye was Doctor Superman in the novel, and in the film. The Hawkeye of the series quickly began to show signs that he wasn't as perfect as he appeared. By the end, he realized that he was never as perfect as he had hoped, but was still a good man doing good work for others. All well and good for a character arc in a television series, but it was no longer the Hawkeye Pierce of Hornberger's making. And most damaging of all, it was the version of Hawkeye that the world recognized now, rather than the Hornberger one. *MASH Mania* is the backlash against all the things that Hornberger feels is wrong with the television character. It's his stake through the heart of this monster created by Hollywood. Have Hawkeye tut-tut racial prejudice in the series? Fine, he'll say the N-word a million times in the novel and think it's a good thing. He's a liberal? Well, the novel has him happy to see liberals beaten up and students protesting a war being physically forced back into the classrooms. The problem is that he lets that agenda get in the way of his storytelling. Thus *MASH Mania* never quite gels the way that the other two novels in the series do.

In his last novel, Hornberger makes his stand. It would be his last. The novel's sales were only tepid, and there would never be another *MASH* novel by the author. For Hornberger, *MASH* was over and—to Hornberger, from all accounts—good riddance.

But other avenues for the concept without its creator had already opened by then, including even competing with himself in the bookstores.

5

Boozing, Cruising, and Cutting Up

The *MASH Goes to . . .* Book Series

As described in chapter 3, Pocket Books was itching to make some money off the success of the *MASH* television series, but after two novels, Hornberger had better things to do with his time. Finally, Pocket Books upped the ante to the point where even Hornberger could not refuse, but only under the stipulation that he didn't have to do the writing and that he got to okay the plots.

William E. Butterworth wrote twelve books in the series, creating histories and backstories for characters that were not so much there because Hornberger had written them, but because they were characters seen in the television series. For this reason, we see a heavy use of Margaret Houlihan in nearly all of the dozen novels, Father Mulcahy popping up every two or three books, and even Frank Burns getting involved in the plots of two novels, although none of these characters had much to do in the original novel. A vague connection to the television series deepens as the novels go along, dropping both Duke and Spearchucker after three books and revamping Trapper to have the backstory of what television viewers would have accepted. Anyone who went from the original novel to one of the Butterworth ones without having the television series as a reference would have been confused, but anyone who was just a fan of the television show would have no such issue. As it is, much of it is still confusing, which is why inconsistencies are listed with each book under review in this chapter.

Butterworth couldn't help adding backstories to the characters in these novels, for the purpose of moving the plots along if nothing else. However, anything that occurs to these characters within the Butterworth novels remains isolated only to this "universe" of novels. The television series would ignore the books (giving Radar a different first and middle name, for

Hawkeye and Trapper from *MASH* (1970). Although the original novel really played up Hawkeye and Duke as a duo, both the film and especially the series would focus on Hawkeye and Trapper instead. This would lead to the *MASH Goes to . . .* book series doing the same, with Duke eventually being forgotten early in the dozen books.

example), as did Hornberger when he concludes the *MASH* series of novels with *MASH Mania* (released just months after the final Butterworth novel). For this reason, it is worth pointing out where the characters end up in this run of novels, as it shows a history that never would be duplicated in any of the other versions of *MASH*.

MASH Goes to New Orleans

Release Date: January 1975 by Pocket Books

The first in the Butterworth series will diverge from the "peace sign on legs" concept of *MASH* and *MASH Goes to Maine* with illustrated covers by the artist Sandy Kossin, painter of both book covers and movie posters, including Clint Eastwood's *Hang 'Em High*, *Becket*, Richard Matheson's *I am Legend*, covers for a series of *The Shadow* and *Fu Manchu* novels, and even artwork in the same issue of *Mad* magazine that did a *MASH* parody. In order to visually tie in the novels with the image people have of the series, all the covers by Kossin suggest that Hawkeye and Trapper spend their civilian years dressed in army fatigues and Houlihan is a stereotyped nurse of the 1950s, even though the novels are set in the 1970s.

Sphere in Britain continued with the "peace sign on legs" motif for this and several of the later books, this time showing the hand holding a banjo, which seems to suggest someone in the art department had seen *Deliverance* rather than *MASH*.

Written by

Listed as by Richard Hooker and William E. Butterworth on the cover. Copyright page has the book being written by Richard Hornberger and William E. Butterworth. As verified through other sources, the novel was written completely by Butterworth, with Hornberger okaying the plot.

Plot

Hawkeye's wife is pregnant, and for the first time he's actually available to be at the birth, which has everyone on edge. To get him out of town during the birth, a con is set to force him into attending the "TA & VD Society" (Tonsil, Adenoid & Vas Deferens) convention in New Orleans, with Trapper John making sure he stays put for the duration.

Coincidences lead to the pair arriving at the same hotel featuring a budget meeting for a missionary hospital in Brazil that Margaret H. Wachauf, R.N., the former Margaret Houlihan, is attending, as well as a Knights of Columbus convention featuring an appearance by the Archbishop of Swengchan, China, better known to the others as John Patrick Mulcahy. The Knights of Columbus event leads to a former MASH patient and now rich owner of Chevaux Petroleum, "Horsey" Jean-Pierre de la Chevaux, rekindling friendships with Hawkeye, Trapper, Mulcahy, and Houlihan. It also leads to an article in the local newspaper that makes mention of Hawkeye and Trapper; drawing the attention of Frank Burns, who is helping to run the TA & VD Society event.

Later, Hawkeye is taken in secret to meet with Mulcahy at a prestigious Catholic hospital, the Gates of Heaven, where it is revealed that Mulcahy has lung cancer. Meanwhile, Trapper and Margaret find out that Cody has colon cancer, but his own hospital will not let Trapper do the work, and it is feared that no one there has the experience or expertise to perform the surgery.

To resolve both situations, Cody is kidnapped to the Gates of Heaven, where Trapper and Margaret perform his surgery in front of a conned group of doctors and nurses, and then Hawkeye performs the extraction of a lung on Mulcahy. All goes well.

The final speech for the convention is being broadcast on local television, and a number of threats have arranged for all possible issues caused by Hawkeye, Trapper, and various others to be washed away. Also, Hawkeye is given a chance to speak to the audience about Burns' statement to the press that he had a much more important role in the war than he actually did. Just as Hawkeye is to speak, he receives word that his wife just gave birth to a boy, so after a quick comment about Burns at the podium, he and Trapper head back to Maine.

Returning Characters

Hawkeye Pierce, Trapper John, Spearchucker Jones (cameo), Duke Forrest (cameo), Margaret Houlihan, John Patrick Mulcahy, Radar O'Reilly (in flashback), Frank Burns, Henry Blake (flashback), Wrong Way Napolitano (cameo), Mary Pierce (cameo), Lucinda McIntyre (cameo), Big Benjy Pierce (mention).

Character Development

- Hawkeye is now chief surgeon at the Spruce Harbor Medical Center, and his wife, Mary, is pregnant with their fourth child (it is established that he had two boys in *MASH*, but no mention was made of a daughter being born "nine months and a day" after Hawkeye returned from Korea in *MASH Goes to Maine*).
- Spearchucker does obstetrics at the clinic when not doing neurosurgery.
- Margaret Houlihan reappears for the first time as a registered nurse and widow of a junkyard dealer after retiring as a lieutenant colonel and with twenty years' service in the army. She is working for Rev. Cody with his missionary hospital in Brazil. As the story takes place in the 1970s and Margaret was already forty at the time of *MASH*, this means that she's still turning heads at the age of sixty-plus.
- John Mulcahy is now an archbishop and is rumored to be personal friends with the pope. He also has cancer of the lung and wants Hawkeye

to perform the operation in secret (it turns out to be the main reason he came to the Knights of Columbus event).

- Frank Burns runs the Burns Loving Family and Zero Population Growth Clinic, where he specializes in vasectomies, and has perpetuated the idea that he was the chief surgeon at the 4077th as well as General MacArthur's personal medical advisor.

Inconsistencies

Finestkind Fishmarket and Clinic is listed as Finest Kind Medical Clinic and Fish Market. The crucifixion of Shaking Sammy is told as if Mulcahy had not yet arrived at the 4077th when in the first novel he had been stationed for a time there and had tried to stop Hawkeye, Trapper, and Duke (rather than Colonel Blake attempting to stop them as suggested here).

Franks Burns is stated to be a major when he was a captain in the first novel, and married with children, which was not suggested in the first novel. It is also implied that he tented with Hawkeye and Trapper, which was not the case in the first novel.

Hawkeye makes mention of wiring Margaret's tent to the public address system at the 4077th while she and Frank were in their "love nest." No such event happened in the novel; further, it is Radar (with the assistance of Trapper and several others) who wires the tent up in the film (Hawkeye was in surgery performing an operation when the event occurred). Considering how briefly Frank appears in the first novel and how fleeting his brush with Houlihan was, the constant reminder of Frank by Hawkeye and Trapper borders on psychotically obsessive rather than merely as a "fond memory." It is safe to assume, as with other aspects of this and later Butterworth novels, that the emphasis was on giving readers the characters from the television program rather than from the first two novels. This is evident when Trapper performs the surgery on the intestines of the reverend, while Hawkeye takes out Mulcahy's lung—the reverse of their specialties in the novels up to this point, but which matches the television series.

"Horsey" Jean-Pierre de la Chevaux may be beloved by one and all in this novel, but the character never made an appearance in any *MASH* novel before this one. Get used to him, though; he's going to reappear in all of the other Butterworth novels.

MASH Goes to Paris

Release Date: January 1975 by Pocket Books

It was released in the same month as *MASH Goes to New Orleans*, but clearly is the sequel to the first Butterworth novel. The illustrated cover by Sandy Kossin shows Hawkeye and Trapper about to run down Houlihan in a car while a "Russian" (no doubt Boris) kneels on the roof of the car. There is no scene like it in the book.

As with *MASH Goes to New Orleans*, Sphere continued with the "peace sign on legs" motif, this time showing the hand holding a cigarette and a brassiere in the colors of the French flag.

Written by

Listed as by Richard Hooker and William E. Butterworth on the cover. As before, the book was solely written by Butterworth.

Plot

Horsey de la Chevaux is back, and he's about to get a medal from the French government in honor of cleaning up what turns out to be Horsey's own drunken mess, which was assisted by Hawkeye and Trapper when down in New Orleans. The secretary of state wants to make sure the award ceremony occurs without a hitch, and with Mulcahy unavailable, the only people Horsey responds to in any manner are Hawkeye and Trapper. To keep those two in check, the U.S. government needs the help of the only man Hawkeye and Trapper will listen to, Major General Henry Blake.

A number of other recipients are on the Air Force One flight to France, including J. Robespierre O'Reilly, the former Radar O'Reilly, who is now the CEO of ROR Corporation, and Margaret Houlihan Wachauf Wilson. In other words, it's a grand reunion of the MASH personnel. But trouble brews as Radar is smitten by Madame Kristina Korsky-Rimsakov, an opera singer who seems to share Radar's talent for reading minds, and whose brother is Boris Korsky-Rimsakov, a famous opera singer that Hawkeye and Trapper also has to keep an eye on until the ceremony can occur. Meanwhile, a pigheaded congresswoman, the Bayou Perdu Council of the Knights of Columbus, and a mistaken Arabian kidnapping collide before the ceremony can take place.

Returning Characters

Hawkeye, Trapper John, Henry Blake, Radar O'Reilly, Margaret Houlihan, Wrong Way Napolitano (cameo), Mary Pierce (cameo), Lucinda McIntyre (cameo), Horsey de la Chevaux (from *MASH Goes to New Orleans*), Ace Travers, and Prudence MacDonald-Travers (from *MASH Goes to New Orleans*).

This is also the first appearance of Prince Hassan, Boris Korsky-Rimsakov and the Bayou Perdu Council of the Knights of Columbus, who will appear in later novels. T. Bascomb "Moosenose" Bartlett, the mayor of Spruce Harbor and boyhood friend of Hawkeye, first appears in this novel. He'll pop up in a few of the others over time.

Character Development

- Margaret is now Margaret Houlihan Wachauf Wilson and is again a widower. Her husband, Rev. Buck Wilson from the first novel, died from overexertion on their wedding night. She is now running a school for nurses and is the "Mother Emeritus" for God-Is-Love-In-All-Forms Christian Church, Inc., which was founded by Rev. Wilson. For the sake of saving printer's ink and any confusion by speed-readers, she'll be referred to as Margaret Houlihan in subsequent entries here.
- Blake is now Major General Henry Blake, commander of the Walter Reed Hospital. He's slightly more scatterbrained than in the first novel.
- Radar is listed in the book as J. Robespierre O'Reilly. He is CEO of ROR Corporation, which is a "fast-food service operation" known mainly for their Mother O'Reilly Irish Parlor franchise.

Inconsistencies

MASH Goes to Paris has Radar being given his nickname after playing cards with Painless, Trapper, and Hawkeye and demonstrating he has ESP. In the original novel he was already called Radar long before Hawkeye arrived, and it was due to his hearing (although ESP was also suggested). He had comics and a teddy bear in Korea, which was the case in the series, but never shown in the first novel or movie (but then again, it was never suggested that he didn't have such items, and comics at least were a staple of GI reading during the war). He is known by those around him to not drink or smoke, but he drops this pretense when with the others and does both (thus allowing the Radar of both the movie and the first three seasons of the show

Margaret Houlihan (played by Loretta Swit in the television series) made only a brief appearance in the original novel and never returned in the Hornberger sequels, but due to the character's popularity in the series will appear in the *MASH Goes to . . .* book series, albeit in the somewhat bizarre development as the head of a religious order that caters to gay men.

to mesh with the later, innocent Radar of the series—it's an act he puts on for people who don't know him).

As with the previous novel, it is implied that Hawkeye and Trapper spent much more time and good fellowship with Houlihan than was ever seen in the original novel. Same as Houlihan with Blake and Radar in this novel.

MASH Goes to London

Release Date: June 1975 by Pocket Books

The third book in the series refers to events in the previous two novels, and all subsequent novels will revisit earlier events in the series as well (sometimes even adding scenes that were to have taken place in earlier novels but did not). The cover by the artist Sandy Kossin shows Hawkeye, Trapper, and Houlihan sitting on a sub that is venturing down the Thames, while a Scotsman, Sgt. Angus MacKenzie, tries to pour a drink from a barrel and a woman (Florabelle Jenkins) looks on from the back of the sub.

Sphere's cover continued with the "peace sign on legs" motif, this time showing the hand with a bobby's helmet rather than the traditional U.S. Army helmet seen in the original version of the theme.

Written by

Listed as by Richard Hooker and William E. Butterworth on the cover. As before, the book was solely written by Butterworth.

Plot

A young British sailor, Hugh Percival Woodburn-Haverstraw, is at the Spruce Harbor Medical Center with a broken arm and sharing a room with Boris Korsky-Rimsakov, who sustained an injury while fishing in the area. As he recuperates, the sailor's uncle dies, leaving him as the Duke of Folkestone, and he is requested to return to England for the burial. As the port in Folkestone is used by the U.S. Military for one pound sterling a year, and that such a deal was only to last as long as the old Duke lived, the U.S. government is anxious to bend over backwards if it means "Woody" (as Hawkeye calls Hugh) will grant them an extension on the lease.

Mary, Hawkeye's wife, likes Woody and refuses to let him be sent back to England without Hawkeye and Trapper in tow to make sure nothing unsavory happens to the poor, sweet kid. With Horsey, Boris, and a few others along for the fun, they make sure Woody gets his title, while also linking him back up with others who will watch over him.

Returning Characters

Hawkeye, Trapper John, Margaret Houlihan, Duke Forrest (cameo), Spearchucker Jones (cameo), Mary Pierce, Lucinda McIntyre (cameo), Horsey de la Chevaux, Prince Hassan, Boris Korsky-Rimsakov, the secretary of state, Wrong Way Napolitano (cameo), the Bayou Perdu Council of the Knights of Columbus (cameo).

This is the first appearance of the wives of Duke Forrest and Oliver Wendell Jones as speaking character in one of the novels, and they are not given first names here. It's the last appearance for Duke's wife in any of the novels, but Jones' wife will reappear in the final novel, *MASH Mania.*

This is the last novel in the Butterworth series to feature Duke Forrest and Spearchucker Jones. From here on out, only Hawkeye, Trapper, and Margaret will be regular recurring characters from the first novel, the movie, and series. Both Duke and Spearchucker will return in Hornberger's final novel, *MASH Mania.*

Character Development

- Boris' marriage to the congresswoman of the previous novel lasted only a short time before they divorced.
- It seems Trapper John and his wife may have finally had children, as he has to appear at the PTA meeting along with all the other fathers, although this is never brought up again in any of the subsequent novels. *MASH Goes to Hollywood* has his wife, Lucinda, working as an eighth grade art teacher, but that's not the implication as to why he has to attend the PTA meeting in *MASH Goes to London.*

Inconsistencies

Part of the plot is based on a mutual long-term understanding between Boris and Margaret that goes back to when she took care of him as a nurse at the 4077th and through her two marriages. This contradicts *MASH Goes to Paris*, where Boris is introduced to Margaret for the first time.

The original novel has Duke's full name being August Bedford Forrest, but *MASH Goes to London* has it as Nathan Bedford Forrest.

Finestkind Fishmarket and Clinic is listed as Finest-Kind Fish Market and Medical Clinic. That's okay—Hornberger himself gets it wrong in *MASH Mania* as well.

MASH Goes to Morocco

Release Date: January 1976 by Pocket Books

The illustrated cover of the fourth book in the series has Sandy Kossin show Hawkeye, Trapper, and Houlihan in front of an oil gusher and giving a drink to a camel, while an Arab sits on top of the camel, watching television.

Sphere's cover shows the "peace sign on legs" motif with two palm trees growing from the fingers of the hand.

MASH Goes to Morocco is the first in the series to go over two hundred pages, as will be the case for the subsequent four books in the series.

Written by

Listed as by Richard Hooker and William E. Butterworth on the cover. As before, the book was solely written by Butterworth.

Plot

Hawkeye wins a trip to Morocco at a medical convention, and with his kids sick with the measles, he is forced to go on the vacation with Trapper (whose kids are also sick with the measles). Their attempt to fake the trip and go golfing for two weeks instead is defeated with the help of the secretary of state, who needs them in Morocco to help with a possible oil deal between Horsey and the Sheikh of Abzub—mainly to make sure no one dies during the sure-to-be scuffle that only Horsey can cause.

Horsey is heading to Abzub with Margaret as "spiritual leader" to help with negotiations. Meanwhile, Hawkeye and Trapper manage to escape the clutches of the military in order to play golf. After much running around and several cases of mistaken identities, things are finally set right, and Hawkeye and Trapper make sure that everyone resolves their problems.

Returning Characters

Hawkeye, Trapper John, Margaret Houlihan, Mary Pierce (cameo), Lucinda McIntyre (cameo), Horsey de la Chevaux, Prince Hassan, Boris Korsky-Rimsakov, the secretary of state, the Bayou Perdu Council of the Knights of Columbus (cameo), Hon. Edwards L. "Smiling Jack" Jackson (from *MASH Goes to London*)

Character Development

- It is clear in this novel that Trapper is now a father and has more than one child.
- While Margaret, Hawkeye, and Trapper are part of the plot, Margaret doesn't appear until 156 pages in, and both Hawkeye and Trapper disappear from the story for nearly a hundred pages. They then disappear again for several chapters before turning up in the final seven pages of

the novel to resolve last-minute problems facing several of the characters. In other words, it is the first nearly *MASH*-less *MASH* novel in the series. It is also the first to not feature Hawkeye and Trapper performing any surgery, although Margaret does help deliver a baby at one point.

Inconsistencies

Finestkind Fishmarket and Clinic is listed as Finest Kind Fish Market and Medical Clinic. The hyphen of the previous novel has disappeared this time around, and Medical is still inserted where it had not been in *MASH Goes to Maine*. It'll remain this way through the rest of the Butterworth novels.

At one point, Hawkeye complains of "having spent sixteen months in Korea" with Trapper. As seen in the original novel and film, Trapper came a bit later to the 4077th, and since sixteen months was the entire length of Hawkeye's stay at the MASH unit, the number of months would be incorrect. It can be assumed that Hawkeye doesn't care for accuracy while jabbing at Trapper in this instance, so not necessarily an inconsistency. However, just a few pages later, it is inferred that Hawkeye returned from Korea with Trapper, when in the first novel he did so with Duke, while Trapper stayed behind to finish his tour of duty.

MASH Goes to Las Vegas

Release Date: January 1976 by Pocket Books

Released in the same month as *MASH Goes to Morocco*, the plot plays off of actions that occurred in the previous novel. Sandy Kossin's cover has Hawkeye and Trapper next to a paying-off slot machine and two showgirls, with a stern-looking balding man in back. It is the first cover to not feature Houlihan.

Sphere's cover shows the "peace sign on legs" motif with a die between the two upright fingers on the hand.

This is the first novel in the series to be dedicated to the memory of Malcom Reiss, the literary agent who got Hornberger and Butterworth together. Every novel after this one will be dedicated to him.

Written by

Listed as by Richard Hooker and William E. Butterworth on the cover. As before, the book was solely written by Butterworth.

Plot

At the Las Vegas casino, Nero's Villa, Radar arrives to see Kristina Korsky-Rimsakov, who is appearing as the nightly entertainment (under a contract the casino wishes to get out of, due to the high cost and little return they have achieved). After winning $81,000 at the poker table, Radar inadvertently proposes to Kris, and they decide to gather the MASH gang together for the wedding.

Meanwhile, Dan Rhotten and his assistant, Monica P. Fenstermacher, want to do a television investigation into the Matthew Q. Framingham Theosophical Foundation, of which Hawkeye and Trapper are members. The foundation is actually a 24-hour-a-day, 365-day-a-year poker game for married men, hidden under the veil of being a charitable organization. The investigation, some shady people who want their $81,000 back. and an assortment of other well-remembered faces turn up at Nero's Villa, with a wedding being the last thing on their minds.

Returning Characters

Hawkeye, Trapper John, Margaret Houlihan, Mary Pierce (cameo), Lucinda McIntyre (cameo), Radar O'Reilly, Kristina Korsky-Rimsakov (from *MASH Goes to Paris*), Don Rhotten (from *MASH Goes to Morocco),* Hon. Edwards L. "Smiling Jack" Jackson, Archbishop Mulcahy, Wrong-Way Napolitano (cameo), Horsey de la Chevaux, Prince Hassan, Boris Korsky-Rimsakov, the Bayou Perdu Council of the Knights of Columbus Marching Band (cameo, and it's the band this time and not the council itself), Sheikh Abdullah (from *MASH Goes to Morocco*), Baroness d'Iberville (*MASH Goes to Morocco*), Esmeralda Hoffenburg (*MASH Goes to Morocco*).

This is the first appearance of Don Rhotten, a parody of Dan Rather, who will appear in several of the later novels.

Character Development

- Radar is now a fully licensed commercial pilot. It is stated that his ability to read minds gets murky during sunspots (it's a plot point that doesn't go anywhere). He marries Kristina Korsky-Rimsakov in this novel.
- Margaret now has waist-length hair.
- Mulcahy is also a licensed jet pilot. (He'll be flying again in *MASH Goes to Miami.*)

- By the end of the novel the casino has been converted into the Archbishop Mulcahy's Home for Wayward Girls.
- Once again, the novel has Hawkeye, Trapper, and Margaret doing very little. In this case, they do not even help resolve the two main crises of the novel. Trapper and Hawkeye do take a look at Boris' head injury at least, but that is the only medical procedure discussed in the novel.

Inconsistencies

Mulcahy's middle name was Patrick in *MASH*, and remains so in *MASH Goes to Las Vegas*. However, the back cover of the paperback states his middle name is Joseph.

The Rhotten Report, featuring Dan Rhotten, was broadcast on the Amalgamated Broadcasting System in *MASH Goes to Morocco*. *MASH Goes to Las Vegas* has *The Rhotten Evening News* broadcasting on the Amalgamated Broadcasting Network (and later in the novel as *The ABN Evening News Starring Dan Rhotten*). Rhotten's ratings in the previous book were described as being the last of the network news anchors, yet second to Cronkite in *MASH Goes to Las Vegas*.

Boris acts as if he has no concept of what a marriage is when told of Kris' upcoming wedding. He may be just forgetting (or wanting to forget) that he got married between *MASH Goes to Paris* and *MASH Goes to London*.

MASH Goes to Hollywood

Release Date: April 1976 by Pocket Books

Sandy Kossin's cover has Hawkeye and Trapper next to a bra and panties–clad woman (it's not Margaret, although she ends up in a bikini by the end of the novel), who is about to sip from a jug of moonshine, while Steve Harris looks on in shock. Oddly enough, Margaret does drink from a jug of moonshine in the following novel released the same month, *MASH Goes to Vienna*.

Sphere's cover shows the "peace sign on legs" motif with a top hat and white tie on the index finger and the hand itself holding a cane.

Written by

Listed as by Richard Hooker and William E. Butterworth on the cover. As before, the book was solely written by Butterworth.

Plot

Steve Harris, a state trooper who served as a medic in Vietnam, catches the attention of Hawkeye and Trapper, and they go to the Framingham Foundation for help to get him into Harvard Medical School. Meanwhile, in Paris, Boris has a disastrous opera appearance that sends him into a rage before he disappears, arriving at the Framingham Foundation while Hawkeye and Trapper are there. To cool Boris down and rack up some money for Steve, they send Boris to live with Steve in his cabin in the woods of Maine.

While the world grows frantic about the missing Boris, Don Rhotten and his old friend Wesley St. James—a producer of soap operas—arrive in the woods of Maine to escape from Hollywood and think up a new show for a manipulative superstar actress. The new show will also need to star Zelda Spinopolous, the daughter of a sponsor who has never acted and is reluctant to do so.

After Steve Harris "saves" St. James and Rhotten in the woods, St. James is convinced that Harris should be the star of his new show. Steve meets Zelda, who tries to sabotage her acting career with bad clothes and makeup. When St. James impolitely makes mention of her looks, Steve knocks him and Rhotten into the lake. Zelda and Steve then run off and get married, forsaking Hollywood.

Returning Characters

Hawkeye, Trapper John, Margaret Houlihan, Mary Pierce (cameo), Lucinda McIntyre (cameo), Don Rhotten, Hon. Edwards L. "Smiling Jack" Jackson, Wrong-Way Napolitano (cameo), Horsey de la Chevaux, Prince Hassan, Boris Korsky-Rimsakov, Matthew Q. Framingham VI (from *MASH Goes to Las Vegas*), Nurse Esther Flanagan (*MASH Goes to London*), Baroness d'Iberville, Esmeralda Hoffenburg, Seymour G. Schwartz (*MASH Goes to Las Vegas*), T. Bacscomb "Moosenose" Bartlett (*MASH Goes to Hollywood*), Stanley K. Warczinski (*MASH Goes to Las Vegas*).

This is the first book with T. Alfred Crumley, the Spruce Harbor Medical Center administrator, who will play a Frank Burns-like role for several of the later novels.

Character Development

- Trapper's wife is now an art teacher for the eighth-grade class in Spruce Harbor.
- Margaret goes by the nickname Maggie now, when "Hot Lips" isn't used (she'll drop this after this novel). Besides her religious role, she now runs the Prudence MacDonald Memorial School of Nursing in New Orleans (see *MASH Goes to New Orleans*).

Inconsistencies

The Rhotten Report has changed in *MASH Goes to Hollywood* to *Waldo Maldemer and the Evening News with Don Rhotten*. It is a half-hour instead of the full hour as listed in *MASH Goes to Morocco*. It's still in second place in the ratings, and the network has reverted back to the Amalgamated Broadcasting System. *MASH Goes to Hollywood* makes clear that Waldo Maldemer was around and doing the news before Don Rhotten turned up, which contradicts the previous two books about Rhotten's rise to power at ABS/ABN.

Although Trapper was granted a membership to the Framingham Foundation in the previous novel, he is merely a guest of Hawkeye's and not a member in *MASH Goes to Hollywood*. He'll have full membership again by the time of *MASH Goes to Texas*.

Very little of the book actually takes place in Hollywood. Most of the action takes place in the vicinity of Spruce Harbor, Maine (well, *MASH Stays in Maine* would hardly have been the best title in the world, even if it had been more accurate).

A plot point is made of the Harvard Medical School's director of admissions, Jasper T. Whaley, refusing anyone connected to the Framingham Foundation as he cannot get membership to the club, yet this is never developed into anything.

Once again, the plot is resolved with little help from Trapper and Hawkeye. Margaret does not physically appear until page 189 of the book (just seventeen pages before the end of the novel).

MASH Goes to Vienna

Release Date: June 1976 by Pocket Books

Sandy Kossin's cover has Hawkeye, Trapper, and Margaret (or perhaps Nurse Flanagan) with a naval officer and a Scottish wolfhound.

Sphere's cover shows the "peace sign on legs" motif with a hat on the middle finger in front of a scene view of Vienna (surprising that they didn't put the legs on a gondola).

Written by

Listed as by Richard Hooker and William E. Butterworth on the cover. As before, the book was solely written by Butterworth.

Plot

Taylor P. Jambon, the famous gourmet and animal lover, has tapped actress Patience Throckbottom Worthington to be in a series of commercials for APPLE, an animal protection company (that is more into profits than caring). Knowing that Boris will be in Vienna, she agrees to the commercials only if they are shot there.

Elsewhere, the secretary of state has requested that Lieutenant (j.g.) Jones chaperone the Duke of Folkestone (Hugh "Woody" Percival Woodburn-Haverstraw) when he decamps to visit Beverly Chambers while in Spruce Harbor. A new doctor at the Spruce Harbor Medical Center, Dr. Richard Wilson, is smitten by the female lieutenant.

Before all this, Angus MacKenzie had broken up a litter of wolfhounds amongst various friends and acquaintances—including Hawkeye, Trapper, and Margaret—and they are all meeting in Venice for a reunion of the full-grown pups, along with a black Bengal tiger that has been raised with them.

In the end, APPLE is exposed, Wilson gets the girl, Woody gets the other girl, the dogs get to have their reunion, and Don Rhotten is thrown into a fountain by Boris.

Returning Characters

Hawkeye, Trapper John, Margaret Houlihan, Mary Pierce, Nurse Esther Flanagan, T. Alfred Crumley, Patience Throckbottom Worthington (*MASH Goes to Hollywood*), Angus MacKenzie (*MASH Goes to London*), Florabelle Jenkins (*MASH Goes to London*), Prince Hassan, Boris Korsky-Rimsakov, the secretary of state, Hugh Percival Woodburn-Haverstraw (*MASH Goes to London*), Beverly Chambers (*MASH Goes to London*), Don Rhotten, Wrong-Way Napolitano, Horsey de la Chevaux, Wesley St. James (*MASH Goes to Hollywood*), Waldo Maldemer (*MASH Goes to Hollywood*),

Seymour G. Schwartz, Baroness d'Iberville, Esmeralda Hoffenburg, Dr. Theophilus Mullins Yancey (mentioned since *MASH Goes to Hollywood*, but this is his appearance as a character involved in the plot of one of the novels).

Character Development

- Margaret has gone a bit loopy with the whole religious design for her outfits. She now has her hair up to resemble a bishop's miter (head-dress), wears a cape (which she has been seen in for a few novels by now), and carries a crosier (an ornamental shepherd's staff). She's still dressed as sexy as ever besides that, however, and is equally likely to use the staff as a weapon or an ornament.

Inconsistencies

Hawkeye mentions the trick pulled on Houlihan in the showers while at the 4077th. This occurred in the movie, but not in the original novel.

Once again, Hawkeye is referred to as an expert "chest cutter," while the Hornberger books and movie have Trapper in that role.

MASH Goes to Miami

Release Date: September 1976 by Pocket Books

Sandy Kossin's cover has Hawkeye, Trapper, and a nurse (possibly Margaret, although she's never dressed this way in the novel) on the beach with a Boy Scout getting a martini from Hawkeye or Trapper, and what appears to be an operatic Spanish matriarch reading a sex manual (it's Dona Antoinetta, a character from the novel).

Sphere's cover shows the "peace sign on legs" motif with a pair of sunglasses.

Written by

Listed as by Richard Hooker and William E. Butterworth on the cover. As before, the book was solely written by Butterworth.

Plot

Hawkeye's quick treatment and concern for a young Cuban refugee who got injured at a Boy Scout camp in Spruce Harbor leads to him getting an award from the boy's rich uncles. They also donate money to the nursing school Houlihan runs, leading to a grand ceremony to be held in Miami, with the assumption that a holy relic will be passed on from Houlihan's school of nursing. As can be expected, this is incorrect, and Hawkeye and Trapper have to come up with a way to save face for all involved while venturing to Miami by way of Paris.

Returning Characters

Hawkeye, Trapper John, Margaret Houlihan, Horsey de la Chevaux, Nurse Esther Flanagan, Wrong-Way Napolitano, T. Bascomb "Moosenose" Bartlett, Boris Korsky-Rimsakov, Walter Kosciusko "Painless Pole" Waldowski (*MASH*), Dr. Theophilus Mullins Yancey, Prince Hassan, Mary Pierce, Lucinda McIntyre, Baroness d'Iberville, Esmeralda Hoffenburg, Don Rhotten (mention), John Patrick Mulcahy, Ace Travers, Prudence MacDonald-Travers, Senator J. Ellwood "Jaws" Fisch (*MASH Goes to Miami*), Senator Christopher Columbus Cacciatore, Reverend Mother Superior Bernadette of Lourdes (*MASH Goes to New Orleans*).

Besides Duke Forrest, the return of Waldowski is the first appearance of a character from the original novel and movie that was not part of the television series.

Character Development

- Hawkeye and Trapper are the official head and deputy surgeons of the local Boy Scout troop. They also hold these designations with other places seen throughout the series of novels as well.
- It is stated here that Margaret has a weakness "for the grape."
- Walter Waldowski is married with a grown daughter. He has gotten chubby and his hair has fallen out, leaving him bald.
- It had been hinted at in an earlier novel, but made clear in this one, that Mulcahy still smokes even after having one lung removed in *MASH Goes to New Orleans*.

Inconsistencies

The back cover blurb on the paperback as well as text in the novel list Waldowski as "the Painless Polack." The original novel has him as "the Painless Pole," and he is referred to as such in this novel, along with "the Painless Polack."

Margaret refers to Nero's Villa as if it is still running as a casino, but this was turned into a school for wayward girls at the end of *MASH Goes to Las Vegas* (perhaps Mulcahy sold it to use the money for better purposes).

MASH Goes to San Francisco

Release Date: September 1976 by Pocket Books

Sandy Kossin's cover has Hawkeye and Trapper watching and dancing with a stripper (Betsy Boobs) while a plastered, older woman (Mrs. Sattyn-Whiley) in jewels and party dress sits in front of them with an empty bottle of bourbon.

Sphere's cover shows the "peace sign on legs" motif in front of a hilly city street with a streetcar on it, which is still an improvement over the *MASH Goes to Vienna* cover.

Written by

Listed as by Richard Hooker and William E. Butterworth on the cover. As before, the book was solely written by Butterworth.

Plot

Colonel Edward Sattyn-Whiley needs a delicate operation that could kill him. Hawkeye and Trapper are called in by a former teacher to do the work, but the colonel decides to steal a plane and fly back from Maine to San Francisco to have his old friend do it instead. Meanwhile, the colonel's son falls in love with a student nurse who's a former stripper, and there's an all-out search for a man who had just suffered a hernia lifting Boris up after a drunken night on the town in Paris.

To further complicate the numerous searches going on, Frank Burns has discovered Houlihan will be in San Francisco, and he wants a chance to spark again with his old flame.

Returning Characters

Hawkeye, Trapper John, Margaret Houlihan, Mary Pierce (cameo), Lucinda McIntyre (cameo), Radar O'Reilly, Kristina Korsky-Rimsakov, Frank Burns, Horsey de la Chevaux, Nurse Esther Flanagan, Wrong-Way Napolitano, Sheikh of Abzub, Dr. Theophilus Mullins Yancey, Prince Hassan, Boris Korsky-Rimsakov, Henry Blake (in flashback), Matthew Q. Framingham, T. Alfred Crumley.

Character Development

- Trapper and Hawkeye learned under Dr. Aloysius J. Grogarty.
- Frank Burns was working in pediatric care before the war, where he had gotten the nickname of "The Bumbling Baby Butcher of Shady Lane." It's the second novel with Burns, and both times he fails to meet face-to-face with Houlihan.
- Trapper and Hawkeye still pull pranks on Frank up to the present day by long distance.
- The wolfhounds once again make an appearance in one of the novels.

Inconsistencies

MASH Goes to New Orleans states that Frank Burns runs the Burns Loving Family and Zero Population Growth Clinic, but in this novel he runs the Burns Institute.

It has been suggested in *MASH Goes to Paris* that Radar refuses to play cards with anyone outside of the MASH team as he can read their thoughts and the game is no fun. But here he plays and loses.

John Patrick Mulcahy is referred to in the text of this novel as John Joseph Mulcahy. It'll be this way from here on out in the novels.

MASH Goes to San Francisco pretty much opens the whole Butterworth range of novels to a reevaluation of where any of them fit into the *MASH* universe. It is clear after this one that the stories told are not canon to anything else officially done for *MASH*, especially when it comes to past events. Unlike the series, film, and even the original novel, it is stated here that Frank Burns and Margaret Houlihan were already at the 4077th before Trapper and Hawkeye arrived (and that the latter two arrived together rather than weeks or even months apart as in the novel and film) and that their relationship lasted six months before Houlihan terminated it after finding out that he had a wife and four children back home. The novel and film have Houlihan arriving months after Hawkeye and Trapper and the relationship between her and Burns a one-night stand at best (and with no suggestion that Burns was married in the novel). Burns is sent home as per normal circumstances rather than after attacking Hawkeye as in the novel and film as well. This novel has Blake making Hawkeye the chief surgeon, rather than Trapper as in the original novel and in the film. It is clear by now that the Butterworth novels have been pegged to showcase these characters as if they were from the series rather the novel or film, but with enough changes that the Butterworth books have to be seen as their own *MASH* universe.

MASH Goes to Texas

Release Date: February 1977 by Pocket Books

Sandy Kossin's cover art has Hawkeye and Trapper drinking behind a buffalo, as a nurse pours a martini while sitting on the animal. To the right is a stereotypical cowboy next to a stereotypical gay man. (Well, it was the 1970s, and it was bound to happen at some point in the novels.)

Sphere's cover shows the "peace sign on legs" motif wearing a sheriff badge and a gun belt. After the scenic view of San Francisco for the last novel, it was at least some type of creative improvement.

Written by

Listed as by Richard Hooker and William E. Butterworth on the cover. As before, the book was solely written by Butterworth.

Plot

Hawkeye wishes to duck out of going to the Dallas Cowboys–New Orleans Saints football game with Houlihan and the Bayou Perdu Council Knights of Columbus Marching Band, so he gives his ticket to Nurse Flanagan. Unfortunately, Mary Pierce wants him and Trapper to go anyway in order to make sure Flanagan stays safe, thus leading to the two meeting up with Horsey, Houlihan, and the Sheikh of Abzub at the game, along with a secret service agent trying to locate the Sheikh, a guy trying to perfect a new animal feed, the daughter of a presidential candidate, the photographers for an ad campaign, the marching band, and a buffalo.

Hijinks occur.

Returning Characters

Hawkeye, Trapper John, Margaret Houlihan, Nurse Esther Flanagan, T. Alfred Crumley, Reverend Mother Superior Bernadette of Lourdes, Bayou Perdu Council Knights of Columbus Marching Band, Horsey de la Chevaux, Mary Pierce, Prince Hassan, Boris Korsky-Rimsakov, Sheikh of Abzub, Esmerelda Hoffenburg (cameo), Stanley K. Warczinski

Character Development

- None to mention in this novel. Most of the proceedings deal with new characters, with the regulars only appearing once in a while to goose the plot along. Even Boris bows out early in the novel, seemingly pretty sick of being around all these people.

Inconsistencies

John Patrick Mulcahy is again referred to as John Joseph Mulcahy in this novel. It'll be this way in the subsequent and final novel in the Butterworth series as well.

MASH Goes to Montreal

Release Date: June 1977 by Pocket Books

Sandy Kossin's cover art has Hawkeye and Trapper sitting on the ground while a Canadian Mountie sings and a Terry-Thomas clone tries to grab at a fleeing nurse with his umbrella (most probably Flanagan and Henri Flambeau). The last two books in the series appear to be much shorter than the 190- to 240-page books from earlier in the series (both clocking in at around 175 pages), but this is due to a smaller font being used than previous.

Sphere's cover shows the "peace sign on legs" motif in front of a maple leaf. They've pretty much given up the ghost on creativity by this point in the series when it comes to the covers.

Written by

Listed as by Richard Hooker and William E. Butterworth on the cover. As before, the book was solely written by Butterworth.

Plot

This novel is a direct sequel to the previous one, *MASH Goes to Texas*, although Butterworth throws in enough references and footnotes to allow the readers to follow the storyline without having seen the previous book.

With Bubba realizing the bean cultivated is perfect buffalo food, he is set to marry the girl of his dreams, Scarlett. The problem is that both have conniving mothers who suspect each other's child is a gold-digger, and both plot in their own ways to stop the marriage. Hawkeye, Trapper, and Margaret work to keep the kids together.

Other interconnecting storylines come into play as well, with Nurse Flanagan flying to Montreal in order to marry a man who is really a shyster, while a rich man—the uncle to Scarlett—wants to marry Flanagan. On top of that, Don Rhotten and former APPLE head Taylor P. Jambon plan to prove that the bean is unsafe for buffalo consumption.

Returning Characters

Hawkeye, Trapper John, Margaret Houlihan, Nurse Esther Flanagan, Frank Burns (cameo), Matthew Q. Framingham VI, T. Alfred Crumley, Josephine Babcock, Bubba Babcock, Scarlett Rose-Marie Jones, Hiram Jones, Ida-Sue Jones, Alamo Jones, Sydney Prescott, Sitting Buffalo, Lance Fairbanks (the previous nine all from *MASH Goes to Texas*), John Patrick Mulcahy, Taylor P. Jambon, Horsey de la Chevaux, Sheikh of Abzub, Don Rhotten, Wrong-Way Napolitano, Stanley K. Warczinski.

Character Development

- Mulcahy's sister is now Sister Saint Francis. In a flashback it is revealed that Sister Saint Francis had fallen ill, which led to Nurse Flanagan first meeting Hawkeye and Trapper, thus setting up her position in Spruce Harbor.

Inconsistencies

"Shaking Sammy" from the original novel is referred to in one chapter repeatedly as "Swinging Sammy."

MASH Goes to Moscow

Release Date: September 1977 by Pocket Books

Sandy Kossin's cover art has Hawkeye and Trapper sitting on the ground and getting refills on their drinks from a nurse while a Russian stereotype and a diplomat argue in the background. This is the last book in the Butterworth series, but Hornberger will be back for one last novel after this, *MASH Mania*.

Sphere's cover shows the "peace sign on legs" motif in front of the Soviet hammer and sickle.

Written by

Listed as by Richard Hooker and William E. Butterworth on the cover. As before, the book was solely written by Butterworth.

Plot

The Soviet Union wants Boris to sing and is willing to make a deal with the President of the United States to do so. The only ones who may be able to talk him into it are Hawkeye and Trapper. They too want to see Boris, but mainly to prank him in meeting a bible-thumping minister's daughter who wants to be an opera singer. Unfortunately, their plan backfires when the girl turns out to be a talented and raving beauty who is far too innocent for the likes of Boris.

In the end, Boris is more interested in the girl for her talent than her beauty and aims to make her a star, while also agreeing to sing in Russia, thus making everyone happy.

Returning Characters

Hawkeye, Trapper John, Mary Pierce, Lucinda McIntyre, Horsey de la Chevaux, Sheikh of Abzub, Prince Hassan, Boris Korsky-Rimsakov, Angus MacKenzie (cameo), T. Mullins Yancey (cameo), Wesley St. James, Nurse Esther Flanagan, Radar O'Reilly, Madame Kristina Korsky-Rimsakov, John Patrick Mulcahy, Don Rhotten, Wrong-Way Napolitano.

Character Development

- This is the first novel to not feature Margaret as a regular character.

Inconsistencies

Trapper is referred to as the "Pecker Checker" by more than one character in this novel as if it's a common nickname for him. This is the first novel such a nickname appeared.

In Review

In conclusion to the Butterworth novels, it is easy to have mixed feelings about the series of twelve books that were written. As seen above, they veer wildly away from the established history of the film, the series, and even the original novel. Characters are dumped that were at the core of the original novel—especially Duke—in order to streamline the novels to feature mainly Hawkeye, Trapper, and Margaret. Even Trapper and Margaret are given less and less to do as the series goes along, with Trapper merely along to voice a line once in a while to prove there's another live body in the room. Instead, the books concentrate more on newly invented characters that are straight-out parodies of celebrities—Boris is a thinly veiled Luciano Pavarotti (world famous opera singer), a secretary of state that is of course Henry Kissinger, a parody of Dan Rather named Don Rhotten, and a new character, Shur-Lee Strydent, is a vicious parody of Barbra Streisand. Further, the new characters are thrown into the mix so often and haphazardly that it is easy to lose sight of who is where and how they're involved with the plots. No wonder by the last novels Hawkeye and Trapper are a bit fed up with dealing with all the others.

Storylines are rushed and heavy on wild goose chases. Contrivances in getting characters to new places are stretched wire-thin. Parodies of people and places are thick and obvious. And every book has the same plots: Hawkeye and Trapper are forced to go somewhere where they come into contact with people who need their help. Meanwhile there is always a plain or ugly woman who believes all men are "male chauvinist, capitalist pigs" and undergoes emotional or physical transformation (in the tradition of a "Marian, Librarian") thanks to the strong, determined actions of a good, Republican man. Margaret always comes in to save part of the day in the last third of each novel, Hawkeye and Trapper appear in the last few pages to

Season three of the DVD collection, showing Radar and Blake.
Both will return in the *MASH Goes to* . . . series, ignoring continu-
ity from the series, including deliberately showing Henry Blake
alive and well in the 1970s after having been killed off in the
television series.

do what they can, and everyone ends up happy and with two characters
ready to get married.

But, really? What can one expect? These books are similar to any other
television tie-in novel series of the time and thus regulated to do a few
things: tell a story, don't change the characters from the series or have
anything affect them in a life-changing way, get a little action, tell a few
jokes, and end on an upbeat note. These are not intended to be epic, fresh

novels that will radically change civilization (of course, the original novel didn't do that either); they are exactly what they are meant to be: the mental equivalent of a bag of chips. Mass produced for consumption by people needing something light and quick to read while on a plane flight or bus.

And in that line of thinking, they do the job. There are some good gags along the way, an occasional twist that shows not everything had to be cookie-cutter in the plotting, and—perhaps most importantly—it is clear that Butterworth is very happy to be getting a chance to not have to worry if the editor is breathing down his neck as he delivers the goods promised. Yes, there'll be a backstory with a girl and a guy who fall in love. Yes, Hawkeye, Trapper, and Margaret will appear. Yes, the novel will incorporate more of what fans know of the show rather than the novel. Once Butterworth put the window-dressing in place, the rest was obviously left to his own devising. So the cliché of the guy getting the girl happens? That's nice.

Besides, it's not like someone would binge-read all the books in a row to see where there were inconsistencies like some manic researcher with too much time on his—oh.

In realistic terms, the readers can't really expect that Mulcahy will become an archbishop and friends with the pope, or Radar will become a millionaire fast-food king, or—most of all—that Margaret will become a religious leader, but Butterworth keeps it light enough in this *MASH* universe, at least for a few hours while reading one, to think of these characters in a dreamlike world where such silly fantasies can come true. Nothing wrong with that, and it certainly does not affect the experience of the previous two novels, the film, or the series.

Over time, it is easy to see that fatigue began to drift into the series, and the last few are a struggle to read. For fans who are curious, the best of the group are the earliest, with *MASH Goes to New Orleans* and *MASH Goes to Paris* (the first two) being the strongest of the bunch. After that, the results decline, with a slight pickup around *MASH Goes to San Francisco*, before fizzling out with *MASH Goes to Moscow*.

Speaking of which, as much as Butterworth sometimes later on would talk about the conservative Republican attitude of the books, this rarely affects the writing beyond some gentle pokes at certain individuals, with the exception of the final novel and its quite pointed disgust by the author that Jimmy Carter was elected president. Still, even there, it's more along the goofy satirical side that Butterworth brought to the earlier novels, so it doesn't quite sting as intended. All in all, the point is to keep things light, and he succeeds.

6

Of Course You Know Me

Characters from *MASH* as Seen in Book Sequels

T he following is a list of characters from the original novels who also appeared at least once in subsequent novels in the series. Only Hawkeye, Trapper, Duke, and Spearchucker will appear in all three of the Hornberger-penned novels. Ho-Jon and Henry Blake will both make return appearances in the final novel, *MASH Mania*. Only character history set up by Hornberger in his three novels is listed here.

Corp. Radar O'Reilly

A recent high school graduate, standing only five feet three inches tall, with ears that stick out at a ninety-degree angle from his head. He joined the army dreaming of quickly becoming a four-star general and giving statements to the press at the White House. Instead, he's serving as a corporal at the 4077th Mobile Army Surgical Hospital. He has the amazing ability to hear things over great distances, although it is not quite clear if this is due to his protruding ears, great hearing, or possibly ESP. He's usually one step ahead of Colonel Blake and, although not mentioned often in the novel, seems to be the go-to man when special supplies are needed. He goes by no other name but Radar in the original novel, with not even a mention of his real first name as with other characters. He does not appear in any of the subsequent Hornberger novels, although he appears several times in the Butterworth series of novels.

Capt. Walter Koskiusko Waldowski (aka Painless Pole)

A dental officer who also runs a never-ending poker game in his tent/clinic. Waldowski is one of the few officers who had a practice before coming to Korea and is greatly admired for his work as a reconstructive dental surgeon (many forget—as did the series eventually—that a dental surgeon was the norm for a MASH unit). He also is respected as a man who knows how to party, and—most of all—for the size of a certain part of his anatomy (so well known that many come from miles around to peek at him when he's in the shower). His only flaw is that of suffering from a monthly depression that lasts from one to three days. The Swamp men appear to cure him of this during the course of the novel. As with Radar, Painless does not reappear in any of the Hornberger novels, but once in the Butterworth series.

Lt. Col. Henry Braymore Blake

Commander of the 4077th and regular army. He is aware that his surgeons are rather loose with regulations, but lets them get away with it as long as they prove themselves as doctors and make him look good. He also makes sure they know that he knows. When very angry he stutters, which happens frequently when dealing with Hawkeye, Duke, and Trapper (this is only seen in the movie when Houlihan bursts into Blake's tent after the shower prank; it was not used at all in the series, nor in later novels). Blake is the only officer higher in rank that the Swamp men respect, which Blake uses to his advantage at times. He will become a major general by the 1970s. He appears once in the Butterworth series and is mentioned several times throughout, but only makes a brief reappearance in the final Hornberger novel. It is hinted there and in the Butterworth series that this was done mainly to counteract the death of the character in the television series (something the producers of the series state Hornberger was livid to see happen).

Capt. Benjamin Franklin "Hawkeye" Pierce

Twenty-eight years old and just a little over six feet tall. Hawkeye is from Crabapple Cove, Maine; has blonde-brown hair that is too long; and wears glasses. He is married, with two sons, and will begin to specialize in thoracic surgery during the course of the novel (and specialize in it back home in the later novels). He went to Androscoggin College (based on Hornberger's own college of Bowdoin). He has six brothers, who appear to frequent the county jail a lot. He also has a sister, although she is not mentioned in the first or second novel. His father, a lobsterman, nicknamed him Hawkeye after the main character in "the only book he ever read," *Last of the Mohicans*. He usually is the instigator of plots by the members of the Swamp and has a tendency to use the phrase "finest kind" when referring to something that he believes is great. Hawkeye will return to Spruce Harbor, Maine, in the 1972 follow-up novel *MASH Goes to Maine* and start up Finestkind Fishmarket and Clinic, with Duke, Trapper, and Spearchucker to join him there. *MASH Mania*, the final novel in the series, will establish that Hawkeye and his wife Mary eventually had four children and quasi-adopted a young man at some point who becomes a surgeon.

Capt. Augustus Bedford "Duke" Forrest

Twenty-nine years old and slightly shorter than Hawkeye. Duke is from Forrest City, Georgia, and he too is married with two children, girls instead of boys as in Hawkeye's case. Duke has short red hair, blue eyes, a nose that had been broken at some point, and a tendency to wear his Southern culture like an amulet. He usually goes along with whatever Trapper and Hawkeye have in mind, although he doesn't really understand the "Northern boys." He is a bit more of a slob than Hawkeye (on the trip back from Korea he repeatedly urinates on things in other rooms just because he can't be bothered to go to the toilet) and is happy to have people believe him to be more of an animal than he really is. *MASH Goes to Maine* will later establish that he joined Hawkeye in Maine at the Finestkind Fishmarket and Clinic.

Capt. John Francis Xavier "Trapper John" McIntyre

No age is given, but since he played college football (Dartmouth College) against Hawkeye's team, it can be assumed they're about the same age. He's from Winchester, New Hampshire, single, and an experienced thoracic surgeon, with his specialty being that of a "chest-cutter." He got his nickname when he and his date were caught having sex in the women's toilet on a train and the woman insisted that he had "trapped" her. (Both Hornberger and Butterworth repeatedly make clear in the later novels that this was consensual, with the woman trying to talk her way out of it when caught, rather than Trapper forcing himself on her.) Trapper will become the chief surgeon at the 4077th. He looks like Jesus when he grows his hair and beard out. Ironically, he'll be trapped into going to Maine to join Hawkeye and

Duke at the Finestkind Fishmarket and Clinic, as well as trapped into marriage (with the woman he loves, so it all works out in the end).

Oliver Wendell "Spearchucker" Jones

The only regular non-Caucasian character in the novel, and this is emphasized repeatedly through the series of Hornberger-penned novels, usually in reference to a racial joke made at Jones' expense. (Ho-Jon also reappears, but only briefly in *MASH Mania*.) No age is given to the man in the novel, but it is mentioned that he was roommates with Hawkeye in college. Even so, with time spent playing professional football—the Philadelphia Eagles—in the mix as well as having the educational background to be drafted into the war as a neurosurgeon, it can be pretty safe to assume that he is older than Hawkeye. It is made clear that his nickname of Spearchucker is based on his ability with the javelin, although obviously the racial designation comes into play as well (albeit never mentioned in the novels). *MASH Goes to Maine* has him returning to his work in Philadelphia after the war before joining Hawkeye in Spruce Harbor, Maine. He is married with children and vacations with Hawkeye and his family from time to time.

Ho-Jon

A seventeen-year-old Korean who is one of a number of "house boys" who help clean up around the MASH unit. Ho-Jon spends most of his time helping out in the Swamp. He is eventually drafted into the South Korean army and wounded, when he is returned to the 4077th and then sent to the States to go to Hawkeye's college. *MASH Mania* will establish that Ho-Jon will become an administrator at the college after graduating.

Father John Patrick "Dago Red" Mulcahy

The Catholic chaplain of the 4077th. Because of his red hair, Duke refers to him as Dago Red, which Mulcahy takes with good humor. Before arriving in Korea, Mulcahy has spent five years in China and seven years before that in Bolivia as a missionary (thus, he is a few years older than most of the other characters). He is trusted and respected by the, surgeons who occasionally have a drink with him in the Swamp. He also seems to have a knack for reviving patients who have been given their last rites by him, thus making Mulcahy a good luck charm to the surgeons, even if they have a disdain for

Catholicism. He does not appear in any other Hornberger novel beyond the first, but many of the Butterworth novels.

Capt. Frank Burns

Being the son of a successful doctor and surgeon, Burns has coasted on his heritage in his own career, arriving in Korea with a $35,000 house, two cars,

An earlier press photo of Houlihan (Loretta Swit) and Burns (Larry Linville) from the television series. Both were relatively minor characters in the original novel—Burns only appears in one chapter and is a captain—and neither appear in the Hornberger sequels, but will become major characters in the film, series, and even the *MASH Goes to . . .* book sequels.

and the assurance that he is a better person and doctor than anyone else at the 4077th. He is also strict with the rules and constantly writes up the enlisted men for minor infractions, which Blake ignores. He's an adequate surgeon, but insufferable and blames others for his mistakes, leading to all the Swamp men taking a punch at him at one time or another (Duke doing the worst damage). There is no indication that he is married, and although he kisses Houlihan, there is also no evidence that they were more intimate than that (it's implied, but no one seems to believe it). When Hawkeye jokes about him and Houlihan, Frank takes his anger out on Hawkeye, leading to him being returned to the States by Blake. Frank appears in only one chapter of the original novel and not at all in the two Hornberger-written sequels.

Major Margaret "Hot Lips" Houlihan

Forty years old and the new chief nurse at the 4077th, arriving eight months into Hawkeye's and Duke's assignment to the division. She looks for order and sees it in Captain Burns, leading to the two teaming up against Hawkeye, Trapper, and Duke. Later she threatens to resign her commission when Trapper enlists others to call her Hot Lips and suggest general innuendo about her, but when that threat is angrily accepted by Blake and a phone call to General Hammond is ignored, she goes about her business. She appears in the middle third of the book off and on before disappearing with no resolution to her character's arc. She does not appear in the two Hornberger-written sequels.

But she'll have surprisingly more to do in the movie and series to come, as will be seen.

7

This Is Mutiny

From Book to Movie and Television

In interviews over the years, Robert Altman has stated the *MASH* film was radically different from the book, but a comparison shows that this is not really the case (same with the oft-mentioned statement that the film has no dialogue from the script). For example, many who read the novel found the chapters dealing with the football game a diversion that upset the balance of the book and could have been eliminated, but that would have meant adding material that wasn't in the novel to the film, and obviously Altman didn't want to make such a radical change. Thus, while the director lambasts the book, what is on the screen doesn't quite match his bravado about how "bad the book is."

It should also be mentioned that the creators of the television series stated over the years that the film used up every possible plot line from the novel so they had to create everything from scratch. Yet both Larry Gelbart and Gene Reynolds have also stated in print that they initially went to the novel for plots before turning to other sources. As seen below, that latter statement appears to be more true for the televisions series.

- The 4077th is referred to as the "Double Natural" (due to the two sevens, with a seven being a natural in a crap game, hence "double natural") in the first novel and many of the Butterworth novels. It is not referred to as such in the film, but Potter refers to it in this manner in the first episode of season eight ("Commander Pierce").
- One of the biggest changes is Duke not making it to the series at all. Ho-Jon, Spearchucker Jones, and Ugly John all appear, but only momentarily in the first season, with Ho-Jon only appearing in seven episodes, Jones in six, and Ugly John actually lasting until the end of the first season with eleven episodes. Also, Painless Pole is mentioned early in the series but never seen.
- Ugly John is American in the novel and movie (even if he is wearing that hat), but an Australian captain in the series. This, no doubt, was the

series' attempt to give the personnel at the camp a more international feel with "foreigners" as part of the cast, but Ugly John was the only long-term holdout on this concept. Usually such characters lasted only for one-shot appearances and commonly to set up gags about foreigners.

• Colonel Henry Blake is not as out-of-touch in the novel as he appears in the film, nor as wishy-washy as in the series. Blake is regular army in the novel and appears to be so in the film. The series never seems quite sure—Blake in the series refers to being sent to the 4077th after making a bad joke to a higher-ranking officer, while he mentions many times his practice at home. However, it would not have been unusual for a doctor already in practice coming in with a higher rank such as major or colonel, so it is possible. Hawkeye's negative reaction to Potter coming in as regular army in the fourth season also implies that Blake was not regular army, however; or at least Blake had been conditioned to not act it.

• Radar is never referred to by any first name, just the nickname of Radar. It will be the series before we find out his first name is Walter, although the subsequent Butterworth series of novels would state otherwise.

• Hawkeye does not remove his captain bars from his uniform as seen in the opening moments of the film, although he is wearing them on the back of his cap by the end of the novel, before substituting them with other insignias on the way back home from Korea.

• Hawkeye and Duke do not steal a jeep when heading to the 4077th in the novel. (To be fair, it's Hawkeye who steals the jeep in the film; Duke assumes the jeep is theirs to take.)

• Hawkeye and Duke get to know each other on the trip to the 4077th; unlike in the film where Hawkeye hides his identity as a prank on Duke.

• In "Dear Peggy" from season four, BJ writes to his wife that Hawkeye says the term "finest kind" all the time. Evidently off-camera, as Hawkeye uses the term only in the pilot and two other episodes besides this reference. In the film, Sutherland uses a wolf whistle instead in most instances where he would have used the term in the novel.

• Biggest change for Hawkeye is that he goes from being married with two boys in the novel and film to single in the series. Meanwhile, Trapper, who is single in the novel and film, becomes married and with girls in the series.

• It should also be mentioned that Trapper is the chief surgeon in the novel and film, but Hawkeye takes on that role early in the series.

- Trapper in the series starts out as a chest-cutter in the novel, film, and series, but that distinction is transferred to Hawkeye early on in the television program—a point of contention that bugged Wayne Rogers (see chapter 16 for more details).
- Hawkeye's father is a lobsterman, while in the series he is a doctor with his own practice in Crabapple Cove. He also has six brothers, most of who are in prison or jail. His family background is never touched on in the movie, while there is a mention of a sister early in the series (who seems to appear or disappear depending on what was needed for storylines). The final Hornberger series will give Hawkeye a sister as well.
- There is no Lieutenant Dish in the novel. She is there mainly to add another female voice to the film. She appears in two episodes of the series as well (and can be glimpsed in the opening credits heading out to the choppers with Hawkeye).
- Because there is no Lieutenant Dish, the resolution to Painless Pole's suicide attempt is completely different in the novel from that of the movie.
- Trapper does hide his identity for a time in both the book and the film—in the book he even has the bottle of olives as seen in the film—but the revelation of his football toss used in the film to clarify Trapper's identity is not enough in the novel, and it is only later that Hawkeye remembers Trapper from the game they played together. The series has the character already established at the 4077th in the pilot.
- "Shaking Sammy" is eliminated from the film. To be fair, audiences at the time probably would not have been ready for a humorous crucifixion scene in a major studio film. The fourth-season episode "Dear Peggy" has Mulcahy being bullied by an overenthusiastic superior into writing a letter to the parents of a wounded soldier who later nearly dies, which plays a bit off of the "Shaking Sammy" storyline.
- Hawkeye's inside knowledge about a battle that will see many casualties arriving and thus allow them to avoid punishment for the "Shaking Sammy" incident in the novel is used in the pilot episode of the series to cover for the party and raffling of a nurse.
- Major Frank Burns is a composite of both Major Hobson—the "holy roller" from the beginning of the novel—and Captain Frank Burns, who appears in only one chapter. Major Burns is carried over to the series, but with more redeeming values, and only ends up being sent home in a straitjacket after his affair with Houlihan ends (and not due to an incident with Hawkeye as seen in the novel and film). In the series,

he becomes a lieutenant colonel upon arriving home, but there is no mention of his destiny in the novel or film.

- Houlihan is forty-ish in the novel, but appears to be much younger in both the series and the film.
- There is no indication that Burns and Houlihan did anything in Houlihan's tent beyond writing the letter to General Hammond and one kiss. (There's the assumption, but never any evidence.)
- There is no incident where Burns' and Houlihan's antics in her tent are broadcast for the whole camp to hear, as seen in the film and referenced in the Butterworth novels.
- Ho-Jon is inducted into the army in both the film and the novel, although there is no attempt to medicate him in order to get him released as seen in the film. In the novel, Ho-Jon returns to the 4077th as a casualty, and it is then that Hawkeye and the others raise cash to get Ho-Jon sent to the U.S. for a college education. The original script has Ho-Jon returning as a wounded soldier as well, but then dying after surgery (it is his body being taken away as the doctors play poker near the end of the film, after the football game). Because this was edited out, the film instead simply has Ho-Jon disappearing from the story. The college storyline will turn up in the series as the plot for the pilot episode, although without the background of Ho-Jon having been wounded in the war. The death in the O.R. of a character who was friends with Hawkeye would eventually turn up in the first-season classic episode "Sometimes You Hear the Bullet."
- Trapper and Hawkeye's trip to Tokyo for golf and an operation, as well as saving a baby's life, appears in both the novel and the film. The film streamlines the material a bit by eliminating some characters involved with the shenanigans, details of a con game during a round of golf, as well as a minor epilogue to the storyline where Me Lay decides to adopt the baby. The sergeant muttering "goddamn army" numerous times made the cut, however.
- While the film briefly shows a patient spurting blood from his neck, the novel develops the circumstances dealing with the patient's surgery in more detail (including Hawkeye having to insert his finger in the hole were the bleeding is occurring).
- Mulcahy's assisting on an operation happens with Hawkeye in the novel, not Duke, and it is Hawkeye who is surprised, not Mulcahy (unlike in the film where Mulcahy fumbles around in shock when Duke demands he helps). It is tempting to suggest this was a linchpin to "Carry On,

Hawkeye" from season two of the series, where Mulcahy has to help out in surgery due to lack of assistance, but that may not be the case.

- Mulcahy is referred to as Red early in the television series.
- Additional background stories on operations, as well as details about Captain Ugly John Black, the anesthesiologist, are also missing from the film. It should be mentioned that the television series reassigned other surgeons to be the anesthesiologist in certain operations instead of having officers who had this as their sole job. This would not be the case in reality, the novel, or the film (but saves time and money in not having to hire another actor for three lines of dialogue in the series).
- Part of one chapter dealing with Hawkeye's multiday concern over a patient after he operates on him is not seen in the film, but does pop up in the first season of the series as the episode "Sticky Wicket." Further, subsequent depressions on the part of Trapper and Duke over losing a patient are glossed over in the film (beyond the scene near the end of the film where the doctors play cards while a dead soldier is driven away . . . which the script has as being Ho-Jon, which makes their response even more sober).
- There is no shower prank on Houlihan in the novel; her anger stems strictly from the name-calling started by Trapper. (The moment where it becomes too much occurs while she is heading from the showers, which is where the notion for the prank came from, no doubt.) One suspects, since they couldn't stick with the Shaking Sammy crucifixion, another elaborate prank had to be staged, and using it here with Houlihan worked the best.
- In connection with Houlihan resigning her commission, the novel does not have her burst in on Blake in bed with a nurse, but rather as Blake waits alone for Houlihan in his tent to discuss the matter.
- Houlihan has no subsequent relationship with Duke as seen in the film, or with Hawkeye, as briefly hinted at in the series. Although the character will be a major part of both the film and television series, she is written out of the storyline a little over halfway through the novel.
- It should also be noted that, while the film and series make clear that Houlihan is a brilliant chief nurse and assistant at the operating tables, there is no indication of this in the novel; she is just a "regular army clown" and nothing more.
- The visiting Colonel DeLong's time as Blake's temporary replacement at the 4077th while he is away in Japan does not appear in the film. It will, however, be the source for two first-season episodes of the television

The gang about to witness the unveiling of Houlihan in the shower. This scene will become one of the best known not only of the film, but of *MASH* overall and would end up being referred to in the *MASH Goes to . . .* series as well as hinted at in the television series. Most interesting of all—no such scene appears in the original novel.

series—"Chief Surgeon Who?" (some of the dialogue is even similar) and "Bananas, Crackers and Nuts"—as well as a likely source for some of "Henry, Please Come Home" that season.

- Ugly John's criticism of the British medical officers and their insistence on giving tea to the wounded (thus resulting in peritonitis for those with stomach wounds) will be given to Hawkeye to use in the sixth-season episode "Tea and Empathy."
- The Swamp men discussing Houlihan's report to General Hammond is moved from Hammond's office in Seoul to the 4077th. Instead of Hammond deciding to ignore the report thanks to the Swamp men's diligent support of Henry, in the film he does so when he finds out that he might be able to con the MASH unit into a football game and a sizable bet on the outcome.
- Speaking of which, instead of Hammond, it is Hawkeye's idea to put together a football team in order to play against Hammond's team.

- Jones' middle name is changed to Harmon in the film. It is never mentioned in the series. The football team he played with is changed from the Philadelphia Eagles in the novel to the San Francisco 49ers in the film.
- Certain elements of the football game are changed, mainly to avoid the amount of discussion about possible plays found in the book during the game. Vollmer (who is seen consistently throughout the film, but only in this one chapter in the book) does walk the ball to the goal line in both the novel and the film.
- Henry telling the Swamp men that even though they continue to thumb their noses at command, they are stuck for the duration of their enlistment due to their skills—a topic briefly mentioned by Trapper and Hawkeye in the pilot of the series.
- Two new surgeons being shown the ropes, as Hawkeye and Duke begin their ending stretch at the camp, is not in the film. However, it can be suggested that the character of Captain Emerson Pinkham, and his resistance to "meatball surgery," as well as the lofty air about him when he first arrives, could be the acorn from which Major Charles Emerson Winchester III of the series would grow.
- Hawkeye and Duke find out they're going home from Henry in the novel, rather than Hawkeye being told by Radar and then Hawkeye telling Duke during the middle of the operation as in the film.
- Hawkeye and Duke salute Henry in respect before they leave. Hawkeye and BJ will do the same to Potter in the final episode of the television series.
- The novel has everyone meeting with Hawkeye and Duke before they leave and then goes through several pages of their departure from Korea (including a final run-in with General Hammond), until Hawkeye at last arrives home. The film instead has a flash-forward of Duke arriving home (or possibly a quick internal fantasy by Duke of arriving home), followed by a short scene with Hawkeye and Duke saying good-bye to Spearchucker and Trapper before taking off in the same jeep they arrived in.

And speaking of the movie . . .

8

Tonight's Movie

The Making of the Robert Altman Film

S elf-promotion is a community effort in Hollywood. In other words, it's hard to be patting someone else on the back when you're busy doing it to yourself. Even so, everyone who worked on *MASH* agreed that it all started with one person reading the novel and seeing it as a movie, Ring Lardner Jr.—a screenwriter who would eventually end up with an Academy Award for the film made of the novel, although many (including Lardner) would later contest how much of it was his work.

The Studio

Lardner was born Ringgold Wilmer Lardner Jr. on August 19, 1915, and was first a newspaper writer for the *New York Daily Mirror* before going to California. In Hollywood, he established himself as a "script doctor" who knew how to fix scripts needing a punch-up here and there before the camera rolled. In 1942, Lardner won his first Academy Award with the screenplay for the classic film *Woman of the Year.* He would continue to do strong work on scripts until the late 1940s, when he was blacklisted as part of the "Hollywood Ten"—a group of writers and directors who had refused to speak to the House Un-American Activities Committee in 1947 about supposed communist infiltration in the American movie picture business. As with many of the other writers, when Lardner was released, he found work overseas and by using pseudonyms, although he was allowed back into Hollywood's embraces with his script for the popular Steve McQueen movie *The Cincinnati Kid* in 1965.

Getting such a known name to review the book and write a blurb for the cover (and which would be used on many of the paperback editions released through the years) was a bit of a coup for the publisher. It would also drive right to the point of what fascinated Lardner about the novel: "Not since *Catch 22* has the struggle to maintain sanity in the rampant insanity of war been told in such outrageously funny terms." Yet, even with that as a basis, there was something more about the novel that attracted Lardner, the very thing that kept the manuscript from being published for years: the ramshackle nature of the plot, which doesn't really deliver a message, but does at the same time. As he states in his autobiography, *I'd Hate Myself in the Morning*: "One of the things that makes a good story, I had always believed, was a character or characters changing in the course of it. In this case, in violation of the rule, the two heroes, Hawkeye and Trapper John, would be exactly the same people at the end as at the beginning." As a scriptwriter, Lardner could not shake Hornberger's book from his thoughts, imagining ways he could write a screenplay for such a novel. Going to his agent, George Litto, Lardner suggested that the novel could make for a great film. From there, the pair went to Lardner's previous agent, Ingo Preminger.

Ingo Preminger (1911–2006) was the brother of famed movie director Otto Preminger (*Anatomy of a Murder, Laura, The Man with the Golden Arm*) and well known for his work as a talent agent, first with the Nat Goldstone Agency and then later on his own. He sold his business in 1961, but kept his literary contacts, including a number of famous writers, many who had been blacklisted like Lardner. This included the team of Ned Young and Hal Smith, who wrote *The Defiant Ones*, and Dalton Trumbo, who wrote the screenplays for *Roman Holiday* (1953), *Exodus* (1960), *Spartacus* (1960), and *Papillon* (1973). Even so, by the end of the 1960s, Preminger was looking to get out of the agent side of the business and pursue a career as a producer. Upon receiving a copy of the novel from Litto, Preminger took it to Richard Zanuck at 20th Century-Fox with a deal in mind.

Richard Darryl Zanuck (1934–2012) was the son of famed movie producer Darryl F. Zanuck. By the age of twenty-four, Zanuck produced his first Hollywood film, *Compulsion* (1959), starring Orson Welles and Dean Stockwell. After becoming the head of 20th Century-Fox, Zanuck was involved in the launching of the successful *Planet of the Apes* series; and after leaving Fox, Zanuck and his partner David Brown would produce the first two theatrical films by Steven Spielberg, *The Sugarland Express* (1974) and *Jaws* (1975). He would also be involved with a number of films with Tim Burton over the years, including Burton's 2001 update of *The Planet of the Apes*. While at Fox, Zanuck got a visit from Ingo Preminger, who passed *MASH* on to the studio executive with the deal he had in mind: If Zanuck liked the book, and was willing to have Ring Lardner Jr. write the script, Preminger was willing to give up his literary agency and produce the film himself.

Zanuck was impressed, as he told Mitchell Zuckoff in *Robert Altman: The Oral Biography*: "He had substantial clients. It was a thriving agency." To leave all that in order to produce *MASH* swayed Zanuck into thinking the novel must be important enough to read and consider, little realizing that Preminger was ready to leave the agency behind anyway. It was a gamble that paid off for Preminger, as Zanuck called him back the following week to let him know that the studio would have an office ready for him. Although H. Richard Hornberger would go on record to suggest that he only got paid a few hundred dollars for the movie rights, most accounts state that 20th Century-Fox paid $100,000 for the rights (which probably was whittled away by the publisher and other assorted individuals, but Hornberger no doubt received more than just "a few hundred dollars"), and Lardner began writing the script in July 1968.

With Lardner quickly turning out a script, the next natural step was to find a director for the project. It was also a major problem. 20th Century-Fox had ideas for the movie that involved turning it into a more traditional type of comedy and eyed the teaming of Jack Lemmon and Walter Matthau—who had been successful together in *The Fortune Cookie* (1966) and *The Odd Couple* (1968)—as Hawkeye and Trapper John. The script Lardner wrote, however, was very much a straight adaptation of the novel, and even with some changes made to take out some of the sting of scenes that no studio would have been anxious to put on film (such as the "Shaking Sammy" sequence being dropped), there was still much hesitation on the part of possible directors for the movie.

Finding a Director

The legend is that fifteen directors were considered for the project, but all turned it down for various reasons, such as the complexity of the script, the attitudes presented in the script, the episodic nature of the script, or simply not liking the script. Who were the fifteen? No one has ever made a complete list, but the directors usually mentioned are George Roy Hill, Sidney Lumet, Bud Yorkin, Sydney Pollack, William Friedkin, and Stanley Kubrick (admittedly, everyone knew that Kubrick was never going to sign on to it, but he is always mentioned as a contender for the film). While all that was going on at the studio, one of George Litto's clients, a director by the name of Robert Altman, met up with Litto at a poker game. Altman had read the script and asked Litto if it was possible to get the movie for him to direct. Litto thought it unlikely that the studio would go for it, but said he would give it a try.

While waiting for a director to appear, Preminger was already thinking ahead to the casting, as was 20th Century-Fox. With any thoughts of turning the film into another Lemmon-Matthau comedy quickly out the window once people actually looked at the script, the thoughts turned to finding younger actors for the main parts and perhaps fill up the rest of the cast with older professionals that the public would recognize. Preminger remembered an actor who played one of the convict soldiers in *The Dirty Dozen*; a scruffy-looking, somewhat goofy character, forced into playing an officer for an inspection, who can't quite take it seriously. The actor was Donald Sutherland, and Preminger was sure that he would make a good Hawkeye Pierce in *MASH*. With the signing of a contract, Sutherland would be the first of the main cast to be hired for the movie.

Yet there were signs that perhaps Sutherland would never get a chance to actually perform in front of the camera in the role. With so many directors turning down the script, the studio was beginning to get cold feet about making the film. For George Litto, this was a blessing. There were faint thoughts on trying to get Stanley Kubrick, who could have done amazing things with the novel and script, but many knew that it was a "Hail Mary" pass at best. Worse, if they approached him and he said no, then 20th Century-Fox probably would pull the plug, figuring no one was interested. On the other hand, Litto had Robert Altman—a seasoned professional with four films as notches in his belt and a long list of television credits. Preminger fought for Altman—having the same agent can be helpful at times—but Zanuck and David Brown were hesitant, even though they liked what they saw in a comedy short Altman had recently shot, which featured everyday people going about their business while toking on joints, *Pot Au Feu*—a small portion of which appears in the documentary film *Altman* (2014).

The downside of hiring Altman (1925–2006) was he was not so much a loose as a deadly cannon. He could direct fast, create good work, and had the arsenal of his television years with programs like *Bonanza* and *Combat!* amongst many others. The problem was that he was steadfast in doing what he wanted to do, when he wanted to do it, in both television and films. If that meant a falling-out with the studio and losing jobs, so be it. Furthermore, doing so only reinforced to him that he was in the right. A spell on the *Kraft Suspense Theater* ended when Altman publicly stated that the program was "as bland as its cheese." An episode of the short-lived series *Bus Stop* directed by Altman, "A Lion Walks Among Us," starring teen idol

Robert Altman, the director of *MASH*, ten years later on the set of his film *A Perfect Couple* (1979).

Fabian as a manic serial killer who happily kills his attorney once his murder trial ends with no conviction, led to the show's sponsor pulling its advertising, stations refusing to air it, and finally congressional hearings on violence in television. Altman began directing *Combat!*, a World War II series, when a script in its first season, "Survival," had been nixed due to the hero of the program (played by Vic Morrow) suffering from "shell shock" after a bombing. Altman was so sure of the script that he waited until those in control were out of town before filming the episode, and in such a manner that the network had no recourse but to air it, even though it presented the show's hero in an unflattering light.

Turning to theatrical films didn't slow Altman's aggression about doing what he wanted and damn the studios, although it started off without issues. In 1956 he made his first film, *The Delinquents*, which he wrote, directed, and produced in Kansas City, Missouri. The film starred Tom Laughlin (who would go on to fame with *Billy Jack*) and was picked up by United Artists, who made changes to the film without Altman's consent. Altman followed it up with some work on the documentary film *The James Dean Story* in 1957 for Warner Brothers. Both films would help lead to Altman getting television work in Hollywood, but it wasn't until 1967 that he would direct another theatrical film.

The film was *Countdown*, released in 1968 by Warner Brothers and starring James Caan as an astronaut forced into a race against time with the Russians to become the first man on the moon. The film costarred Robert Duvall and Michael Murphy, both of whom would go on to appear in *MASH*, and was based on a novel called *The Pilgrim Project*, which was written by Hank Searls (who also wrote *The Crowded Sky* and other aviation-oriented novels). It was a story already beginning to show its stiffness and antiquity as America was preparing to land on the moon (this would happen on July 20, 1969, just seventeen months after the film premiered), further compounded by being turned into a soap opera centering around the space program on the script page. Still, Altman attempted to do what he could with the film, with a team of actors who felt as he did.

The results seen by the studio made them furious, especially the tragic ending Altman staged, which was in the script okayed by the studio. The script has James Caan's character landing on the moon, in search of a beacon where supplies and oxygen awaits him. Realizing that he is rapidly running out of air, the character chooses to walk off in hopes of finding the beacon, only for the camera to pull back and show the audience the beacon in the opposite direction, thereby guaranteeing his death as the film fades out. The studio was unhappy with the downer ending, feeling that the audience would not be content to have sat through the film only to find out that their hero dies due to bad luck. Further, Altman wanted to sink some reality into the numerous talking-head scenes (and, by golly, there are a lot of them in *Countdown*) by having the actors say their lines in the manner people in reality do—talking over each other, skipping over words, and stumbling on statements. It would be something that Altman would do again in *MASH* that would find critical favor, but in 1967 the world, or rather Warner Brothers, wasn't ready for it. Altman was fired from the film, with editing done to give audiences the happy ending Warner felt they wanted, as well as toning down as much as possible the overlapping of dialogue.

In 1969, Altman moved on to an independent film starring Sandy Dennis called *That Cold Day in the Park*, which too offered overlapping dialogue and snippets of conversations that had no impact on the main story beyond adding color to the overall film. *That Cold Day in the Park* is actually a slow-boiling horror film, dealing with a woman (Dennis) who takes in a young man, only to attempt to keep him locked up in her apartment. Longing for his affection, the woman eventually turns to madness and murder to get what she wants.

That Cold Day in the Park was released in June 1969 but little seen, and faced harsh critical analysis at the time (it is still a type of film that people will either love or hate). Even Ingo Preminger would go on record years later to say that if he had seen the film at the time, he probably never would have agreed to Altman as the director. Still, *That Cold Day in the Park* (which featured Michael Murphy in a small role) demonstrated one trait that had always been in Altman's favor—he knew how to draw out performances from his actors, including allowing them to shape their lines and characters in ways that were not always present in the scripts. He also was willing to take suggestions from anyone as long as he felt they were trying to make the film better. Even so, if cornered, Altman could be defiant, and that's when trouble would begin.

Which gets back to Donald Sutherland. Altman liked having the same people around him working on shows and movies as they knew his methods and he knew theirs. This is why so many of the actors who appeared in his films returned to do others over time, such as Elliott Gould starring in three of Atman's films (and briefly popping up in others) and Tom Skerritt

Hawkeye (Donald Sutherland) with Lt. Dish (Jo Ann Pflug) messing around in the Officers' Club. Dish was a character created specifically for the film and is not in the original novel.

playing Duke after having worked with Altman on *Combat!* and becoming friends. Altman planned to bring in fresh faces, which makes sense for a war film that deals with mostly people in their early to mid-twenties. However, he wanted to bring in people he knew he could work with without reserve. There were also rumors that he saw James Garner playing the role of Hawkeye, but these have never been confirmed (plus, it is counterintuitive to the look of the film, where Garner would have looked much older than most of the cast, who were supposed to be of similar age to Hawkeye). Whatever Altman planned, he wanted to be there for the casting. But Sutherland was already hired to play the lead, and that did not go over well with Altman. He would attempt to have Sutherland replaced before finally conceding on the issue. Even so, it would begin a rift with the star of the film that would fester as the movie began production.

Furthermore, although Altman had requested to direct the film, he began to back off as the deal for him was being made. It was not helped that Altman was first told he would get $125,000 plus a percentage, before the studio made clear that they would only pay him $75,000 with no percentages. To Altman, this was what a studio did best—stab the artist in the back when he's vulnerable; to the studio, a promise of percentages to a director with no hits on a small-budgeted film (in an era when only the most profitable directors could even ask for such a thing) was insane. Altman attempted to back out, but his agent talked him into staying with what looked to be a good stepping-stone film for his career.

Zanuck also felt a good amount of anxiety from Altman as well. Altman wanted to shoot the picture in Korea, but was shot down and told that they would film it on the Fox Ranch in Malibu—just a short distance from Hollywood. Next, Altman told Zanuck they should at least shoot the Tokyo golf game in Tokyo, but Zanuck again nixed the idea. As Zanuck stated in *Robert Altman: The Oral Biography*, "I said, 'No, we're not. We're going across the street to Rancho Park. There's a golf course. All you have to do is get a couple of Japanese girls and dress them up and they're caddies.' One golf course looks like another. Why would we ever do that?" Altman was also less than happy with studio people telling him the best way to shoot the picture. Yet, with the help of Preminger negotiating elements of the shooting to Altman's preference, Altman finally—and literally—said, "Oh fuck it, I'll do it." With that, he began working with Preminger and Lardner on some changes for the script, and the production was ready to get started.

Casting

After Sutherland, there was still the rest of the cast to put into place. There have been rumors that James Caan was asked to play the part of Trapper John, which would have made sense given Altman's attraction to recasting earlier players in new films (as he would do in *MASH* for Robert Duvall and Michael Murphy), but if so it never went past merely an ask, as Caan had signed in February 1969 to played the lead in the film adaptation of the John Updike novel *Rabbit, Run* (1970). In the *Altman* book, Tom Skerritt states that the studio was pursuing Burt Reynolds for the role of Trapper John, but if so, it would have been like a kid on a scooter chasing the ambulance that was Reynolds' career at that point. At the beginning of 1969, when casting was being done, Reynolds was busy making the film *Skullduggery* and would immediately follow that filming with kneecap surgery in April when filming on *MASH* began (as well as getting ready to film his ABC series *Dan August*). Thus, it seems unlikely that hiring Reynolds went past the suggestion phase and not even to the level of something official, if at all.

The first real news of someone being cast for the film came in January 1969 when *Variety* stated that Bob Newhart had been signed for the film and would start immediately after completion of his work on what some saw as the "never-ending" filming on Mike Nichols' *Catch-22* (see chapter 12 for more details). Then in April 1969, *Variety* reported that Newhart had pulled out of *MASH* as he didn't want to conflict with himself in another military comedy. In February 1969 came word that Dan Blocker, who played Hoss on the NBC western series *Bonanza*, had backed out of the film as well, due to the network refusing to let him out of his television series contract for a few weeks in order to do the film. Blocker had become friends with Altman when the director was working on the series in the 1960s, and there was talk of him finally making an appearance in an Altman film, but he passed away before he could appear in *The Long Goodbye* (1973). It's intriguing to guess what roles both Newhart and Blocker would have played in the film, although one could guess that Blocker would have made for a good General Hammond (which went to G. Wood in the film), while Newhart would have bought his own subtle look of confusion to the role of Henry Blake (Newhart used stammering in his stand-up routines in a manner that would have suited Henry Blake's stutter from the novel well).

Altman would later state that he believed Elliott Gould was cast before he even signed on, but there's evidence that Gould had to do at least a screen test (as seen in one of the documentaries on the *MASH* special edition DVD and Blu-ray), and it should be noted that *Variety* announced

Trapper John (Elliott Gould) and Hawkeye (Donald Sutherland) are about to go on an adventure to Japan.

Gould joining the cast in March 1969, two months after Altman had officially signed on. Gould also confirmed that he had been brought in to
discuss playing the role of Duke, but felt he could never effectively pull off
the Southern accent needed for the role. Looking at the role of Trapper,
Gould thought he could easily fit into the character and asked if it was still
up for grabs. Altman had no complaints with the idea and handed him the
role. Soon after, Altman got a call from Tom Skerritt, who was working on
a screenplay and wanted the director's advice on it. Altman abruptly ended
their call nearly as soon as Skerritt said hello, telling Skerritt he would call
him back later. A short time later, Altman offered Skerritt the role of Duke.

Sally Kellerman had already been working in television in various roles
(including a substantial one in the second pilot of *Star Trek*) when she was
asked to audition for the role of Lieutenant Dish in the film. Kellerman
remembered in her autobiography, *Read My Lips* (Weinstein Books, New
York, 2013), that she didn't even know who she was auditioning for when
Altman told her, "I'll give you the best role in the picture: Hot Lips."

Kellerman was happy until she paged through the Lardner script to find that Houlihan had only "nine lines" in the film (the character actually has a little over thirty lines, but mainly in reaction to other characters and little in the way of dialogue to hang a performance on). She was livid that her career had devolved to only being offered such a small role, and she told Altman point-blank that she was offended. She felt she had proved herself to be able to do comedy, and instead what was being offered to her was just a cartoon that gets pushed around and mentally beaten down until she disappears midway through the picture (to be fair to Lardner, he was merely following what Hornberger himself had written for Houlihan in the novel, as discussed in a previous chapter). Demanding to know why Houlihan couldn't do more and couldn't react like a real person, Altman replied, "Why couldn't she? You could end up with something or nothing. Why not take a chance?" Taking the risk that Altman would be true to his words, Kellerman signed on for the part of Hot Lips.

As for Lieutenant Dish (who is only briefly referred to by her actual character name of Maria Schneider), Altman already had seen someone he felt was right for the part, actress Jo Ann Pflug. According to an online interview with the actress, Pflug had a career in radio and television for a few years when one day as she was eating in the 20th Century-Fox commissary, an agent asked her to come with him to meet Altman and Preminger for the role. Showing she could act as well as being attractive, she quickly landed the part.

Robert Duvall was already a recognizable star from television and movies at the time, but still struggling to make ends meet. Moreover, he was getting tired of working mainly in television, especially after having had a taste of working in film earlier in his career (such as playing Boo in *To Kill a Mockingbird*). "Around the time of *MASH*," Duvall told Marlow Stern at the SXSW event in 2013, "I was always looking for the next job. I thought, 'When's the next one coming?' I did TV and then I wanted to get into movies, but it was TV, TV, TV. Come on! Some of the old episodic shows were good to do, but it got to be repetitive." Having worked with Altman before for *Countdown*, it was a logical choice to ask him to be in the film, and he quickly snatched up the offer to play Frank Burns. The same occurred with Michael Murphy, who had appeared in Altman's last two films at that point and would play Me Lay in *MASH*. Murphy would go on to perform in many other Altman projects, such as starring in the HBO series, *Tanner '88*.

Gary Burghoff had gained praise off-Broadway as Charlie Brown in the musical *You're a Good Man, Charlie Brown* during the late 1960s, and it led to a chance to audition for Otto Preminger to costar in a film with Liza Minnelli. Burghoff thought he was sure to get the part in *The Sterile Cuckoo* (1969), but he later found out in the trade newspapers that Wendell Burton was cast instead. Sometime later, he received a call from one of his agents to let him know that he had been asked to audition for *MASH*. Not knowing the director or even why he had been asked to audition, Burghoff arrived to talk to Ingo Preminger. As it turns out, Preminger didn't even ask Burghoff to audition; after "two minutes" (according to Burghoff in his autobiography *To MASH and Back: My Life in Poems and Songs*), Preminger told him to go. Still, there was something pleasant about the conversation, and Burghoff had a nagging feeling the name of Preminger meant something. Soon after, his agent called to tell him that he had gotten the part of Radar in the film. When Burghoff asked who Preminger was, he was informed that he was the brother of Otto, and Burghoff realized that Ingo's brother must have recommended him to his brother based on his earlier audition. As it turns out, he wasn't the first one asked to play the role, however.

Austin Pendleton had just appeared on Otto Preminger's anti-classic *Skidoo* and thus was on the mind of Ingo when asked to audition for the role of Radar. Pendleton was told that he had the part, but he was working on *Catch-22* in Mexico at the time. Further, he didn't care for the script. When Altman found out that Pendleton was leaning toward saying no, Altman moved on. Pendleton had been advised that he had made a mistake, and when his agent saw him as the lead for Altman's follow-up, *Brewster McCloud* (1970), Pendleton knew Altman would never cast him. Instead, Altman would cast the actor who would be another discovery for *MASH*, Bud Cort.

Bud Cort would go on to star in Altman's *Brewster McCloud* as well as the cult favorite *Harold and Maude* (1971), but in 1969 he was looking for work and took buses to get to the audition for *MASH*. While he recognized Ingo Preminger (mainly as being related to Otto), he brushed off the other man watching his audition and would do so again when he won the role of Private Boone (the young man who Frank tells killed a patient). When Altman told him to get his hair cut and get cleaned up for the role, Cort wondered "What is with this hairdresser?" only to find out it was the director.

For Spearchucker Jones, it was understandable to go after someone who could not only act but play football. Altman also had another issue—he didn't know how he was going to shoot the football game as he didn't really know the sport that well. Fred Williamson had been a professional football player before becoming an actor, playing for the Oakland Raiders and Kansas City Chiefs, so he certainly knew the game, which is what Altman needed. As Williamson told Tom Clark for *This Is Infamous*, "I was doing a television series with Diahann Carroll called *Julia*. It was shot on 20th Century-Fox lot. I happened to be sitting in the commissary; a guy walks by and says, 'I'm doing a movie. It's got football in it. I don't know anything about football. Would you help me out? Put the football game [and] put the players together and direct it?' I said, 'Sure.' That guy was Robert Altman and the movie was *MASH*." (Keep reading for another version of who directed those football scenes.)

With Altman in place as director, as well as most of the main cast set, there was still a lot to do in the way of casting the various smaller but still important roles in the film. Altman wanted to build on the organized chaos of dialogue and action intended for *Countdown* and used to good effect in *That Cold Day in the Park*. For this reason, getting Roger Bowen as Henry Blake was a step in the right direction. Bowen was a writer who eventually became one of the members of the Compass Players in Chicago back in the mid- to late 1950s, an improv group that would eventually transform into the famous Second City theatrical group (and which featured Mike Nichols, who would be busy finishing *MASH*'s rival film, *Catch-22*, in 1969, and later Alan Alda). He brought with him the ability to make lines naturally flow off the tongue, which put him in good graces with many of the other actors added to the film at this point, several of whom came by way of the American Conservatory Theater (A.C.T.) in San Francisco.

A.C.T. was and remains a theater company started in 1965 that featured several productions as well as a number of acting classes with a very restricted enrollment. Many popular actors have come out of the not-for-profit company, including several that would be asked to audition for *MASH* by Altman after seeing several of the members in a "highly improvisational" performance at one of its theaters. Those included John Schuck (Painless Pole), Rene Auberjonois (cast as Father Mulcahy after Malachy McCourt was nixed by Ingo Preminger for the role), and G. Wood (General Hammond). The rest of the cast fell together quickly: David Arkin as the well-meaning but ineffectual Staff Sergeant Vollmer (and PA announcer), Tamara Wilcox as Captain "Knocko" McCarthy (a character with a bigger part in the novel than film), Corey Fischer as Captain Bandini (Fischer will briefly turn up in the television series as another character, but still with a guitar), Danny

Goldman as Captain Murrhardt, Carol Gottlieb as Ugly John, and Timothy Brown as Corporal Judson (Brown, a former professional football player, went on to play Spearchucker in the first few episodes of the television series, as well as turn up in Altman's 1975 film *Nashville*). From there, the production was ready to go, with filming to begin April 14, 1969, at the Fox Ranch in Malibu.

Filming

With rehearsal came the revelation that there were issues with the script, which had been batted about even as Lardner was working on it. Lardner states in his autobiography that he and Preminger tossed around the idea of moving the setting to Vietnam, but "the current war was just too close for us to be funny or properly irreverent about it." Lardner's aim was to stay vague enough that people would recognize it was of an earlier time and still tie it into the then-current Vietnam War. Altman went on to obliterate even that wall of safety, hoping that people would leave thinking it was about the Vietnam War (even going so far as to have the locals wearing clothing from Vietnam rather than Korea, such as the conical straw hats, in order to blur the line). It was only after the film was finished that the studio balked; they wanted to make sure people knew it was the Korean War for the very reason Lardner and Preminger concluded. To do that, they added the rolling titles a few minutes into the film that state it is Korea. It also positions the timeline so that, given the text of MacArthur's speech and Eisenhower's statement of going to Korea, anyone who knows history will assume that the film takes place in the final year of the war, just as the book takes place in roughly the last year and a half of the war. Better yet, since the titles come a few minutes into the film, and in a rather flip manner, it appears as a type of afterthought—that, "Yes, it's the Korean War, but that doesn't really matter to the story we're telling here." Which works perfectly with what Lardner, Preminger, and the studio wanted, plus what Altman was trying to achieve in the film.

The bigger problem turned out to be the dialogue. The scenes were fine, and reflected the book for the most part, with some additions here and there, such as adding the shower scene for Houlihan (as discussed in the previous chapter). The issue was that Lardner, as a writer respecting another writer's work, stuck with a certain percentage of dialogue from Hornberger's novel. This became a problem as the actors tried to say their lines; it was clear that a lot of it was not sounding "real." Here was the director already known for wanting to make dialogue realistic and with a cast that included many improvisers, yet the script was restricting their movements. That's exactly what Altman had in mind, though—to work with the cast and crew to take what was written on the page and make it "real" by changing dialogue and even changing scenes, in order to get them to work on-screen.

For the improvisers and other actors just starting out, it made sense and was perfectly geared toward what they had been doing before the film. They didn't have to just say their lines and perform rehearsed movements, they could develop their characters to make the things they said and did look more natural. Further, Altman wanted to make sure the other actors got to do more than window-dress the background of scenes by placing microphones all over the sets and letting the camera follow any action taking place. Tom Skerritt knew what was up and made sure the cast was aware that anything said may be used in the film, so "pay attention and come up with stuff on your own." It gave the actors an additional sense of belonging, knowing that what they did could end up in the film rather than on the editing floor due to them just being background players for the "stars."

This helped to liberate the other actors, especially Rene Auberjonois with Father Mulcahy. The novel and script play up the priest as an old-timer who was fair—in other words a traditional cinematic priest who could have fitted into *Going My Way* or *Boystown*; the kind but firm priest who is hip to the world. Auberjonois, on the other hand, came into the role thinking of the priest like someone he knew who had been a priest that was soft-spoken, humble, and had the best intentions at heart. This reshaping would be reflected in the character once it got to the television screen as well, and the authoritative Father Mulcahy of the first novel (and certainly of the later Butterworth novels) would cease to be. Ironically, although Auberjonois thought the changes he made served the character well, some viewers took it to be a mockery of religion and/or Catholicism, since Mulcahy seems blissfully unaware of some of the activities around him in the MASH unit as well as going to Hawkeye to resolve Painless' concerns rather than doing so himself. Such accusations would follow into the television series as well, but in the case of both Auberjonois and William Christopher later on, the point was to show a human side to such a figure, which makes his devotion much more meaningful than the cliché everyone was used to seeing. Auberjonois also added the prayer heard at the end of the film where Mulcahy blesses the jeep Hawkeye and Duke use to leave, which was added when Auberjonois found a prayer for travel that—with a minor alternation—seemed perfectly in character for Mulcahy to use.

Such allowances would transform the destiny of another character in the film. After Sally Kellerman made her complaints to Altman about Houlihan having nothing to do in the film besides being abused by the other characters, the director looked to find more for her to do. According to Kellerman in her autobiography, *Read My Lips*, it was Altman who came up with the line during Houlihan's discussion with Pierce that "the Army is my home" (it is neither in the novel nor in Lardner's script). In one sentence, the audience is given a definition of Houlihan that better explains Hawkeye's response (which is from the novel) that Houlihan is a "regular army clown." Houlihan is proud to be that clown and doesn't recognize how stifling she had made herself to others and even herself. Later, when Houlihan comes out of the shower, Kellerman improvises a long, gawky run for the character from the showers to Blake's tent, full of panic, anger, and awkwardly funny at the same time. Although Kellerman delivers her lines about the "insane asylum" that is the MASH unit exactly as in the script (and in the novel), she then falters after Blake tells her to resign her commission. She begins to break down, knowing that her commission is essentially her lifeline, her life. And that lifeline doesn't mean anything to anyone. Nor does anything else she has done. Kellerman in the space of two minutes of film develops Houlihan into a real person—she doesn't really know how to act in this world where no one seems to do what life has told her is reality. She's suddenly no longer a cartoon, as seen in the novel and as appeared in the script, but a vulnerable person who you actually do want to comfort.

Altman saw it as well. According to Kellerman in her book, Altman was thrilled with her response on film and told her that he would make sure she stays in the movie instead of disappearing, as the character does in the novel. From there, Houlihan begins to develop into just "one of the guys," showing that Duke always had an interest in her, and her eventually becoming part of the team as head cheerleader for the football game (none of which was in the novel or in Lardner's script). Houlihan is fleshed out and—a rarity for the film—gets a character arc that most of the others do not. All due to Altman being willing to let the actors steer the characters and the plot to some extent.

To the newcomers to film, getting to work through material and make it their own was a dream job that they were very happy to do. It also gave them false hope for the future. "For all of us who had never been in a movie," Rene Auberjonois states in *Altman*, "other than being a day player, it's almost as if he ruined us for the rest of our lives. We thought that's the way movies were." Kellerman, who had done extensive television and some films before *MASH*, states in the same biography that she knew that it was outside the norm, "I came from television, and in those days you couldn't change one line and if you did, the entire suite of suits from Universal had to come down to the set to check it out. . . . "

It was also unusual to the two main actors of the film, Donald Sutherland and Elliott Gould. Both had been working in films and elsewhere for years at that point, and neither had known Altman before beginning the film (unlike Skerritt, Duvall, and Murphy). To them, filming meant shooting the script, centering the camera on the main players, getting it right, and moving on to the next setup. Now there was Altman, looking for advice, making changes on the set, and welcoming cast members plugging in their own dialogue when it was felt to help the film. The rest of the cast saw all this freedom to experiment; to Sutherland and Gould, they saw a director who was lost and about to destroy their careers with a bad movie. Further, they had been hired to be the stars of the film, but the director was spending more time filming the secondary cast only briefly to be seen in the picture rather than concentrating on the performances of the main actors. Tie into that the fact that Sutherland already had some ill feelings about Altman after the director tried to get him fired from the movie, and it was very easy to feel like they were aboard a sinking ship with a lot of insane people willing to drown with it.

Things nearly came to blows when Altman was having difficulty in getting a crane shot involving Sutherland and Gould walking through the compound. Breaking for lunch, Altman confronted Gould for not being like one of the other actors who was flexible enough to do the walking scene the way Altman wanted. Gould, throwing his lunch into the air, pushed back; getting into Altman's face that he didn't appreciate being told to be like another member of the cast. Altman relented, saying that he made a mistake. The actor accepted the veiled apology, but it was the breaking point for Gould and Sutherland, who shared the same agent. The two reported to the studio that they thought Altman needed to be terminated from the film. Calmer heads smoothed things out for the stars, but no one told Altman as they continued filming what they had done. With the director already feeling a bit defensive about working on the film, thanks to the studio changing his salary and dictating locations, he later stated that if he had found out, he probably would have walked off the picture. Later, once the two stars of the film saw the dailies (footage that was run for the cast, crew, and executives to see how a movie is coming along) and how Altman was managing to pull the pieces together, Sutherland and Gould realized they had made a mistake. "We thought you just didn't know what you were doing," Gould told Altman when the director finally found out about their visit to the studio heads behind his back.

On April 30, 1969, two weeks into filming, the crew and cast began to shoot the opening sequence of the movie, which shows casualties being brought in by helicopter. Contrary to the look on film, the area where the copters land is very small, leaving little room for those standing on the ground to be at a safe distance. Watch the opening credits in the television series for an example of this—you see Hawkeye and several others leaning down as they head to the helicopter, but you don't see that the helicopter has already landed, making the stance of the actors relatively safe. It would be less dangerous for everyone to be down the hill, and—according to Gary Burghoff in his autobiography *To MASH and Back*—Altman was safely in a ditch a good forty feet away from the action when the sequence commenced. The plan was to have the helicopters appear over the mountain ridge and then land on the pad, as the cast ran out under the whirling blades and began to take the "patients" (actually stuntmen) off the 'copters and away.

The first attempt did not go well, with no one really sure of their actions and stumbling about. A strong wind that had built up in the area didn't help with the confusion, and Altman asked that everyone return to their places and they would reshoot the sequence. At that point, Burghoff bowed out, feeling the shot was unsafe and refusing to risk his health again after getting his knitted cap knocked off by one of the blades the first time. An extra was then pulled in to substitute for him, and the helicopters were told to take off. According to Burghoff, one 'copter made it up with no problem, but the second had a rotor blade malfunction while ten feet off the ground, sending the helicopter sideways toward a group of extras waiting nearby before crashing into a rocky stream a few yards away. The pilot, Van Honeycutt, and the two stuntmen in the stretchers, Ed Smith and John Ashley, received minor injuries (at least according to *Variety* the next day), while Altman shouted to the cameraman to make sure he got it all on film. The first attempt was used in the film, and one can see Burghoff, John Schuck, and others scurrying away and Burghoff briefly looking back without his cap. Meanwhile, the crash site came into use later in the film where the men are sitting by the stream discussing if Hot Lips is a natural blonde, so it didn't go to waste.

Other scenes went much smoother, including the famous suicide attempt of the Painless Pole—the first sequence shot for the film. Written to take place as a small gathering, Michael Murphy reported in the *Altman* oral biography that he arrived on the set to find Altman snickering over a copy of *The Last Supper* painting by da Vinci (footage appears of Altman doing exactly this in several of the *MASH* documentaries from over the years). The image was not necessarily sacrilegious, but as a parody of a well-known religious artifact of the Christian faith, it certainly was not something seen often in American cinema at the time (or still to this day).

The most memorable filming experience would be the shower scene, although Altman tried to keep the antics around the shot to a minimum. Sally Kellerman was anxious about shooting the sequence, never feeling comfortable with her body (as discussed in her autobiography) and now was about to do something rarely seen in American studio films at the time—a nude scene. Sure, it was a side view and she would quickly cover up, but it was still a big moment in American cinema, and she was going to be the "poster child" for the movement. Altman decided to use a skeleton crew (only the necessary crew members to help film it being there) and asked the actors to avoid the set for a while in order "not to spook her." Gary Burghoff then suggested a way that might help her feel better about being naked in front of others.

With the shot ready, the tent wall came down and Kellerman flew to the ground with it. In doing so, she had been so quick that the camera didn't get anything on film, and the shot had to be reset. Meanwhile, Kellerman was shocked to see Gary Burghoff standing next to the camera naked. For the second shot, Burghoff changed things up a bit by having Tamara Horrocks stand topless by the camera instead of himself. Kellerman later stated that she still had Burghoff's body in her thoughts, so to see Horrocks standing there made her momentarily think she was seeing a hermaphrodite. Needing to shoot it one more time, Kellerman looked up to see Horrocks now fully clothed, but being "dry-humped by actor Kenny Prymus." It was enough to get the take needed for the film, and Kellerman claims in her autobiography that it was Burghoff and the others doing what they did that helped her get through the filming.

To give the operations the authoritative feel of the real thing, Dr. David Sachs was enlisted as the technical adviser and also appears as one of the surgeons in the O.R. at one point. Sachs was a heart surgeon, working in Beverly Hills and teaching at UCLA in their medical center. He had appeared briefly on the soap opera *General Hospital* before *MASH* and would go on to appear as a biker in the film *Hell's Angels '69,* and other walk-on roles on television (mainly hospital and doctor dramatic series). He would later run into trouble with the law in 1975 due to a cocaine charge related to the treatment of hemorrhoids for acquaintances in Hollywood.

The filming for the football game was kept to the end of the schedule, with *Variety* announcing on June 4, 1969, that G. Wood had been hired to act in the film (as General Hammond, the central villain of the last third of the film). Gearing up production for the sports sequence was occurring before then, with *Variety* in its May 12 issue announcing that Altman was working with E. T. Grant of the 20th Century-Fox grip department on a portable camera in a steel frame that could be tossed around like a football for the filming of the game. If the camera was completed, it appears it was never used in the actual film, however.

Hired to help direct the football game was Andy Sidaris, who had worked for ABC in their sports department and had directed early episodes of *ABC's Wide World of Sports* as well as *Monday Night Football.* Sidaris would go on to direct a number of television dramas in the 1970s before working on a series of direct-to-video action films in the 1980s. Sidaris would be directly involved with the filming of the game to the point that he would later sue 20th Century-Fox for not crediting him for directing it. (Sidaris' involvement also conflicts with Williamson's earlier statement in this chapter that he had been asked by Altman to direct the football scenes.) Sidaris—following in Altman's footsteps—made many suggestions to the cast as to what to do and say during the filming, including the suggestion to John Schuck that he say something really offensive to his opponent out on the field as they lined up for a play. With that in his head, Schuck leaned down and said the immortal line, "All right, bub, your fucking head is coming right off!" to real-life professional football defensive tackle Buck Buchanan. Buchanan then nearly did the same in reality to Schuck, sending him flying several feet back into the air, and later apologizing to the actor for clicking into defense mode after hearing Schuck mouth off like someone would during an actual game.

Editing the film with Altman was Danford B. Greene, who had worked with the director back in the days of the *Kraft Suspense Theatre* for two episodes and then edited *That Cold Day in the Park* for Altman before performing the same function on *MASH.* When going through the dailies, Greene was happy to put the shot of Schuck using the f-word into the dailies, mainly as a joke, since no one figured it would make it into the movie. Altman, however, loved the line; even more so when others commented that there was no way the studio would allow him to keep it in the final film. Besides, there was a bigger issue to worry about as the filming came to an end on June 11, 1970 and the postproduction started—the episodic nature of the film came through in the completed cut. Due to this, the film seemed to be jumping around with not much really to hold it together. Something needed to be done to help link the pieces so that it read as a whole, rather than bits and pieces.

Fortunately, Altman and crew had filmed several shots of the loudspeaker system, and essentially made it a character in the movie, with David Arkin heard making announcements in-between musical numbers on the MASH loudspeaker system (other announcers were used in other scene locations, including Ted Knight, who would go on to play Ted Baxter on *The Mary Tyler Moore Show*). These sequences worked so well that Arkin even does the ending cast list in character to wrap up the film. With the editing of completed, Altman was ready to show off the final product to everyone.

One of the first to see it was Ring Lardner Jr. Depending on who discusses what happened next, Lardner was either mildly upset (his opinion) or violently outraged (everyone else) as to what had happened to his script when it went to screen. Lardner had worked with Altman on alterations to the script before filming, and knew that there would probably be more to come when the actual filming started (as can be typical for many Hollywood films), but he was surprised at how much had changed. Recalling what occurred on *Countdown* with the studio and the director, he was also a bit miffed Altman had mixed the soundtrack in such a way that many of what Lardner considered to be his best lines were muffled under other dialogue and sound effects. When the screening ended, Elliott Gould would find Lardner looking at him and the others saying, "How could you do this to me? There's not a word that I wrote on screen."

As will be seen in another chapter, there is plenty of what Lardner wrote that made it into the film, and thus it is proper that he would eventually pick up an Academy Award for the screenplay. However, that never quite set well with Altman, who felt additionally abandoned by the writer when Lardner gave no thanks to the director when accepting the award. In some ways, this was par for the course for Altman, who felt he had to be the outsider to everyone, even someone like Lardner, who had seen the worst in the studio system during the blacklist. Over time, Altman would enhance the story to make it bigger and better. By the late 1990s, he was telling others that Lardner had been outraged from the time he had read Altman's draft of the script—a version that Lardner told *The New York Times* in June 1997 he could not have ever seen because Altman never wrote such a draft.

Lardner did point out in his autobiography certain things that Altman brought to the film that were not in the script: the stealing of the jeep by Hawkeye and Duke; Blake having an affair with one of the nurses; everyone in the camp singing "Onward, Christian Soldiers" (a misstep that ruined the scene, according to Lardner); and Mulcahy's famous line "He was drafted." Nevertheless, the script holds the film together, and many of Lardner's lines and general action do appear in the film, so the notion some fans get that *MASH* was improvised by the actors and Altman—a notion that even the actors dismiss—is not correct. A team effort from writer on down—even Lardner would later state that he should have given Altman more credit for the script than he did at the time—but hardly a film that emerged out of Altman's head like the birth of Athena.

Altman would also misremember later the studio's reaction to the film's progress as he was shooting. His statement has always been that "*MASH* wasn't released; it escaped." As he would state in various interviews over the years, the film was made for $3.5 million at the studio ranch and hidden away from the studio as they prepared bigger war pictures for the year—*Tora! Tora! Tora!* and *Patton*. Altman's stance was that if they just kept their heads down and didn't cause waves, they would be able to make the film he wanted to make. In his eyes, the film was made without 20th Century-Fox knowing what they had.

Zanuck disagreed with this assessment, stating that he was watching dailies every day and knew exactly what was going on with the film. It also conflicts with Gould and Sutherland going to the studio to complain about Altman, as that certainly would have sent red flags to the studio heads that they needed to check in on Altman's "little film." One could also argue that, if staying low-key was the point, then why was Altman wanting to film in Korea and Japan in the first place? (In response to that question, it could be said that he figured if he was overseas, the studio heads would leave him alone, just as they did on the studio ranch anyway.) But that was Altman—a man who liked butting heads, and if changing some minor details help to give him a good story to tell to demonstrate that image, so be it.

As it stood, he had plenty of heat to worry about from the studio anyway. A script never could convey the type of blood and gore that would be on display in the operating room scenes (and even as the beginning titles play and we see the wounded being taken down the hill to the O.R.). No doubt the studio assumed they would get the type of sterilized operation scenes as had always been the norm in even war pictures up to that point—plenty of hand gestures and action happening below the camera, with a swipe or two of blood here and there. Instead, Altman wanted to make viewers aware of the ugliness involved, not only in real war, but also to better explain/excuse the actions of the doctors in needing to break the rules in order to relieve the stress they were under. Even so, it was a new element for a major studio picture, and the studio was unsure if the audience would buy it. A comedy with gore? Would anyone want to see it?

To make matters worse, the head of the studio, Darryl Zanuck, came to the same showing where Lardner had first seen it. As Lardner remembered him saying at the time, "You simply can't combine broad comedy with bloody operating-room scenes," and that was going to be the end of the matter. He had good reasons for saying so beyond his own judgment—*Variety* reported in January 1970 that audience members at a studio screening fled when the O.R. scenes started, so Zanuck was right in his assumption that some of the audience would not be able to take it. He suggested everyone meet with him at 10 a.m. the next morning to go over what needed to be cut and refilmed in order to make the movie releasable.

When the time came to meet, however, Darryl Zanuck's attitude had done a 180. It turns out the young woman (or women, as the story is sometimes told) who had watched the movie with Zanuck disagreed with him about the blood. She felt that it was necessary to the story and would be fine with the young audiences going to movies. Her ability to convince Zanuck saved the film from being recut and becoming probably a different movie.

Release and Response

As it stood, the film was ready to go to the promotion department, who had their own issues with it, not knowing exactly how to sell it to American audiences. Yes, it was a comedy, but it wasn't traditional "Bob Hope" military wackiness. The cast was largely unknown, and the director known mainly for television. There was blood, nudity, and the f-word, leading to an R rating in the fairly new ratings system by the Motion Pictures Association of America (MPAA) that would keep a good percentage of people out. (Keep in mind that although an R rating in 1970 would be nearly a PG today, at the time people were still unsure if an R meant a fairly traditional movie or the worst horrors ever to be witnessed on the screen.) Even the name of the movie was a problem. "They first challenged the title," Richard Zanuck stated in *Robert Altman*, "'What is this? Mash potatoes? We can't sell this.'" Nor were things helped when Altman announced in *Film/TV Daily*. "All the studios are going broke and I love it. The studios waste their money. When they go on location it costs them a fortune. When I go on location I know my costs even before I begin to shoot." This from the man who tried to force the studio to send him, his cast, and crew to Korea to film. Such talk did him no favors with 20th Century-Fox

There were at least the early critical responses to be thankful for when it came to promotion. At the time, critics were having a field day with a heady number of remarkable films coming out of Hollywood, thanks to the older men in control simply not knowing what America wanted anymore and beginning to throw anything up on the screen to see if it would stick (in ticket buyers' minds). True, there were many duds among the offerings, but just as many brilliant directors, writers, and actors would come out of the period, and the critics had something to talk about beyond traditional "this comedy is funny" and/or "the new western has a lot of action." They could discuss ideas going on within the films, a function reserved mainly for foreign films up to that time. *MASH* was another example of this, and the critics were anxious to talk about the little film that seemed completely outside the norm for Hollywood.

Pauline Kael was one of the first to come out in its favor. When asked by a 20th Century-Fox executive after an advance screening what could be done with the film, Kael reportedly said, "What are you crazy? You release it!" Her quote from her review in *The New Yorker* would headline the *MASH* newspaper ad, "*MASH* is the best American war comedy since sound came in." Richard Schickel from *Life* magazine was also featured in the ad and made mention of the changing times in Hollywood by disclaiming, "*MASH* is what the new freedom of the screen is all about." Roger Ebert focused his review in early January 1970 on the sadistic nature of the characters (a point that many fans of the television series have stated as a reason they have a hard time watching the movie): "There is perhaps nothing so exquisite as achieving (as the country song has it) sweet mental revenge against someone we hate with particular dedication. And it is the flat-out poker-faced hatred in *MASH* that makes it work. Most comedies want us to laugh at things that aren't really funny; in this one we laugh precisely because they're not funny. We laugh, that we may not cry."

Of course, not all critics were in love with the film. *Variety* concluded that the film missed more than hit with the mixture of "reality and slapstick," while still thinking that a young audience may find something of value in it (the paper would also state that the character of Mulcahy was saved "from being an insulting absurdity" only due to the skill of the actor playing the part). Vincent Canby, whose *New York Times* review is quoted in the *MASH* ad, actually turned in a negative review, calling the film "unsuccessful" and saying it "simply runs out of steam, says good-bye to its major characters, and calls final attention to itself as a movie—surely the saddest and most overworked of cop-out devices in the comic film repertory."

Only hinted at the time, but aggressively reprised in later years, is what some felt was a misogynist attitude within the film. It is certainly an understandable topic in terms of how viewers sometimes see the women as being portrayed in the film. However, this argument misses the forest for the trees. Lieutenant Dish may be enticed to have sex with Painless Pole, but this was at her own discretion (she is left with Painless to decide what she wants to do, and could have just as easily left or pretended to have done something in order to help Painless; her smiling in the copter does not show her being pleased to be submissive, but pleased that she did something). The rants toward the nurses in Tokyo by Trapper are not against women but against authority (he's the same way with the head of the hospital, but tolerant with those who work with him without having to following the "rules"). And of course, there's Houlihan, who is mistreated, yet Ebert's review perhaps puts even this into a better focus: "Hot Lips, who is all Army professionalism and objectivity, is less human because the suffering doesn't reach her. . . . Her façade offends them; no one could be unaffected by the work of this hospital, but she is." To Hawkeye and the others, she's not a woman to mistreat, she's a monster that needs to be knocked back down to a human level. Look again at the shower scene. It is not just men in that crowd waiting for the tent to rise, but women as well. And women who are happy to see it happen to someone like Houlihan because they too despise her for her inability to be human. Keep in mind as well that the Swamp men give her an out—they ask her to join them looking at pictures of their kids, but she refuses (as they rightly expect, but still . . . if she had turned around and conveyed any interest, would the shower prank have even occurred?).

Altman in later years would confound this concern by excusing what was done in the film by claiming it was how men acted at the time. Yet, if this was the purpose of such scenes, then why weren't they addressed in some manner to show how wrong it was? If anything, it should have led to something that provoked a response by the audience to being participants in watching the shower scene—and let's face it, there were as many people there in the theater to see Kellerman naked as to laugh at the comedy. Because Altman tried to divert attention, he lessens the overall message—that Houlihan eventually does become one of the gang; she becomes human, and is the better for it. Certainly better than simply being invisible once her use as a joke is over, as in the novel.

With critical reviews in as the film was moving to general release in April, the promotional department at 20th Century-Fox at least had something to chew on for the pressbook, which littered the ads with the critics' (sometimes veiled) rejoices. The pressbook also emphasized the professional football players in the film, hoping to get sports fans into the theaters just to see the athletes.

Along with the critical quotes, the poster and film ads all feature the famous "peace sign on two legs" that would be transferred to the book series. The original work can clearly be seen as a composite of a hand with a pair of woman's legs in high heels. Due to the somewhat racy nature of the artwork, the pressbook contained a variation available that puts the movie title over the "hips" of the legs in order to avoid showing . . . well, not really showing anything, actually, but still, the image was considered a tad scandalous at the time. A later reissue of the film that was edited to achieve a PG rating would go even further, by attaching a sheet in the pressbook of the "peace sign on legs" covered in a glove. This "gloved" artwork appeared in the revised pressbook in various sizes to be cut-and-pasted over the "offensive" version for more delicate newspaper editors (the page in the pressbook states, "Use this art where newspaper censorship exists").

While various black-and-white as well as color stills were available upon request, only one print-ready photo was included with the pressbook, showing Sutherland and Gould in a posed shot, face-to-face, with Gould shirtless. The photo was by Lawrence Schiller (famous for some of the last photos of Marilyn Monroe), who took a number of pictures of the actors from the film, including a re-creation of the "Last Supper" scene. A few of the photos feature the actors, including Kellerman, in various stages of undress, along with pictures of the male cast watching a woman (not Kellerman) showering in the foreground. Of these photos, usually just the one of Sutherland and Gould has been featured in promotion for the movie, however. Speaking of exploitation, the pressbook states that "word of mouth" would help spread the news about the film. The pressbook also gives the novel a backhanded compliment by pointing out that it's available but that the film "is even faster, funnier and more fantastic than the original." Also mentioned is a soundtrack album (the opening theme being a song "by The MASH"—more

A promotional flyer sent with some pressbooks that incorporates a number of the quotes from critics, as well as one shot from the Lawrence Schiller photo shoot that featured a number of the actors in various stages of undress.

on that in the next chapter) on Columbia Records, open-ended interviews with Donald Sutherland and Elliott Gould on record, radio and TV spots, as well as a "5-minute featurette" for television stations to air.

Sneak previews of the film to help with that "word of mouth" began in October 1969, leading to a showing for the Directors Guild in early November and the Sutton Theatre in New York later that month. The response was greater than expected, and soon 20th Century-Fox began pushing to move the movie's national release from March to February and then went with January 25, 1970, for a world premiere and exclusive run at the Baronet in New York.

In March, the film was screened by the Army and Air Force Motion Picture Service to decide if it would be shown at base theaters. The group of twenty to twenty-five officers had mixed emotions about it—younger officers believed that the majority "took the film too seriously" but did agree that it had no socially redeeming value and that "the bad guys triumphed" in the picture. Ironically, the same group reviewed *Medium Cool*, a film rated X at the time that ends with the real-life police riot at the 1968 Democratic

National Convention, and gave it an A-OK to be shown on bases. At the same time, the reviewer for *The Army Times*, John Greenwald, gave the movie three-and-a-half stars out of four, but cautioned that the film "cuts deep, obviously too deep for the officers who, in effect, banned the movie. And I have a feeling I might have reacted the same way to a film which ridiculed my life and my career." The navy, on the other hand, had no issues with the film being shown on ships at sea or in land installation. Then again, there certainly were no sailors in the film to knock. Less than a week later, the Defense Department announced that *MASH* would be allowed in base theaters after "senior staff officers" reviewed the film again. It should also be mentioned that such a restriction on base would have no hold over anyone in the army going to see it in a civilian theater, so the fuss was relatively mild overall.

The film finally went national April 3, 1970. Also in theaters at the time were *Cactus Flower* (Walter Matthau and Goldie Hawn), *Frankenstein Must Be Destroyed* (Hammer horror film with Peter Cushing), *Marooned* (Gene Hackman, Gregory Peck), Franco Zeffirelli's *Romeo & Juliet*, *Paint Your Wagon* (Lee Marvin and Clint Eastwood), *Easy Rider* (Peter Fonda and Dennis Hooper), as well as Disney's *The Computer Wore Tennis Shoes*. *Airport* and *Hello, Dolly!* would debut while *MASH* played in theaters through the summer of 1970, while finally the film many were waiting to compare *MASH* to—*Catch-22*—came out as *MASH* was winding down its initial run in June 1970. Although the movie had been playing to turn-away business in New York, there was still surprise when it did better than anyone expected in general release, with lines forming around blocks at theaters for those wanting to buy tickets. With a budget of just $3.5 million, the film would make over $36 million in its initial run around the world; earning over $86 million up to the current day.

In May 1970, *MASH* played in competition at the Cannes Film Festival, which was a controversial year because of Russian and Japanese films being ineligible to compete due to the sameness of the genres done in each ("Slavic Spectacles and Japanese Samurai Flicks"). With Altman alongside Jo Ann Pflug and Sally Kellerman, Altman picked up the most prestigious award at the festival, the Palme d'Or. *MASH* won as "Best Film—Musical or Comedy" at the 1970 Golden Globe awards in February of that year. The big one, however, was the 1971 Academy Awards, where *MASH* had received five nominations, but won only in Best Adapted Screenplay. The other categories were: Best Film Editing (won by *Patton*), Best Supporting Actress (won by Helen Hayes for *Airport*), Best Director (won by Franklin

J. Schaffner for *Patton*), and Best Picture (*Patton*). Altman was asked if he was disappointed, but he would go on to say he was relieved at the time, as winning so early in his theatrical career would mean people would be looking for him to fail.

The film would push the career of everyone in some manner, although most of the supporting cast would go on to roles in television rather than other films. Elliott Gould and Donald Sutherland—both of whom were on the upswing in popularity before filming *MASH*—had the most success out of the actors in the film over time. As for the director, he would announce that his next picture would be one called *Interiors*, but that was pushed back in order to do *Brewster McCloud* (1970), which would be a critical and financial flop at the time (although considered a cult favorite today by many). Altman would continue with films through the 1970s, including the hit *Nashville* in 1975 (which nearly starred Sally Kellerman and Robert Duvall at various points of production, but in the end only featured Michael Murphy from the *MASH* cast). He stumbled with the expensive wreck *Popeye* (1980), but continued to make films and eventually received renewed praise for his 1992 movie *The Player*, a comedy about the evils of Hollywood. He died in 2006, leaving a legacy of films that may not have always won over the public or critics, but were done the way he wanted.

As for *MASH*, it was edited in 1974 and rereleased to theaters with a PG rating. In the process, it lost a little bit of the blood (mainly the squirting blood seen in the film), left only a snippet of nudity, and eliminated John Schuck's "fuck." The film premiered on CBS—the network airing the television series—on Friday, March 5, 1976, with the *TV Guide* ad using a composite of one of the Lawrence Schiller photos in order to show Houlihan, Hawkeye, and Trapper together. *MASH* was one of the first movies people could own through the magic of videotape when Magnetic Video Corp released it on VHS and BETA along with fifty other titles. Over the years it has been released in CED videodisc, LaserDisc, DVD, and Blu-ray, with special editions featuring additional documentary material on some editions of the Blu-ray and DVD. By the early 1980s, it was also not completely uncommon for the film to air on television stations unedited (including the nudity and f-word unbleeped). But that's the ramification of the liberal 1970s for you, and we reversed track pretty quickly on that front as the 1980s went along.

20th Century-Fox was extremely happy with the success of the film, and immediately looked to bringing the sequel novel, *MASH Goes to Maine*, to the silver screen, but a workable script was never produced, and the cast and director who made the first a success were long gone on to other projects. Instead, the focus went to television, which would see the transfer of the characters and location to a new world. It would also move over the theme song to the new series as well. A song that was supposed to be idiotic on purpose, and yet would become one of the biggest legacies of the *MASH* phenomenon.

9

We Can Do Stupid

The History of "Suicide Is Painless"

J ohnny Mandel had been working in the recording business for years when asked to write "the stupidest song ever" for Robert Altman's new movie.

Born November 23, 1925, Mandel had become interested in learning to arrange music while playing trumpet and later trombone in jazz bands and orchestras in the 1940s. As the 1950s approached, Mandel was performing, writing, and/or arranging for such performers as Buddy Rich, Woody Herman, Artie Shaw, and Count Basie. In the mid-1950s, Mandel stopped performing in order to concentrate on arrangements and would work with Hoagy Carmichael and Frank Sinatra (the album *Ring-a-Ding-Ding!* in 1960). He also began writing scores for movies, starting with the Robert Wise film *I Want to Live* (1958, with Susan Hayward). From there, Mandel would bounce around between television and films (including two years on *Your Show of Shows*). He went on to write the score for *The Americanization of Emily* (1964), *The Sandpiper* (1965)—which featured a hit theme song, "The Shadow of Your Smile," written by Mandel and Johnny Mercer—*Harper* (1966), *Point Blank* (1967), and many others. In 1969, he did the score for *That Cold Day in the Park* for Robert Altman, and with Altman's tendency to use people again—especially those that he became friends with, such as Mandel—the musician was asked to do the same duties on *MASH*. "I was brought in before the movie was even shot, which was highly unusual," Mandel told Marc Myers in an interview for the *JazzWax* website. "In most cases, you're the last one in the line to see the film when scoring it."

According to Mandel, Painless' suicide dinner was to be one of the first (if not the first) scenes shot for the film. Altman told Mandel that he needed to do something in the scene when everyone is walking by Painless' casket with last words and mementos. "There's just dead air," Altman said. Knowing that actor Ken Prymus (Private Seidman) could sing and that Corey Fischer (Captain Bandini) could play "three chords" on the guitar,

Altman decided the two would perform a song during the mourners' portion of the scene. The main stipulation Altman had was that "it's got to be the stupidest song ever written." Mandel responded, "Well, we can do stupid."

Robert Altman went home to work out lyrics for the song for Mandel, but came back the next day empty-handed. "There's too much stuff in this forty-five-year-old brain of mine," Mandel recalled Altman telling him in the *Altman* biography. "I can't get anything nearly as stupid as I need. But all is not lost. I have this kid who is a total idiot. He'll run through this thing like a dose of salts."

Michael Altman was fifteen years old at the time and going through the artistic angst of most teenagers in writing poetry when his father asked him to write the lyrics for the song. His first few attempts were "atrocious crap" and told his father that he'd have to find someone else to do it, but then a week later everything fell into place—lyrics as well as some of the chords. Michael Altman recorded his version of the song on a cassette recorder, and the tape was sent to Mandel to piece together as quickly as possible, since filming was to start very soon on the scene and the actors would need a version they could imitate on film.

Mandel listened to it and then got drunk. "I had to get loose enough to come up with that," Mandel stated in the *Altman* biography. "I had to get bombed and wrote it. I don't recommend that." He made a few changes to what Altman had in order to "make it sound homemade" and gave it to the director to use. The director liked it so much that he began tinkering with the idea of having a version of the song play over the opening credits. Mandel was against it and tried to talk them out of it for a short time before admitting defeat and letting them do what they wanted.

The recording of the song for the opening titles was with an orchestra conducted by Johnny Mandel, with Thomas Z. Shepard producing. The group of tenor singers used would be listed on the soundtrack album and single as "The MASH," but they were mostly made up of members of the Ron Hicklin Singers, who did a variety of session work, sometimes with the famous Hollywood session group the Wrecking Crew. Ron Hicklin, John Bahler, and Tom Bahler were the three tenors in the group, who did a variety of work in television and films, including the themes for *Love, American Style* (listed as the Charles Fox Singers), *Batman*, and *Wonder Woman*. They were augmented by Ian Freebain-Smith, who had been a member of the Eligibles, a group who sang "The Ballad of Gilligan's Island" in the second and third seasons of that series.

Besides appearing on the soundtrack album, the song would be released over the years and in a number of countries as a single under the name most know it by, "Suicide Is Painless," although it has also been released as "Song from MASH" and "Theme from MASH (Suicide Is Painless)." The single's B side was typically "The MASH March" by Johnny Mandel, although there have been at least two costarring singles over the years: a 1984 Netherlands single with John Barry's theme from the television series *The Persuaders* on the B side and a U.S. reissue from 1990 that featured on the B side "Yakety Sax" by "Boots" Randolph (popularly known as the theme to *The Benny Hill Show*). The single reached #4 on the Dutch Top 40 chart in 1970, but a push by Noel Edmonds in the UK in1980 helped get it to #1 on the UK Singles chart when reissued that year.

The soundtrack album for the film.

In 1973, jazz pianist Ahmad Jamal recorded an instrumental version of "Suicide Is Painless" that was released on some1974 reissues of the soundtrack album. His version was popular in some quarters, but there have been dozens and dozens of recordings of the song by a slew of artists over the years, including Bill Evans, Marilyn Manson, Roger Williams, and a 1992 version by rock band Manic Street Preachers that got to #7 on the UK charts.

"Suicide Is Painless" would become the theme of the television series, although in a much shorter and slightly upbeat variation of the movie theme. The pilot features the longest version of the television theme, but over the years of the

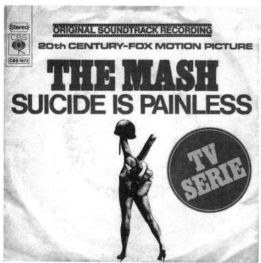

The single released for "Suicide Is Painless," featuring the group the MASH. The MASH was made up of session players who had worked on theme songs from *Gilligan's Island*, *Love American Style*, and *Wonder Woman*.

series the song was recorded again and used sometimes even in the middle or end of a season, or for just a few episodes. Since the television version had no lyrics, only Johnny Mandel was listed in the credits for it.

Mandel had not expected much out of the song, but eventually was pleased with Altman and others wanting to use it as the theme song of the film. Without that, it may not have made its way into the series, and thanks to that and the multiple recordings, both Michael Altman and Johnny Mandel made millions based on their fifty-fifty split on the song's royalties. Michael Altman would admit that he made $2 million on the song over the years, but eventually had to sell his rights to his father for $30,000 in order to pay off taxes he owed from the royalties. As for Mandel, it became his biggest copyright and he continues to make money off of the only song that he wrote drunk.

10

And Introducing

A s mentioned a couple of chapters back, so many actors were being "introduced" in *MASH* that many of the credits simply say "And introducing. . . . " While chapter 8 took a look at some of the auditions and other practices that took place when hiring the actors for the film, it should be mentioned that not all those being "introduced" were actually appearing in films for the first time. Nor does the focus on the making of the film really allow for the longevity in careers for many of those performers who appeared in *MASH*.

Donald Sutherland as Capt. Benjamin Franklin "Hawkeye" Pierce

Born July 17, 1935, in Saint John, New Brunswick, Canada, Donald McNichol Sutherland spent his early years fighting a variety of ailments, including polio until his teenage years. In college, he majored in engineering as well as drama, figuring to go into the engineering field after graduating. Instead, at the age of twenty-two he moved to England, where he studied at the London Academy of Music and Dramatic Art for a time before starting to seek work in the theater and television. One of his first film appearances came in *Castle of the Living Dead* (1964), starring Christopher Lee and featuring Sutherland in three roles. From there he bounced around between film and television—there have even been rumors he appeared as one of the blonde, mascara-wearing aliens in *Dr. Who and the Daleks* (1965), as well as a verified rather large role in an episode of *The Avengers*, "The Superlative Seven" (1967). Then came his role as Vernon Pinkley in *The Dirty Dozen* (1967) that would lead to him being cast in *MASH*, which he filmed after costarring with Gene Wilder in the comedy *Two by Two*, released in 1970 as *Start the Revolution Without Me*. With those two films, along with his role as Oddball in the Clint Eastwood World War II comedy *Kelly's Heroes*

(1970), Sutherland would establish himself as a leading man in movies. He would appear in *Klute* (1971), *Don't Look Now* (1973), *Fellini's Casanova* (1976), *Invasion of the Body Snatchers* (1978), *Ordinary People* (1980), *JFK* (1991), and the *Hunger Games* series (2013–2015). He also had a memorial supporting role in *Animal House* (1978), as well as reappearing with Elliott Gould in two other films, *Little Murders* (1971) and *S*P*Y*S* (1974).

Elliott Gould as Capt. John Francis Xavier "Trapper John" McIntyre

Born in Brooklyn on August 29, 1938, Elliott Goldstein began working on the Broadway stage in his late teens as Elliott Gould in a number of musical-comedies, starting with *Rumple* in 1957 and on to his first starring role in the 1962 production of *I Can Get It for You Wholesale*. It was during this show that he met his future wife Barbra Streisand, whom he married in 1963 and divorced in 1971. He would continue to work on Broadway up through a short-lived production of Jules Feiffer's comedy *Little Murders*, which Gould would turn into a film in the early 1970s.

His work in films really took off after appearing in *The Night They Raided Minsky's* (1968) and with a starring role in a 1969 hit comedy by Paul Mazursky, *Bob & Carol & Ted & Alice*. Gould would appear in four films released in 1970, including the heavily promoted *Move*. He continued to make movies through the 1970s and 1980s, including *The Long Goodbye* (1973) and *California Split* (1974) with Robert Altman. While not all of his films were commercial successes, some have achieved cult status, such as *Little Murders* (1971) and *The Silent Partner* (1978). After appearing on *Saturday Night Live* several times in the 1970s, Gould would revisit medical humor with the CBS series, *E/R* (not to be confused with the later NBC dramatic series that costarred George Clooney). One episode of that series aired before the finale of *MASH*, and a *TV Guide* ad paired off the film Trapper John against TV's Hawkeye in a two-page spread. The series lasted twenty-two episodes before being canceled.

Gould has continued to work in both television and movies over the years, including the successful *Ocean's* film series with George Clooney.

Tom Skerritt as Capt. Augustus Bedford "Duke" Forrest

Thomas Roy Skerritt was born August 25, 1933, in Detroit, Michigan, and made his debut in the Korean War action film *War Hunt* in 1962. He spent

Lt. Margaret "Hot Lips" Houlihan arriving at the 4077th in the film. Sally Kellerman initially refused the part, angry that it did not give her anything to do before disappearing. Her argument won Altman over, and the script was rewritten to end up featuring Houlihan through the rest of the picture.

most of the 1960s working in television in roles that usually required someone in a uniform or to look rough and tough, including several episodes of *Combat!* directed by Robert Altman. It was their friendship that would lead to Skerritt being hired to play Duke in *MASH*, but unlike some of the other main cast members of the movie, Skerritt would continue to bounce back and forth between films and television in the 1970s and subsequently up to the present date. Memorable and successful films such as *Alien* (1979), *The Dead Zone* (1983), *Top Gun* (1986), and *Steel Magnolias* (1989) have followed, as well as the popular CBS series *Picket Fence* (1992–1996).

Sally Kellerman as Maj. Margaret "Hot Lips" Houlihan

Born June 2, 1937, Sally Claire Kellerman in Long Beach, California, Kellerman followed much the same path as Tom Skerritt in working through network television series in guest roles through the 1960s (including the much-remembered second pilot to *Star Trek*). She immediately returned to the Robert Altman stable of actors with his follow-up film in 1971, *Brewster McCloud* (with Bud Cort). *Brewster McCloud* would follow a chain of films that Kellerman did in the 1970s that have achieved cult followings, including *The Big Bus* (1976), *Foxes* (1980), and *Serial* (1980). She continues to work mostly in television, along with the occasional film. She has sung in several of her films, along with having two musical albums released over the years. Her autobiography, *Read My Lips* was released in 2013 by Weinstein Books.

Robert Duvall as Maj. Frank Burns

Robert Selden Duvall, born January 5, 1931, in San Diego, California, started acting in New York in his early twenties after serving in the U.S. Army from 1953 through 1954 (this has sometimes led to people mistakenly assuming Duvall fought in the Korean War, but the war was over before he even got into the army). Once out, Duvall went to New York to study acting, where he met fellow young hopefuls such as James Caan, Dustin Hoffman, and Gene Hackman (the latter two he would roommate with at one time or another during those years).

As with Kellerman and Skerritt, Duvall too began working in television programs, but in 1962 he received much notice for his small role as Boo in *To Kill a Mockingbird*. Duvall got the secondary lead in Altman's *Countdown* (1967), while later getting to face off against John Wayne in the classic *True Grit* (1969), before getting the role of Frank Burns in *MASH*.

Having already appeared in a number of classic films, Duvall continued with a role in George Lucas' first theatrical film, *THX 1138* (1971), and defined his star status with the role of Tom Hagen in *The Godfather* (1973, his third film with James Caan and second for Francis Ford Coppola). From there, the list of films is one of many classics, such as *Network* (1976); *Apocalypse Now* (1979); *The Great Santini* (1979); *Tender Mercies* (1983, which earned him an Oscar for Best Actor); as well as the popular television miniseries *Lonesome Dove*.

Roger Bowen as Lt. Col. Henry Braymore Blake

A writer at heart, Roger Bowen was born Mary 25, 1932, in Attleboro, Massachusetts. It was while writing reviews of improvisational theater in Chicago for the University of Chicago newspaper that he was introduced to the Compass Players. The Players, made up of Mike Nichols, Elaine May, Alan Arkin, and Barbara Harris, were looking for writers; and when asked what it paid, he was told "nothing, but actors got $25 a week." So he began to act with the group in order to help pay for his writing. The group would evolve into Second City, while Bowen would move to San Francisco in 1966 to participate in another well-known improv group, the Committee.

He began working in television and movies in the second half of the 1960s, usually playing clueless men in authority, much like Colonel Blake. He played such roles as a regular in television series, such as *Arnie* (1970–1972), *The Brian Keith Show* (1973–1974), *House Calls* (1979–1981, with a post-*MASH* Wayne Rogers starring), and a military comedy series with J. J. Walker called *At Ease* in 1983. He also appeared in such films as *Foxes* (1980), *Zapped!* (1982), and *What About Bob?* (1991). An expert chess player, Bowen played in tournaments in the 1970s, and also wrote a number of comedic novels in the 1970s and into the 1990s. He died February 16, 1996, the day after McLean Stevenson, who had played the role of Colonel Blake in the *MASH* series, making him the first member of the main cast in *MASH* to pass away.

Gary Burghoff as Cpl. "Radar" O'Reilly

Born Gary Rich Burghoff in Bristol, Connecticut, on May 24, 1943, Burghoff first came to notice at the age of twenty-four when he appeared as Charlie Brown in the original off-Broadway production of *You're a Good Man, Charlie Brown*. He also excelled as a drummer (he can be seen playing in a couple of episodes of *MASH*) and performed in Las Vegas in a band called the Relatives in 1968, the lead singer of which was Lynda Carter (who would go on to play the lead in *Wonder Woman*). After *MASH*, Burghoff appeared in the film *BS, I Love You* (1971), but was having trouble finding work when asked to reprise the role of Radar for the television series based on the movie.

And more as to what happened after that in chapter 17.

René Auberjonois as Father John Patrick "Dago Red" Mulcahy

René Murat Auberjonois was born June 1, 1940, in New York City. His family moved to Paris after World War II before returning to New York, where Auberjonois began to concentrate on acting. He began appearing in

Radar O'Reilly (Gary Burghoff) is the only character to be played by the same actor in both the movie and television series.

Broadway shows in the late 1960s, winning a Tony award for Best Featured Actor in *Coco* (starring Katharine Hepburn) in 1969.

One of his first movies was a small role in *Petulia* (1968), which also featured Roger Bowen. After *MASH*, Auberjonois appeared in *Brewster McCloud* and Altman's *McCabe & Mrs. Miller* (1971). *MASH* ties didn't stop there: he appeared in an episode of *McMillan & Wife*, "Once Upon a Dead Man" (1971), a series costarring fellow *MASH* alumni John Schuck; costarred in the television comedy movie *Shirts/Skins*, with McLean Stevenson and Loretta Swit from the *MASH* series; and costarred with Sally Kellerman in *The Big Bus* (1976). Television took up a majority of his time in the 1970s, with his role on the series *Benson* (1980–1986) cementing his recognition for a lot of viewers. He later appeared in one of the *Star Trek* films, *Star Trek VI: The Undiscovered Country* (1991), where he again acted with John Schuck, as well as a regular stint as Odo on *Star Trek: Deep Space Nine* (1993–1999). He continues to bounce between theater, film, and television, along with voice work for animated series and novels on tape.

Jo Ann Pflug as Lt. Maria "Dish" Schneider

Born May 2, 1940, in Atlanta, Georgia, Pflug began in radio, where she did an interview show, which led to her doing a weekly talk show on KHJ-TV in Los Angeles. Besides some earlier appearances on network television, she was also the voice of the Invisible Girl in the 1967 animated cartoon of the Marvel comic book superhero series *Fantastic Four*. After *MASH*, for which she was heavily promoted, Pflug stuck mostly with television work, including a costarring role in *Operation Petticoat* (1978–1979), an ABC adaption of the military comedy film. One of her last television projects was the notoriously bad soap opera *Rituals* (1984), which she left when storylines conflicted with her religious beliefs. She continues to work in radio and is working on a biographical book about her years in the business.

John Schuck as Capt. Walter Koskiusko "The Painless Pole" Waldowski, DDS

Conrad John Schuck Jr. was born February 4, 1940, in Boston, Massachusetts. As mentioned in an earlier chapter, he was part of the American Conservatory Theater in San Francisco when Robert Altman hired him for *MASH*. He would reappear in *Brewster McCloud, McCabe & Mrs. Miller,* and *Thieves Like Us* for Altman over the next several years. Unlike several of his fellow *MASH* performers, Schuck has concentrated mostly on television work rather than the theater, with an occasional venture into films over the years. He was a regular on the NBC Mystery Movies series *McMillan & Wife* and played the robot in the notorious comedy-crime series *Holmes and Yo-Yo* (1976–1977). While he didn't have much better luck with *Turnabout* in 1979 (a series about a husband and wife who switch bodies) or *The New Odd Couple* (where he played Murray the Cop), he did much better with the syndicated *The Munsters Today* (1988–1991), where he played Herman Munster, as well as a semiregular part in a few seasons of *Law & Order: Special Victims Unit*. He has also appeared in several *Star Trek*-related projects, including two of the films, *Star Trek IV: The Voyage Home* and *Star Trek VI: The Undiscovered Country*, as well as *Star Trek: Deep Space Nine* and *Star Trek Voyager*. He'll always be remembered for being the first actor to say the word "fuck" in a movie filmed and released by a major American studio.

David Arkin as SSgt. Wade Douglas Vollmer

David George Arkin, who played the ineffectual Ssgt. Vollmer and did most of the announcements heard in the film, was born December 24, 1941. Besides *MASH*, he appeared in secondary roles in *I Love You, Alice B. Toklas!* (1968), *The Long Goodbye* (1973), *Nashville* (1975), and *All the President's Men* (1976). His final film credit was another Altman picture, *Popeye* (1980). On January 14, 1991, he committed suicide.

Fred Williamson as Capt. Oliver Harmon "Spearchucker" Jones

Frederick Robert "The Hammer" Williamson was born March 6, 1938, in Gary, Indiana. He signed with the Pittsburgh Steelers in 1960, where he gained the nickname "The Hammer" for the way he "hammered" through opposing players. He would move on to the Oakland Raiders (1961–1964), then the Kansas City Chiefs (1965–1967), before playing for a year with the Canadian football team the Montreal Alouettes and then retiring in 1968.

With his good looks in a period where American television and films were looking for minority actors, Williamson quickly moved to acting in front of the camera, gaining a regular role on *Julia* as the boyfriend of the title character. *Julia* was the first network series to feature a black woman as a nonstereotypical lead and starred Diahann Carroll. Williamson talked his way into the role when suggesting that Julia having a rotation of boyfriends made her look easy, an early sign of the type of negotiating skills that would come in handy later in his career.

From *MASH*, Williamson would appear in a number of films that herald the beginning of the "blaxploitation" genre, starring in such films as *The Legend of Nigger Charley* (1972) and *Black Caesar* (1973). In 1975, he produced his first film (which he also wrote and starred in), *Boss Nigger*, and the following year he would direct his first film, *Mean Johnny Barrows* (1976). Over the years, Williamson has appeared in dozens upon dozens of films, mainly action films, and continues to produce and direct films as well as act.

Michael Murphy as Capt. Ezekiel Bradbury "Me Lay" Marston IV

Born in Los Angeles, California, on May 5, 1938, Michael George Murphy began acting after working as a schoolteacher for two years. One of his earlier roles came in *Combat!*, where he met Robert Altman and developed a friendship with him that would last throughout Altman's career. Besides *MASH*, Murphy appeared in *Countdown* (1967), *That Cold Day in the Park* (1969), *Brewster McCloud* (1970), *McCabe & Mrs. Miller* (1971), *Nashville* (1975), *The Caine Mutiny Court-Martial* (1988), *Tanner '88* (1988), *Kansas City* (1996), and *Tanner on Tanner* (2004)—all for Altman. He also appeared in substantial roles in *Count Yorga, Vampire* (1970), *Phase IV* (1974), *An Unmarried Woman* (1978), *Manhattan* (1979), *Salvador* (1986), and has frequently narrated documentaries for PBS' *American Experience* series (mostly set in the West of the nineteenth century).

Bud Cort as Pvt. Lorenzo Boone

One of the youngest members of the *MASH* cast, Walter Edward Cox was born on March 29, 1948, in New Rochelle, New York. Needing to change his name so as to not be confused with comedian/actor Wally Cox, when beginning to work in the theater and on television (in commercials and the soap opera *The Doctors*), Bud Cort would be "introduced" in his film career with *MASH*, although he had actually appeared briefly in two earlier films, *Up the Down Staircase* (1967) and *Sweet Charity* (1969). With his round face and large eyes, Cort conveyed an innocence that would help him become the lead in Altman's follow-up film, *Brewster McCloud*, as well as playing the depressed Harold in the cult classic *Harold and Maude* (1971). He would star in the successful Canadian film *Why Shoot the Teacher?* in 1977, but a car accident in 1978 led to multiple plastic surgeries and a delay in his career that turned him to more personal roles that were not always the lead. He later cofounded the LA Classic Theatre and continues to work in films, such as *Dogma* (1999) and *The Life Aquatic with Steve Zissou* (2004).

G. Wood as Brig. Gen. Charlie Hammond

George Wood was the next-to-oldest member of the *MASH* cast; born December 31, 1919, in Forrest City, Arkansas. He was acting with John Schuck and others at the ACT in San Francisco when he caught the attention of Robert Altman and was cast in the part of Brigadier General Hamilton Hammond in the film. He subsequently would play a General Charles Hammond three times in the first season of the *MASH* television series, making him one of four actors from the film to appear in the series (although it appears not playing the same General Hammond from the film). G. Wood appears in Altman's *Brewster McCloud* and in *Harold and Maude* with Bud Cort, as well as appearing in the pilot episode of *Holmes and Yo-Yo* with John Schuck. His last film appearance was in 1989 in the television movie *False Witness*, where he used his full name of George Wood. He passed away on July 24, 2000.

Corey Fischer as Capt. Dennis Patrick Bandini

Corey Fischer is another of the four actors who appeared in both the film and television series of *MASH*. Fischer was born in 1945 in Los Angeles and studied at UCLA in Theatre Arts. He would eventually begin working with The Committee, while also acting in television shows such as *Daniel Boone* and *Mod Squad*. After *MASH* he would appear in *McCabe & Mrs. Miller* and *Brewster McCloud* for Altman, while also doing television work, including his appearance as the guitar-playing Captain Phil Cardozo in the classic *MASH* episode "5 O'Clock Charlie." While he has done television and movie work since then, he has concentrated most of this time on the theater, directing and writing, mainly for the Traveling Jewish Theatre, which he cofounded.

Ken Prymus as Pvt. Seidman

Ken Prymus, who sings "Suicide Is Painless" at Painless' suicide attempt, has done some television work, but is mainly known for his years on Broadway, especially in *Ain't Misbehavin'* and later in a seven-year stretch as Old Deuteronomy in *Cats* (in both cases replacing Ken Page in the roles). He continues to work in television and in the theater.

Timothy Brown as Cpl. Judson

Born May 24, 1937, in Richmond, Indiana, Thomas Allen Brown was picked along with several other professional football players by Fred Williamson to appear in the football game segment of *MASH*. He would be the final actor from the film to also appear in the series, where he played Spearchucker Jones in several early episodes of the first season. Brown played with the Green Bay Packers in 1959, then spent 1960–1967 with the Philadelphia Eagles, before having one final season with the Baltimore Colts in1968. He had appeared in an episode of *The Wild, Wild, West* in 1967 ("The Night of the Bubbling Death"), but *MASH* was his first film. He would go on to appear three times on the police series *Adam-12* (which also featured Jo Ann Pflug in one episode) and a few exploitation action pictures—such as the blaxploitation/kung-fu epic *Dynamite Brothers* (1974), before appearing again for Robert Altman in *Nashville* as Tommy Brown, where he sang. He has mostly done television work since then.

Carl Gottlieb as Capt. John "Ugly John" Black

Born March 18, 1938, Gottlieb was another member of The Committee who joined the cast of the film. He mainly has been known as a comedy writer, and has helped write the scripts for *Jaws* and *The Jerk*. He also directed the 1981 Ringo Starr comedy *Caveman*, which he wrote. He also cowrote musician David Crosby's two autobiographies, *Long Time Gone* (1989) and *Since Then* (2006).

Bobby Troup as Sgt. Gorman

The sergeant who repeatedly says "Goddamn army" in *MASH* is Robert W. "Bobby" Troup Jr. Born October 18, 1918, making him the oldest member of the cast, Troup was raised in Harrisburg, Pennsylvania, and became known as a jazz musician who wrote the popular song "(Get Your Kicks on) Route 66" as well as the title song sung by Little Richard in *The Girl Can't Help It*. He began to do more acting as the years went by, eventually becoming best known to television viewers as Dr. Joe Early in the series *Emergency!* (1972–1978), in which he costarred with his wife, Julie London. He passed away on February 7, 1999.

Not a Word I Wrote

Differences Between Scripts to Screen

Ring Lardner Jr. was a writer who respected what others had done before him, but could also go his own direction with a script if necessary. As mentioned in an earlier chapter, Richard Hornberger himself would state that he loved what was done to his novel in the film (not the series, but at least the film), so he was obviously working in the correct direction at least from the standpoint of the author and his fans. Lardner also got the whole ball rolling on *MASH* as a film mainly to see if he could take the story structure of the novel—which had little of what is common for story structure in the sense of arc(s), character development, and resolution—and turn it into a script that would work as a film.

Robert Altman, on the other hand, felt a script should be a foundation to a movie. Strong, sturdy to hold the weight of the actions, but needing to be built upon depending on where the film took him. A script can't predict the cast hired, the weather conditions, or even dialogue and actions that work better in front of the camera than in the mind of the screenwriter. There is always a chance for improvement, and Altman certainly did make changes to the script in order to pull together the film that we know today as *MASH*. To the point that Lardner felt there may have been so many changes that the movie hardly reflected that of his script.

Of course, that's an exaggeration. The film and the script ultimately follow the same course of actions as the novel in many ways. Hawkeye and Duke arrive at the 4077th and are soon joined by Trapper. Frank Burns bum-rushes Hawkeye and gets sent home in a straitjacket. Houlihan is humiliated and threatens to resign her commission. There's a football game against General Hammond's team that brings in Spearchucker Jones. Finally, Hawkeye and Duke have served their time and get to go home.

And yet so many changes occurred as well. These changes have already been discussed in a previous chapter of this book; in this chapter the changes between what Lardner had in his script and what appeared in the film are examined. In review, the scenes of the film are listed below, followed by what Lardner had envisioned in his script.

Scene One—Choppers arriving at the 4077th

Altman

The movie's title comes into focus briefly before cutting to the helicopters coming in to land at the 4077th with wounded. As the wounded are being taken away, Blake tells Radar to call General Hammond. If Blake hears Radar repeating the orders slightly before Blake, he doesn't appear to notice it. After Radar runs off, Vollmer asks what needs to be done and Blake tells him that Radar has the information.

Lardner

The script calls for the film to start on a sign that reads "This is where it is—Parallel 38," and signs pointing in the directions of North and South Korea, as the helicopters descend at the 4077th. The camera was to focus on the helicopter, which would bring another sign into place that shows the word "M-A-S-H," the "4077th," and then "Mobile Army Surgical Hospital." Blake starts giving his command to Radar and is angered by Radar getting ahead of him (something Blake in the series would do so often). Radar registers that more choppers are coming and then announces Blake's order about new surgeons without Blake even saying them. Vollmer is not in the scene. (According to Burghoff, he was the one suggesting that Radar overlap what Blake is saying rather than say it before him or without him. Either way, Roger Bowen plays Blake as not caring if Radar does this, rather than how Lardner wrote it.)

Scene Two—325th Evacuation Hospital

Altman

Titles appear to say, "And then there was—Korea" along with a passage from MacArthur's speech after he left Korea and Eisenhower's famous "I will go to Korea" quote (placing the film near the final year of the war, although a later P.A. announcement makes it out to be 1951). This runs as Hawkeye appears from the officers' latrine and heads to a jeep. He piles it with his stuff, which ruffles the feathers of the head of the motor pool. Duke appears and, thinking Hawkeye is the driver, tells Hawkeye to head on out. Hawkeye agrees and leaves with the jeep. The motor pool head alerts the MPs to stop them, but a blown tire leads to the MPs having to subdue the motor pool head, as Hawkeye and Duke travel to the 4077th.

Lardner

Hawkeye talks with a thick Maine accent (that will disappear in the next scene to help audiences understand him, as per Lardner's script). A motor pool sergeant hands off the jeep to Hawkeye and wishes him luck. Hawkeye and Duke introduced themselves to each other and share some booze, while discussing Blake as being "regular army" and needing to be put in his place so they can get their work done. They take off when the MPs notice them drinking and, with Hawkeye's map, head to the 4077th. (This does at least explain why Hawkeye knew where to go to get to the 4077th. There is no stolen jeep, however—a plot point that Lardner readily admits was an Altman touch. As the jeep is theirs, the scene is set up much differently and Duke knows full well who Hawkeye is before they get to the camp.)

Missing is a scene where Lardner has the two going by a house of prostitution that offers "curb service." Several prostitutes are standing outside while a soldier is seen going at it with one of them in the back of a truck by the road. Hawkeye asks Duke if he wants to stop, but Duke says he "did his shopping in Seoul" the night before.

Scene Three—Mess Tent Greetings

Altman

Arriving at the camp, Duke offers Hawkeye a chance for some lunch in the Officers' Mess. They spot Dish, with Duke making a play for her, while Hawkeye readily backs off upon seeing Dish's wedding ring. Blake, who wonders who the men are, goes over to them and receives their orders (allowing Hawkeye to prove he just put one over on Duke). Everyone is introduced to each other, while Hawkeye and Duke repeatedly cut Blake off to learn more about the camp situation.

Lardner

Hawkeye and Duke do sit with the nurses, but there is no indication that Dish is married at this point, nor dialogue for the nurses. Hawkeye says

"Finest Kind" for the first time in the script (Sutherland only says it once in the film, and whistles here and elsewhere instead). With the exception of the gags dealing with the stolen jeep, much of the dialogue is very similar to what appears on the screen, although overlapping to speed it along. Hawkeye makes plain his plans to go after Dish in the script, rather than Duke swinging and missing as in the film.

Scene Four—The Swamp

Altman

Duke and Hawkeye head off to the Swamp, where they run into Vollmer—who mistakes them for enlisted men—and then Lieutenant Leslie, a nurse Radar informs them is involved with Blake. They hear Ho-Jon reading from the Bible and meet Frank. Duke gives Ho-Jon a nudie magazine and Ho-Jon leaves, with Duke telling him to have fun.

Lardner

Missing from the script is the meeting with Vollmer and Leslie. Hawkeye and Duke walk in on Ho-Jon reading the Bible, although Ho-Jon doesn't leave as in the film. Hawkeye and Duke toss a bat to see who has to sleep near the door, with Duke losing, which doesn't appear in the film.

Scene Five—The O.R.

Altman

Hawkeye and Duke are shown working on patients in the O.R. The nurses find Duke's accent and attitude "cute." Meanwhile, Hawkeye asks Lieutenant Dish to scratch his nose as he saws through a soldier's leg.

Lardner

Lardner makes clear that the sights and sounds of the O.R. should be "almost unbearable" for the audience. (So it is clear from the start that Lardner saw the surgeries as being intense and it was not just an Altman idea.) Hawkeye saws through a leg as in the film, but with Duke assisting and Dish being so upset that she has to leave the O.R. Hawkeye goes after her, and they talk about both being married and so far from home, as well as how many hours surgeons usually have to work at the MASH unit. Dish admits she is attracted to Hawkeye, and Hawkeye hints that there's no harm in them being there for each other. Dish interprets this as meaning in friendship and thanks him for saving her from making a terrible mistake by giving in to her urges. Hawkeye is appalled with himself over how the conversation has turned.

Beyond this conversation, also missing from the film are three scenes in the script: the first shows a major (possibly Burns, although it isn't clear in the script) overseeing the surgery but showing no sign of wanting to actually do any work, while Hawkeye and Duke juggle as many patients as they can. The second scene follows the talk between Hawkeye and Dish, and is more of the surgeons working in order to make clear that they've been in the O.R. for many hours.

The third scene shows Hawkeye and Duke wearily walking back to the Swamp while there is an announcement over the P.A. (showing that Lardner had the P.A. in mind, but it would be Altman who would turn it into a series of comical announcements, while Lardner kept them straight in his script). Ho-Jon is there and bows to them, whereupon Hawkeye tells him to stop bowing. (This is the dialogue you can see and hear Elliott Gould perform in his screen test for the film that appears in one of the documentaries on the *MASH* special edition DVD and Blu-ray, but was dropped from the film.) They instead teach him how to make martinis, which slides into the next scene that does appear in the film.

Scene Six—Back at the Swamp

Altman

As another announcement is heard on the P.A., Frank arrives and is not happy to see the two have Ho-Jon fixing them drinks. Ho-Jon leaves and Franks prays. And prays some more. Finally Hawkeye and Duke begin singing "Onward, Christian Soldiers," which is picked up by people outside the tent, who then parade away, while Frank shows signs that he may be edging toward a breakdown.

Lardner

With a slight change in dialogue, most of the scene is the same. Hawkeye and Duke break into Frank's prayer with the hymn, but stop when they realize Frank is still praying. The scene ends with Frank saying that he'll be praying for them, and there is no parade of others outside to further needle Burns.

Scene Seven—Henry's Office

Altman

Hawkeye and Duke ignore Vollmer and go in to see Henry, who has Lieutenant Leslie with him as he works on some fishing lure. They ask that Frank be moved out of their tent and that Henry get a chest-cutter to help out. When Radar appears to tell Blake that more wounded are coming, he's under pressure and agrees to what the two want just to get them out. The ending of their discussion is overheard as the scene cuts to Hawkeye and Duke looking at the wounded arriving.

Lardner

Scene and dialogue are essentially the same, with the exception that Henry is not working on the lure, and there is no cutting to the wounded as in the film. The discussion Henry has with Leslie about the wounded is actually from a much later scene in the script, around what would have been the 74-minute mark.

Scene Eight—Mulcahy in O.R.

Altman

Mulcahy arrives in the O.R. to give last rites to a dead man. Duke needs assistance and calls for Mulcahy to help, telling him that the other man is dead and the one he is operating on is alive and needs the extra help. Mulcahy queasily agrees.

Lardner

This scene, which is similar to one found in the novel, is not in Lardner's script.

Scene Nine—The Arrival of Trapper John

Altman

As Hawkeye and Dish fumble around with their clothes in the Officers Club, Ho-Jon arrives to tell Hawkeye to "haul ass" to the Swamp to meet the chest-cutter. When Dish leaves, she is fixing her clothes, and there is comical business with two nurses watching her and then Mulcahy throwing her sweater back into the tent. Hawkeye arrives as Trapper is putting up a nude photo. Hawkeye and Duke get the runaround from Trapper as to who he is and where he is from. When offered a martini, Trapper pulls out a jar of olives.

Lardner

Hawkeye and Dish just arrive inside the Officers' Club when Ho-Jon gets him, so all the business with the nurses and Mulcahy is missing, as they don't get a chance to do anything. The script has a panning shot of Hawkeye's family photos, then Duke's family photos, and then Trapper putting up his nudie photo, so Altman threw out the setup for Lardner's gag. The rest of the action and dialogue is nearly the same as in the film, including the jar of olives (which is also from the book).

Scene Ten—Trapper in the O.R.

Altman

Trapper performs surgery as everyone watches in awe. He and the others chatter as the work on the soldier's chest is done.

Lardner

Same as in the film, only with no mention of dialogue. Blake is also seen watching and is happy with the results, although unsure about the surgeon himself.

Scene Eleven—Trapper Is Found Out and Painless Is Watched
Altman

With a football from a game the enlisted men are playing, Trapper tosses a pass to Hawkeye, who instantly recognizes the man who threw it as Trapper John McIntyre. Hawkeye explains to Duke how Trapper got his name. Trapper notices a line of men at the shower and is told about the legend of Painless. Hawkeye begins telling a story that everyone has heard before.

Lardner

Very much as in the film, with some refinement—Hawkeye forgets to hand the ball back to the enlisted men, while in the film he hands it off to Duke; Duke and Hawkeye have more background details about Painless, which are dropped in the film. Hawkeye doesn't have a redundant story to tell at the end of the scene.

Missing is the next scene that shows the surgeons in the O.R. calling for Mulcahy to give last rites, whereupon the patient is saved. This is then followed by a scene (also missing) where Mulcahy joins the men in the Swamp for a martini and an explanation—as in the novel—as to Mulcahy's magical ability to save lives whenever he does the last rites (although this is straight from the novel, it conflicts with the film, where Mulcahy is giving last rites to a dead man and is pulled away to save another man's life instead). While in the Swamp, Mulcahy mentions that he is concerned about Painless, whereupon Hawkeye decides to go visit him. Part of this scene will appear in a bit in the film. Instead, what is next is. . . .

Scene Twelve—The Arrival of Hot Lips Houlihan
Altman

Blake, Mulcahy, Dish, and others arrive to welcome Major Houlihan from a chopper. All but Dish—who is in full dress uniform while seated inside a truck nearby—welcome her.

Lardner

This scene appears in the script exactly the same, but after that of Painless' suicide dinner and his visit from Lieutenant Dish. This is why we see Dish in the truck but not greeting Houlihan, as the scene was shot as per the script, with Houlihan arriving as Dish is leaving. This also explains some earlier actions in the O.R., where Dish is clearly the chief nurse and is giving orders to others—Houlihan is Dish's replacement. Because the film is edited differently, however, it appears the Houlihan arrived and is stationed there for a time with Dish (but note that we never have a scene with the two together, nor do we ever see Dish in any scenes related to Houlihan beyond this "greeting" scene).

Scene Thirteen—Trapper Loses His Punch

Altman

Frank, pounding on a patient's chest, tells Boone to get him a CC of adrenaline and a cardiac needle. Boone doesn't quite hear the request, but heads off just as Trapper arrives. By the time he has come back, the patient is dead. As he has the wrong needle as well, Frank takes out his anger on Boone as Frank tells him that he killed the patient (watch Duvall; it appears for a moment as if even Frank can't believe he went that far before he stomps off). Boone begins to cry, and Trapper is exasperated over what he just saw.

Blake shows Houlihan the O.R. and then moves through the Pre-op Ward when they pass Trapper decking Frank (falling into boxes of tampons, incidentally). It's a clumsy punch, getting Frank in the forehead and looking to hurt Trapper more than Frank. Frank wants to finish the fight alone, but Blake tells them to knock it off. It's a bad first impression for Houlihan.

Larner

Plays much like in the film, only in the script Trapper asks Frank to join him in the utility room instead of seemingly ending up together there. Gould's dialogue is less smug and with more anger than in the script (Trapper pretty much smirks at being put under arrest, while in the film he blows it off as if he can't believe anyone would seriously have a problem with him punching Frank).

Scene Fourteen—Trapper Becomes Chief Surgeon

Altman

Blake goes into the Swamp wanting to know what happened and plans to take disciplinary action. Everyone agrees that Frank is a menace, but thanks to Trapper punching Frank, Blake will have to wait a week before making him chief surgeon. It becomes clear that Blake is more concerned about his coffee by that point than the assault.

Lardner

Same as in the film with some minor changes to dialogue and the addition of coffee.

Scene Fifteen—Hawkeye Meets Houlihan

Altman

Vollmer finds Blake fishing in a stream and tells him that General Hammond is at a football game. The camera then ventures into the camp, where Hawkeye sits down to lunch and is joined by Margaret Houlihan. Her concerns about the lack of military discipline and her endorsement of Frank lead to Hawkeye calling her a "regular army clown." (The script has Duke calling Blake this while traveling to the 4077th, but it only appears here in the film.) Her response leads to Mulcahy's famous line about Hawkeye being drafted. Between all this, there's a brief interlude in the O.R., showing the power going out and everyone singing as lanterns are brought in. Eventually, it is mentioned that someone will have to tell the patient that he no longer has anything between his legs.

Lardner

Scenes in the O.R. with the lights going out and the dialogue about the patient with nothing between his legs appear, but much later in the script (around the 75-minute mark) rather than at this point, nor is there singing as in the film. Kellerman added the line about the army being her home, but much of the remaining dialogue is the same or very similar. In the script,

Hawkeye respond's to Houlihan's last line, but the change to Mulcahy makes for a better punch line.

Scene Sixteen—Blake Leaves for a Conference

Altman

Henry leaves for a conference and Vollmer asks for orders, to which Blake offhandedly tells him that Radar has everything. Blake stops long enough to mention some shirts in his tent to Lieutenant Leslie, who offers to mend them. She asks about his new jacket, and it is clear that he is about to say his wife sent it to him, but he stops himself as the jeep speed off.

Lardner

No such scene appears in his script.

Scene Seventeen—Trapper's Party

Altman

As Houlihan and Burns get dinner in the mess tent, Trapper is paraded into the tent in celebration of him becoming chief surgeon. He demands a woman and points to Houlihan, calling her the "sultry bitch with the fire in her eyes." She and Burns leave, going to her tent to write a letter to General Hammond about the lack of discipline there. Burns mentions that it is almost suppertime, which leads to them sharing a passionate kiss before Houlihan goes to mail the letter.

They mail the letter, then separate, with Burns promising to check in on Houlihan later. The scene cuts back to the party and shows Radar arriving.

Lardner

In the script, Vollmer announces Trapper becoming chief surgeon, and everyone congratulates Trapper except Houlihan and Burns. They plan to meet at Houlihan's tent to write a letter to General Hammond, but Burns think people may get the wrong idea. Houlihan says she doesn't care if people talk, as long as they "give them something to talk about."

The next scene in the script is Houlihan and Burns writing the letter then briefly sharing a passionate kiss before Houlihan "is all business again" and goes to send the letter off. This is followed by Radar arriving at the start of a party for Trapper and handing the letter to Hawkeye, who tears it up.

The next scene in the script is the party seen in the film. The opening song is the same, but the dialogue and jokes after that are much different, with Trapper's request for someone being jokingly misunderstood by Hawkeye to mean Frank. There is no dialogue from Trapper demanding "the sultry bitch with the fire in her eyes" as heard in the film (and which works better to make Houlihan so angry she leaves). No final dialogue about shingles by Duke either.

It does seem odd that Burns would mention it almost being supper-time when they were just seen getting supper in the mess tent. Obviously a dialogue error that came out of the editing of the scene to after where it appears in the script.

Scene Eighteen—Margaret's Tent

Altman

Burns arrives at Houlihan's tent and they talk for a while before embracing. Radar places a microphone under the cot in Houlihan's tent and then goes back to the communication room where everyone else is waiting. Everyone listens in the room, including Mulcahy, who quickly leaves when he realizes what is going on. Margaret demands that Frank kiss her "hot lips." Trapper suggests the audio be shared with the rest of the camp over the P.A., surprising Hawkeye and others in the O.R. who are doing an operation, as well as a poker game in Painless' tent. Houlihan also figures it out and pushes Burns out her door, and the scuffle inside the tent alerts the group in the other room to turn it off and put on some music, as the show is over.

Lardner

In the script, Burns never leaves Houlihan's side and is in her tent when they decide to become passionate. It is Duke who offers to share the audio with the camp, and there are some other minor changes in dialogue, as well as Mulcahy not being there. The scene in the script ends with Burns being unable to prematurely stop himself, and saying so to the whole camp, instead of being pushed out of the tent in the confusion.

Scene Nineteen—The Next Morning

Altman

Blake arrives back at the 4077th and Vollmer states that there was nothing he could do about what happened. Blake has no idea what that means but shrugs it off, which is good enough for Vollmer.

In the mess tent, Duke calls Houlihan "Hot Lips" for the first time, while both Trapper and Hawkeye needle her until she leaves. Hawkeye then sits with Burns and begins hassling him about the night before (including the information—which does not appear in the novel or in Lardner's script—that Burns is married). As Blake watches from the outside with Radar and Lieutenant Leslie, Burns reaches his breaking point and attacks Hawkeye. Hawkeye begs for Burns to be pulled off him, while Trapper suggests that Burns is sexually molesting Hawkeye. In a quick cut, we see Burns being taken away in a straitjacket, as Boone smiles in satisfaction and Duke asks if hitting Hawkeye and "nailing" Houlihan will get him sent home as well (he'll do one of the two by the end of the picture and ends up being sent home, incidentally). Trapper and Hawkeye watch, almost as if sorry to see Frank go, then enter the Swamp.

Lardner

Radar and Leslie join Blake as in the film, but there is no Vollmer. In the mess tent, Burns and Houlihan are seated at different tables, but within arms' reach. Burns is ready to make a move, but is held back by Hot Lips. As she leaves, Hawkeye begins ribbing Frank, who threatens to kill him. Through all this, as in the film, Blake, Leslie, and Radar are outside looking in as Radar tries to "explain" what is being said. Frank throws a coffeepot at Hawkeye and attacks him, leading to Frank being taken away and Duke's comment, although there is no sign of Boone as in the film, or Hawkeye's and Trapper's reactions to Burns leaving.

Scene Nineteen—Bleeding from the Neck

Altman

Similar to a scene found in the novel, Hawkeye has to operate on a man who is gushing blood from his neck.

Lardner

This scene appears much later in the script (around the 79-minute mark) and plays out much like in the novel, along with Mulcahy helping out with the surgery. Most of that does not appear in the film, however.

Scene Twenty—Mulcahy Confesses to Hawkeye

Altman

Mulcahy talks to Hawkeye about Painless, who is acting so melancholy that during a poker game he says, "It's only a game." This raises fears that something is wrong with Painless, and Mulcahy asks Hawkeye to talk to him. Hawkeye agrees and pats Mulcahy on the head. (This is also the first time the audience sees Lieutenant Dish again since being seen in the truck when Houlihan arrived, as she's inside the Swamp with Trapper.)

Lardner

Some of the dialogue between Mulcahy and Hawkeye is similar to that found much earlier in the script. As it is, Lardner has Painless' storyline happening about a half-hour into the film and before the arrival of Houlihan and Burns' meltdown.

Scene Twenty-One—Talking to Painless

Altman

Hawkeye bypasses a poker game in Painless' dental tent and goes to discuss Painless' problem. Essentially, he had issues "rising to the occasion," and although Hawkeye assures him that it happens to everyone, Painless assumes it is because he is a homosexual.

Back at the Swamp, everyone discusses what to do about the "jaw-breaker" when Painless arrives. He announces that he plans to kill himself (Hawkeye, in the background, tries to keep from laughing at Painless, as do others). Everyone humors him and suggests that the best method is that of a "black capsule."

With the introduction of Lt. Dish to the script, the "Black Capsule" ceremony for Painless (John Schuck) is resolved in an entirely different manner than in the novel.

Lardner

Much is the same as in the film. The woman Painless was with is a Korean in the script, but a nurse from the 325th in the film. There's no Man-of-War story in the script (which is just as well, as it's a joke that falls very flat).

Scene Twenty-Two: Painless' Suicide Dinner

Altman

In the dental tent, the group gathers for Painless' taking of the "black capsule." Mulcahy is arguing with Hawkeye that he cannot give absolution to a man who is committing suicide, but Hawkeye assures him that if things work, there won't be a suicide and he'll actually be helping to save a life.

The group poses like *The Last Supper* before a brief speech for Painless, Mulcahy's performance of the viaticum, then Painless getting into a coffin and taking the "black capsule" as "Suicide Is Painless" is performed, and the others leave things for Painless in his coffin as they say their final goodbyes.

Lardner

A scene was to appear before the dinner where Trapper and Hawkeye go to Mulcahy to convince him to help. Some of this dialogue is the same as found in the film at the beginning of the suicide dinner with Mulcahy and Hawkeye. Besides the speeches at the beginning, most of the dialogue is different; Lardner has a lot of unnecessary exposition that is replaced in the film with visual gags, the song, and some spoken gags by the men as they pass by the casket.

Scene Twenty-Three—Painless' Resurrection

Altman

Hawkeye meets up with Lieutenant Dish, who is leaving the next morning to go home and back to her husband. They make out a little, but Hawkeye is mainly there to convince her to go to a tent lit in red lights, where the drugged Painless awaits. Dish is creeped out, but enticed when Hawkeye leaves her there alone and she sees what is under the sheet. The next morning, one of the nurses gives her a gift and Vollmer fails to give Dish her traveling orders. Hawkeye sees a very peppy Painless in the mess tent and can tell that things are all right with the world again. At the helicopter, there's a final shot of Lieutenant Dish, who sighs and smiles at the camera as the chopper takes her away.

Lardner

The tent is blue-tint instead of red, and Hawkeye assures Dish that Painless has "so much dope in him by tomorrow he won't know fact from fantasy." Some of the dialogue is cut—again, too much exposition—but the results are the same and Lieutenant Dish leaves in the script just as she does in the film.

Scene Twenty-Four—Back in the O.R. and Waiting for Blood

Altman

In the O.R., a prisoner of war is needing blood, so Radar goes to siphon some off of Blake while he sleeps. Trapper compliments Hot Lips for being a good nurse, showing that feelings are changing between the Swamp men and Houlihan. Trapper and Hawkeye argue over what to do with no blood available when Radar arrives with the blood.

Lardner

This O.R. scene appears at the 82-minute mark in the script, and the patient is Ho-Jon, who talks briefly before being put under. The scene goes on much longer, with Trapper and Hawkeye working to save Ho-Jon's life. They succeed and decide they need to raise money for Ho-Jon so he can go to the American college Hawkeye did.

Instead, the scene is matched up with earlier dialogue from a discarded O.R. sequence where Hot Lips exclaims that the patient is a prisoner-of-war, whereupon it is mentioned that she is one too but doesn't realize it. The patient's face is blackened from debris, so it's not quite noticeable that it is the same actor who plays Ho-Jon.

Scene Twenty-Five—At the Crash Site, Discussing Houlihan

Altman

Duke, Hawkeye, Trapper, Ugly John, and a few others are sunbathing by a stream that is also covered in debris from a crashed helicopter (an actual crash that occurred during filming, as discussed in an earlier chapter). After a brief discussion about the crash and the pilot, the conversation turns to Houlihan. Duke swears that he nearly pukes when he sees her, and is willing to bet she isn't a natural blonde. The others agree to the bet, but need to devise a way that they can all determine the truth of the matter.

Lardner

The scene comes much later in the script, around the 88-minute mark. It features only Duke, Hawkeye, and Trapper, and there is no reference to a 'copter crash, but most of the dialogue is the same.

After the shower prank, Houlihan interrupts Henry Blake (Roger Bowen) and Lt. Leslie (Indus Arthur) in bed. In the book, Blake is alone and is waiting for Houlihan.

Scene Twenty-Six—The Shower

Altman

It's a group effort, including nurses, in setting up Houlihan to be in the shower by herself. (Hawkeye says "Finest kind" for the first and only time in this scene.) A complicated contraption lifts up the tent wall to reveal Houlihan naked. She falls to the ground and slithers out, putting on a robe and running to Blake's tent as everyone else starts rushing to clean everything up.

In the tent, Houlihan finds Blake in bed with Leslie. Houlihan threatens to resign her commission, and Blake tells her to do so. Houlihan wanders off in shock, while Blake offers Leslie some more wine.

Lardner

It is only an effort by Duke, Hawkeye, and Trapper, but they do convince the nurses to stop, and even Houlihan is offered a chance to do so as well.

Their contraption is also less complicated, but the results are the same. Duke tells everyone to pay up as Houlihan stomps off to Blake's tent and finds Blake and Leslie together (Lardner states in the script that this would be the point where the audience would realize why no one else makes a pass at Leslie, although Altman makes it pretty clear through earlier moments in the film). There is no mumbling in shock by Houlihan as seen in the film (which Kellerman states she added herself and was the moment where Altman decided to rewrite some of the script so Houlihan would remain through the end of the film). The business with Mulcahy coming out of the shower and having trouble with the sign was added on-set as well.

Scene Twenty-Seven—Ho-Jon's Induction

Altman

Hawkeye goes with a few others to drop Ho-Jon off for his induction to the South Korean army. While waiting, a woman reporter with a camera asks Hawkeye some questions and then asks if he wants to say hello to his mother on film. Hawkeye mentions that his mother is dead, but does say hello to his dad. (Sutherland would later tell the story of his dad seeing the scene in the film and standing up and saying "Hello, Son!" while in the movie theater.)

Inside the building, a doctor looks at Ho-Jon. He comes out with him and tells Hawkeye that Ho-Jon's blood pressure is dangerously high; however, it is noted that he works at an American hospital, so he assumes "somehow" Ho-Jon got into the medicine there. As Hawkeye tries to talk the doctor out of keeping Ho-Jon, the doctor makes clear that he sees through the con and takes Ho-Jon away. Hawkeye throws down his hat in defeat.

Lardner

Getting back to the point in the script that appears right after Burns' breakdown and thus before Ho-Jon would arrive as a patient in the OR, Hawkeye takes Ho-Jon to the induction center as in the film. He only has Lieutenant Scorch with him. There is dialogue in the induction center as the doctor is shown recognizing what is going on. He comes out to tell Hawkeye that Ho-Jon obviously took some medication he shouldn't have and that he should say goodbye. (Although it is not as clear as in the movie, the doctor knows what is up.) Hawkeye says goodbye to Ho-Jon, but promises to find the money to get him into college once he is out of the army.

Scene Twenty-Eight—X-Ray from Seoul

Altman

Trapper and Hawkeye are hitting golf balls off the helicopter pad when a chopper lands, upsetting their playing. A soldier runs down the hill, only to come back up with Vollmer, who points out Trapper.

Turns out a congressman's son was practicing with grenades when one went off and shrapnel entered his heart—or, rather, that's what the doctors in Japan thinks happened. They want Trapper to come do the surgery as he has been recommended. The x-ray tells Hawkeye and Trapper that the injury is not nearly as bad as diagnosed, but they're willing to take the trip to Japan with their golf clubs.

Lardner

Pretty much exactly as in the script, with some minor changes to the dialogue. The "Shirley" comment was added by Gould, who had been joking with Sutherland over the name while on the set.

Scene Twenty-Nine—Driving by the Golf Course

Altman

In Japan, Hawkeye and Trapper are in a jeep with a sergeant who repeatedly says "Goddamn army." The pair talk in Japanese nonsense while stopping by a golf course.

Lardner

The script has the two arriving in Japan and meeting the sergeant. They are heading to the hospital when they see the golf course and discuss whether to shoot nine holes or go directly to the hospital. They decide to go to the hospital. None of this dialogue is in the mock Japanese of the film, but the sergeant's profanity is certainly in the script.

Scene Thirty—Arriving at the Hospital

Altman

Hawkeye and Trapper arrive at the hospital but have problems getting to the patient at first. Fighting off a pretty WAC, they arrive at the bed of the patient when the head nurse comes to tell them that nothing will be done until Colonel Merrill is back from lunch. Trapper goes into instructions that are forceful but also shows that he knows his business. The head nurse stumbles into another nurse before stomping off. The other nurse asks them how they would like their lunch.

Lardner

Nearly the same, including the speech Trapper gives to the nurse. There is a little additional dialogue between the two and the one nurse, while the stumbling over her by the head nurse (actually a nurse corps captain) and the punch line about the steaks are missing.

Scene Thirty-One—Meeting Merrill

Altman

The pair are operating on the congressman's son when Merrill arrives. Hawkeye asks that the "dirty old man" be removed from the operating room. Merrill leaves. The anesthesiologist asks who they are, and Hawkeye says he is Dr. Jekyll and Trapper is Mr. Hyde (Trapper grunts). The anesthesiologist is actually on old friend of Hawkeye's, Me Lay Marston. They ask him if he golfs, but he says he's too busy working there and at Dr. Yamachi's New Era Pediatric Hospital and Whorehouse.

The scene cuts to Me Lay giving them a card with the address to the place and tells them to come by. The pair decide to play golf first and head off with their golf clubs, but two MPs trail them as they walk unsuspectingly into Merrill's office, where an MP is waiting, along with the WAC. They play it out with good humor as they go to wait in Merrill's inner office.

When Merrill arrives, they are putting in his office. They lay the cards on the table that Merrill's people misdiagnosed the injury and will inform Washington of that fact if Merrill decides to discipline them. They announce they are off to the golf course and to contact them there if needed.

Lardner

The scene is written more toward what was in the novel, although Hawkeye says he is "the Ghost of Smokey Joe" and Trapper is "the pro from Dover" instead of the Dr. Jekyll and Mr. Hyde line in the film. Me Lay explains his functions at the whorehouse, and then Hawkeye and Trapper are asked to go to Merrill's office. There's no chase to the office by the MPs, and it is only when they get there that they realize they are being detained. Altman's changes make for a much funnier scene. Lardner does have the pair getting out their clubs for some putting while they wait, and the rest of the scene with them telling Merrill what's what plays much like in the film, with some minor dialogue changes.

Scene Thirty-Two—At the Clinic with an Emergency

Altman

Trapper, Hawkeye, and Me Lay are at a table, having dinner with some of the women from the clinic when Me Lay is told of the sick baby. They decide to take the baby straight to the hospital, where the nurses ask why the baby is there. Before anyone can explain, Merrill arrives to protest and is held by Me Lay as Trapper gasses him.

Merrill wakes up in the clinic with a prostitute in bed with him as Me Lay takes pictures, thus ending any chance for Merrill to protest any further.

Lardner

Lardner has a scene at the Pro Shop with Trapper and Hawkeye that was filmed (the special edition DVD shows a photo of the actors filming the scene in the Pro Shop set) but then cut from the film. In it, the pair buy golfing outfits (seen later in the film when they return to the 4077th) and meet a couple of young women who are to be their caddies. Hawkeye sees them walking into trouble and talks Trapper out of golfing after dark with the young women and instead going over to the clinic/whorehouse where Me Lay works.

The script has Trapper stuffed with food and refusing more (instead of stuffing his face as in the film). As he makes his moves on one of the women, Me Lay is called away to attend to the baby. In talking with Hawkeye and Trapper, they decide to take the baby to the army hospital. Once there, Hawkeye explains what they want to do, and the O.R. nurse agrees to help (this explains why no one comes to Merrill's aid in the O.R.; the nurses are already on Hawkeye's and Trapper's side). Merrill arrives to protest and is gassed by Me Lay, with the others helping. The scene cuts to Me Lay and Hawkeye putting Merrill in a bed with one of the prostitutes ready to jump in when the time comes. As Merrill comes to, she jumps in, Hawkeye takes pictures, and Hawkeye explains the blackmail situation to Merrill.

Cut from the film were additional scenes after this point: the first is of the prostitute ready to have some fun with Trapper, only to find that he's fallen asleep. The second has Hawkeye and Trapper visiting the congressman's son the next day while wearing their new golf outfits. They figure to play a round and relax, but a message comes for them to report back to the 4077th.

Back at the 4077th, we get the early scene of Blake asking Leslie about the wounded. Radar appears to tell him that there are multiple helicopters coming, including one "from the south" that carries Hawkeye and Trapper.

Scene Thirty-Three—Back to the O.R.

Altman

Hawkeye and Trapper arrive back at the 4077th and are immediately in the O.R. in their golf outfits, working. Mulcahy asks how the trip went, and Trapper mentions "screwing a Kabuki dancer." Mulcahy asks Blake if he can be of assistance, and Blake isn't even paying attention beyond blowing Mulcahy off.

Lardner

Lardner has ten pages of script at this point, going through the various stages of a fifteen-day stretch in the O.R., including Ho-Jon's surgery, Blake being put to bed and then having his blood siphoned, the patient with the gushing neck wound, Duke performing cranial surgery to save a soldier's life, having patients die as they are operating, and Mulcahy assisting Hawkeye in an operation. Obviously, Lardner's intent is to show the pressure place on the surgeons, and how the football game will end up becoming a release for them. Instead, Altman broke up the material to place in earlier parts of the film and by doing so, makes the same point without overloading the audience with ten to fifteen minutes of rather depressing surgery material.

Scene Thirty-Four—A Surprise Waiting in the Swamp

Altman

Trapper and Hawkeye head back to the Swamp, but can't get in. Duke is surprised to see them, and there's enough fumbling around inside the tent to make Hawkeye and Trapper suspicious. Looking around the side, they see Duke leading someone out of the tent with a blanket over her head. It is revealed to be Houlihan. Hawkeye and Trapper razz Duke, who takes it as best he can.

Lardner

There is no such scene in Lardner's script. Nor in the novel. This was the result of Kellerman's performance in the earlier shower scene, with Altman agreeing that her character should stay through the remainder of the film, and showing a shift that allows Houlihan to become one of the group.

Scene Thirty-Five—Hammond calls

Altman

Blake is in his office, working on some fishing lure when a call comes in. He asks Radar to hold the fishing line so he can take the call, and Radar does so absentmindedly while reading. Hammond tells him that the battle for Old Baldy is over, and Blake asks who won. Hammond ignores the question and mentions that he got a report from Houlihan that makes accusations he finds hard to believe. Blake happily tells him not to believe them and hangs up. Radar lets go of the line when Blake thanks him for his help, and Blake realizes that the line is now gone.

Lardner

The scene is similar, expect Hawkeye, Duke, and Trapper are in his office as well—they're all there hoping that the battle that has put them in the O.R. for fifteen days straight is over. Hammond calls to tell them that it is, and Blake hangs up. Hammond is surprised that Blake doesn't ask who won.

There is no mention of the complaints by Houlihan that set up the final portion of the film with the football game.

It is at this point in the script that Houlihan's shower was to have occurred. This leads to her writing a letter (offscreen) to Hammond, who decides, in the next scene of the script, to visit the 4077th to deal with the situation. Gathering the staff in the mess tent, Hammond suspends Blake and takes over the 4077th himself.

The script paraphrases the segment in the novel dealing with Blake's temporary replacement and Hawkeye waiting to perform surgery on a soldier. Hawkeye performs the surgery with an impressed Hammond watching. Hawkeye points out that Blake may be regular army, but he knows to leave the doctors to do their work, and that's more important than anything else that occurs there.

Scene Thirty-Five—Hammond Visits the 4077th

Altman

Hammond arrives and says that he is looking for Blake, but ends up having a drink with Duke, Hawkeye, and Trapper. Discussing the Houlihan situation, football is mentioned, and Hammond talks them into playing a game against the 325th for money. He leaves to find Blake, mainly to discuss setting up the game. His talk with Blake is intercut with Hawkeye, Duke, and Trapper setting up the con with their "ringer," of Spearchucker Jones. Duke is aghast at having to share a tent not only with two Yankees, but also a "negro boy." Back in Blake's office, Blake asks about Houlihan's complaint and Hammond brushes it off with "screw her." (Roger Bowen calls her "O'Houlihan," although it is not clear if this was a mistake on his part of that of the character.)

Lardner

Plays much like in the film, although Duke's dialogue in the script is altered and some given to Trapper and Hawkeye in order to allow Duke to defend Houlihan's honor when the others begin to dig at her. Also cut is additional exposition from Hawkeye to explain who Jones is and why no one knows about his football past.

Scene Thirty-Six—Spearchucker Jones

Altman

A crowd is gathered around Jones as Radar, Hawkeye, Trapper, Duke, and Blake arrive in a jeep. Blake tries to be in command, but at the first chance he is willing to let Jones do all the work. A brief montage takes place showing the men going through their paces, while Houlihan works with the nurses to be cheerleaders. Blake has more encouraging words for the cheerleaders than the men, and both he and Jones agree that the men look pretty lousy.

Hawkeye comes up with a plan that they put up half the money and keep Jones hidden until the second half, whereupon they bet the rest of the money, raise the odds, and "clean up." Blake agrees. Blake asks Jones for plays and Jones has them all ready to go. Blake is impressed, but obviously has no idea how to read them.

Lardner

Most of the discussion heard in the film is between Henry and Jones in the script. As Houlihan remaining in the movie at this point came while filming, Lardner does not have her appearing here or in the rest of the film. There are no cheerleaders. Hawkeye does make the offer of setting up the betting, but he mainly makes the point that the betting is to raise money for Ho-Jon's college education. There is no mention of plays from Jones.

Scene Thirty-Seven—The Game

Altman

Obviously any action in the film dealing with physical activity like a football game is going to have moments that play out differently from the script. The MASH men take out one of the opposing football players with an injection, but are still playing terribly. They make it to the half at 16 to 0. Blake tries to give a speech but has to finish the bet, and Radar gets spit on by one of the players. Jones comes in, and with his touchdown the game becomes a free-for-all, with more injuries showing up on the field than in the O.R. scenes earlier in the movie. In the final play, Vollmer is given the ball and he makes a touchdown, winning the game for the 4077th.

The main characters playing cards near the end of the film. Both the concept of Houlihan becoming one of the gang as well as the identity of the dead man being driven out of the camp in the background were not present in the novel.

Lardner

Lardner has the action play out more like in the novel. He has the injection of the player (although not the swabbing that only adds to the humor), the betting, and the final play with Vollmer are all there. In the script, but missing from the film, is Jones admitting he's out of shape, and Radar using his ability to hear over long distances in order to make out the 325th's plays. Missing from the script is that of the zonked-out player tackling the cheerleaders, Radar being spit on, Painless' rant with the f-word, Judson being called a "coon" along with his response, and the running gag of Houlihan repeating the score after Blake does as well as her other misunderstandings during the game, including thinking that the ending of a quarter means someone's been shot.

While in the film, the team celebrates in the locker room with Blake showing off the money, the script has Hawkeye talking about how the money will help pay for Ho-Jon's college and Blake talking about how he outcoached Hammond.

Scene Thirty-Eight—Back to Camp

Altman

The team arrives back at the 4077th celebrating. The scene then cuts to a group—including Duke with Houlihan—playing cards. They notice a jeep taking a dead body away, but then go back to playing their game.

Lardner

When the team returns to the 4077th, the script has Hawkeye and Trapper finding out that Ho-Jon (who earlier in the script had returned to the camp as a wounded soldier) has relapse and there's nothing they can do for him. Ho-Jon asks if they will have to open him up again, and Duke is the one to tell him that there's no point.

The next scene is of everyone playing cards as they see an ambulance parked outside where Ho-Jon's body is tossed into the back like a sack of potatoes. Hawkeye and Trapper watch and hesitate, but the others force their attention back to the game as the ambulance pulls away.

Scene Thirty-Nine—Going Home

Altman

Hawkeye gets the news he and Duke are going home from Radar and runs off to find Duke, who is assisting Jones in the O.R. As Duke looks up, a flashforward (or what he imagines is yet to be) occurs, showing Duke arriving home and meeting his wife and kids. Duke looks at Houlihan, and Hawkeye can see that he just made things very awkward and leaves.

In the final scene, Duke and Hawkeye say goodbye to Trapper and head off in the same jeep they stole at the beginning of the film, for which Mulcahy does a prayer. Blake notices them stealing the jeep, but Radar reminds them that it's the same one they came in, so it's okay. Leslie grins at Radar putting one over on Blake, as Radar walks off with a whistle much like the one Hawkeye does throughout the film.

The ending credits are done as a P.A. announcement from Vollmer, and the screen goes to black.

Hawkeye returns home to his wife and sons in a scene directly from the novel that was filmed and then discarded. Even so, publicity stills were released featuring the sequence.

Lardner

Hawkeye bursts into the O.R. without the benefit of Radar being shown telling him the news. As there's no relationship with Houlihan for Duke, the dialogue is more about him wanting to skip out of the surgery and leave, with some additional dialogue about stealing a chopper. Duke and Hawkeye say goodbye to Spearchucker and Trapper as in the film, although Trapper says four months in the script and five in the movie. They then head out.

The next scene in the script has Duke and Hawkeye waiting to board ship. They are clean, with new haircuts, and wearing fresh uniforms. They are asked to help out with inspections on ship, but Hawkeye stops Duke from giving their real names so they can avoid the service. On board the ship, they replace their Medical Corps insignia with that of a cross and masquerade as chaplains. In a crap game, they are recognized but the soldiers who spot them are willing to trade places with them for the inspections.

On a flight, Duke and Hawkeye pass a bottle of scotch back and forth. In a men's room in Chicago, they split off, saying that they may run into each other again sometime. Duke is next seen arriving home and running to his wife and daughters. The final scene in the script has Hawkeye arriving and greeting his wife and sons. His five-year-old asks, "How they going, Hawkeye?" "Finest kind," Hawkeye says and the script comes to an end.

As seen in the film, Duke's arrival home was filmed, but placed earlier in the movie. Stills exist of Hawkeye's arrival home as well, although this, along with the scenes of the pair on the ship and the plane, was cut. It should be noted that the main photo used for promotion from Hawkeye's arrival has him whistling, instead of saying "finest kind."

From a look through the script and the film, it is obvious that the story about the film not having any of Lardner's dialogue is untrue. A lot of it appears in the film, or at most is worded slightly differently to make the dialogue more believable. It is also noted that the type of exposition Hornberger did often in the novel was carried over by Lardner, but disappeared from the film due to it sounding exactly as it is—stilted dialogue that is there only to tell the audience details they really don't need to know.

It is pretty clear that the script was improved upon by Altman and the cast when filming. Yet, as many from the film have pointed out, *MASH* would not have worked without what Lardner had laid out on the page. The tweaks he made from the novel helped make it into the film it is. And the additional changes by Altman and the others helped set the groundwork for the series that was to follow. The film would also be influential on many movies to come, as discussed in the next chapter.

Yankee Doodle Doctor

Movies (and Two TV Shows) Connected with *MASH*

There is no argument that both *MASH* the film and *MASH* the series were major players in the way movies and television changed in the 1970s. This was partially due to the evolution in the creative centers of both media, with the generations that had been in charge of the studios and networks—some from even before World War II—were realizing that they needed to gear products toward younger viewers. To do so in the radical world of the late 1960s and early 1970s meant having to take risks. Not all of them worked out—for every breakthrough like Mike Nichols' *The Graduate* (1967, a film that pushed Dustin Hoffman and Simon & Garfunkel to stardom, looked at the changing American culture, and gave us Anne Bancroft's bare midriff), we'd have a mind-warping blunder like Otto Preminger's *Skidoo* (1968, featuring a drug-soaked script that involves LSD, Jackie Gleason, Groucho Marx as "God," and Carol Channing in a see-through bra). Even so, the wheels slowly began turning to help make things just a tad more accessible to adults rather than just families or kids.

MASH, along with other more adult-oriented comedies of that era, changed the way humor would be used in films. As with the series after it, it became okay to throw a dash of drama and even material usually seen as too dark for comedies in a realistic fashion into a film that was set to make people laugh as well. Comedies had made us think in the past, such as Chaplin's *The Great Dictator* (1940) and Kubrick's *Dr. Strangelove* (1964), but even then there was a distancing effect that allowed the audience to not quite engage the seriousness (even Chaplin would later regret allowing his Hitler-like villain in *The Great Dictator* to be funny instead of the monster Hitler was). *MASH*, along with films like *The Graduate* and others, was challenging the perception that comedies could not get close to reality. Now here was *MASH* showing us blood and the horrors of war while at the same

Battle Circus (1953). The story of a surgeon helping to run a MASH unit during the Korean War. If you ever wonder how Humphrey Bogart would have played Hawkeye Pierce, this is the film for you.

time delivering jokes and visual humor. In other words, *MASH* was in the forefront when it came to black comedy, to being able to laugh at the darkness within our souls.

MASH would be reflected in many comedies to come over the years— mostly those dealing with the military in some sense or medicine. In many cases, *MASH* would be tied directly to such films and television series to try to find a common ground that audiences would recognize. "Hey, you liked *MASH!* Here's something kinda like it." It would continue to leak into promotions and critical analysis of other films for years to come. Even a movie like the warped comedy by Lindsay Anderson about the British National Health Service in 1982, *Britannia Hospital*, was promoted in the U.S. as "the *MASH* of Socialized Medicine" to try to get people into the theater.

Below is a list of films that hold a link to *MASH*, featuring at least two television series that tried to play off of the *MASH* influence. Including one that took on the story of a MASH unit long before the novel was even a thought in the author's head.

Battle Circus (1953)

Filmed in 1952 with the cooperation of the military and with technical advice by K. E. Van Buskirk, the commanding officer of the 8076th (the third MASH unit in Korea). The movie features Humphrey Bogart as the boozing, driven, womanizing Maj. Jed Webbe of the 8066th (a fictional version of the 8076th) who falls in love with naïve Lt. Ruth McGara (played by June Allyson) while working in a MASH unit during the Korean War. The film followed the unit as it evacuates twice in order to stay ahead of the North Koreans (a common situation for the MASH units in the early days of the war).

The director, Richard Brooks, has stated that the MGM film was originally to have been called *MASH 66*, but the studio decided the name would be too confusing for audiences, so it was changed to *Battle Circus*, a nickname for the MASH units due to their constant travel and raising of tents, much like a circus does. Oddly enough, although the film's central love story is not very authentic, the look of the unit is closer to the appearance of a MASH unit and how one operated than seen in *MASH*. Fans of *MASH* may also wish to give the movie a look not only to see how Hollywood was looking at the Korean War at the time, but also to witness Humphrey Bogart's interpretation of Hawkeye Pierce, as his Major Webbe is very much in the same mode (with similar jokes and pickup lines).

Catch-22 (1970)

The war novel *Catch-22* was written by Joseph Heller and released in 1961, several years before the release of Richard Hornberger's *MASH*. The two were commonly compared in reviews, as both deal with the insanity of . . . not so much war, but rather the mind-set of the military; one that seems to reward those in the wrong and punish those who are sane. The main thrust of *Catch-22* is the phrase itself, which has become part of common speech—a catch-22 in the novel and film deals with the idea that only sane pilots could go on a dangerous mission; yet, if you went, you were crazy and shouldn't be carrying out the mission. In more modern terms, it means any function that loops around itself in a manner that makes it impossible to happen (such as not being able to become a member to a club unless you're already in the club).

The film was directed by Mike Nichols after the success of *The Graduate* and written by Buck Henry (who also had worked on *The Graduate*). The film starred Alan Arkin as a bombardier during World War II who wants to stop flying dangerous missions but can't because he's proven to be one of the few sane men around that can do the job. For those unfamiliar with the novel or film, it is even blacker comedy than *MASH*, which may have been why some people stayed away from the theaters when it came out. Most of the film deals with characters in insane events, but ultimately it is about the crushing of the spirit and acceptance of evil; *MASH* deals with keeping people alive, looking at naked ladies, and winning a crooked football game. One can sense why audiences preferred one over the other.

Costarring Jon Voight, Charles Grodin, Bob Newhart, Richard Benjamin, Martin Balsam, and Orson Welles, the movie was set to be released by Paramount as a big moneymaker in 1970. However, filming took much longer than expected, leaving the actors in a state of exhaustion over time, as well as being one reason why Bob Newhart passed on doing *MASH*. Ironically, although *Catch-22* started filming before *MASH*, *MASH* had been in theaters for months before *Catch-22* premiered to underwhelming critical and box-office appeal. The novel is written in a nonlinear fashion that also made it hard to bring to the screen (just as Ring Lardner had problems taking the episodic nature of *MASH* and building a script out of it), and production was revamped several times to try to make the film work. While it is considered a more critical success decades later, it was deemed the lesser of the two war comedies released by a major studio in 1970 and a box-office failure. Thus, although *Catch-22* was not influenced by *MASH*, its critical appraisal and audience appreciation at the time certainly was. To put a capper on it, when *Mad* magazine finally parodied the movie, it ended with Hawkeye and Trapper appearing in the final illustration, delivering the punchline that they "had been there first, and were funnier."

As with *MASH*, a sitcom adaptation was attempted in 1973, with Richard Dreyfuss in the Alan Arkin role. It did not get past the pilot stage, with only one episode filmed.

The Hospital (1971)

This film directed by Arthur Hiller from a script by Paddy Chayefsky (*Network*) stars George C. Scott (fresh off of *Patton*) as the chief of medicine at a hospital that is falling apart due to red tape and the ignorance and disregard the staff has toward the sick and suffering. Diana Rigg plays the daughter of a man who is wanting to die, while Scott's character has to deal with a series of murders involving doctors and nurses. While the film treats the serious breakdown in the hospital and a possible one for Scott's character, there are many comedic moments in the movie as well, which naturally led to comparisons to the previous year's release of *MASH* in reviews. *Variety* called it "a civilian mis-*MASH*," while Roger Ebert referred to early scenes as if "the *MASH* gang was demobilized and went into private practice."

In some ways, the aforementioned *Britannia Hospital* (dealing with a maddening hospital system, but in more slapstick fashion) is a sister to *The Hospital*, while Martin Scorsese's *Bringing Out the Dead* (1999, about a depressed paramedic dealing with crazy associates and patients) plays not so much as a sequel, but as a bastard child to *The Hospital*, with all three films finding some parentage with *MASH*.

S*P*Y*S (1974)

This comedy stars Elliott Gould and Donald Sutherland as two bumbling CIA agents who are marked for death by their own agency, the KGB, the Chinese, and a terrorist group. Cowritten by Lawrence J. Cohen, who also cowrote *Start the Revolution Without Me*, which also starred Sutherland. Directed by Irvin Kershner, who is probably best remembered as directing *The Empire Strikes Back* (1980). Originally called *Wet Stuff*, the title was changed to play off the success of *MASH*, with asterisks between each letter as in the original movie title. Some poster art for the film also used the slogan, "Now they do to the CIA what they did to the Army in *M*A*S*H*."

To be fair, the movie isn't that horrible, but pales in comparison with *MASH*. It may have done better without the link being made between the two. As it is, it's a mixture of some dull spots with some genuinely funny material, and Gould and Sutherland prove they could be a very likable team

S*P*Y*S (1974) featured a reunion of Donald Sutherland and Elliott Gould in a neat little comedy that was hurt by trying to promote it as another *MASH*.

together, but most fans would be advised to pass it up if expecting anything along the lines of *MASH*.

Oddly enough, writer Lawrence J. Cohen would also cowrite the script for the movie *The Big Bus* (1976), which features Rene Auberjonois and Sally Kellerman. His cowriter on *S*P*Y*S*, Malcolm Marmorstein, also wrote the next film on the list.

Whiffs (1975)

Whiffs stars Elliott Gould as a human guinea pig for the army's chemical warfare department. When let go because he's become immune to everything given him over the years, and with no job prospects, he decides to steal a gas that makes people go spastic and use it to rob the banks in a town.

Such a plot sounds like it has potential. It costars Eddie Albert, directed by Ted Post, written by Malcolm Marmorstein, and . . . well . . . it's hard to sit through. Still, it was promoted by way of the movie poster as "The most hilarious military farce since *M*A*S*H!*" Yes, similar to how *S*P*Y*S* was promoted, but *S*P*Y*S* is the better film.

The most hilarious military farce since M·A·S·H!

The Army's prize human guinea pigs turn on the gas

GEORGE BARRIE PRESENTS A BRUT PRODUCTION
ELLIOTT GOULD in WHIFFS CO-STARRING EDDIE ALBERT
HARRY GUARDINO GODFREY CAMBRIDGE
AND STARRING JENNIFER O'NEILL
PRODUCED BY GEORGE BARRIE DIRECTED BY TED POST WRITTEN BY MALCOLM MARMORSTEIN MUSIC BY JOHN CAMERON
Made without the cooperation of the US Army PG PARENTAL GUIDANCE SUGGESTED

Whiffs (1975) is a weak comedy showcasing Elliott Gould as a military "guinea pig" that uses an experimental gas in a bank robbery. As seen from the poster, there was an attempt to play off of *MASH* in hopes of attracting people to the theaters. It didn't work.

Mother, Jugs & Speed (1976)

Directed by Peter Yates, the film stared Bill Cosby (Mother), Raquel Welch (Jugs), and Harvey Keitel (Speed) as employees of a private ambulance service who are competing against another ambulance service for a contract to service part of Los Angeles. For this reason, everyone is doing anything they can to obtain more patients than their competitor.

While the film never tried to promote itself with *MASH*, the creative team's attempts to copy the style of *MASH* by presenting dramatic medical emergencies mixed with dark comedy did not go unnoticed by the critics and audiences. Critics were not kind to the film; Roger Ebert stated, "if it thinks it's imitating *MASH* it's wrong. . . ." While Vincent Canby at the *New York Times* said in his review, "It's essentially a fraud, and typical of so many post-*MASH* comedies that assume that a lunatic juxtaposition of slapstick, brutal realism, obscenities, romance and bad humor automatically make an important statement about the world we live in. Mostly it makes a mess of a film."

Even so, the film was successful enough to earn a pilot on television, which failed to become a series. The scriptwriter, Tom Mankiewicz, who is best remembered for working on a number of James Bond films and *Superman* (1978), directed the 1991 John Candy comedy *Delirious*, which was written by Lawrence J. Cohen. It's a small world.

Bad Medicine (1985)

Directed and written by Harvey Miller, this movie starring Steve Guttenberg is about a premed student who blows his chances to get into a number of medical schools and ends up at one in Central America. From there, he slowly begins to gain a better understanding of life and helps to build a clinic for the poor in the area that those in authority are against. Costarring in the film was Alan Arkin (*Catch-22*). The 1980s saw a number of medical school comedies, but many tended toward a more slapstick approach (*Young Doctors in Love* from 1982 is more in the style of *Airplane!* [1980], for example). *Bad Medicine* shares some of that as well, but the storyline soon becomes one about social commentary and being antiauthority for a greater cause, much as seated at the heart of *MASH*.

Good Morning, Vietnam (1987)

Directed by Barry Levinson, written by Mitch Markowitz, and starring Robin Williams, the film follows an Armed Forces Radio disc jockey who disregards authority and attempts to bring humor to the soldiers listening to his show. While the film is not related to medicine, it was hard to not look at the mixture of drama, violence, and dark humor and see the connection to *MASH*. Critics certainly picked up on it and commonly pointed to *Good Morning, Vietnam* as one of the best military comedies since *MASH*.

It also is similar to *MASH* in that it's a fictional account based on a real person—H. Richard Hornberger in the case of *MASH* and Adrian Cronauer, who was a DJ for Armed Forces Radio during the Vietnam War, in the case of *Good Morning, Vietnam*. In the 1970s, Cronauer attempted to interest networks in his story for a sitcom based on how well *MASH* was doing, but was turned down as the Vietnam War was still too recent to be seen as a good setting for a comedy. (They had good reasons to think so;

check out *The Six O'Clock Follies* listed below.) The movie was a success and was eventually attempted to be turned into a sitcom, but things never gelled.

Article 99 (1992)

Directed by Howard Deutch (*Pretty in Pink*), this medical drama/comedy dealing with a veterans hospital and the doctors there who avoid red tape in order to help patients even stars a Sutherland—Kiefer Sutherland, the son of Donald Sutherland. The film actually combines an element of *Catch-22* into the film (the movie's title is a dead giveaway there), with a fictional government regulation that says no treatment can be given to a veteran if the ailment is not due to military service. The doctor bypasses this regulation, leading to comedic high jinks and tragic losses along the way. Any way you look at it, although *MASH* is not mentioned, it is obvious where some elements of the film came from.

Animal House (1978)

Seems like an odd choice, doesn't it? Certainly not much in the way of medicine here, but it does deal with a couple of main elements from *MASH*. The first is the antiauthority status of our protagonists (and there are several, just like in *MASH*) who do things in an enclosed environment—thereby allowing us to laugh without feeling threatened—against villains that are just this shade of being cartoons (thus allowing us to laugh at the horrible things done to them without regret). Before *MASH*, our comedy heroes had to be put in a position where their methods are accepted as they have no other choice. In *MASH,* our heroes do what they want because they're Teflon—nothing can hurt them, so they can get away with everything. Same in *Animal House*—the actions taken would put everyone in jail, but none of that occurs because the characters cannot be hurt.

Further, the gross-out element of the humor in some specific areas of *MASH* is there in *Animal House* as well. We accept it because we're not hurt by it, and *MASH* pointed out that dark comedy can be played for positive results. Of course, *Animal House* sets up a type of antiauthority humor that would become a genre on to its own, especially in dealing with military comedies. *Private Benjamin* (1980) and *Stripes* (1981) are both antiauthority military films, but they are in the spirit of the progression of such comedy found in *Animal House* rather than *MASH* (yet still with the Teflon-shielding to the characters as in *MASH*). *Animal House* is the parent of such later films—and many after them—but *MASH* remains the godfather of them all.

Animal House also went to television; at least getting past a pilot to land for a short time on ABC in 1979 as *Delta House*. And in relation to television, there have been two sitcoms that were influenced by the success of *MASH* as a television series.

Roll Out (1973–1974)

This CBS series, which was created by Larry Gelbart and Gene Reynolds (who helped develop, write, and produce *MASH* for television), sprang from the slowly emerging success of *MASH* on the network. The producers wanted to capitalize on that success as well, but didn't want to simply give the network a carbon copy of *MASH*. Instead, they decided to do a comedy about a staff of supply drivers during the European advances in World War II. Most of such drivers were African Americans, and thus the series not only dealt with elements of that war, but also racial topics that affected us then and in the 1970s.

The series starred Stu Gilliam and Hilly Hicks, while a number of actors who would go on to bigger things appeared, such as Ed Begley Jr. and Garrett Morris. The show lasted only twelve episodes due to being placed against *The Odd Couple* on ABC's invincible Friday Night lineup. The series re-aired briefly on the BET! cable network in the 1980s.

The Six O'Clock Follies (1980)

Another series bouncing off the success of *MASH* lasted an even shorter time than *Rolling Out*. This series for NBC, which aired on Thursday nights, took place in 1967 Saigon and dealt with a news program filmed for the Armed Forces Vietnam Network. Starring were

The Six O'Clock Follies (1980) would be an attempt to do a comedy series based on the Vietnam War. Its claim to fame was an early use of actors Phil Hartman and Lawrence Fishburne (the latter eventually turning up in an episode of *MASH*).

Randall Carver, Joby Baker, and Laurence Fishburne (just after finishing *Apocalypse Now*, which also takes place during the Vietnam War). Each episode would feature comedy with dramatic moments dealing with the war, leading many to see it as *MASH* for another war. In the series was also a young Phil Hartman, who would later work with Fishburne on the Pee Wee Herman series *Pee Wee's Playhouse*. *The Six O'Clock Follies* lasted five episodes before being canceled.

As can be seen, *MASH* as a television series was also influential on other programs, just as the novel and the movie were influential on others in their medium as well. 20th Century-Fox could feel the heat coming off the movie in the early 1970s and were ready to see if a sitcom version could work.

But before heading into the area of the *MASH* phenomena that be best remembered today, one final side trip.

13

One of Those Traveling Medicine Shows

MASH Onstage

Everyone has to start somewhere. A person doesn't find a writer, a stage, and an audience in order to become instantly known as an actor, he or she has to train and learn the skills of becoming an actor. Same with those who wish to design sets, or costumes; perhaps run lights or other production duties behind the scenes; even get involved with promotion and producing. All of these things have to be learned, and many start off by doing so in school or community productions of plays and musicals.

Of course, there are a variety of such plays and musicals that can be purchased for use by groups who wish to stage them. Some can be pretty expensive, and also can be done so often that it isn't feasible for groups to do them (in other words, if the high school down the road is doing *Sound of Music*, there's no point in the community theater troupe putting it on as well). So a variety is needed, and furthermore, sometimes performing material that is a bit more offbeat can be a good way to help with training as well and can give the actors, production designers, costumers, and so on a chance to do something that is "new" to them in a way that may help them develop new plays and musicals as well.

The thing is to find them. Fortunately, there are companies that publish new plays for such use, including a number based on television shows. The Dramatic Publishing Company out of Woodstock, Illinois, does exactly this, featuring monologues, plays, and musicals for different types of groups (children through adults), genres, and size of the cast. They also have musical accompaniment, posters, and other equipment available for productions as well.

MASH is one such play that is available. Actually, it's available in two forms—a one-act play running roughly thirty minutes, and a full-length two-act play running approximately ninety minutes. Yet, before anyone reading this starts wondering how a high school performs the shower scene, it should be noted that the play is not quite a simple adaptation of the movie. Or of the novel. Or even of the series.

If one can say that the Hornberger novels represent *MASH* in its original universe, and the Butterworth novels represent another universe where the characters do things differently; just as the movie version of the characters are from another *MASH* universe, and so too with the characters from the television series; then the characters in the *MASH* play are just one more in the multiverse of *MASH*.

Both versions of the play were written by Tim Kelly (1937–1998), who wrote more than three hundred plays over time, many of them for the Dramatic Publishing Company and several adaptations of earlier plays, movies, television, and books; from horror to comedy to musical. Since many of these plays are known to be done by small groups on the cheap and with small staging available, such elements are taken into consideration in the playbook that can be bought when a group decides to perform such a play.

The full-length play for *MASH* comes in a plain white cover with an illustration of the original cast from the television series on the back. What is interesting about this drawing is that it has been altered. The drawing shows the cast hanging on to a rope ladder from a helicopter. The revised version shows the same, but the drawing of Frank Burns has been altered to show him with a mustache and beard. Looking at the playbook, Frank hardly appears in the play at all, while Duke does. Thus, the drawing has been altered to make Frank Burns into Duke. Even so, one look at the playbook can show that the characters appearing therein are not the same ones from the series.

The playbook for the full-length play—first published in 1973—has thirty parts in order to give a good size number of students a chance to get up onstage and perform, but which can also be done in such a way that some of the actors can play more than one part if needed. The stage is set up so that the main action takes place in the Swamp, with nurses' tents stage left and the mess tent stage right. All other actions take place in front of the curtains to suggest other areas. Costumes and scenery are pretty easy, with mostly army green and camping gear. No doubt there would be some concerns about Ho-Jon and Spearchucker, as they do suggest some racial

An illustration by Gordon Currie to help promote the television series in the early days of the show. It would later be used as the back cover of the stage-play scriptbook, only with the illustration of Frank Burns altered in order to represent Duke with a beard.

stereotyping even if the play makes clear that racism is never a good thing. Interestingly, the playbook suggests getting a local football celebrity to play the part of Spearchucker. As for the play itself, Tim Kelly took elements from the novel and, using those spare parts, built his own version of the story dealing with Hawkeye and Duke arriving at the 4077th, their stay there, and going home.

The play starts with Henry Blake being portrayed more in the spirit of Potter than Blake—a bit of a hardnose who wears sunglasses through and barks orders at everyone. Opening at a poker game with Painless and

Radar, Trapper John is with them, thus making him already at the 4077th before Hawkeye and Duke get there. (it's never mentioned, but suggested that Trapper got his name because he trapped lobsters in Maine alongside Hawkeye). Boone, the character that is told by Burns that he killed a patient, is promoted to be Henry's assistant and follows him around throughout the play. Radar has his ESP and super-hearing, while Hawkeye and Duke are pretty much as is from the film and novel, although less willing to make waves. As in the novel, Frank Burns is a captain, who acts more in the tradition of the naïve blunderer of the series than the nearly psychotic character of the film.

The opening scene also has two nurses discussing things (thus giving females more to do in the play than in the novel or movie). One mentions about sometimes wanting to pass out during surgery from exhaustion, but the other says to do so would lead to the doctors betting on how long she'll stay under or using her to obtain blood. This pretty much tells you right there that this is going to be a much cleaner version of *MASH* than seen previously or even in the television series.

Burns' dressing down someone for "killing a patient" comes quickly, appearing in Scene Four of Act One, but instead of Boone, it involves a nurse who breaks down over it. Instead of the violence Burns gets for this in the novel and film, Hawkeye and Duke leave a dead cat in Burns' locker, then retrieve it before Burns can report it, making it appear that Burns is cracking up. Blake sends him packing, but there's trouble brewing with the new chief nurse, Houlihan, whom Hawkeye warns to stay away from his crew (as in the novel and in Lardner's original script). Hawkeye gets to call her a "regular army clown" here as in all other sources.

Ho-Jon is drafted and says goodbye, while Painless is suffering from melancholia (as in the novel; the film went in a different direction with the impotence angle). The whole suicide business is in the play, but it's due to simple sadness and nothing more. They give him the black capsule, knocking Painless out. When he awakens, he is wearing a Frankenstein mask and is told that Hawkeye brought him back from the dead. Thinking something has happened to his face due to the mask, Painless runs out and smack into a congresswoman who is visiting the 4077th, scaring her.

Ho-Jon returns as a wounded soldier, and the doctors are worried, but they do eventually succeed in saving his life. Elsewhere, three women who are entertainers are stranded at the camp, leading to a musical number in the play. The nurses get fed up with the prima donnas and convince them that the Swamp men are disgusting to be with. The entertainers flee.

After being told that they can't leave because of how good they are at surgery, Hawkeye devises a plan to make himself look insane by discussing mermaids. Henry sends him to be evaluated (this is all straight from the novel, except it was not Blake who sends him). Hawkeye goes to the 325th for evaluation and meets Spearchucker, who snaps Hawkeye out of his con, and they go off to talk about old times. Back at the 4077th, Hawkeye announces the football game to be held against Hammond's team, with all the money going to get Ho-Jon to the States and college. In doing so, he mentions that Spearchucker will be joining them to help with the game. The game itself is all off-stage, but the results are the same, only with Spearchucker winning the game for the MASH unit.

The final scene has Hawkeye and Duke getting ready to leave and go back to the States. In a final prank, the pair send Henry five hundred pounds of live lobsters from Maine C.O.D., which leads to Blake rattling on about them as the play comes to a close.

The play definitely finds its own way to tell the story of *MASH* and yet avoid certain areas that would have probably gotten the cast in trouble if they had stayed true to the original plot. Oddly enough, Kelly follows Lardner's plot for Ho-Jon over what Hornberger and Altman did, including the football game's betting being for Ho-Jon's education (although Kelly avoids killing off Ho-Jon as Lardner would do). The whole bit with the female entertainers is new and really serves only the purpose of allowing a musical number to take place that would not have been there otherwise (Hawkeye and Duke get to sing a bit earlier in the play as well when making up a song about Blake and Houlihan). Kelly does get rid of Burns as quickly as both Hornberger and Lardner did, although in a less offensive manner than in the other sources. Houlihan's survival to the end of the play also shows that Kelly may have seen the film and thought it best to keep her around, as well as soften her character as Altman did.

Of course, Painless' resurrection is different, although rather anticlimactic (no pun intended). Houlihan never gets in the shower, understandably, and there certainly isn't any of the profanity or off-color humor found in the novel and movies. Spearchucker's role in the play is even less than in the movie, which seems like a bit of a cheat for those paying to see the play (especially if they did advertise it as a local celebrity in the role). All the material with Ho-Jon and the other Koreans shows all the signs of 1970s "we're trying to be so aware, while still being a bit blind to how to portray Asians" writing, unfortunately. One would suspect that there would be some minor retooling of lines there these days.

It makes for a fascinating variation of the story Hornberger told in his novel, as well as the Altman film. It would not be alone, for the television series would need to retool the characters and events from the original source as well in order to make it work for the small screen. But first, there was the need to figure who could even make those changes and get them to work.

14

Put It Over There by the Television Set

The Five Military Sitcoms That Influenced *MASH*

M*ASH* took off at the box office, and—as always—there were two immediate thoughts from the studio about it. No, not "Should we try to make more movies that are as different and exciting as Robert Altman's film?" And definitely not "Should we rethink what America wants to see in movies?" The thoughts were "Can we do a sequel?" and "Can we cash in with a television tie-in?"

As mentioned in previous chapters, as soon as H. Richard Hornberger finished the second novel, *MASH Goes to Maine*, 20th Century-Fox snapped up the rights and went about putting together a film that would follow Hawkeye and the gang back to Maine, where they set up shop. That dream crashed pretty quickly for the studio, however. First, the cast were already scattered to the wind, doing other projects, and with both Gould and Sutherland suddenly in very high demand. Also, Altman was definitely not coming back for a sequel as he was already working on his next film (which probably would have been fine with the studio, but still would have put a dent into expectations). But most of all, the script Dick Zanuck saw, just as he was on his way out the door of 20th Century-Fox, didn't work at all. Which wasn't that big of a surprise—the novel is once again episodic, only this time about backward people in a small town in Maine who are all having sex with their neighbors. Plus, Hawkeye, Trapper, Duke, and Spearchucker didn't have the level of authority to fight against that to make audiences root for them. One thing to fight the army in a war zone; another to get heated over minor problems at the hospital.

So the film was out. And television was in.

Which wasn't that outlandish an idea. Many successful movies had at least gotten pilots made for possible television versions. After all, if people loved the film, they'd like the idea of revisiting those characters, and television offered the chance to do that for twenty-six episodes a year if a pilot got picked up.

There certainly had been military comedies done in the past on television. The problem was that none of them were like *MASH*. *MASH* as a film dealt with some serious topics pertaining to warfare and medicine in a crisis situation. Military comedies that played theaters and on television weren't really into the whole idea of being serious. Sometimes playfully poking at the regulations and procedures of the military; perhaps even sometimes dealing with the consequences of war, but mainly they were comedy of errors. Which is perfectly natural; after all, what better setup for a comedy than to have a disciplined organization and then place a misfit into the middle of that to muck it up. Look at most of the comedies dealing with the military and that's the story—the slow-burn sergeant or officer who has to deal with the idiot recruit. From Charlie Chaplin, to the Three Stooges, to Abbott and Costello, and Martin and Lewis; from *Carry On Sergeant* to *No Time for Sergeants*, and through more recent years with *Stripes* and *Private Benjamin*, the concept really hasn't changed that much.

There were exceptions, of course. *Mister Roberts*, a film that was closer in spirit to the MASH novel than most military comedies, and *Operation Petticoat* were more traditional in certain ways, but still dealt with oddballs who have to rise to the occasion (as would commonly occur in the earlier type of military comedies discussed above). And the same held true for television. Most dealt with misfits struggling against authority, some dealing with those who knew how to subvert the higher-ups to get what they want. The main thing is that most of them didn't last very long, even those that were based on successful films, such as *Mister Roberts* and *No Time for Sergeants*—both of which only lasted a season each. Audiences grew tired of the same setup and payoff every week, and such shows had to offer something unique to keep them running.

Below are five series that did last for a time due to finding their niche amongst all the "screwball" military fun. (As an aside, one could add long-running British favorites as *'Allo 'Allo* and *Dad's Army*, but since Americans did not see these programs until later in the 1980s—if at all—they didn't have the same influence as the other American ones listed here.) All had *some* influence—mainly as things to avoid when it came to putting *MASH* together for television, but that's still an influence. When the time had come for the series to be put together, the discussion became "How do we avoid this being *McHale's Navy?*" Such questions extended to the actors as well, as Alan Alda's first meeting with Larry Gelbart and Gene Reynolds was wrapped around Alda's concerns that the show would end up being *Sgt. Bilko* every week (and for a time the show was veering dangerously close to that). Thus, even though none of these five shows are much like *MASH* beyond dealing with the military, they all affected how *MASH* would turn out. They also all have direct connections to *MASH* in the form of people who have worked or appeared on these programs.

Sgt. Bilko/The Phil Silvers Show (CBS, 1955–1959)

Phil Silvers as Sgt. Bilko in an ad for Camel cigarettes. Bilko's con games would be the basis for many military comedies to come, including *MASH*.

Created by Nat Hiken, this series not only made Phil Silvers a superstar as Sgt. Bilko, but would essentially set up the premise of several similar characters in other programs. Both *F Troop*'s Sgt. O'Rourke and McHale in *McHale's Navy* were variation of the con man who uses military red tape to get things to help lead a cushy life and make some money on the side.

Most episodes of *The Phil Silvers Show* deal with Bilko and the soldiers under him at the army post's motor pool, looking for means to swindle others, although almost always with Bilko finding himself on the losing end of things at the end of each episode (and typically with too much of a conscience to con innocent people who are the only ones that really fall for his swindles). *The Phil Silvers Show* featured characters in Kansas during a time of peace, so there wasn't much call to see the character in any real danger, unlike a couple of others programs listed here and *MASH*, but the objective of conning the upper brass would be one of the benchmarks of *MASH*, especially in the early years of the show. "To Market, To Market" and "Major Fred C. Dobbs," both from season one, could readily have been episodes of *The Phil Silvers Show* with minor changes (some would say that's part of the problem with an episode like "Major Fred C. Dobbs," however).

Of course, any series dealing with a group of men and women in the military that lasts for a few seasons is going to end up incorporating a lot of actors over time. Thus, the chances of someone from one of many from one program to appear on the other are pretty good. In the case of *The Phil Silvers Show*, at least fourteen actors appeared on both programs over the years. In most cases, this meant a one-off appearance in both shows, including some familiar names to some readers, such as Bruno Kirby and Pat Hingle.

There are three more prominent names in that group: Ronny Graham, an actor who appeared once on *Bilko*, would later become a writer and pen seven episodes for *MASH* in the later 1970s. Herb Voland, another one-timer on *Bilko*, would go on to be a semiregular in the first season of *MASH* with seven appearances as General Crandell Clayton. Finally, the last one-off performer with a connection to *MASH* on *The Phil Silvers Show* was a young Alan Alda, as a rich young man who wants to become an artist, with Bilko as his manager, in "Bilko, the Art Lover."

McHale's Navy (ABC, 1962–1966)

One of the producers of *The Phil Silvers Show*, Edward Montagne, would walk away from that series with the idea of doing something similar only based around the navy. In this case, the Bilko-like character was Lt. Cmdr. Quinton McHale, who commanded a group of men stationed on an island in the Pacific (and in the final season in a town in Italy) during World War II. Although the series took place during a war, McHale and the men usually didn't see much fighting and instead concentrated on various schemes to raise money to help themselves and the natives, while flying under the radar of Capt. Binghamton (Joe Flynn), who was determined to send McHale and his men packing. The series was popular enough to last four seasons and result in two theatrical movies while the series was ongoing: *McHale's Navy* (1964) and *McHale's Navy Joins the Air Force* (1965), as well as a remake in 1997.

The series certainly could be as silly as *The Phil Silvers Show*, but there was still an element of danger possible for the characters (although that was quickly pushed aside in knowing that none of the regulars would have to worry about getting killed off). The initial pilot episode, "Seven Against the Sea," which aired on *Alcoa Premiere* in 1962, was much more of a drama, with McHale settling in with the natives on the island, but mainly to keep alive the surviving members of the base hit by the Japanese; showing some of the effects of war on the survivors. The element of drama and comedy found there had been seen before in films like *Mister Roberts* and would play a vital role in *MASH* years later.

The people linked between *McHale's Navy* and *MASH* not only involve actors, but some of the behind-the-scenes people as well. Director Earl Bellamy would do six episodes of *McHale's Navy* and two early episodes of *MASH*. Rick Mittleman, who was a script consultant for twenty-three episodes of the older series, would write one 1975 episode of the latter, while Jerry Mayer and Burt Styler—who wrote one episode each for *McHale's Navy*—would write two episodes each between 1972 and 1973 of *MASH*. Ralph Sylos decorated sets on both shows: fourteen episodes for *McHale's Navy* and thirty for *MASH*. Richard A. Kelley was the director of photography on one episode of *McHale's Navy* and three episodes of the first season of *MASH*.

Fifteen actors also shared duties between the two shows. Popular Japanese actor Mako made nine appearances on *McHale's Navy* and four on *MASH*, each time playing Japanese in the first and either Chinese or Korean in the second (Mako is probably best remembered by *MASH* fans as the Chinese officer who is trading patients with the 4077th in the episode "Rainbow Bridge"). Yuki Shimoda and John Rujioka would perform similar multiple parts in both shows as well. Robert F. Simon played different parts in three episodes of *McHale's Navy*, but would play only one in three early episodes of *MASH*, General Maynard M. Mitchell (as the general who gives the 4077th the Officers' Club in "Officers Only"). Best known by *MASH* fans, however, is Mike Farrell, who made a one-off appearance in "Washing Machine Charlie" on *McHale's Navy*.

F Troop (ABC, 1965–1967)

A series that was a bit different from the others listed here, as the emphasis was on being incredibly silly rather than the usual "man vs. the military" agenda of the other programs. The Native Americans talked Yiddish, the commanding officer of the Western fort in the late 1880s is a bumbler who can't stop tripping over himself, the sergeant is a con man out to swindle everyone around him (thus keeping up the *Bilko* aspect). It was slapstick and shenanigans, set in the old West, with occasional moments that tied back to the general military theme.

But besides con games, *MASH* too would sometimes resort to slapstick in a manner similar to *F Troop*: the 4077th sign falling down and narrowly missing MacArthur's car in "Big Mac"; the destruction of the stockpile of artillery thanks to Frank's weapon in "Five O'Clock Charlie" (not to mention a two-episode appearance of the Five O'Clock Charlie character—the enemy who couldn't bomb straight—who would have fit right in with the supposed enemies in *F Troop*); the dimwitted commander who can be talked into anything (more early episodes of *MASH* than later ones, even those with Blake). All these elements are certainly a reflection of earlier comedies such as *F Troop*.

That connection is definitely supported by who had worked on both series. Gene Reynolds, who helped make *MASH* happen on television—producing, writing, and directing for the series over the years—directed four episodes of *F Troop*. *F Troop* producer Hy Averback would go on to direct twenty episodes of *MASH*. William Wiard, who edited one episode of *F Troop*, ended up directing six episodes of *MASH*. Richard Baer, writer of three episodes, and Arthur Julian, writer of twenty-nine, would both write one episode each of *MASH*.

Of the twelve actors shared, Mako once again pops up—this time as a Samurai warrior—on *F Troop*. Dennis Troy, a regular utility player on *MASH* who popped up in several earlier episodes (the guy with the glasses and the mustache; getting a letter from his wife as he was attempting to hit up a nurse in "Hot Lips and Empty Arms" is a good frame of reference for fans), also made one appearance on *F Troop* as a medicine man. Movie and television fans no doubt recognized James Gregory ("Iron Guts" Kelly) in three episodes of *F Troop*. But the biggest actor connection is spotting Jamie Farr in two episodes of *F Troop*, both times as an Indian, and naturally enough, once again making it clear that he had no interest in getting himself killed fighting.

Hogan's Heroes (CBS, 1965–1971)

In some eyes it would be even more of a stretch to compare *Hogan's Heroes* to *MASH* than *F Troop*. The series, essentially a variation of *Stalag 17* (1953) with a dash of *The Great Escape* (1963), dealt with a group of World War II prisoners of war being held in the German camp, Stalag Luft 13. As viewers discovered in the first episode, the prisoners are there on purpose—an undercover operation with various gizmos in the camp to be used to help prisoners from other camps escape and to go on dangerous missions for the Allies.

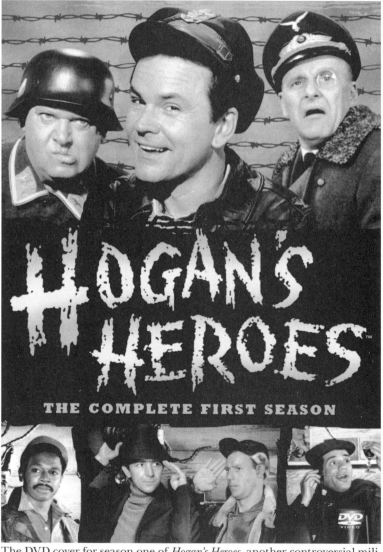

The DVD cover for season one of *Hogan's Heroes*, another controversial military comedy from CBS. Many people behind the scenes and even in front of the camera would move from this series almost directly on to *MASH*.

Colonel Robert Hogan is the leader of the prisoners, who uses a variety of con games and other resources to keep the clueless German officers at bay while performing his duties. The double-talk and con games also play into *Bilko*-like, and the series—like *MASH*—takes place during a war, but the threat to the characters was pretty much on the level of *McHale's Navy* in that audience were assured that nothing harmful would happen to the "heroes" in the show.

Still, the thrust of the comedy was vastly different from that of *MASH*, just as *MASH* was vastly different in its view of serving in a war as *Stalag 17*. Perhaps more important to this review of the shows is the people that worked on both. Once again, Gene Reynolds was there with thirty-four episodes directed for *Hogan's Heroes*. Bruce Bilson, who directed one episode of *MASH*, would direct twenty-five episodes of the WWII series. Arthur Jillian, who also worked on *F Troop* and one episode of *MASH*, wrote twenty-four episodes of *Hogan's Heroes*, while Richard Powell, who wrote twenty-nine episodes of *Hogan's Heroes*, would write one episode of *MASH* as well. The champ when it comes to scripts is Laurence Marks, who wrote sixty-seven episodes of *Hogan's Heroes* and twenty-eight episodes of *MASH* (including such classics as "Rainbow Bridge" and "Adam's Ribs").

Naturally, getting closer to the time period when *MASH* was filmed means that more actors turn up in both, with a total of nineteen in all. Bernard Fox may have only appeared in one episode of each, but these include *MASH*, *F Troop*, *McHale's Navy*, and *Hogan's Heroes*. Bruce Kirby appeared in *MASH*, *Hogan's Heroes* (three times), and *The Phil Silvers Show* (twice). James Gregory turns up again, after also appearing on *F Troop*. Buck Young appeared in three episodes of *Hogan's Heroes* and three of *MASH*; two where he played a helicopter pilot (O'Brien in "Dr. Pierce and Mr. Hyde" and Dan in "Dear Mildred," so the character's name could be Dan O'Brien). Bonnie Jones was in only one episode of *Hogan's Heroes*, but was Lt. Barbara Bannerman in several early episodes of *MASH*. Lynette Mettey also only did one episode of the former, but six episodes of *MASH*, where she mainly played Lt. Nancy Griffen, then Nurses Anderson, Baker, and Able in that order. John Orchard, who played Capt. Ugly John Black in eleven episodes of *MASH* (along with one other character a few years later) appeared in three episodes of *Hogan's Heroes* as various characters. Johnny Haymer was a general in one episode of *Hogan's Heroes* before being demoted to sergeant as Zale in twenty episodes of *MASH*. Roy Goldman was a background player for *Hogan's Heroes* in one episode, then went on to appear in forty-four episodes of *MASH* in similar roles, and (no doubt an inside joke) was eventually listed as "Private Roy Goldman" as his character's name. The biggest of all is William Christopher, who appeared in four episodes of *Hogan's Heroes* as various characters and then would become Father Mulcahy on *MASH*.

Gomer Pyle, U.S.M.C. (CBS, 1964–1969)

Hogan's Heroes created controversy by being a show that was seen by some as treating Nazi Germany as a joke. Also on CBS during many of the same years was another military comedy that faced a backlash as well, only from a younger generation who thought *Gomer Pyle, U.S.M.C.* was promoting war during a period where the Vietnam War was becoming increasingly unpopular. In other words, *Hogan's Heroes* wasn't treating the war with respect, while *Gomer Pyle, U.S.M.C.* was too respectful toward the military. As an aside, with both shows on CBS, it perhaps shows that the network could court controversy (maybe not that well, as the censorship problems of the Smothers Brothers going on in the late 1960s would contest, but at least they could stand their ground when they wanted).

Gomer Pyle, U.S.M.C. was a spin-off series from *The Andy Griffith Show*, where Gomer was a simple farm boy who ran a gas station and never lost his innocence (even when in the Marines). The series was different in that Pyle was not the typical military comedy showing a con artist trying to get the better of his superiors in the military, but mainly someone so good-natured that good karma seemed to follow him everywhere, leading him to the right decisions. In many ways, it was similar to *No Time for Sergeants*, which was about a young man from the backwoods who may have sounded uneducated, but proved himself smarter in many ways than those around him in the military (and which helped to bring Andy Griffith to national attention in the Broadway and movie versions of the novel it is based; also look for Jamie Farr and William Christopher in small roles in the film). Gomer was usually placed up against his sergeant, Vince Carter (Frank Sutton), although at heart Carter knew Pyle was a good man and a good Marine. *Gomer Pyle, U.S.M.C.* also could veer into dramatic moments—never about the ongoing war, but rather on a more emotional level (like a two-parter crossover with *The Andy Griffith Show*, where Opie runs away from home and joins Gomer at the base). Certainly an element that would pass over to *MASH* as well (not to mention itself also being controversy for the way it treated a war).

Three individuals, Lee Philips, Alan Rafkin, and John Erman, all directed one to five episodes for each series. Six writers would work on both shows as well, with Bill Idelson, Rick Mittleman, Carl Kleinschmitt, and Richard Powell—a few of whom had worked on earlier series mentioned in this chapter—writing a total of fifty-four episodes for *Gomer Pyle, U.S.M.C.*, and six between them for *MASH*. On the other hand, James Fritzell and Everett Greenbaum wrote one episode of *Gomer Pyle, U.S.M.C.* together, but would go on to write twenty-four episodes together of *MASH*, including the episodes that see the last of Henry Blake and introduce BJ, Potter, and Winchester. Fritzell was also the creator of *The Doris Day Show*, which costarred McLean Stevenson. Earle Hagen, who wrote music for *Gomer Pyle, U.S.M.C.* (and *The Dick Van Dyke Show*), wrote incidental music for the *MASH* episode "Captain Pierce and Mr. Hyde."

Thirty actors worked on both series. Buck Young again appeared in a series, this time with ten episodes in various roles on *Gomer Pyle, U.S.M.C.* Yuki Shimoda, who was mentioned much earlier in this chapter, reappeared in *Gomer Pyle, U.S.M.C.* for one role. George Lindsey, who played a memorable one-off role on *MASH* as the temporarily assigned Captain Roy Dupree ("Temporary Duty"), was—of course—Goober on *The Andy Griffith Show* and also appeared a couple of times on *Gomer Pyle, U.S.M.C.* Pat Morita, who many remember from *Happy Days*, appeared only once on *Gomer Pyle, U.S.M.C.*, but had what was looking to be a semiregular role on *MASH* for two separate episodes before disappearing. Eldon Quick, who played the bureaucratic Captain Sloan in three episodes of *MASH* ("The Late Captain Pierce," for example) appeared in one episode of *Gomer Pyle, U.S.M.C.* Also appearing once was Wayne Rogers, who would go on to play Trapper John for the first three years of *MASH*. Jamie Farr would appear twice on *Gomer Pyle, U.S.M.C.* William Christopher remains the champ for the regular cast of *MASH*, appearing in fifteen episodes of *Gomer Pyle, U.S.M.C.* and nearly all of them as the same character—Private Lester Hummel.

Thus, the connections were there. The people who worked on one or more of these shows can be seen as slowly starting to tie together into what will become *MASH*. Perhaps most important was that cast and crew from all these shows merged into one and said, "Let's not do a show like *these* shows."

So with the past behind them, the time was ripe to begin looking into the future for the television version of *MASH*. The future of 1970.

15

If I Can't Get the Girl

The Creative Team Behind the Series

The television series adaptation of *MASH* would last for eleven seasons—from September 17, 1972, through February 28, 1983. In that time, the show grew from what started as a smarter version of television military comedies that had come before it to one that shaped how many comedy and dramatic series would be done in the future. The characters would move from a core group of six characters (Hawkeye, Trapper John, Hot Lips, Frank, Henry, and Radar) and slowly involve additional ones until those in minor roles were given more to do and major characters could be replaced in a natural manner with new characters that won over audiences.

In television, it is not very common for those who initially put a show together to stay with it in a central role for a certain length of time before moving onward. If a program is lucky enough to stick around for a few years, such individuals may be ready to leave the show to others who they know will have the show's best interest at heart. At least, that's the pleasant way it is sometimes done. In most cases, people just get bored, want more money, and/or have a chance to move on and try other things. Just like any job, after a while, it's nice to do something a little different, especially for those in a creative field. Additionally if it means that people want to pay you more.

Thus is the case with *MASH*. Just as certain actors left and new ones came in to help shape the series in their own ways, so too did producers, directors, script consultants, and writers behind the scenes. That said, *MASH* was a series that found most if not all those involved happy to be there for the time period that they were. As for the fans, however, sometimes it is hard to remember who was around when and what else they have done before and after *MASH*. For example, as much as Larry Gelbart helped develop it for television, he was only there for the first four years of the show (a fact Gelbart himself usually pointed out to interviewers so as not to take any glory away from those who came after him), but many viewers—if they note the existence of anyone behind the scenes at all—would see his name popping up in later episodes (due to his "developed for television" notice in the ending credits of each episode) and assume he was the mastermind from Day One.

But that wasn't the case. In fact, he wasn't even there when the concept of turning the novel and film into a series was discussed.

William E. Self (1921–2010)

William Self had been an actor when he first arrived in Los Angeles, and had appeared as an extra in *Battle Circus* (see chapter 12 for more details as to why that's of interest) when he decided to move to behind the camera as producer for *Schlitz Playhouse of Stars*. In 1957, he would work as a program executive at CBS before moving on to run the television division of 20th Century-Fox in 1959. Self would be involved in a number of hit television series for the studio, with a particular interest in taking popular films and transforming them into shows that would run for a good number of years each, such as *Voyage to the Bottom of the Sea* and *Peyton Place*.

In 1970, he decided to run a yet-to-be-released 20th Century-Fox movie for a few friends, picking *MASH* after hearing Dick Zanuck rave about the film. Much like Ring Lardner Jr. when he first read the novel and envisioned a film, Self finished watching the movie and thinking it was a perfect candidate for television. He also knew that 20th Century-Fox had left the outdoor set standing at the Fox Ranch, and that most of the props were readily available, so the cost of making the show would be on the cheap. He immediately contacted Zanuck about television rights to *MASH*, but was informed that the studio was set to turn the sequel novel into a film, and thus television rights would be a few years in coming.

When that sequel film notion died, however, Zanuck contacted Self to see if he was still interested. Self grabbed at the chance and began contacting the networks. As a former network man and head of 20th Century-Fox Television, Self was well respected and known for producing shows that had healthy ratings. Yet Self wanted more than the standard commitment that was made for shows at the time (and used today) of agreeing only to read a script for a new show. If the network liked the script, they would okay a pilot (a test episode that commonly would introduce the characters, etc. of the program). Then, if that went over well enough, they would okay the show to "go to series," and x-number of episodes would be made to be put on the network schedule.

Self wanted more than just a script okay; he wanted a firm offer of being able to do a pilot rather than having to get an okay on a script first. CBS Vice President of Programming Alan Wagner was surprised that someone would want to turn *MASH* into a television series. As he told Allan Neuwirth in *They'll Never Put That on the Air: An Oral History of Taboo-Breaking TV Comedy*, "You'd had *Gomer Pyle, Hogan's Heroes*, things that really were farcical. Not a show that took the problems of people who were facing death." Even so, he was intrigued by the idea, and CBS agreed to Self's terms, as did ABC. Self had to choose between the two networks, but had a history with CBS, and had recently run into issues with ABC over *Room 222*—a series dealing with issues at a high school—due to it becoming less of a comedy than a dramatic series. Things had gotten so negative at ABC about the program that they forced the producer out in 1971. Self saw that *MASH* at its heart was a comedy in spite of its drama, and if the dramatic moments were to be taken away, the show would no longer reflect what brought people to it in the first place; the film and even the novel had moments that were not played for laughs. Self went with CBS and got an agreement to go straight to pilot on the program. So he immediately turned to a writer/producer at 20th Century-Fox, Anthony Wilson.

Anthony Wilson (1926–1978) had written for television since the early 1960s, including episodes of *The Twilight Zone*, *The Fugitive*, *The Addams Family*, and even Robert Altman's old stomping grounds, *Combat!* He had moved up to being a story editor on *Lost in Space* and a consultant on *Lancer* and had just completed a year on *The Immortal* (a series about a man with a rare blood type that allows him to live forever on the run from others) when Self asked him to develop *MASH* for television. Wilson was uncertain how they could put together a show using the same characters when the actors in the movie were so good. As Self told Ed Solomon and Mark O'Neill in their book *TV's MASH: The Ultimate Guide Book*, "A few days later, Tony came to me with his solution to the problem. He had decided that there were no many great characters in the book that our TV version wouldn't use any of the characters from the movie." Knowing that wouldn't work, Self parted ways with Wilson and began looking for someone else to help get *MASH* ready for television.

After *MASH*

In 1974, Self left 20th Century-Fox in order to go back to producing films (including John Wayne's last film, *The Shootist*), then went back to CBS as

Vice President Head of the West Coast and later as Vice President in Charge of Movies and Miniseries. In 1982, he was the president of CBS Theatrical Film Division. In 1985, he went solo to produce television films including *Sarah, Plain and Tall* (1991) before finally retiring.

Gene Reynolds

With Wilson gone, Self started thinking of someone else who could help get the ball rolling on the pilot. As it turns out, the producer that ABC just axed from *Room 222*, Gene Reynolds, was available. He appeared to be an ideal fit for the job.

Reynolds was born in Cleveland, Ohio, in 1923 (another Ohio boy—Self was born in Dayton), but grew up in Detroit for the first ten years of his life, where he was already bitten by the acting bug after performing in commercials for radio as a child. In the early 1930s, his family moved to Los Angeles, where he worked as an extra in *Babes in Toyland* and a handful of *Our Gang* comedies. As he got older, he began getting more movie parts, leading to a career in television. In 1958, Reynolds began his move behind the camera, becoming a casting director for *Peter Gunn* and *Steve Canyon*. He would also be involved on the creative end as writer and one-off director for the western series *Tales of Wells Fargo* (1957–1962), starring Dale Robertson, along with co-creator James Brooks (who would go on to work on many other series with Reynolds and help created *The Mary Tyler Moore Show*, *The Simpsons*, and *Taxi*). *Tales of Wells Fargo* would first appears as part of the *Schlitz Playhouse of the Stars*, which William Self was doing at the time. He soon would be directing a number of different programs, mostly sitcoms through the 1960s, including three episodes of the series *Hennesey* (1959–1962), which starred Jackie Cooper, the former *Little Rascals* child actor who would go on to direct thirteen episodes of *MASH* in its first and second season. In 1968, he and James Brooks would create the series *Room 222*, for which Reynolds would produce as well as direct some episodes. With an emphasis on drama more than comedy—including losing a laugh track after the first season—ABC asked that Reynolds be fired.

Self, knowing that Reynolds could produce a comedy show that leaned toward drama, and that Reynolds had worked on other military comedies before (see last chapter for more details), believed Gene Reynolds would be a good person for the job. Reynolds accepted and immediatcly got in touch with Ring Lardner Jr. to see if he would be interested in helping. Lardner, busy with another project, turned it down, but suggested Reynolds get in touch with Ian Hunter (who, besides writing scripts on his own, had worked as a front for Lardner and Dalton Trumbo during the blacklist). Reynolds instead had an old friend in mind, Larry Gelbart.

After MASH

Reynolds would stay with *MASH* as a writer and director, as well as producer and then executive producer until 1977. As Reynolds told Tom Goldrup in his book *Growing Up on the Set: Interviews with 39 Former Child Actors of Classic Film and Television* (2002. Jefferson, North Carolina, McFarland.), "Then I had money problems with Fox. I had a percentage of the show that they beat me out of—a very unorthodox, very dishonest manipulation. At any rate, they worked me over, so I got sore at Fox." While remaining a creative consultant on *MASH*, Reynolds moved directly from it to work on James Brooks' follow-up to *The Mary Tyler Moore Show*, *Lou Grant*. From there, Reynolds slowed down, doing an occasional directing job here and there as well as producing.

Larry Gelbart (1928–2009)

As it happens, Gelbart was getting fed up. He had been in England for years at that point and was now finding himself quickly being backed into a corner with the series he was doing in 1970.

Born in Chicago, Gelbart moved to California with his family in his teen years. His first venture into writing comedy came when his father, a barber who cut comedian Danny Thomas' hair, gave Thomas some of his son's jokes. From there, Gelbart began writing for Thomas and then later for Bob Hope—including a tour of Korea during the Korean War, where Gelbart and other writers wrote topical humor for Hope to use in his USO shows. In 1954, Gelbart began writing for Sid Caesar on his post-*Your Show of Shows* program, *Caesar's Hour*. The program included such writers as Mel Tolkin, Mel Brooks, Carl Reiner, Selma Diamond, and Neil and Danny Simon.

Gelbart would continue to work for various television programming and began to dabble in the theater when he got a chance to help put together a musical-comedy that would become *A Funny Thing Happened on the Way to the Forum*. The musical would be a smash, and in 1963, Gelbart moved to England to work on the production of it over there. He would remain for years, while writing for shows on both sides of the ocean (as well as the

Larry Gelbart, the comedy genius who would help reshape *MASH* into the television success that it would become.

Peter Cook-Dudley Moore-Michael Caine comedy *The Wrong Box* with Burt Shevelove in 1966).

Working with ATV, Gelbart became the producer of a fourteen-episode comedy series called *The Marty Feldman Comedy Machine*. The concept was to create a British show for comedian Marty Feldman that would play in America, thus leading to Gelbart's involvement, as he knew television from both sides of the waters. The series, featuring writing from Gelbart, Barry Levinson, Spike Milligan, Tim Brooke-Taylor, and Feldman, had moments (including opening credits done by Terry Gilliam of *Monty Python* fame), but Gelbart was rapidly losing faith in the product. Feldman was going through a phase of excessive partying that was leading to bodily injuries that slowed down production. Feldman also had a tendency to muck with the writing at times, trying to rewrite material after he got bored by it in rehearsal, and thus sometimes making results that were not as funny as originally conceived.

While working on the show, Gene Reynolds contacted Gelbart about doing the pilot script for *MASH*. Gelbart was interested but unsure, "If they want another *Hogan's Heroes*—which was one too many *Hogan's Heroes*—*McHale's Navy*, then no," Gelbart remembered telling Reynolds on the phone. Still, it intrigued him, as Gelbart had been to Korea during the war, thanks to his time with Bob Hope, so felt he had a better handle on the topic than many other writers that could be asked to do it. Reynolds went over to England and spent several days talking with Gelbart during breaks on the Feldman program in order to see what they could come up with for the script. Looking at the film and reading the novel again, the two noted that both avoided saying anything about the war itself, and thus seemed to give the impression that it was all fun and games—something they felt they could address in their version of *MASH*. Eventually they threw together enough ideas that they had the concept of the pilot in hand—that of a raffle for Lieutenant Dish in order to raise money for Ho-Jon's trip to America to go to college. They called Alan Wagner at CBS with the pitch for the pilot, and Wagner told them to go ahead and get a script ready.

Then Gelbart went back to working on the Feldman show and completely forgot about the *MASH* project. Two months later, he got a call from Reynolds asking about the script, and Gelbart told him that it was in the mail. Gelbart then went home and wrote it. Having thought about the project so long and having fleshed it out, as well as having the movie set (which would be used in the show) fresh in his mind, he felt comfortable in taking only a day and a half to complete the script and mailed it off to Reynolds in November 1971. The script was almost immediately approved and the pilot could go forward for filming that December. Reynolds and Gelbart then needed to cast the show, and the next important figure in the series' history would soon be added, Burt Metcalfe.

After *MASH*

Gelbart would remain with the program until after the fourth season (the first with both Potter and BJ) as producer, as well as the executive script consultant during its first season, and—as many fans know—always listed as having "developed for television" the series. He would write the script for *Oh, God!* (1977 and directed by Carl Reiner) and the cult classic *Movie Movie* (1978) before making the dramatic comedy series *United States* in 1980 (considered an early experiment in what would be called "dramedies" later in the decade). After screenplay credits for *Tootsie* (1982) and *Neighbors* (1981), Gelbart would come back to work on the series *After MASH* (1983–1984), and then find renewed success with his script for the HBO movie *Barbarians at the Gate* (1993). His last film would be for television, *And Starring Pancho Villa as Himself* (2003).

Burt Metcalfe

Born in Saskatchewan, Canada, in 1935, Burt Metcalfe began acting as a youngster and eventually found himself working in television in the mid-1950s, including an episode of *Steve Canyon* that had Gene Reynolds as a casting supervisor. Appearing on such shows as *The Twilight Zone* and *The Outer Limits*, Metcalfe was also a regular on *Father of the Bride* (1961–1962). After appearing on *Perry Mason* three times and a recurring role on *12 O'Clock High* (1964–1965), Metcalfe turned to becoming a casting director, working on both *Bewitched* and *Here Come the Brides*. It was this background that helped land him the job as associate producer on *MASH*, with him and Reynolds choosing the cast while Gelbart was working to get back to the States to help run the show. (Reynolds also asked Metcalfe to cast a half-hour series with Yul Brynner that was based on *The King and I* called *Anna and the King*—and which aired on CBS right before *MASH* for a half season in 1972.) We'll return to this series a couple more times in this book.

When Gelbart left, Metcalfe would sign on as a full producer on the show, and then executive producer after Reynolds left. As it turns out, Reynolds had asked Metcalfe to join him in moving over to *Lou Grant*, but CBS had offered Metcalfe the chance to run *MASH* on his own. While he worried about moving out of his comfort zone as a second to Reynolds—as well fearing he would be known as the man who "presided over the demise of *MASH*"—he decided he needed to break out on his own. Metcalfe would also write a handful of episodes and direct thirty-one through the years. Of all the behind-the-scenes people, Metcalfe would be the only one to be there essentially from Day One until the final episode was over. For the moment in 1971, the trinity of Reynolds-Gelbart-Metcalfe would gather to fine-tune the pilot for filming, interview doctors and nurses who had been in MASH units during the war in order to authenticate stories for the series, and begin pulling together the cast that would launch the program (and more about that cast in the next chapter).

Burt Metcalfe, Alan Alda, Loretta Swit, and Harry Morgan, would be there for the series from nearly Day One straight on through the finale.

After *MASH*

Metcalfe would continue with *After MASH* as an executive producer and director of thirteen episodes. He did some directing as well as produce a comedy series about a barber shop called *Cutters* in 1993.

Producers

Although Burt Metcalfe would stay the entire run of the series, it is not as if the program suddenly became a one-man effort after Reynolds and Gelbart left. Additional producers would join over time, many of whom had been story consultants or editors before becoming producers. Some would stay only a season, while a few would stick it out until the end of the series.

Allan Katz and Don Reo

These two writers came in as a team to help produce *MASH* in the fifth season, after Larry Gelbart left the series. Don Reo had first worked on the *Jimmy Durante Presents the Lennon Sisters* series in 1969–1970, before joining Allan Katz on *Rowan & Martin's Laugh-In* as part of the stable of writers working on the show in its last few seasons. The pair would occasionally work separately, but mainly worked as a duo on scripts for *All in the Family*, *Sanford and Son*, and *The Mary Tyler Moore Show*. The two would also co-head and produce episodes of Cher's variety series in 1975.

This would lead directly to their work on *MASH*, where they also wrote two episodes for the series ("Movie Night" and "The Abduction of Margaret Houlihan"). They would leave the series after the one season to do similar duties on a season of the series *Rhoda*. After that, the two would break off to work on an assortment of other series, before reteaming as executive producers on *Blossom*. Don Reo would also produce *The John Larroquette Show* (1993–1996), the cult favorite *Action* (1999–2000), *Everybody Hates Chris* (2007–2009), and the final seasons of *Two and a Half Men* (2011–2015).

Stanford Tischler (1921–2014)

An editor who had worked on *Schlitz Playhouse* and *Tales of Wells Fargo* would eventually edit 239 episodes of *MASH*, including the pilot and the finale. He would also edit the Radar pilot, *W*A*L*T*E*R*, and eight episodes of *After MASH*. He became an associate producer on *MASH* from 1977–1983 and did the same function for the episodes of *After MASH*.

John Rappaport

John Rappaport also was a writer on *Rowan & Martin's Laugh-In*, from 1969 to 1971. He would write episodes of *The Bob Newhart Show, The Odd Couple,* and *All in the Family* before signing on as a writer and producer for *MASH* in 1979. His first script was "Period of Adjustment" in season eight (the first episode after Radar left the series). He would contribute to the finale in 1983. He remained a producer until 1981, and then became a supervising producer from 1981 to 1983.

Rappaport was executive producer on *Gung Ho* (1986–1987), based on the popular comedy film. He was also a creative consultant on *Night Court* for a season.

Jim Mulligan

Jim Mulligan was another *Rowan & Martin's Laugh-In* writer, working on that program from 1967 to 1971. He also wrote scripts for the Filmation cartoon series *Sabrina and the Groovie Goolies* and *Will the Real Jerry Lewis Please Sit Down* before that. More variety work followed with *The Sonny and Cher Show* (1973–1974) and *The Jacksons* (1976–1977), amongst other shows. He also wrote the pilot and was the producer for *In the Beginning* (1978), a short-lived series for a post-*MASH* McLean Stevenson.

Mulligan was one of the producers of season eight of *MASH*, where he would cowrite "Period of Adjustment" with John Rappaport, and write two other episodes. He moved on to writer for a few other shows, including one episode of *Trapper John, M.D.* in 1984.

Dan Wilcox, Dennis Koenig, and Thad Mumford

All three writers jumped on-board *MASH* as executive story editors in 1979. Dan Wilcox and Thad Mumford eventually became story consultants. The three moved together into the role of producers in 1981, with Wilcox and Mumford sticking it out until the finale, while Koenig moved on after the tenth season.

Thad Mumford's career stretches just a bit further back than the other two, starting with writing on the PBS children's series *The Electric Company*. In 1974, Thad worked on a script with Dan Wilcox for the sadly short-lived ABC comedy *That's My Mama* ("Clifton's Con"), and they would begin writing off and on together, including four episodes of *The Waverly Wonders*

(1978), *Roots: The Next Generation, Angie,* and *Alice.* The pair would then move on to write seventeen episodes of *MASH,* starting in 1979 with the script "Are You Now, Margaret?" After their run on *MASH,* they would write an episode of *Bay City Blues* together in 1983 before going in their own directions. Dan Wilcox would write and produce for *Newhart, Growing Pains,* and cocreate the series *FM,* which Burt Metcalfe was briefly involved with as well. Thad Mumford would produce a season of *Alf* and work as a supervising producer for one season and co-executive producer for two seasons on *A Different World,* as well as writing eleven episodes. Mumford would then go on to write for such series as *Roc, NYPD Blues,* and *Judging Amy.*

Dennis Koenig also worked on an episode with Dan Wilcox and Thad Mumford for *The Waverly Wonders* before joining *MASH* as a writer and story editor in the 1979–1980 season with the other two. He would become a producer on the show for the 1981–1982 season and then move on, but would contribute one more episode to the final season of *MASH* as well ("Give and Take"). Koenig also contributed scripts for *Rhoda, Barney Miller, Night Court* (on which he was also executive story editor for two seasons), and *Anything but Love,* which he helped develop. Koenig would also produce *After MASH* and write ten episodes for the series.

Production

Most fans will have noted Mark Evans' name in the credits for the series over the years. That's no surprise, as he would work on 250 episodes of the program, so it was hard not to notice his name flying by on the screen with those freeze-frames from the episode. That said, many may not really understand what Evans' job was on the show. Both a production manager and production supervisor are there to make sure that a program is scheduled and completed on time and within the budget. In other words, the production manager is there to make sure everyone stays on track so that plans for filming are not too extravagant, and that everyone completes their work to avoid additional costs. Joining Evans for much of this was Joseph Silvers, who worked on 227 episodes as a production supervisor and post-production supervisor and executive in charge of production. Because such individuals were working mainly for the studio to make sure producers were not flying off the rails, they tended to work on a number of shows at once (but, to be fair, were usually working as much to get the producers what they wanted as making sure they didn't spend like crazy).

Mark Evans (1915–1993)

Mark Evans started his career as an assistant director for movies back in the early 1940s before moving on to television in the same role in such shows as *Dragnet* and *The Real McCoys*. In the mid-1960s, he would move on to becoming a unit production manager at 20th Century-Fox, working on *The Green Hornet* and *Judd for the Defense* before performing the same role in the first year of *MASH*. He would advance to become the production supervisor for seasons two through four, and then executive production manager from seasons five through eleven. He would also function as such for the Radar pilot, *W*A*L*T*E*R*, and *After Mash*. Other series he was involved in a similar function were *Planet of the Apes* (the television series), *The Paper Chase*, *The Fall Guy*, *Trapper John, M.D.*, and *L.A. Law*.

Joseph Silver

Joseph Silver became an editor in the 1950s, working on a variety of mostly westerns, including *The Adventures of Rin Tin Tin*, *Circus Boy*, *Bat Masterson*, and programs like *Men into Space* and *Julia*. After working as an assistant to the producer and then as an associate producer on *Daniel Boone* (1965–1970), he would move into production as a supervisor in the 1970s, working on *MASH* and several of the same shows Mark Evans was associated with.

Medical Consultants

Just like the movie before it, those working on the television series wanted to make sure that the procedures discussed and seen on the program at least made sense to those who would know better. Typically, this meant someone calling a doctor friend for a quick resolution that would work for a script, but in cases of programs that dealt so heavily with medical needs and practices, it was obvious to have someone the writers could turn to when help was needed, as well as to read the scripts (and sometimes be there on the set) to make sure things were being said and done in a correct manner. For a show like *MASH*, such a specialist would also have to make sure that the characters did not perform or discuss procedures that had not been invented yet.

Essentially, the writers would write a script, knowing how they wanted an operation or disease to go with a character, but not the best way to make that work. The script would leave space (sometimes in clever ways) in the dialogue and actions for the medical advisor to review and then pitch in with his or her thoughts as to what should be said and done. In the case of *MASH*, a nurse would also be on-set to make sure no one handled the instruments like . . . well, like an actor.

In some such cases, it was not unusual for the doctors to get the bug and contribute in other ways to a show as well, as was the case with the first advisor listed below.

Walter D. Dishell

Dishell, an otolaryngologist (ears, nose, and throat doctor for those of us who can't untie their tongue long enough to say the real name) specializing in plastic surgery (well, it is Hollywood), first began working with the studios back in the late 1960s as a medical advisor on the program *Medical Center*, where he also appeared in one episode as an assistant surgeon. He would be the regular advisor for *MASH*, working on 251 episodes and doing such an extensive job on the episode "Life Time" (discussed in chapter 24) that he is listed as cowriter with Alan Alda. He would also work as an advisor on *House Calls*, *Knots Landing*, *After MASH*, and *Trapper John, M.D.*

For the finale of the series, due to the intricate plot dealing with Hawkeye's breakdown, Dr. Michael J. Gitlin, a professor of clinical psychiatry at the UCLA School of Medicine, and Dr. Robert S. Pynoos, a psychiatrist out of UCLA's Neuropsychiatric Hospital, helped as advisors as well.

Additional Consultants

Most of the additional consultants were also those who wrote episodes for the series or had other involvements that were so extensive, it was understandable for these people to be able to add their voices to the creation of episodes for the series. Many worked as script consultants, or executive script consultants, such as Laurence Marks (twenty-four episodes, with Larry Gelbart as executive script consultant in the first season of the program); Jay Folb (seasons four and five); David Isaacs and Ken Levine as both consultants and story editor (seasons five and six); Ronny Graham as a consultant for both stories and the program (seasons five and six); Larry Balmagia as story editor (season six); Elias Davis (season ten); David Pollock (season ten); and Karen Hall as story editor and then executive story consultant for seasons ten and eleven).

And some guy named Alan Alda would be a creative consultant from season six through eleven. But more about him in the next chapter.

16

We Tried to Get Pat O'Brien

The Main Cast Over the Years

W hen Burt Metcalfe was made the casting director for the series at the pilot stage, it was partially due to Gene Reynolds and Larry Gelbart needing to free up their time to finish other projects. In fact, Gelbart arrived only in time to try to convince one actor to take a role, as all the other characters had been cast while he was still in England settling up accounts with the Marty Feldman show. But more importantly, Reynolds knew that Metcalfe would find the people needed for the job. He would be the one to decide who should be added to play all of the major regular cast members, up through the final change of Major Charles Emerson Winchester in season six.

As mentioned in chapter 15, a series dealing with a military medical camp during a war that runs eleven seasons is bound to cast a lot of actors over that period. Hundreds. The list on the Internet Movie Database (imdb.com) goes on for more than seven hundred lines, each describing another actor who played at least one role (sometimes more) on the program. Some characters would be introduced early on that eventually vanished without fanfare; others would manage to stick around for many years and be given a line or two. In some cases, certain actors who appeared on *MASH* would go on to further fame (or at least in one case, to renewed popularity). Actors who fall into these categories will be covered in subsequent chapters. Instead here, the focus is on the original six regular characters, then a seventh, an eighth, and subsequently, replacements for three of the originals.

MASH did have the luxury of being able to drop characters and add new ones easily thanks to the idea that people were bound to go home at some point—or attempt to and die as in the case of Henry Blake. What is fascinating is that usually when shows, especially comedy shows, attempt to eliminate one character and bring in a new one, viewership falters. A new character usually fails due to the production side of the show being too self-conscious of what to do with a new characters. Too close and viewers will think it's a poor carbon copy of the original. Too opposite and it looks like the show is trying too hard. Referencing the old character in an attempt to compare (which, admittedly, *MASH* did a bit with Colonel Potter when first introduced) and people may long too much for the previous character. *MASH* avoided this with characters who evolved in ways that made them different, BJ being the best representation of the three that would eventually join, as he had a personality that was vastly different from Trapper John. Potter was essentially a steadier version of his one-shot character, the crazed General Steele from "The General Flipped at Dawn" in season three, but more inclined to try to steer the others into doing things the military way, while giving them rope to be a bit freer due to many of the doctors not being regular army (as was the case with most commanding officers of MASH units during the war). Winchester was the most obvious in being an attempt to create someone totally the opposite of the character being replaced, the sniveling and mediocre doctor hitting on Margaret, Frank Burns, which only partially worked as Winchester was a sniveling and better doctor who was hitting on Margaret (at least in the character's first season). His character would take longer to evolve, but came into his own as time went by.

Yet none of this would matter if the cast really had not come together under the guidance of Metcalfe, Reynolds, and Gelbart in the beginning. As it was, the actor most associated with the show was close to being the last one cast.

Captain Benjamin Franklin "Hawkeye" Pierce (age 28)— Alan Alda (age 35 at time of pilot)

Alan Alda was not the first actor to eye the role of Hawkeye. In fact, two other cast members campaigned to take on the role.

But more about that later on.

Alphonso Joseph D'Abruzzo was born on January 28, 1936, to Joan and Robert Alda in New York City. His father, Robert Alda, had started as a singer-dancer, working his way through vaudeville and burlesque and taking his young son with him on the road. Later, Alan became interested in writing, which would eventually lead to earning a bachelor of arts degree

Alan Alda in his first hit success—as the lead with Diana Sands in the Broadway hit *The Owl and the Pussycat* (1964–1965).
Used courtesy of Playbill

in English from Fordham University in New York. Even so, as Alda told *TV Guide* in 1977, "I wanted to be an actor for a simple reason—my father was."

After serving in the army for a year and a half, Alda reentered the civilian world by joining the Compass Players in the 1950s (Roger Bowen, Colonel Blake of the movie, was also a member for a time), and would make his first television appearance as a young artist looking to break through in an episode of *The Phil Silvers Show* in 1958. By 1959, he was starting to work on Broadway, first in a play called *Only in America*, and beginning to rise through the ranks of players with his turn in the comedy *Purlie Victorious* (written by Ossie Davis), which was eventually turned into a movie (also known as *Gone Are the Days!*) in 1963 with Alda in the same role he played on Broadway. His breakthrough came with obtaining the lead in the comedy

The Owl and the Pussycat, which ran for a year (1964–1965). The play, by Bill Manhoff, dealing with a writer who shares an apartment with a prostitute and their growing admiration for each other, was somewhat controversial due to the prostitute being played by Diana Sands, an African American woman, making their growing romance a biracial one (this aspect was jettisoned from the eventual movie adaptation with Barbra Streisand).

The Owl and the Pussycat led to a lead role in the comedy *The Apple Tree* for a year. In the meantime, Alda would make occasional guest star appearances on various television shows. His first lead role in a movie was playing writer George Plimpton in the adaptation of his *Sports Illustrated* article about posing as a quarterback for the Detroit Lions. The film *Paper Lion* (1968) would find Alda working with a cast full of real-life football players (including Alex Karras, who would later appear in an early role on *MASH* as a soldier who becomes Hawkeye's bodyguard and servant after saving his life). It was rough work, with Alda explaining in his autobiography *Never Have Your Dog Stuffed*, "In one scene, eleven of them piled on top of me, and when I finally got up, I had been kicked in the ankle so many times, my left foot was asleep, and it stayed that way for half an hour."

He also worked on a film called *The Extraordinary Seaman*, which costarred David Niven, Mickey Rooney, and Faye Dunaway, as well as directed by John Frankenheimer. It would go on to be listed in *The Golden Turkey Awards* by Harry and Michael Medved as one of the "Worst Films You Never Saw" due to being held back for two years before quickly being released and forgotten. Alda would continue making films, including *Jenny* (1970, with Marlo Thomas, whom he would work with on her award-winning TV special *Free to Be . . . You and Me* in 1974), *The Moonshine War* (1970, and costarring Teri Garr, who would make an appearance as a nurse on *MASH* in season two, "The Sniper"), the supernatural thriller *The Mephisto Waltz* (1971), and the misfired psychological thriller *To Kill a Clown* (1972, with Blythe Danner, who would appear on *MASH* as Hawkeye's former love, Carlye, in "The More I See You"). He would also make the 1972 television comedy film *Playmates*, featuring Roger Bowen in a small role. Then he worked on the controversial made-for-television film *The Glass House* (1972), costarring Vic Morrow and Billy Dee Williams, which dealt with prison life and contains a brutal gang rape scene as well as a suicide.

It was while making *The Glass House* that Alda got the script for the *MASH* pilot. Alda was hesitant, even though he felt the script was excellent. He had been married for a few years by this point, with his wife and daughters living in New Jersey; a series would mean possibly uprooting the family to California or him being separated from his family during filming (Alda would go with the second choice, commuting every weekend to his family in New Jersey). He was also worried that a pilot script could only convey the pilot and not the series. Alda asked to meet with Gene Reynolds and Larry Gelbart at the Beverly Wilshire Hotel coffee shop the night before rehearsals were to begin to discuss the show. "What Alda was saying was," Reynolds remembered in the book *They'll Never Put That on the Air*, "'I don't want to do *McHale's Navy*. I don't want it to be one of these jerkoff things. The pilot is very good, but are you gonna stick with it? What's it going to be?" After talking for hours, all three agreed that the show needed to avoid falling into the standards of the military comedies that had come before it, even though some of them were classics in their own way. It had to be about people facing the ugliness of the war and struggling to stay sane.

By the time they were finished, Alda had agreed to sign on. In December 1971, the cast and crew would be filming the pilot at 20th Century-Fox and the remaining set still standing at the Fox Ranch in Malibu Creek. After the series was picked up, CBS insisted that the program stay "viewer-friendly" by avoiding dramatic topic and direct links to the ongoing Vietnam War. All connected to the show were hesitant, but they finally reached a compromise where the first season would feature a heavy mix of less serious scripts, and they would evolve from there once a viewership was established. Even so, Alda and the others were relieved to see the show moving away from some earlier episodes that hinted at a backslide into *Sgt. Bilko* territory, and before the first season was out, he had written his first script for the series, "The Longjohn Flap." Over time, Alda would write/cowrite nineteen episodes for the series, most of a psychological nature and which dealt with Hawkeye learning a bit about himself: "Dr. Pierce and Mr. Hyde" (Hawkeye unable to sleep and deciding to deliver a latrine to North Korea), "Fallen Idol" (Hawkeye's guilt over Radar getting hurt, leading to a new awareness between them), "Comrades in Arms" (Hawkeye and Margaret avoiding the enemy and having a brief affair), "Inga" (Hawkeye being shown up by a Swedish female doctor and learning to accept that women can be as smart or smarter than him), "Dreams" (featuring Hawkeye dreaming about being unable to save everyone), "Hey, Look Me Over" (Nurse Kellye showing Hawkeye to get beyond looks when it came to women), and of course the finale, "Goodbye, Farewell, and Amen" (Hawkeye's final breakdown).

With season two's "Mail Call" episode, Alda would also work as director on the series, leading to him directing thirty-one episodes (including the finale). While starring—Alda would be the only actor to appear in every single episode of *MASH*—directing, and scripting on the series between 1972–1983, Alda would also create the series *We'll Get By* (a comedy about a family living in New Jersey), star in *Kill Me If You Can* (1977), *Same Time Next Year* (1978), and *California Suite* (1979), and write and direct both *The Seduction of Joe Tynan* (1979, with a young Meryl Streep and his former *The Apple Tree* co-star, Barbara Harris) and *The Four Seasons* (1981).

After MASH

Alda would write and direct *Sweet Liberty* (1986), *A New Life* (1988), and *Betsy's Wedding* (1990), while appearing in three Woody Allen films, *Crimes and Misdemeanors* (1989), *Manhattan Murder Mystery* (1993), and *Everyone Says I Love You* (1996). He would appear as the villainous Senator Brewster in Martin Scorsese's *The Aviator* (2004), appear five times in the series *ER* (1999), as Senator Vinick in twenty-eight episodes of *The West Wing* (2004–2006), and three episode of *30 Rock* (where he famously made fun of the "Chicken/Baby" storyline from the *MASH* finale).

Alda would also return to the theater, starring in Neil Simon's *Jake's Women* in 1992, which he would reprise for a 1996 movie adaptation, the one-man show *QED* (2001–2002), and revivals of *Glengarry Glen Ross* (2005) and *Love Letters* (2014, with Mia Farrow). He would also host the PBS series *Scientific American Frontiers* from 1993 through 2005. He also has been involved with feminist projects over the years, including work on the Equal Rights Amendment. Alda has been nominated over fifty times for various awards—including an Academy Award nomination for his role in *The Aviator* (2004)—and won over thirty, many of which were for *MASH* (including from the Directors Guild of America, Emmy Awards, and the Writers Guild of America). He has written two books about his life and thoughts: *Never Have Your Dog Stuffed* (2005) and *Things I Overheard While Talking to Myself* (2008).

Captain John Francis Xavier "Trapper John" McIntyre (age 28)—Wayne Rogers (age 38 at time of pilot)

Wayne Rogers had tested for the part of Hawkeye. As it stood, if Alan Alda had turned down the role, Rogers was set to take it and someone else would play Trapper. But whatever the result, Rogers was fine—the script had been written to give everyone something to do, and there was an assurance that

Trapper and Hawkeye would work as in the film—as part of a duo who had equal footing in life and in the show. That worked for Rogers. Besides, his main concern was to make a little bit of money from the pilot in order to help with some investments he wanted to make.

Born William Wayne McMillan Rogers III on April 7, 1933, in Birmingham, Alabama; his father a lawyer. After attending the Webb School in Bell Buckle, Tennessee; "A school for rich young near-incorrigibles," as he called it in an interview with *TV Guide* in 1974. Wayne graduated from Princeton University with a bachelor of arts degree, before serving in the navy for three years (mainly as a navigator on a cargo ship in the Mediterranean).

Settling in New York, Rogers had plans to get involved with the financial world when his roommate, Peter Falk, and other friends convinced him to study acting at the Neighborhood Playhouse. Rogers soon was getting work in television, including appearing as a regular on the western series *Stagecoach West* (1960–1961) as "Luke Perry." Even so, Rogers knew not to focus all his energy on just one thing, and would instead remain heavily involved with investments and the stock market for himself and friends, building an impressive portfolio as he continued his acting career.

In the early 1960s, Rogers would become acquainted with exploitation director Ted V. Mikels, for whom he would cowrite and coproduce two scripts that became films: *Dr. Sex* (1964, and written under the pseudonym of Juan Rogero) and the notoriously oddball *The Astro-Zombies* (1968, and starring Tura Satana of *Faster, Pussycat! Kill! Kill!*, with John Carradine). Bouncing around through guest-star roles in westerns and cop shows—including several appearances on *The F.B.I.* (1966–1971)—as well as turning up in *Cool Hand Luke* (1968), Rogers went in to test for the role of Hawkeye in the *MASH* pilot. Looking at the role, Rogers was also seriously leaning toward that of the Trapper John character as well, especially when it was mentioned that the producers were looking to cast Alan Alda for the role of Hawkeye.

Although of different political ilk, with a cast and production team leaning more liberal while Rogers was a strong conservative, he got along well with the cast and used to drive to and from the studio with Alda (spending morning drives discussing their dreams from the night before and evening drives going over what worked and didn't work when filming). Yet, while early episodes gave both Hawkeye and Trapper punch lines, it was slowly becoming apparent that the emphasis was moving toward Hawkeye getting more to do with Trapper being reduced to Hawkeye's audience. In

Wayne Rogers as Trapper John. Rogers was a contender for the role of Hawkeye, but was happy to be Trapper until it became clear that the character would also play second fiddle to Hawkeye in the program.

episode four, "Chief Surgeon Who?" Hawkeye was made chief surgeon, which was Trapper John's role in both the movie and novel. This was followed in episode twelve, "Dear Dad," with Hawkeye and Trapper changing specialties, with Hawkeye becoming a thoracic surgeon. "They took away Trapper's credentials, his identity," Rogers told Suzy Kalter in *The Complete Book of MASH*. "It didn't bother me that they chose to make Hawkeye more important, but don't emasculate my character."

Early on, Rogers asked if he was being written out of the show. Larry Gelbart told him at the time that he was "kicking the lines around a little" and throwing off the rhythm of the gags, which Rogers attempted to rein in. The scripts began to use Trapper more, but it was clear that fresh reminders were necessary to make sure Trapper was remaining a part of the storylines. At the end of the first season, Rogers told the production team, "I came here with the understanding that this was a show with primarily two characters and their relationship with the McLean Stevenson character, and if that's not so, I have a solution to your problems. I can do less shows and be more involved in those, that saves you money and I won't feel like I'm wasting my time and I won't feel like I'm being treated in some half-assed manner."

The writers and producers assured Rogers that season two would be better, but things merely repeated themselves, with only reminders to the production team being enough to get them to give Trapper something to do on the show. At the end of the second season, it was clear that things were not going to change, and Rogers saw no point in continuing to spend time better spent in pursuing other things than becoming a background player. Further, he had no financial reason to stay, as his investments in a variety of different things, including a vineyard, were paying off in a manner that made it so he didn't have to worry about keeping in the good graces of the studio or network. "I know who I am and where the hell I'm going," Rogers told Bill Davidson in 1974 for *TV Guide*. "If both CBS and 20th Century-Fox burned down tomorrow, I'd retire to a small intellectual community—probably Princeton or Cambridge—and be a professional student for the rest of the my life."

Rogers was convinced to come back for third season, but it simply felt like more of the same, and eventually he made it clear that he wanted out. The studio stated he had to stick to his contract, which Rogers pointed out he had never signed. A lawsuit and countersuit between 20th Century-Fox and Rogers would take place but were eventually dropped, while the production team continued to hope that Rogers would come back for another season. Instead, it was the end, and the fourth season had Trapper written out off-camera in the first episode, "Welcome to Korea." Oddly enough, the character that replaced Trapper, BJ, would begin to have whole episodes wrapped around things that happen to him, which was what Rogers wanted for Trapper in the first place. Years later, Rogers would say that if he had known at the time how the show would evolve and that it would last eleven years, he probably would have had second thoughts about leaving when he did. Not that events after leaving *MASH* left him crying to come back.

After *MASH*

Rogers would jump from *MASH* to star in the short-lived, but well-remembered by crime show fans, detective series *City of Angels* (1976). The program obviously was inspired by the success of Roman Polanski's *Chinatown*, with

Rogers as a private detective in Los Angeles in the 1930s. After several television movies, Rogers would hit upon a popular comedy series, returning to the role of a doctor in the television adaptation of the Walter Matthau movie *House Calls*. The series would run three seasons and suffer its own internal star problems when costar Lynn Redgrave requested to bring her newborn to the set for regular breast-feeding. The studio and Redgrave would sue each other over the situation (recalling Rogers' own issues with *MASH*), and Sharon Gless replaced Redgrave's character after the original character left off-air (again like Rogers' departure from *MASH*). Rogers also had a five-episode run on *Murder, She Wrote* in the early 1990s, while also appearing in other films for television and in theaters. In 2005, a star was named for him on the Hollywood Walk of Fame.

Out of the sight of the camera lens, Rogers had been a producer on Broadway (including a female-reversal version of Neil Simon's *The Odd Couple*, starring Rita Moreno and Sally Struthers) and worked with a number of investment projects, including being the chairman of Wayne M. Rogers & Co., Stop-N-Save, LLC (chain of grocery stores), and Kleinfeld (wedding dress emporium), while also on the board for Vishay Intertechnology and his alma mater, The Webb School. He was a frequent analyst on Fox News about financial matters and in 2011 cowrote a book about business and investing with Josh Young called *Make Your Own Rules*.

Wayne Rogers passed away on December 31, 2015 at the age of 82. Although he rarely discussed elements of his time on MASH, he also didn't shy away from respecting the work done on the program. Nevertheless, he was certainly much more than Trapper John, and certainly more than a guy who once wrote a script called Dr. Sex.

Lt. Col. Henry Braymore Blake (44, at time of "Henry in Love")—McLean Stevenson (44 at time of pilot)

The producers wanted Alan Alda as Hawkeye. Wayne Rogers also had eyes on the role, but felt Trapper would suit his talents just as well. McLean Stevenson, on the other hand, really wanted to break out of the pack and saw the role of Hawkeye as a chance to finally become the lead in a series after years of being the second banana.

Edgar McLean Stevenson Jr. was born November 14, 1927, in Normal, Illinois. His father was a cardiologist and his mother a nurse, although McLean never got used to medical issues as his parents had (he once told a story on *The Tonight Show* of going to watch an operation in preparation for *MASH*, only to faint at the first sounds of the scalpel cutting into the

McLean Stevenson with Doris Day in a promotional photo from her CBS series *The Doris Day Show* (1968–1973). Stevenson quickly grew tired of playing bumbling leaders, and fought to win the role of Hawkeye only to settle for Henry Blake in the *MASH* series.

patient's skin). After high school, he joined the Navy in the final days of World War II and was assigned to the medical corps, where "I saw a lot of things that were the result of war that were just awful," he told David Reiss in *MASH: The Exclusive Inside Story of TV's Most Popular Show.* After being released from the service, Stevenson went to Northwestern University, where he gained a degree in theater arts, but his family disapproved of his interest in acting, and he spent the next few years working in a variety of odd jobs, including as a press secretary to his cousin Adlai Stevenson's political campaign. After accepting a job as assistant athletic director at Notre Dame, Stevenson took in a Broadway show (*Do Re Mi*) and realized that he was about to go down the wrong career path. Already in his early thirties, he started at the American Musical and Dramatic Academy and began working in cabaret and plays before finally getting a break as a writer for such shows as *That Was the Week That Was* (which usually featured Alan Alda on the panel), and then *The Smothers Brothers Comedy Hour.*

Stevenson's big break came in 1969 when he appeared briefly in an episode of *That Girl* ("My Sister's Keeper"), playing a bumbling and somewhat ineffectual representative for a cola company. It would lead directly to him playing the part of the bumbling, somewhat ineffectual magazine editor Michael Nicholson on *The Doris Day Show* in the last two seasons of that program. An attempt to get a role on *Room 222* went belly-up, but Stevenson was remembered by producer Gene Reynolds when the time came to put together the cast for *MASH*, and he was sent the script and told to see the movie. As it was, the theater running the film was projecting it in Spanish with English subtitles, and Stevenson came out hating the movie. However, he loved the pilot script and thought he'd be perfect as Hawkeye.

Stevenson went in to see Reynolds, campaigning for the part of Hawkeye, but Reynolds soon sent him back to Earth. Another actor (two, if you count the potential of Wayne Rogers getting the part if Alan Alda had backed out) was already set for the role, and Reynolds saw Stevenson instead in the role as the commander officer, Henry Blake. (No doubt as well that, in his early forties and looking it, Stevenson just didn't fit the physical aspects of Hawkeye, but did of Blake.) Stevenson was unsure, as he felt Roger Bowen's depiction of the character in the movie made Blake out to be a mindless idiot, and Stevenson was looking to get away from being pigeonholed as the always awkward businessman. He too was worried that the show would likely fall back on becoming another standard military comedy. Upon hearing from the production staff that his concerns were theirs as well, Stevenson signed on.

He would stay with the program for three seasons, contributing a story ("The Army-Navy Game") and a script ("The Trial of Henry Blake"). The others in the cast took to Stevenson, who always tried to keep the atmosphere relaxed in front of and behind the camera. Many have tales of Stevenson going into improvised business while off-camera, and more than one have attested that Stevenson added bits of business in scenes as they were being filmed. Look no further than the O.R. scene with Blake and Ginger in "Five O'Clock Charlie"—the actress playing Ginger hands over too many instruments, but Stevenson smoothly works it into the scenes and moves on without a hiccup in the action. Also, watch Wayne Rogers in the third-season episode "Crisis" as Henry begins to repeat the list of missing provisions to see him start to crack up.

Over time, however, Stevenson became restless. The show was not as focused on Blake as he had been told it would be, and he was also resentful about how he felt the studio—not the production team, but the studio—treated the cast, especially after the show started doing better in the ratings during seasons two and three. An incident early on with director Jackie Cooper, where Stevenson called up William Self to complain about Cooper keeping background actors standing out in twenty-degree weather in t-shirts and shorts, only to have Self smugly insist he didn't know who Stevenson was, was one of several breaking points for Stevenson. "I could not understand 20th Century-Fox," Stevenson told David Reiss. "I wasn't asking for anything very odd. I was asking for a place to dress. I was asking for some kind of air to be pumped into the stage to combat the 110-degree heat we endured there during July and August. . . . I wasn't asking for a place to park my car, I just wanted a place to go to the bathroom." Jeff Maxwell, in his book *Secrets of the MASH Mess* (1997, Cumberland House Publishing, Nashville), mentioned Stevenson's generosity, describing an incident where he ran into Stevenson while auditioning for an NBC pilot and Stevenson walking Maxwell into the producer's office and hard-selling Maxwell for fifteen minutes in order to get him the role. Such concern for others was normal for Stevenson.

But further, more personal issues were also arising as time went on. Stevenson had started getting offers for other work. He appeared in the excellent television film (costarring Loretta Swit) *Shirts/Skins* (1973), was getting film offers, and he was a recurring guest host on *The Tonight Show* when Johnny Carson was off. There was even speculation that he might take over for Carson (a reason Stevenson would sign to NBC after leaving *MASH* just in case Carson did finally go forward with the retirement he had been threatening NBC with at that point). He was approaching fifty and finally starting to see himself as a leading man, while being stuck within an ensemble back on *MASH*. "I'm tired of being one of six," *TV Guide* quoted him as saying, "I want to be one of one." In David Reiss' book, Stevenson went on to say, "I felt there was a lot more money to be had with a lot less aggravation. And that turned out to be true."

Seeing Stevenson's exit, the producers decided it was time to show the audience that the characters could move on. More importantly, it was time to show that war can destroy, and to make this point, it was determined to have Henry Blake die, his plan crashing in the Sea of Japan as he was heading home. The story surrounding this is probably the best known to *MASH* fans: in filming the episode, the final scene was to take place in the O.R., with Radar coming in to read a letter from Henry announcing his safe arrival back home. Gary Burghoff, in his autobiography, took Stevenson aside and asked him if he really wanted to go through with it: "If they kill you off, you can never change your mind. If you don't want me to, I'll refuse." Stevenson told Burghoff to do it, as it was for the integrity of the program they show that war kills indiscriminately, and that good people die just as bad.

Stevenson watched Burghoff rehearse the scene once, then actually film it before walking back to his dressing room to cry. "Not because I died," he told David Reiss, "but because it was all over." There was a season wrap party, but Stevenson soon left, never returning. For a time, he felt anxious about the decision. "I felt it was vindictive," he told Reiss. "That the real motive was to prevent me from doing a show where I might want to continue being Henry Blake, M.D.—which I didn't." This was understandable, as the rumor flying around at the time was that it came about in order to make sure Stevenson never could return to the show.

Fans were shocked, and many wrote to the show in anger and frustration over the death of the character. As mentioned earlier in the book, H. Richard Hornberger immediately was upset over the killing of one of his characters from the novel; and both in the Butterworth novels and *MASH Mania*, Hornberger made sure that it was shown that Henry Blake was alive and well. As for Stevenson, he would even joke about it on the May 4, 1975, episode of the variety series *Cher* (some sources state it was *The Carol Burnett Show,* but this is incorrect) where Cher announced that McLean Stevenson was supposed to be a guest that night, but couldn't appear after being shot down in the Sea of Japan . . . only for the camera to cut to a bird's-eye view of Stevenson dressed as Blake in an inflatable life raft waving to the camera and shouting he was alive.

Yet, over time, Stevenson knew the initial response to let it happen was the right one. "It did make one hell of a show and one that a lot of people won't forget." It still is remembered today as one of the most shocking events on American episodic television, more than forty years on.

After MASH

Stevenson's first show after *MASH* was *The McLean Stevenson Show,* which lasted twelve episodes (1976–1977). It was followed by *In the Beginning* (1978), which lasted nine episodes. This was followed by the infamous *Hello, Larry* (1979–1980), which actually lasted a season and a half at thirty-eight episodes; and crossovers with *Diff'rent Strokes*; thirteen episodes of *Condo* (1983); eleven episodes of *Dirty Dancing* (1988–1989); and hosting the short-lived talk show *America* (1985). Sprinkled between all this were game shows such as *Match Game* and talk shows. Stevenson also worked with his replacement on *MASH* Harry Morgan in the Disney film *The Cat from Outer Space* (1978), wrote a story used in an episode of *The Love Boat* ("Love Below Decks," 1983), and did a handful of pilots for other series that never panned out. There was talk of other projects, such as a dramatic film he was supposed to do with Richard Dreyfuss and Jack Lemmon in 1981 that never happened, but Stevenson always kept pushing to find something, although he realized that leaving *MASH* probably was not the best idea. "I've never been able to work with a group that's as talented or scripts that are as good," he told Mary Corey for the *Baltimore Sun* in 1990 ("McLean Stevenson Reflects on His Roller-Coaster Career 15 Years Since Leaving Hit Series"). He also knew that he got razzed for leaving when he did. "Some of it was justified," he told Corey. "I made the mistake of believing that people were enamored of McLean Stevenson when the person they were enamored of was Henry Blake."

McLean Stevenson would be nominated in each year he appeared on *MASH*, including one nomination for writing "The Trial of Henry Blake." He also won a Golden Globe in 1974 as Best Supporting Actor in a television series. McLean Stevenson passed away on February 15, 1996, suffering a heart attack while recuperating from surgery due to bladder cancer. He would be the first main cast member of the *MASH* series to pass away and one day before the death of the movie's Henry Blake, Roger Bowen.

Corp. Walter Eugene "Radar" O'Reilly (age 19)—Gary Burghoff (age 28 at time of pilot)

Burghoff had already been around once in *MASH*, thanks to playing Radar O'Reilly in the Robert Altman film (and more about his history before the film and series can be found in chapter 10). Burghoff was looking for work when he heard that there was interest to do a pilot of the movie. Soon after, he heard from his agent that the production was interested in getting Gary to reprise his role, if he wanted "to do television." Gary had worked with Gene Reynolds before in a screen test for another project, knew of Larry Gelbart, and had run into Alan Alda while Burghoff was in *You're a Good Man, Charlie Brown*, so everything sounded promising. His portrayal of the character would evolve over the years, however, going from the scuzzy maker-of-deals who drinks and smokes when no one is looking in seasons one through three, to the teddy-bear-carrying wide-eyed youth of seasons

four through eight (which was slowly being hinted at in the first three seasons); Radar managed to leave Korea more innocent than when he arrived.
Yet this was not a case of forgetfulness, but rather a rational approach by
Burghoff to the character in keeping with the evolution of the other characters on the program. The show was moving swiftly from the devil-may-care
wackiness of the early episodes (see Radar like an evil alternate universe
version in the pilot, for example) to where the characters were feeling
more and have mature things to say between the jokes. Burghoff knew the
character had to change quickly in order for him to have anything to play on
the show, and to do that, he decided there needed to be a character who was
not corrupted by the world, who could see things as black and white/good
and evil. Burghoff also was instrumental in giving Radar his first name,
Walter, in the episode "Quo Vadis, Captain Chandler?" from season four,
feeling that after so many years it was time the character became more of a
whole person than just a nickname.

The character was a success, and Burghoff would be nominated for an
Emmy each season he was featured in *MASH*, winning in 1977 (he was not
there to receive the award, with Alan Alda accepting in his place). But as
time went on, Burghoff was starting to get burnt out on a character he had
been playing since 1969. People on the street referred to him as Radar,
while personal issues (mainly concerns about raising his family) were piling
on. By the fourth season, he had gotten a raise along with an agreement to
a reduced number of episodes to film—an agreement he later admitted
in his book was probably not the best way to go, although it did give him
more time with this family. (This also explains why episodes in seasons four
through seven see only so much of Radar, with his character either said to
be elsewhere or not even mentioned.) For some on the program, this was
just as well, as his feelings of being overwhelmed and frustrated with some
of the things occurring on the show caused him to lash out, even in the
early years of the program. (A *TV Guide* interview from the second season
mentions an argument between Burghoff and Wayne Rogers that climaxed
with Rogers throwing his chair forty-five feet after Burghoff had mouthed
off to him.) Unfortunately, everybody needs a villain, and although the
cast respected his work and dedication, his temperament—which Burghoff
himself admits was out of control at times—gained him a reputation as
someone not easy to work with. One of the most famous stories came by
way of *TV Guide* again ("The Troops Scatter—But the Memories Linger," by
Burt Prelutsky, Feb 12–18, 1983), where an unnamed member of the cast

stated that Burghoff would be rude to everyone, but if anyone said anything to him, he'd have a tantrum. When Mike Farrell, according to the source, told Burghoff he could "dish it out, but he couldn't take it," Gary replied, "And I'm getting real sick and tired of dishing it out." To the person making the remark, it was meant to say how confused Burghoff was, but it could also be read as showing how he felt he was the only one trying to point out issues with the show. He had been there the longest of them all; he knew his character well. And yet the show had grown without him there half the time, and he faced the dual edge of being perceived as the youngest child (as Radar) and the grumpy old man.

When season eight rolled around, Burghoff had decided it was time to go. He was rapidly approaching forty and still playing a kid, while finding little satisfaction in his work on the program. He had also found financial security in real estate investments and didn't need to keep doing Radar in order to fulfill his life. He would bow out with the eighth-season two-parter, "Goodbye, Radar" (in fact, he only appears in this two-parter and in some brief scenes in earlier episodes of the season, where Radar is shown being on R&R). In the story, Radar's uncle passes away, leading to him being sent home to his family. Even so, Burghoff would feel comfortable enough with the character to return to it three times, twice on *After MASH* and then in a short pilot for a series called *W*A*L*T*E*R*, thus showing that he didn't have a problem with the character as much as other elements of the program.

After MASH

Leaving the show, Burghoff would find inner peace through his Christian faith, while still actively pursuing work in movies and television; appearing in a few episodes of various series like *Fantasy Island* and *Love Boat*, as well as starring in and codirecting a crime film called *Small Kill* in 1991. He became the spokesperson for BP gasoline and would later reunite with nearly all of the cast of the *MASH* series in a number of commercials for IBM computers in the 1980s. Picking up painting, he established a career as a wildlife painter in the 1990s, and beyond an appearance in a film in 2010, *Daniel's Lot*, he would retire from acting. In 2009, he released a book called *Gary Burghoff: To MASH and Back, My Life in Poems and Songs (That Nobody Ever Wanted to Publish)* through BearManorMedia, which is an autobiographical review of his life, his faith, his art, and his poems.

Maj. Margaret J. "Hot Lips" Houlihan (age 40+)—Loretta Swit (age 34 at the time of pilot)

When her agent told her about some producers wanting to interview her for the role of Houlihan on the television version of *MASH*, Loretta Swit's response was "Well, I'm going to Saks Fifth Avenue anyhow and Fox isn't too far away from there—so okay."

Loretta Jane Swit was born November 4, 1937 in Passaic, New Jersey, to Polish immigrant parents, who were less than keen on the idea of their daughter wanting to go into the entertainment business. She had studied dancing as a child and had taught it while still in high school, then attended the American Academy of Dramatic Arts in New York. She moved on to the Repertory Theatre for a couple of years and then performed in national productions of various plays, including *Any Wednesday* in 1967 and *Mame* with Susan Hayward (later Celeste Holm), which played at Caesar's Palace in 1968–1969, where Swit played Agnes Gooch. Swit has stated she had planned to return to New York when friends convinced her to move out West and try to get into television and the movies.

Her first work in television came by way of *Hawaii Five-O* in 1969, where she appeared four times over four years, as well as multiple appearances on *Mannix, Gunsmoke, Mission: Impossible*, and others. Initially, Houlihan would be the main antagonist alongside Frank Burns, but even in the first season there was evidence that—just as in the film—Margaret was eventually going to be swinging over to the good guys (check out "Sticky Wicket," where Houlihan is the only one to help Hawkeye as he agonizes over a patient that isn't getting better for an early change of heart). It would take time, but eventually the love affair between Houlihan and Burns would be dropped, and Margaret would go through a marriage and divorce, as well as a brief fling with Hawkeye in a later season. As the main female character on the show, it was noticeable to many viewers that Margaret was changing, but Swit renounced the idea that her character changed the most over the seasons as it meant an emphasis on "the woman changing" rather than noting that all the characters went through emotional and personality changes over time. Perhaps the one thing that could be said is that Swit always portrayed Houlihan as someone who cared about the patients first (sometimes less than about her nurses and even the doctors), and while other aspects of her personality did evolve, Houlihan was always a "damn good nurse" (as mentioned in the film).

As the series went on, Swit appeared in two movies that have some cult status today with certain viewers: the oddball James Caan and Allan Arkin cop comedy *Freebie and the Bean* (1974) and the horror thriller *Race with the Devil* (1975, with Peter Fonda and Warren Oates). In 1981, she appeared in the Blake Edwards comedy *S.O.B.* and starred in the *Cagney & Lacey* pilot, which went to series with Meg Foster and later Sharon Gless (who had replaced Lynn Redgrave on *House Calls* before that) taking on her role.

After MASH

Swit would continue with television for the most part, appearing in *The Best Christmas Pageant Ever* (1983), the apocalyptic comedy *Whoops Apocalypse* (1983) as a woman president, and episodes of *Murder, She Wrote* and *Diagnosis Murder*. For several years she has been dedicated to work involving animal protection. Over her time in *MASH*—in which she was one of only two actors to have appeared in both the first and final episodes (Alan Alda being the other)—Swit was nominated for an Emmy ten times, winning twice (1980 and 1982). In 1986, she wrote a book with Ellen Appel, *A Needlepoint Scrapbook*, detailing various needlepoint projects she had worked on over the years, including while on *MASH*. She was awarded a star on the Hollywood Walk of Fame in 1989.

Maj. Franklin Delano Marion "Frank" Burns (approximately early 30s)—Larry Linville (age 32 at time of pilot)

Many of the others listed here have had training that led to Broadway, but Larry Linville (Lawrence Linville, as he was notably listed in some credits during the early 1970s) came by way of another direction—from the Royal Academy of Dramatic Arts.

Lawrence Lavon Linville was born September 29, 1939, in Ojai, California, but grew up in Sacramento, California, near an Air Force base, which nurtured his passion for flying. Flying gliders by age eleven, Linville became fascinated by engineering and went to the University of Colorado to studio engineering, hoping to become a test pilot, but his dreams were curtailed by color blindness. Instead, he turned his attention to theatrics, winning a scholarship to the Royal Academy of Dramatic Art between the years of 1959 and 1961 (his classes included students such as David Warner, John Hurt, and Ian McShane).

Returning to the U.S. in 1962, Linville struggled to find work for a few years, once even stealing a Christmas tree due to being broke. "You haven't seen anything funny," he told *TV Guide* in 1976, "until you've seen an actor try to jump a subway turnstile with a Christmas tree." Things picked up in 1967, however, when he obtained a role on Broadway in the drama *More Stately Mansions*, starring Ingrid Bergman. He then appeared in a production of *The Matter of J. Robert Oppenheimer* in Los Angeles, which got him noticed by the studios. Soon he started working in television, playing a series of either doctors, bad guys, or both. "I spent three years," Linville joked with David Reiss, "throwing old ladies down stairs, poisoning Greg Morris, and pounding Darren McGavin. . . ." A break came from the villains with his role as Lieutenant George Kramer on *Mannix*, playing a sympathetic police officer to the private detective hero.

Even so, after playing bad guys for so long, 20th Century-Fox balked when Linville won the part after auditioning (Burns has so little to do in the pilot that Gene Reynolds had him audition with the part of Henry Blake instead). The assumption was that the audience would never buy him as being funny after having killed so many characters in the crime shows over the past three years. Finally the studio relented, and Linville would make Frank Burns a lasting impression on sniveling comedy foils ever since.

Linville's perception of the character was actually somewhat different from the way most actors take to their role as the villain, To them, the concept is to find what makes the character "right" in what he was doing. To Linville, Burns was someone everyone needed to see as looking normal at first, but hiding a monster inside. "Frank is a dangerous man because he acts without reason," Linville told David Reiss, "often without true intelligence, and perhaps more importantly, with no real knowledge or perception of what consequences an action will bring about."

As the show moved through the years, relationships between the characters morphed as well, and it became clear that the affair between Burns and Houlihan would have to be phased out. Doing so allowed Houlihan to become one of the "good guys" (which, as the only stable female presence in the series, made sense), but it left Burns as the sole nut, the sole antagonist. Although the writers would sometimes give Burns a break and let him have a "moment of clarity," the character became more cartoonish as season five started. Further, Linville has been known as a man who wanted to explore other things in his life, and he was finding the risk of settling into a "safe place" as being dangerous. "A year and a half ago, I was on the verge of being trapped by money and security," Linville told *TV Guide* at the time he was leaving *MASH*. "I went after the golden apple on the American dream tree, and it's rather bitter." More importantly, as to his acting career, he knew he had to move on, even though he liked the part. He didn't want to have to be Frank Burns for the rest of his life, however.

After MASH

Linville would move on to the short-lived family comedy series *Grandpa Goes to Washington* (1978–1979) and as the antagonist in *The Jefferson* spin-off *Checking In* (1981). There were also the villain role in the *Herbie, the Love Bug* series (1982) and in the short-lived series *Paper Dolls* (1984). In between guest roles on various series, he appeared in the comedy *Rumors* on Broadway (replacing Ken Howard in the cast for a time).

As is typical with good actors in villainous roles, Linville was never nominated for an award. He would continue to fly in his off-times and made an appearance with Larry Gelbart and David Ogden Stiers in Korea when the final MASH unit was deactivated in 1997. In 1998, it was discovered he had cancer, leading to his death from pneumonia on April 10, 2000. He was the second original cast member of the series to pass away.

First Lt. Francis John Patrick Mulcahy (age approximately mid-40s)—William Christopher (age 39 at time of pilot . . . in which he didn't appear)

Father Mulcahy appears in the pilot episode of *MASH*, and thus the character lasts through the entire series from Day One to the finale. It's just that the part wasn't played by the actor who would become known for the part, William Christopher.

William Christopher was born on October 20, 1932, in Evanston, Illinois. He obtained a bachelor of arts degree at Wesleyan University in Middletown, Connecticut, and was a struggling actor for many years before getting a break working on Broadway in *Beyond the Fringe*, the classic British ensemble comedy revue featuring Peter Cook, Dudley Moore, and Alan Bennett. This would put Christopher on the national tour and eventually find him in Los Angeles, where he appeared in a number of television shows, commonly comedies. He also appears briefly in the classic Billy Wilder comedy *The Fortune Cookie* (1966) as an intern, and in Bob Hope's awkward military comedy of the late 1960s *The Private Navy of Sgt. O'Farrell* (1968). Roles in *Gomer Pyle: U.S.M.C.* and *Hogan's Heroes* got him noticed, but Christopher was already working as a semiregular on the short-lived but well-regarded James Garner series *Nichols* in 1971. When that series folded, the production team was looking to recast the role of Father Mulcahy after using George Morgan in the pilot (Morgan had no lines in the pilot and was dropped).

Christopher went in to audition, but nearly lost out. Having spent much time working with an improvisation class at the Harvey Lembeck Comedy Workshop, Christopher decided he would wing the audition by foregoing the lines written by Larry Gelbart and do his own. Feeling strongly he had won the production team over, he was asked to audition again, and cautioned by Burt Metcalfe to stick with the lines written by people who really cared about their lines being stuck to. He tried out again and was given the role.

Mulcahy turned up every so often in the first few seasons, and Christopher (along with Jamie Farr, who played Klinger) was paid as a "day player" (someone who gets a line and perhaps a credit at the end of the show) for several seasons before finally being contracted as a regular part of the cast in season four (and not billed as such in the opening credits until season five, the same season Gene Reynolds would sneak into the opening credits as executive producer). While the money and credits changed, so did the emphasis on Mulcahy, who began to do more than being there either to help set up a gag or tie into the punch line. No doubt, Christopher himself wanted to do more than being there to set up awkward religious humor and wanted to show a more human side to the religious faith—and one in wartime that was rarely discussed in movies or television. Yet, even early on, it was clear that Mulcahy brought something to the show, and it was an early confrontation with Klinger in episode 12 of the first season, "Dear Dad," that demonstrated the humor of the character and the ability to show the weariness of the war on his face, while at the same time showing a determination to carry on by Christopher as Mulcahy that really locked the character in place as a major one for the show. As mentioned earlier in the book, Christopher developed hepatitis while filming season five, but had already filmed exterior scenes for several episodes and thus appeared in many episodes in the season even though he was sick in bed for two months (Father Mulcahy would also be diagnosed with hepatitis in the same season, although after Christopher was well enough to appear on the show again).

After MASH

Christopher would join Jamie Farr and Harry Morgan in the sequel series, *After MASH* from 1983 to 1984, then do a variety of guest shots on various television shows through 2012. In 1989, William Christopher wrote a book with his wife Barbara, *Mixed Blessings* (1989, Abingdon Press, Nashville), about raising their sons, one of whom has autism, and the various frustrations and triumphs they had.

Corp. Maxwell Q. Klinger (no age given)—Jamie Farr (age 37 at time of first appearance on MASH)

He was supposed to be a one-off character—a ripe punch line about a crossdresser. He would end up sticking it out much longer than the gag itself.

Born Jarmeel Joseph Farah on July 1, 1934 in Toledo, Ohio. Although he would use Klinger's character to project Toledo as a tough town—which it is, actually—Farr himself excelled in school: three years as class president, manager of both the football and basketball teams, member of the National Honor Society, star tennis player, and writing and acting in two variety shows as part of the drama society. He left high school and went out to California, where he was spotted by a talent agent for MGM at the Pasadena Playhouse, leading to a role in *Blackboard Jungle* at the age of twenty-one. A small number of roles followed, but it wasn't until he got hired onto *The Red Skelton Hour* in 1956 that he began popping up more and more often on television. He would appear four times on *The Dick Van Dyke Show* as a delivery boy in 1961, as well as other shows, including two appearances in *F Troop*, where he would work with Gene Reynolds.

In 1972, the script for "Chief Surgeon Who?" in the first season called for a gag where the night patrol at the 4077th would turn out to be a guy wearing a dress, which doesn't surprise the officer who meets him as he realizes the guy is trying to get a Section 8 (a discharge due to insanity) in order to be sent home. When Reynolds read the script, he immediately thought of Jamie Farr as the joke would just seem funnier if the guy in the dress was as hairy as Farr. Farr came in to do the part and was asked to do it in a stereotypical manner as a homosexual, lisp and all. Reynolds, upon seeing the footage, was appalled. To him, Klinger was a con artist first and foremost, who wanted to be out of the army and just happened to be wearing a dress to do it. It was funnier that way. The scene was reshot, and it went over so well that Farr was asked to come back in "Dear Dad" that same season. In this instance, Klinger came off as possibly being about ready to lose his mind, threatening to shove a grenade down Burns' throat for touching a red beret he was wearing that his mother gave him, then ready to pull the pin when Mulcahy asks for the grenade. It would be the last time Klinger was played so close to the edge, however, and from that point forward he would usually be one of the sanest character in the show (as well as usually representing all non-com if Radar was not around). It did give an early indication of the camaraderie of Klinger and Mulcahy to come as the seasons went on.

From there on out, Klinger increasingly became part of the regulars, and was the first character to join the cast from outside the core group that had appeared in the film. As the seasons progressed, the emphasis on crossdressing began to disappear, with the "Bug-Out" episode that kicked off season five—in which Klinger gave up most of his dresses to a group of prostitutes for the sake of the unit—a turning point for the character who would increasingly find other methods to get out of the army. After Radar was let go, Klinger would take his place as Potter's second in the show and the character stabilized even more, reverting to army green for most of the remainder of the series.

Farr would also work as a writer in the 1970s, coming up with stories for the animated series *The Amazing Chan and the Chan Clan* in 1972, as well as writing two episodes of the 1976 series *Swiss Family Robinson*. He also had a fun part on the made-for-television movie *Murder Can Hurt You* (playing a traumatized parody of Starsky who had lost his Hutch) and also in the two *Cannonball Run* films. Over time of the series, Farr would never forget his Lebanese and Toledo roots, incorporating those elements into the character of Klinger.

After MASH

As with Christopher, Farr would return to the role of Klinger in the two seasons of *After MASH*. He appeared in a number of guest shots on television since then and wrote an autobiography with Robert Blair Kaiser in 1994, *Just Farr Fun*, which works as a good primer on the making of *MASH*, besides detailing his life. He received a star on the Hollywood Walk of Fame in 1985.

Capt. BJ Hunnicutt (approximately late 20s)—Mike Farrell (age 36 in season four)

In 1974, Mike Farrell was looking forward to being in a new series that would focus on philosophical questions pertaining to humans. Then things happened and *The Questor Tape* was out of the question for him.

Born February 6, 1939, in St. Paul, Minnesota, Michael Joseph Farrell Jr. and his family moved to California when he was two years old. His father would end up working as a carpenter for film studios (no definitive studio names have ever been mentioned), and Farrell went to Hollywood High School before going on to serve for two years in the U.S. Marine Corps. He returned from his stint to study drama at UCLA and Los Angeles City College, as well as the Desilu Professional Workshop. After working in theatrical productions around the area, Farrell began getting jobs in television, usually in military roles or as government officials, including *McHale's Navy*, *Combat!*, and even as a secret service agent in an episode of *The Monkees*. He also appeared briefly in films such as Mike Nichols' *The Graduate* (1967) and Peter Bogdanovich's *Targets* (1968).

Regular television roles started coming his way in the 1970s, first on *The Interns* (1970–1971) and then in *The Man and the City* (1971–1972), but then it was back to the grind of guest shots until he was offered a role in a television movie that was a pilot for a series created by *Star Trek*'s Gene Roddenberry. *The Questor Tapes* (1974) dealt with an android whose creator has disappeared and half of his programming erased. The android, Questor (Robert Foxworth), teamed up with a man named Jerry (Mike Farrell), and the pair soon went on the run from government officials. In some ways it was like "Spock from *Star Trek* meets *The Fugitive*," but the pilot had done well and there were signs of a series being done. Then, suddenly, Farrell was out, as the studio felt that the show would be better with no "human support" for the android. Eventually, the series failed to materialize (some would say because losing Farrell's character lost the "heart" of the show).

Meanwhile, Farrell was getting calls about *MASH*. The third season was starting up, and there were concerns that the arguments between Wayne Rogers and the studio would lead to him walking out. If so, would Farrell be interested in joining the cast? Farrell had seen the program and was anxious to be on a show that had writing as good as *MASH*, but would only say yes if everything was clear-cut about Rogers deciding to leave. As it turned out, Rogers stayed on for another season, and Farrell thought that was the end of things until the question was again asked of him at the end of the third season. When Rogers was definitely out, Farrell was happy to come in . . . but he was under contract with Universal. Universal okayed his release for the show, and Farrell auditioned for the part with Alan Alda (others who auditioned were Alan Fudge, Sam Elliott, and James Cromwell—who would appear in the season six episode "Last Laugh" as BJ's practical joker friend). Farrell soon was given the part.

Both Farrell and the production staff agreed that the worst thing to do would be to have the new character, BJ Hunnicutt, be a carbon copy of Trapper John. Both were married men with kids, and both surgeons, but that's pretty much where the comparison ended. While Trapper was loose with women (and it was clear that he probably would not be with his wife long once he got back home), BJ was devoted to his wife. Trapper was an extrovert who could resort to violence if needed; BJ was low-key but could have moments of rage when pushed. Trapper tended to be straightforward, while BJ loved puns. After much frustration on Hawkeye's part, he discovered that BJ's full name is BJ (his father was Jay, and his mother was Bea, hence BJ).

Furthermore, Farrell felt he could ask for changes and guide his character in ways that were not always evident from the writers' point of view. In keeping BJ faithful, it took Farrell to suggest that BJ should face temptation and how he would react to that instead of keeping him a clean slate through the series. A seventh-season episode, "Preventative Medicine," was written with Hawkeye and BJ stopping a colonel from getting his men killed by performing an unneeded appendectomy on the colonel, which would sideline him. As it was, it was old hat for the show—Hawkeye and Trapper had done the exact same thing to Colonel Flagg in the season three episode "White Gold," but in this case Farrell balked. He didn't think a doctor should do such a thing and fought the production team on having BJ assist in it. As it turns out, it moved the story to another level, and instead of simply copying the conclusion of another story, found Hawkeye and BJ on opposite ends of a conflict, and giving them more to do.

Farrell would contribute to the series as a writer (with four episodes) and direct five others, while staying with the series until it ended in 1983.

After MASH

Farrell has been and continues to be a strong political activist, working on various causes dealing with human rights, from gay rights back in the mid-1970s (when celebrities didn't do such things) to helping with refugees in El Salvador. He has also worked with PETA, Human Rights Watch, and Death Penalty Focus, amongst others.

He was a regular on the series *Providence* (1999–2002), played the voice of Jonathan Kent (Clark Kent's father) in various animated series over the years, and played a regular in the series *The Red Road* in 2014. He was nominated twice for an Emmy and once by the Directors Guild of America for *MASH*, and received a Humanitarian Award in 1993 from the organization Women in Films. In 2007, he wrote an autobiography about this acting and activism careers called *Just Call Me Mike*. He followed that one up with a book detailing the book tour he did for the first, called *Of Mule and Man*.

Col. Sherman Tecumseh Potter (age is anywhere from 51 to 62)—Harry Morgan (age at time of joining the series, 59)

Harry Morgan had a most fortunate life in acting, falling into it at an early age and never looking back.

Born Harry Bratsberg on April 10, 1915, in Detroit, Michigan, Morgan had gone to college at the University of Chicago in order to become a lawyer. Instead, he found speaking in front of audiences was what he enjoyed most and started acting at a theater in Washington, D.C. during the Great Depression. He soon was appearing in productions of *The Petrified Forest* and others and felt that acting was an easy street. In 1937, he appeared on Broadway in *Golden Boy*, which ran for several months, but after a series of productions that folded quickly, Morgan—who was still going by the name of Bratsberg at the time—decided to move to Hollywood.

In 1942, he signed with 20th Century-Fox and began appearing in a series of films, usually westerns or crime films and under the name of Henry Morgan, including *The Ox-Bow Incident* (1943), *The Big Clock* (1948), *High Noon* (1952), and even the military comedy *The Teahouse of the August Moon* (1956). A bigger break came in 1954, when Morgan appeared (this time going by the name of Harry Morgan) in the hit comedy series *December Bride* (1954–1959). It would lead to the spin-off series *Pete and Gladys* (Harry played Pete) in 1960, while Morgan appeared in films like *Inherit the Wind* (1960).

Morgan would hit series gold again with a return to *Dragnet* by Jack Webb in the late 1960s. The show is remembered today for being a bit out of sync with the times (especially when it came to the hippie culture big at the time), and Morgan at one point said it was the biggest grind of a show he worked on, but it lasted from 1967 to 1970 and continues today in reruns.

Additional television and movie work continued to come his way, including a run on the series *Hec Ramsey* (1972–1974), when he was asked to play General Steele in the immortal season three episode "The General Flipped at Dawn." Morgan was so good in it that when it was clear that Stevenson would be leaving, Morgan was approached to become a regular as his replacement. Col. Sherman T. Potter was obviously an extension of what Morgan had already done before with General Steele—only on a saner plane. Potter still had a tendency to whip out a story (commonly a topper to anything happening at the moment) that related to an event happening on-screen, but the main difference was that Potter was a military man who knew that doctors were not soldiers, and that regulations had to be stretched in order to keep such a unit functioning.

After *MASH*

Morgan would be back immediately after *MASH* in *After MASH*, joining William Christopher and Jamie Farr in the series (making it only one original character from *MASH*—Father Mulcahy—in the cast of characters). He would also be a regular on *Blacke's Magic* (1986), with Hal Linden, about a crime-fighting magician, and turn up as his old *Dragnet* character Bill Gannon in the Dan Aykroyd/Tom Hanks comedy version of *Dragnet* (1987), as well as three episodes of *3rd Rock from the Sun*.

There was a domestic violence report against Morgan in 1997 that left a mark on his career, but charges were dropped after he completed a counseling program, and he and his wife remained married until his death. He died at the age of ninety-six on December 7, 2011.

Harry Morgan directed nine episodes of *MASH*, and all evidence points to him being loved as a friend and father figure to everyone who worked on the program. He was nominated eleven times for an Emmy award, winning once in 1980 for Best Supporting Actor in a Comedy or Variety series.

Major Charles Emerson Winchester III (age early 40s)—David Ogden Stiers (age 34 at time of joining cast in season six)

There's a good reason to see Winchester performing magic in the season eight episode "Dreams": David Ogden Stiers had already been there and done that.

David Ogden Stiers (whose name seems impossible to not pronounce as one) was born on October 31, 1942, in Peoria, Illinois. Struggling after high school, Stiers finally found his career when he began to perform in Community Theater in Eugene, Oregon. He then acted in the California Shakespeare Festival in Santa Clara for seven years, playing only classical parts, before joining The Committee for part of a year and then going to The Julliard School in New York to help him work on his voice.

Appearing in several short-lived Broadway productions, Stiers finally broke through with his performance as a villainous alcoholic magician in the Doug Henning magic-musical *The Magic Show,* which he left after nine months. Back in Oregon, Stiers' agent convinced him to do some television work (he had already appeared in two movies in 1971—one as just a voice in George Lucas' *THX 1138,* and the other in Jack Nicholson's *Drive, He Said*). He first appeared as a regular on the comedy series *Doc* (1976) before getting noticed in his three appearances as the station owner who fires everyone in the finale of *The Mary Tyler Moore Show* (1976–1977). When Burt Metcalfe began looking for an actor to replace Larry Linville, Metcalfe and the production team decided that the new character needed to be someone who would be a "far more formidable opponent for Hawkeye and BJ" Metcalfe told *TV Guide,* "I had an image of William Buckley in mind. Then I saw David."

Stiers was not at first drawn to the idea of being part of the show, however. "I hated the idea of the TV show *MASH,*" Stiers told David Reiss, "because I had seen and loved the film. It was only after I started, when the possibility of joining was imminent, that I began screening shows, and I began to realize that I loved it in advance of anything I'd seen in the movie." Stiers saw the characters in the film as being crazy no matter where they went, but the ones in the show were crazy because they had to be in order to get through the pain of what they were experiencing while trying to help the wounded in the war.

The character of Winchester would prove a strong one, lasting until the end of the series, and help change the focus in that Hawkeye was not always the one to get the last word any longer (not that Winchester did instead, but he helped move that barrier away in the series). The writer still got stuck sometimes with the character in later seasons; too often making Winchester drunk in order to avoid having to justify clever dialogue for him; but over time the character went from being one that was just a stuck-up, to a caring man who began to understand life better than all that his upbringing has brought him beforehand.

After *MASH*

Stiers would continue working in television and movies, doing voice work in animated films, such as Disney's *Beauty and the Beast* (1991). He appeared in a number of *Perry Mason* movies in the 1980s as D. A. Michael Reston; worked in the miniseries for *North and South, Books I & II*; and appeared as a regular in *Two Guys, a Girl and a Pizza Place* (1998), *Love & Money* (1999–2000), and *The Dead Zone* (2002–2007). Stiers has performed as a conductor for orchestras around the world over seventy times. He was nominated twice for an Emmy for *MASH* and directed two episodes of the series.

 MASH was fortunate. Twice it found a cast that worked together and kept viewers coming back every week, even after well-loved characters left the series. But casting choices didn't stop there. There were plenty of guest stars, and semiregulars along the way as well. Some who arrived only to disappear; some, like Klinger, who stayed for the duration once they popped up; and even those who just turned up every week, running toward the camera as the opening credits played out.

17

The Running of the Nurses

The Actresses in the Opening Credits

There is one question that fans and even nonfans of *MASH* regularly ask when the show is brought up. No, not why did Frank leave, or why was Henry killed off. The question typically is, "Who were those women running toward the camera at the beginning of the show?"

The image suggested is so iconic that it doesn't even have to be explained to readers here, but for those unaware: the opening credits always featured wounded arriving at the 4077th. As the helicopters land, Hawkeye and . . . whoever was the second lead (be it Trapper or BJ) run toward them, look grimly at the wounded, nod, and then we'd get a bird's-eye view of the patients being taken down by jeep as the names of the cast appeared on the screen. Before the landing of the helicopters, however, we see a number of personnel in the camp head toward the wounded, including a group of young nurses running as if their lives depend on it. One of these actresses would remain with the series for the entire run of the program. The rest would disappear after a couple of background cameos. But they were always there in every season's opening credits, and when the opening was partially refilmed after Radar left (as his image was the first you would see through seasons one through seven), it was agreed that anything else could change, but the nurses running had to stay.

As you can guess now—this is their story.

Fortunately, the website MASH4077TV.com had done a bit of legwork in tracking down much of the needed information about these actresses in the shot and was gracious enough to let me use some of it here. As pointed out on their website, although much of the footage in the credits is from the pilot, the shot of the nurses running to get to the helicopter is not. There is a similar shot in the pilot, but Lieutenant Dish is in the forefront, and with her disappearance early in the series, this had to change (she also pops up behind Hawkeye as he's looking down at the chopper patient in the pilot, which was edited out of the credits as well). Instead, the stampede of nurses (as well as a shot of soldiers running up the steps to get to the helicopter) came from the first few minutes of the season one episode "Sticky Wicket." Actually what you see in the episode is a nurse flying out the door of the nurses' quarters and that's it. You don't see them tearing toward the camera as in the opening credits. However, when a matchup is made of the shot from the episode with that of the opening credits, it is clear that the two are from the same footage.

Of course, it should be made clear that none of the actresses seen in the opening credits would become well-known regulars on the show. So the best way to describe them is by their positions in the shot.

The Leader—Kathy Denny Fradella

This is the woman who is winning the running of the nurses. She's in front of all the others and will be our guide to point out the rest in the shot. There was a rumor at one time that actress Michelle Lee (*Knots Landing*) was the woman in front in the opening credits, but this is incorrect. As MASH4077TV.com found, in the April 16, 1978, edition of a newspaper column called "TV Talkback," Kathy Denny Fradella wrote to respond to an earlier question from a reader who wanted to know who the actress was in the opening credits. Fradella stated that Gene Reynolds had "lined up about twenty girls and we literally raced for the job. I had run in high school, so I was more than eager to compete." Reynolds himself stated that the shot was done for the opening credits, and that Fradella would always wind up in front no matter how many times they filmed it. This also helps explain why everyone is not "stage running," but running as fast as hell—as they knew the faster they ran, the better chance they would be picked up by the camera and make it into the opening credits of the show. Kathy Denny Fradella would go on to do some acting in *Starsky & Hutch* and *Kojak*. She still lives in California.

Left of the Leader, Gritting Because She Lost Her Hat— Gwen Farrell

The woman stage left of Fradella is Gwen Farrell, also known as Gwen Adair, who appeared in several episodes, from "For the Good of the Outfit" in 1973 up through "Goodbye, Farewell and Amen," the finale in 1983.

She occasionally had lines on the show as well, but her character's name changed from Butler to Wilson to Gwen to Able (yes, she was one of the many Nurse Ables on the show) and back to Gwen. She also appeared in the film *Billy Jack Goes to Washington* (1977).

Just to make clear, although Mike Farrell's wife at the time did appear as a nurse in several episodes, she is not Gwen Farrell, but Judy Farrell.

Right of the Leader and Behind, but Still Holding Her Hat— Marcia Gelman

This one is not an absolute, but the actress lagging behind and a bit obscured by the others appears to be Marcia Gelman, who played Nurse Jacob in two first-season episodes, "Carry On, Hawkeye" and "The Sniper."

The Blonde—Sheila Lauritsen

This is the woman to the right of Gelman and the only blonde in the group. She would appear in eight episodes between season one and two. As with Gwen Farrell, her character was a nurse, but of many names, from Hardy, to Watson, to Sheila (as you can see here, the series tended to start naming the nurses after the real names of the actresses playing them). She would also appear in one episode of *Starsky & Hutch* in 1977.

The One on the Far Right—Lori Noel Brokamp

The final actress is Lori Noel Brokamp, who also went by the name of Lori Noel. She also worked as an extra, usually playing a nurse, on such shows as *Marcus Welby, M.D.*, *Emergency!*, and *Medical Center*.

And as for all those men running up those stairs? Uh-huh. Let's move on.

18

Going AWOL

Nine Recurring Characters Who Disappeared

A s seen in chapter 16, it's not completely unusual for a television program to have characters leave at some point and be replaced by others. Maybe unusual for those characters to win over audiences, as most shows struggle when bringing in replacements, but it's still part of the test of a long-running show.

It's also not completely uncommon for programs to have characters brought in at the beginning or at different points in the series who eventually disappear. There are more reasons for this than simply the audience not growing to love them, however. The writers can't get a firm grip on the characters, the focus of the show is damaged, actors just end up not being right for the program—these are all things that can account for an actor disappearing from a show. For *MASH*, there were plenty of attempts in the first season to showcase a number of characters who ultimately were scrubbed from the show, with many listed below coming solely from season one. In all cases, the reasons were never given as to where the characters disappeared to or why they were never even referred to again. No doubt, as in reality, the characters simply went home.

Captain Oliver Harmon "Spearchucker" Jones— Timothy Brown

Timothy Brown had appeared in the film version of *MASH* as Corporal Judson (best remembered as the football player who turns the tables on the opposing player who calls him a "coon"). Born on May 24, 1937, Brown played professional football with the Philadelphia Eagles and Baltimore Colts before he began appearing in various television shows by the early 1970s, including three appearances on *Adam-12*. He would take over the role of Spearchucker Jones from the movie when the television show started,

An early cast photo from the series. Even then, it was clear that many secondary characters in the first season of the series would never be considered part of the main cast.

but it was pretty clear by his fourth episode that the writers really had no idea what to do with him (except pair him up with the African American Nurse Ginger). Jones would only appear in six episodes before disappearing, leaving the Swamp with an extra bunk seen from time to time (officers commonly would bunk four to a tent, but *MASH* made it appear that three was just fine and dandy . . . then again Corporal Klinger got a tent to himself, which seemed very unlikely). See season ten's episode "The Tooth Shall Set You Free" for a rare view of the fourth cot in the Swamp.

Of course, the story told is that they got rid of the character when the production team was told that there were no African America surgeons at MASH units in the Korean War. This actually is incorrect; there were African American doctors and (especially) nurses working at the MASH units during the war, as General Ridgway (who took over as supreme commander after MacArthur) was quick in looking to desegregate the army. That being said, many who came to serve arrived later in the war instead of in 1950, when the series was established as taking place in the pilot. Keep in mind as well who the production team and writers were—men who felt strongly about trying to bring issues to the forefront. Race certainly was discussed on the show—"Dear Dad Three" in season two dealt with a patient who didn't want the "wrong color blood" and is given a makeover in order to scare him straight on the issue, and the aforementioned "The Tooth Shall Set You Free" featured a commander who kept sending his African American soldiers off on dangerous missions in hopes of getting rid of them. But the focus of race was usually the Koreans and Chinese versus the Caucasians there, which in some ways shows that there was a missed opportunity. It is interesting to think how the story would have turned if Dr. Jones had still been around. No doubt there could have been plenty of things to deal with on the show with him around (even down to the use of his nickname), but it was not to be.

Brown would move on to exploitation movies (*Bonnie's Kids*, *Dynamite Brothers*), but would return to the world of Robert Altman with the strong role of Tommy Brown in the Robert Altman film *Nashville*. After that, Brown would bounce back and forth between television and movies and is now remembered more for his football career than his acting one.

Captain John "Ugly John" Black—John Orchard

Ugly John was another character from the film who made the transfer to the series, only to be wiped from the show after the first season. He did manage to last longer than Spearchucker, though, turning up in eleven episodes in the first season—from the pilot through to the final episode in the season—usually getting a few lines in and looking to be a regular part of the show. (Or, at least, a regular part of the poker games he seemed to always be a part of in that season.)

As mentioned in a previous chapter, the character was written in the novel as being an American. Same as in the film, where Ugly John is played by Carl Gottlieb. Then came the series, and it was decided to make him Australian, which is actually in keeping with the reality of the U.N. forces in Korea during the war (albeit, it was more common to see units with the same nationality than one person being split off into an American unit as Ugly John evidently had been). John was played by John Orchard in the pilot and in a number of subsequent episodes, making a total of eleven appearances as "Ugly John."

Orchard was born November 15, 1928, in Kennington, London, England. He popped up in American television in the early 1960s, including episodes of *Combat!*, *Get Smart* (where he appeared as a parody of John Steed from *The Avengers* series), and even *The Beverly Hillbillies*. He also appeared in an episode of *Hogan's Heroes* directed by executive producer Gene Reynolds ("The Prisoner's Prisoner"), which may have been a link to his run on *MASH*.

After the first season, it was decided to drop the character, and Orchard moved back to guest-starring roles in television and movies, even appearing in a Disney film with Timothy Brown, *Gus* (1976). In 1979, he returned to

MASH, not as Ugly John, but as an MP who gets on the wrong side of Charles and ends up closing Rosie's Bar. Oddly enough, all of Orchard's dialogue is mainly with characters that were not around in that first season.

Orchard passed away on November 3, 1995 in Kent, England.

Ho-Jon—Patrick Adiarte

Ho-Jon also made it from pilot to the final episode of the first season . . . which was strange as he should have been in the States by then if they had raised all that money for him to go to college in the pilot. (Fan creed states that to make it work in canon Ho-Jon would stay until a particular date for family reasons or logistical ones; the customary Hollywood reason would be they just forgot that he should not have been there anymore.) Ho-Jon turns up in seven episodes of the series and then is never seen again. The concept of a house boy (common in units like a *MASH*) pretty much disappeared in the series as well, although Charles at one point attempted to have one in the season seven episode "Dear Comrade," where it turned out the "house boy" is actually a spy who eventually gives up trying to figure out the craziness of the unit and goes to have a drink with everyone.

As mentioned previously, Koreans did a lot of work at the MASH units, including preparing meals and manual labor, but you rarely saw that in the series (you did see Koreans serving in the mess tent in the film at least). Typically, the only place the Koreans worked in the 4077th seemed to be the laundry in *MASH*, which may speak of hidden stereotypes in and of itself.

Speaking of which, the actor who played Ho-Jon, Patrick Adiarte, got to break stereotypes in the late 1960s, even if he was systematically stuck in Asian roles for most of his film and television career. Adiarte was born on August 2, 1943, in Manila, Philippines. He became a singer and dancer, appearing first as a young adult in *The King and I* on Broadway, and would play the same role in the film version from 1956. He followed this up with a starring role in *Flower Drum Song* on Broadway, and again repeated his role in the film version of 1961 (Jack Soo, who is discussed in chapter 20, also appeared in *Flower Drum Song*). In 1965, he performed for a year as a singer and dancer on the teenage music–oriented series *Hullabaloo*, and then moved on to other roles in television, including two in 1972 on *The Brady Bunch*. In 1971, he joined *MASH*, playing the young Ho-Jon at the age of twenty-eight in the pilot. After *MASH*, Adiarte bounced around in television for a bit, including a well-remembered *Kojak* two-parter, "The Chinatown Murders" (which featured Robert Ito, who is also covered in chapter 20), but then decided to branch off into the field of photography, where he has worked since.

First Lt. Maria "Dish" Schneider—Karen Philipp

It wasn't a bad idea—the series had only one regular female character, and since it was Houlihan, it meant the series' sole female character was also one of the two main villains. There had to be a counterpart, and what better one than the other lead female role from the film—Lieutenant Dish?

Dish from the series was a bit different from the movie—turning blonde and taller—but both devastatingly beautiful (as a character nicknamed Dish should be). Dish is a major player in the first episode, where Hawkeye is actively pursuing (okay, in today's world, stalking in a sexually harassing manner) her. Although Dish is given a close-up in what would be partially used for the opening credits during the pilot episode, she would be edited from such a close-up in all subsequent episodes. She appears only in one other episode, "Germ Warfare," before she disappears for good.

Dish was played in the series by Karen Philipp, who was born on September 7, 1945, in Salina, Kansas. She graduated from Redlands University in 1967 and then became part of the band Brasil '66 in 1968. In 1972, she decided to branch out into acting and landed the role of Lieutenant Dish in the pilot for *MASH*. She would continue working in television and appeared several times on *Quincy M.E.* between 1977 through 1981. One of her final credits was in the 1985 film *Moving Violations*, which was cowritten by her husband Pat Proft (*Police Academy, Naked Gun, Star Wars Holiday Special*) and costarred Sally Kellerman.

Nurse Margie Cutler—Marcia Strassman

So Lieutenant Dish didn't work out, but there was still a feeling that someone had to be there to represent a positive female voice, and thus entered Nurse Margie Cutler into the third episode of the series, "Requiem for a Lightweight." Antagonizing Houlihan and drawing the romantic interest of both Trapper and Hawkeye, Cutler was bound to fall into the "good guys" way of thinking (and would be seen as a leader for the nurses in episodes like "Edwina"). Cutler would be put to good use in the series, taking on actions in storylines that were more than simply saying a gag and moving along (as most of the nurses did throughout the series). Even so, it was rapidly becoming clear that Cutler was shaping up to be a romantic interest to Hawkeye, and that would cut down on the situations Hawkeye could have with various female guest stars on the program. There was also another issue, as Larry Gelbart himself said on the alt.tv.mash google group back in 2000: "We just had too many regulars on our hands." By the next to last episode of the first season, "Ceasefire," the writers would have Hawkeye burn any romantic link with Cutler by telling her he is married. After six appearances in the first season, Cutler would not return for the second. As for finding a counterpart to Houlihan, the show ended up doing exactly what the movie had done before it—and the shift began to make Margaret one of the good guys, although it was a slow metamorphosis.

Cutler was played by Marcia Strassman, probably best remembered as Kotter's long-suffering (suffering from hearing bad relative jokes, that is) wife, Julie Kotter, on *Welcome Back, Kotter* (1975–1979). She was born April 28, 1948, in New York City and began acting at an early age, appearing at fifteen on *The Patty Duke Show* in two episodes. She would be sidetracked for a time with a music career, including a minor hit with "The Flower Children" in 1967, but soon returned to acting at the beginning of the 1970s. After *MASH*, Strassman would appear in several television series, including an episode of Wayne Rogers' *City of Angels* show in 1976, as well as landing the costarring role of Julie on *Welcome Back, Kotter*. As it turns out, the actors playing the students became the real focus of the show, and Strassman fought to get more things to do. Oddly enough, when the star of the series, Gabe Kaplan, had a contract dispute in the final season, the program began to focus more on Julie, giving Strassman more work on the show.

Strassman would appear in several other programs, including the pilot to the Elliott Gould series *E/R* in 1984, and in a recurring role on *Providence*, which costarred Mike Farrell. She is also remembered for her role in the *Honey, I Shrunk the Kids* series of movies. She died on October 24, 2014, from breast cancer.

Brig. Gen. Crandell Clayton—Herb Voland

Brigadier General Crandell Clayton was brought into the program very early on to be a regular foil for the *MASH* heroes (this wasn't unprecedented—General Hammond turns up multiple times in the novel in such a capacity, again in the stage play and even in the series for three episodes, so General Clayton was merely following in earlier footsteps). The general was usually played for a stooge (who—much like many other generals in the show—had been with Houlihan in less than a military fashion), but his next to last appearance, in "For the Good of the Outfit," showed that Clayton wasn't a stupid man. Faced with a scandal about a "friendly fire" bombing of a Korean village, Clayton blocks Hawkeye and Trapper's investigation and explains that there are bigger issues at stake for them all. Yet, when it is clear that Houlihan and Burns have more evidence that proves the bombing, Clayton accept that "the army has to take its lumps sometimes" and agrees to let the press know about the bombing. A rare chance to Clayton to be more than someone to mock.

And in his final appearance, Hawkeye drags him around in a latrine to take to the North Koreans. Well, at least there was one episode that took Clayton a bit more seriously.

Clayton was played by Herb Voland, who would have been a lock at Spiro Agnew and did play him (doing an excellent Stan Laurel at the same time) in Bob Einstein's comedy *Another Nice Mess* (1972). Voland was born on October 2, 1918, in New Rochelle, New York, and spent most of his acting career as a guest star in a variety of both comedies and dramas. He was a regular on *Love on a Rooftop* in 1966, which costarred Judy Carne and Rich Little (Little played Nixon/Oliver Hardy to Voland's Agnew/Stan Laurel in *Another Nice Mess*) and *Arnie* (which costarred Roger Bowen . . . who seems to keep popping up in the history of *MASH*, as detailed in other parts of this book). Voland would continue with his television career after *MASH*, and make some rare appearances in films such as *Airplane!* (1980). He passed away on April 26, 1981.

Nurse Ginger Ballis (Bayliss)—Odessa Cleveland

There were several nurses who came and went in the series, and several were played by actresses over a number of episodes, but Ginger was an early one noticed by fans. She certainly is the one who commonly comes up as to "whatever happened to so-and-so on the show?" (Probably even more than Cutler or Dish.) She appears in the pilot up through the fifth episode of season three ("O.R.") and usually had dialogue, including nice bits in both "Five O'Clock Charlie" with Blake and the shutting down of the racist in "Dear Dad Three." Twenty episodes in all; more than three times that of Spearchucker, who was looked upon to be a romantic lockup with Ginger early in the series. Then she just disappeared.

Ginger was played by Odessa Cleveland, who was born on March 3, 1944, in Louisiana. Her career started at the Watts Writer's Workshop and Theater in Los Angeles, where she was a receptionist and writer. Later she began appearing in productions by the Studio Watts Theater, which eventually led to her being cast in *MASH* as Ginger. After *MASH*, Cleveland worked in television for a few more years, playing nurses for the most part, including an episode of *Trapper John, M.D.* in 1986. Cleveland would continue to write, having poems published in various magazines over the years. She also taught for many years with the Los Angeles Unified School District, with a bachelor of science in physical education and English, as well as a master's degree in business management and education.

Capt. Calvin Spalding—Loudon Wainwright III

Every so often, *MASH* attempted to branch out with new characters, and this was the case with Captain Spalding, a character who was written up in an issue of *TV Guide* as being a new regular on the show. As it turns out, Spalding may have gotten a lot of screen time—he's given a showcase to perform songs in each of his three episodes—but then disappeared; obviously a sign that what looked good on paper—a surgeon who sings and plays guitar—didn't really work well in the show. (As it was, the stories would have to pretty much stop cold so that Spalding could do a number.)

Spalding was played by Loudon Wainwright III, who was born on September 5, 1946, in Chapel Hill, North Carolina. Having learned to play the guitar at an early age, he found himself writing and performing folkrock in the late 1960s in the Boston–New York area. Because he had been brought up on the music of comedic performers like Tom Lehrer and Stan Freberg, he was just as likely to write humorous material as more straitlaced, and it was this disposition that led to him achieving a top twenty hit in 1972 with the song "Dead Skunk (in the Middle of the Road)." No doubt that type of humor led the production team on *MASH* to hire him for the role of Spalding.

Wainwright would write and perform songs in each of his three episodes: "Rainbow Bridge," "There Is Nothing Like a Nurse," and "Big Mac." From there, he returned mainly to music, although he has popped up in various movies and television over the years, including as a regular characters on the series *Undeclared* (2001–2002) and in films like *Big Fish* (2003), *Knocked Up* (2007), and *The Aviator* (2004, which costarred Alan Alda). Wainwright has recorded over twenty albums, and his children are all musicians as well, with his son Rufus Wainwright being the best known.

Lt. Col. Sam Flagg—Edward Winter

The baddest of the bad guys on *MASH* turned up when Col. Flagg started causing problems at the 4077th in his own paranoid military way. Although he didn't start that way.

In season two, the episode "Deal Me Out" featured Frank Burns refusing to operate on a man who works for the CID (Criminal Investigation Command—think of it as the FBI for the army), as another CID man has to be present in case the wounded man gives out military secrets during the operation. Captain Halloran, played by Edward Winter, arrives at the 4077th for this reason, but by the time he gets there, Hawkeye and Trapper have already worked on the wounded man. Trying to make the best of the situation, Halloran joins in a card game already in progress—which includes Major Sidney Freedman as one of the other players.

At the end of the season, Winter returned as Colonel Flagg, an intelligence officer who suspects that something is up in the camp because a competing intelligence officer, Pratt (an old friend of Trapper's), is there. As it turns out, Pratt is there pretty much because Flagg is there, and Hawkeye and Trapper rig things so that they each come to the conclusion that Frank is a traitor in order to prove to them how crazy they're behaving. Flagg and Pratt both take it with good humor and end their investigations (although we see Flagg taking pictures of the Swamp before he goes).

Up to this point, Flagg is shown to be a bit obsessive, but not crazy. He certainly could be brought back to human terms at least, and would rather play cards or go for a drink than get all wrapped up in conspiracy theories. Then season four comes around, and suddenly Flagg goes off the deep end. In "Officer of the Day," he arrives with a wounded prisoner he wants patched up so he can then have the man executed in Seoul. (A season eight episode, "Guerilla My Dreams," would use this same plot, only with a South Korean officer wanting to have a wounded female prisoner fixed up so he can then take her to be tortured . . . and in that case, he turned out to be 100 percent correct that the woman was a guerrilla). In "White Gold," Flagg arrives once again—as if no one recognizes him from his previous appearance—in order to steal a shipment of penicillin to use in exchange for military secrets. (Hawkeye and Trapper would fake an appendectomy on Flagg to get him out of the game for a bit, just as Hawkeye would do in a seventh-season episode, "Preventative Medicine," only with different ramifications. See under BJ Hunnicutt in chapter 16.)

Flagg would turn up in three more episodes of the series for a total of seven. There are fans who insisted that the Halloran appearance marks a different character completely, however, thereby making only six appearances for Flagg (and there certainly have been actors who played more than one role on the show, such the various Nurse Ables and Bakers, and even this chapter shows John Orchard being a regular in season one and then reappearing as another character in a subsequent season, thus making Orchard having appeared twelve times, but Ugly John only eleven). Fans who insist that they are one and the same point to dialogue in "Quo Vadis, Captain Chandler?" in season four, where Flagg and Major Freedman meet up and discuss having played cards together once (and they did when Winter played Halloran in "Deal Me Out"). Fans who argue against "Halloran is Flagg" mention that they could have played cards another time, and besides, Flagg arrives in "A Smattering of Intelligence" as if no one know him, thus proving that they are not the same. Yet he also arrived in "White Gold" thinking no one knew him, when he had been there twice before (possibly three times—Hawkeye and Trapper discuss Flagg nearly killing himself the last time in an offscreen incident the last time he was there).

Then, in his final appearance, Flagg is shown trying to kill a helpless wounded man, and suddenly the jokes stop coming. Flagg stepped over the threshold of being merely an insane incompetent who is all talk with no bite, to that of homicidal lunatic (sure, he may have been before, but we never saw any of that; just him being a blowhard about how macho he is). Flagg would end the episode making a fool of himself (with a little help from Charles) and then disappearing into thin air. Yet this wasn't quite the end for Flagg—he would turn up in the series *After MASH* to testify against Klinger in a court trial. Flagg now has gone on to be pretty much a secret agent. Just as we all expected he would someday be.

Flagg was played by Edward Winter, who was born on June 3, 1937, in Ventura, California. Winter began working on Broadway as a performer in various plays, but really hit pay dirt with his casting in the original production of *Cabaret* (as Ernst Ludwig, a character who eventually is revealed to be a Nazi). He would earn a Tony nomination for the role, as he would for the musical *Promises, Promises*, in which he starred as the villainous Sheldrake in 1968. He then appeared in *Night Watch* in 1972 before moving completely over to television and movies, although he had appeared as a running character on the soap opera *Somerset* in 1970.

With his stern but handsome looks, Winters usually got pegged with roles as authoritative figures when not playing villains (sometimes even both), including playing a senator in the movie *The Parallax View* (1974) and the series *Karen* in 1975, as well as a congressman in *Soap* (1977–1978). He would also be seen as an FBI agent in an episode of Wayne Rogers' *City of Angels* in 1976. So it is no surprise that when the role of Flagg came up, Winter was brought in.

Winter would continue in television and movies, starring in the series *Project U.F.O.* (1978–1979), appearing several times in a season of *Dallas* (1981–1982), and appearing in the film *A Change of Seasons* (1980), which featured an appearance by Karen Philipp (Lieutenant Dish). He later was a regular on shows like *Herman's Head* (1991–1994), *Nine to Five* (1986–1988), and *Hollywood Beat* (1985). In his later years he would do voice work in a number of animated series. He passed away on March 8, 2001, from Parkinson's disease.

At least Flagg had a reason to disappear into the ether; with his character, it was easy to see him vanish off the face of the earth (and he would have been proud to do so). As to the others, such as Spearchucker and Cutler, it was a shame that more was not done with them. Yet that's how things happen in television sometimes—one minute you have a character who seems to be there for the duration, and then the character simply doesn't work out. On the other hand, sometimes a background actor can find him or herself suddenly being asked to do more on a show and end up staying for years. Which is exactly what happened to those listed in the next chapter.

19

Reenlisted

Minor Characters That Stuck It Out

As many times as there were characters that started or were brought into *MASH* over the years to remain but then disappeared, so too were there those who came into the program for what were simply background parts—people just standing there to fill up space in scenes—who would go on to have regular speaking roles.

In several cases, these were actresses who played nurses many times on the program, but the names changed every few episodes as no one suspected anyone would bother keeping track of such things while watching. Over the years, there was a Nurse Able and a Nurse Baker, but these characters were played by various actresses. Nurse Able was played by Mike Farrell's then-wife Judy in eight episodes, but before that, the character was played by eight other actresses, including Gwen Farrell (who was not Mike's wife) and Kellye Nakahara—both of whom would have their own recurring character names eventually in the show (Gwen's history in the program is listed in chapter 17, as she also participated in the "running of the nurses" at the beginning of each episode). It was only in later seasons that the naming of nurses really settled down to particular actresses. Thus, while we have Ables and Bakers all over the place in *MASH*, they do not quite fit the definition of a recurring character. After all, maybe the 4077th just had the luck of getting Able after Able as nurses there.

Below are seven actors who eventually found themselves spending more time on the Fox Ranch and Stage 9 than they probably thought was likely.

Private Igor Straminsky—Jeff Maxwell

Jeff Maxell, born in 1947, had started off working at 20th Century-Fox in the print department. While working there, he was given the nickname Igor due to a routine he would pull when the touring buses came by the printing office where he acted like Charles Laughton in *The Hunchback of Notre Dame*.

Leaving Fox for a time to work as a stand-up comedian, where he toured Asia—including Korea—as part of a comedy duo, Maxwell returned to find work as an extra on *MASH*. His first appearance came in the second episode of the second season, "Five O'Clock Charlie," and he eventually began appearing regularly. The loss of Alan Alda's stand-in (a person of the same height and build who literally stands in for an actor before filming so that lighting and other essentials can be set up properly, thus allowing the actor to not wilt under the hot lights before the camera rolls) led to Maxwell taking over the position, and left him there most days for filming anyway, so it was only natural for Maxwell to get more screen time in episodes as he was there anyway.

As the season wore on, Jeff Maxwell was given dialogue in "Crisis" (as well as a little visual business) when his character is asked where he got desk drawers to burn as firewood. In the second episode of season three, "Officer of the Day," Maxwell's character finally got a name—Igor. It was around this time that several of the regular background performers—mainly those who played nurses—were given characters that were based on their real ones, so it made sense that Maxwell would get Igor. In the fourth-season

Give that man a cigar! Jamie Farr took a one-shot character from early in the first season, the crossdressing Klinger, and turned it into a major feature character in the series. Even so, it would take many seasons before Farr would get a credit in the opening of each episode.

episode "The Price of Tomato Juice," Igor tells Frank Burns that his name is Maxwell. It was later revealed to be Straminsky. Perhaps his name was Maxwell "Igor" Straminsky? Perhaps, as with the desk drawers in "Crisis," he was putting one over on Burns? The world will never know. No matter what his name, he would appear in over eighty episodes of the series.

Igor in the series would do various jobs around the camp, usually in a manner that caused near-disasters (such as shooting Radar's bugle out of his hand in "Officer of the Day"), and he usually turned up in the mess tent, serving inedible food and managing to get fresh corn on the cob and then cream it in the season nine episode, "A War for all Seasons." Although his job as a stand-in eventually disappeared, Maxwell stayed with the series until the finale in 1983. He can be seen as a medical student in *Young Frankenstein* (which featured Teri Garr, who appeared in one earlier episode of the series) and even popped up in an episode of Wayne Rogers' series *House Calls* in 1981. One of his best roles was in the 1977 film *The Kentucky Fried Movie*, (featuring Donald Sutherland as "The Clumsy Waiter"): a movie patron who wanders into a showing of a film in "Feel-A-Round" and finds his life in danger along with the main character in the film he's watching.

Fans usually point out that two episodes in season six feature Peter Riegert (*Animal House*, *The Sopranos*, and several Broadway shows) as Igor— "War of Nerves" and "Change Day." However, Riegert's Igor is much different from Maxwell in personality and could simply be someone with the same nickname. True, Maxwell did not appear in that season, but he would be back soon enough, and one can just assume he was in the back of the mess tent, figuring out what else he could serve in a creamed form.

Jeff Maxwell also published a recipe book called *Secrets of the MASH Mess* (1977, by Cumberland House Press, Nashville). The book also contains several photos from the show and a brief autobiography by Maxwell on his career before, during, and after *MASH*.

Nurse Kellye—Kellye Nakahara

Born in 1950, Nakahara would make her first appearance on *MASH* one episode before Jeff Maxwell, in the first episode of the second season as Lt. Kellye Yamato. In more than 160 episodes, Nakahara would play the same character, although she did appear as Nurse Able in "As You Were" in 1974 and Nurse Charlie in "Bulletin Board" in 1975. (Perhaps she was just too polite to correct everyone? Well, anything is possible.) She would appear often in the O.R. and in scenes where people were having fun in their off-time. Eventually, she got dialogue in the series, and the episode "Hey, Look Me Over" in season eleven would showcase her as the central character. She would continue with the series until the end, then appear in television and movies (including *Shattered* in 1991 and *Doctor Dolittle* in 1998). She is an artist and works in oil and watercolors, although she occasionally acts when a part comes along.

Staff Sgt. Luther Wilson Rizzo—G. W. Bailey

The Louisianan Rizzo was the head of the motor pool, and first turned up in the eighth season of the program ("Yalu Brick Road"), but he would make it to the end of the series, announcing that he planned to breed frogs for restaurants in the party scene and left the camp in a garbage truck with Winchester riding shotgun. In some ways he was similar to Zale (see below), but with less of a temper. As Zelmo Zale (and Johnny Haymer, the actor who played the part) bowed out of the series earlier in season eight, it is easy to see that Rizzo was in some way a continuation of Zale.

G. W. Bailey, born in 1944, had been acting in bit parts on television since the early 1970s. He was a regular on *St. Elsewhere*, *Goodnight, Beantown*, and *The Closer*, but probably still best remembered as Harris in the *Police Academy* movies.

Maj. Sidney Theodore Freedman—Allan Arbus

Sidney Freedman was only in twelve episodes, but appeared just often enough that he seemed more of a regular than some who were there more often, notably because he was more pivotal to the episodes' resolutions than other characters.

Freedman first turned up as Milton Freedman in the season two episode "Radar's Report," where Klinger finally gets to talk to a psychiatrist in order to—hopefully—get a Section 8. Friedman isn't fooled, in fact, he's a bit ticked off that they brought him out to talk to a guy who was obviously faking it. He finishes by giving Klinger the Section 8, but not the way he wants, and Klinger refuses to sign. Freedman would return a few episodes later in season two for "Deal Me Out," where his first name was changed to Sidney (and where he first runs into the man who may or may not be Colonel Flagg). In the third-season episode "O.R." the audience finds out that he has surgical experience, as he is tasked to help out when the camp is short-handed. It is also the episode where he tells the surgeons and nurses to "take my advice—pull down your pants and slide on the ice!"

Freedman would pop up in subsequent seasons when a psychological diagnosis needs to be made, including of various issues that trouble Hawkeye over the seasons such as the "chicken" incident in the finale. In all that time, Freedman was calm, jokey when needed, and one of the few psychiatrists in sitcom history who wasn't portrayed as crazier than the patients. (Freedman probably did more to send people to psychiatrists in the 1970s than any real doctor did.)

The character was played by Allan Arbus, born in 1918, who had two careers—one as a photographer, which lasted from 1946 through most of the 1960s and ended with his first marriage. Looking for something new, Arbus decided to begin a career in acting at the age of fifty. A role in Robert Downey Sr.'s *Putney Swope* (1969) would lead to a starring role as Jesse in Downey's 1972 cult film *Greaser's Palace*. He played a villain in the Pam Grier blaxploitation film *Coffy* (1973), and also appeared in films like *The Electric Horseman* (1979) and *Volunteers* (1985). He was also a regular in the television version of Alan Alda's *The Four Seasons*, which ran for thirteen episodes in 1984. An amazing dual career for a man who lived to be ninety-five, passing away in 2013.

Staff Sgt. Zelmo Zale—Johnny Haymer

Zelmo Zale was the supply sergeant at the 4077th and pretty much a nemesis to everyone else in the camp who wanted supplies, but in particular had issues with Klinger. Zale first turned up in the season two episode "For Want of a Boot," and appeared in twenty episodes over the years until the first part of "Good-Bye Radar" in 1979. Zale's best episode came in season four's "Of Moose and Men," where BJ writes Zale a letter to send to his wife, who had admitted to an affair in a letter. As it turns out Zale, has a "moose," a Korean woman he spends time with, thus showing his true colors.

Zale commonly would snark at Klinger, pushing his buttons in hopes of starting a fight, although the two could get along when motivated to do so—as in season five's "End Run," where the two realize that Frank Burns is setting them up in a boxing match mainly to feed his own ego and the two "accidentally" knock Burns out together when the fight occurs.

Zale was played by Johnny Haymer, born in 1920, who had been working in television since the mid-1950s. He appeared in pretty much everything, including *Star Trek*, *The Wild Wild West*, *Hogan's Heroes*, *S.W.A.T.*, and even did the voice of Highbrow on *The Transformers*. Haymer passed away in 1989.

Rosie—Shizuko Hoski/Frances Fong/Eileen Saki

This is a bit of a trick entry, as we have the same character here but played by three actresses. Still, Rosie was an important character; certainly so in later seasons, for a total of eleven appearances over the years.

Rosie was the owner of a bar on the outskirts of where the 4077th was located. In early episodes, it was seen as not a very safe place to go, but over time the hut that stationed the watering hole would become a common center of activities for those stations at the camp.

Rosie was first played by Shizuko Hoshi, who was married to Mako, the actor who appeared in the series a couple of times (see chapter 14 for more details about him). "Mad Dogs and Servicemen" was the episode from the third season that featured Rosie for the first time, as she helps Radar and Blake locate a dog that had bitten Radar. It was the only time Shizuko Hoshi played the role, although she would appear in three other episodes over the years, and always as a mothers ("Hawkeye," "BJ Papa San," and "Private Finance"). She has directed theater in California and off-Broadway in New York, and appeared in films like *M. Butterfly* (1993), *Come See the Paradise* (1990), and *Memoirs of a Geisha* (2005).

The second Rosie appeared in the season four hour-long opener, "Bug-Out," where Hawkeye, Houlihan, and Radar are left behind to care for a patient that cannot be moved while everyone else leaves due to the enemy approaching (leading to the battle line becoming the 4077th itself). With the camp mostly deserted, Hawkeye and Radar go to visit Rosie's and manage to get a drink as Rosie hurries with packing. The actress this time around was France Fong. Fong, born in 1927, had a number of movie and television roles in her past before appearing as Rosie, such as *Man from U.N.C.L.E.*, *Mod Squad*, and *Kung Fu*. She also has appeared in the Jackie Chan film, *Rush Hour* (1998). She would play Rosie in the season six episode "Fallen Idol" before moving on.

The final Rosie was the one that lasted the longest—Eileen Saki, who had earlier appeared as the "Madam" (as Potter calls her) of the prostitutes that end up taking Klinger's wardrobe in season four's "Bug-Out." Saki would take over in the role with the season seven episode "A Night at Rosie's," which takes place completely inside the confines of Rosie's Bar. She would play the role again in the following episode, "Ain't Love Grand?" and then two episodes in season eight, three in season nine, and a final one in season ten. Although Rosie and her bar would be mentioned in various other episodes, "Snap Judgement" would be the final episode to actually show Rosie.

Eileen Saki also appeared in *Meteor* (1979), *History of the World: Part I* (1981), and *Splash* (1984) besides parts on television.

Private Roy Goldman—Roy Goldman

Roy Goldman had appeared in two episodes of *Hogan's Heroes*, a cameo in the Peter Bogdanovich film *At Long Last Love* (1975), and as a workman quickly seen in the television movie *Sherlock Holmes in New York* (1976). His last big role was a cameo as Hitler in the 1983 remake of the comedy *To Be or Not To Be*.

Goldman was mainly known for one role in particular—as a soldier at the 4077th who usually went by the name of Goldman, and was referred to as Roy sometimes. In other words, he played Roy Goldman (although on occasion his character was given a different name). Roy would appear in episodes from first season to last, commonly as a character watching the main characters do something outrageous (for example, he's the soldier who drops his food tray upon noticing Hawkeye naked in the mess tent in season one's "Dear Dad, Again"). His character would eventually get a few lines in the show, including more of a showcase in the episode "The Red/White Blues." His last episode was the finale of the series, and he passed away in 2009.

The past few chapters have covered both major and minor characters of the 4077th. Yet some of the best-known moments of the show occurred with the guest stars that appeared over the years, as covered in the following chapter.

20

I Don't Know Your Name, But . . .

Thirty Famous Guest Appearances

N ot surprisingly, for a show that lasted eleven years and considered a good notch in the belt for up-and-coming actors, *MASH* had a lot of guest stars that had been or would go on to big things in both television and movies. No doubt, there are even more than thirty for such a list, but in order to end up not spending half the book discussing the many others, below is a good sampling; showing thirty individuals that viewers remember, or are surprised to see once again when watching reruns of the program.

Leslie Nielsen

Leslie Nielsen was only in one episode of *MASH*, the first season's "The Ringbanger," but even that short diversion was enough to demonstrate that there was a comedian longing to come out of the actor typically stuck in dramatic roles.

Nielsen was born in 1926 and began working in television in 1950 in a variety of dramatic roles. His first film appearance was in a small role in *Ransom!* (1956) with Glenn Ford, and he followed that up as the star of the science-fiction classic *Forbidden Planet* (1956). The occasional comedic part would pop up over the following years, such as in *Tammy and the Bachelor* (1957), but for the most part, with his good looks and smooth voice, Nielsen etched out a career as the determined good guy in many roles, including a semiregular one on *Walt Disney's The Wonderful World of Color* in 1960 with the character "The Swamp Fox." It was this cliché that Nielsen had fallen into as always playing the dashing lead (he played the dashing captain of the ill-fated *Poseidon* in *The Poseidon Adventure* in 1972, for example) that led to him being cast in the comedy *Airplane!* In 1980. The role as the doctor

Harry Morgan as Col. Sherman T. Potter. Morgan had been so successful in a guest-starring role in season three that he was asked to play a sane version of essentially the same character in season four onward, a case of a guest star who changed the show in an effective manner.

was a parody of many roles Nielsen had done straitlaced in several other movies and television shows, and it demonstrated that Nielsen has comic chops that had been rarely used.

He would follow that up with the series *Police Squad!*, which became the *Naked Gun* series of films later in the 1980s and 1990s. From there, he would appear mainly in comedies, and most of the parody films similar to *Airplane!* He would happily continue with his second career as a comic actor for the rest of his life, until his passing in 2010.

In the *MASH* episode, Nielsen plays a colonel who seems likable enough, but is known for disastrous campaigns in battle that see a lot of casualties. Hawkeye and Trapper decide to convince the colonel and everyone else that he is going crazy in order to get him sent back to the U.S. for a while to clear his head.

Shelly Long

Shelly Long is best remembered from the series *Cheers*, which she appeared on for five seasons. Born in 1949, Long was a member of Second City and had appeared in an episode of *Trapper John, M.D.* in 1979 before popping up on *MASH* in the eighth-season episode "Bottle Fatigue," as a nurse that Hawkeye is interested in but drives off from after complaining about her drinking. She would star in Ron Howard's *Night Shift* (1982) as well as *Caveman* (1981), and appear in a number of other film and television roles.

Andrew "Dice" Clay and George Wendt

Andrew "Dice" Clay, born in 1957, may be remembered as a raunchy comedian who hit it big in 1988, but for a time he was actively pursuing a career as an actor before fame hit with his character "the dice man." One of his first roles was a short part as a drunken Marine who is injured when driving backwards. His scene in the episode is solely with Mike Farrell, a former Marine in real life. As "the dice man" character was still pretty much in the future, Clay is listed in the credits as Andrew Clay.

The episode was from the final season of *MASH*, "Trick or Treatment," which also featured George Wendt as a private who ends up with a billiard ball stuck in his mouth. Wendt, born in 1948, started with Second City as an actor and then moved on to television and the movies, such as a small role in *Somewhere in Time* (1980) and as a regular on the show *Making the Grade* (1982). He's best remembered as the character Norm Peterson on the sitcom *Cheers* (1982–1993).

Ron Howard

Born in 1954 in a showbiz family, Ron Howard would achieve stardom by the age of six in the role of Opie Taylor on *The Andy Griffith Show*, and then compound that by landing the role of Richie Cunningham in *Happy Days*.

He also appeared in the film *American Graffiti* (1973) and began directing films with *Grand Theft Auto* in 1977. He has since directed such films as *Splash* (1984), *Apollo 13* (1995), *The Da Vinci Code* (2006), and *Cocoon* (1985, and featuring Brian Dennehy, who is listed in this chapter).

In 1972, he appeared in the famous *MASH* episode "Sometimes You Hear the Bullet" from season one. He played a soldier that Hawkeye finds out is underage, and during the course of the episode decides to rat on the kid in order to save him from possibly being killed after Hawkeye watches an old friend die from a battle wound.

Teri Garr

Appearing in the season two episode "The Sniper," Garr had already spent years in television and was a year away from gaining stardom in the film *Young Frankenstein* (1974). Born in 1947 to vaudevillian Eddie Garr and his wife Phyllis, a former Rockette, Teri would first begin appearing as a dancer in various Elvis Presley movies of the 1960s, while occasionally getting lines on shows, including a costarring role in the 1968 *Star Trek* episode "Assignment: Earth" that was a backdoor pilot. In 1970, she appeared with Alan Alda in the film *The Moonshine War*, while first really being showcased as one of the actors in *The Sonny and Cher Comedy Hour* (1971–1972). After *Young Frankenstein*, Garr would costar in the Larry Gelbart–written film *Oh, God!* (1977) and as the wife of Richard Dreyfuss' character in *Close Encounters of the Third Kind* (1977). She also had a role in the Gelbart-related film *Tootsie* (1982) and costarred with Gregory Harrison (also in this chapter) in the comedy miniseries *Fresno* (1986).

Blythe Danner

Born in 1943, Blythe Danner was a star of Broadway, having won a Tony Award for *Butterflies Are Free* in 1970. In 1972, she appeared in the film *To Kill a Clown* with Alan Alda, making her appearance as Hawkeye's college girlfriend (and the one woman he can't forget) in the season four episode "The More I See You" a reunion in a way. She has appeared in several roles on television and movies, including the film *The Great Santini* (1979) with Robert Duval and in the *Meet the Fockers* series of films. She's also known as the mother of actress Gwyneth Paltrow.

John Ritter

Born in 1948 to the famous country singer Tex Ritter, John Ritter will forever be remembered as Jack Tripper on *Three's Company* (1976–1984), whose pilot was written by Larry Gelbart. He had many television roles before that, usually in sitcoms where he got memorable parts (the waiter dissing Bob for only ordering one scoop of ice cream on *The Bob Newhart Show*, the tennis-playing reverend for Ted and Georgette's wedding on *The Mary Tyler Moore Show*). He was also a semiregular on *The Waltons*, playing Reverend Fordwick. Other roles included starring in *Hooperman* (1987–1990), one of the first sitcoms done specifically without a laugh track, and appearing on *Anything but Love*, which was cocreated by *MASH* writer Dennis Koenig. He also appeared in two films with Billy Bob Thornton, *Sling Blade* (1996) and *Bad Santa* (2003).

Ritter appeared in the season two episode "Deal Me Out" as a soldier who takes Frank Burns hostage after Burns refuses to listen to his pleas to not have to go back to combat.

While working on a new series, *8 Simple Rules for Dating My Teenage Daughter* in 2003, Ritter fell ill on the set. At first it was assumed to be a heart attack, but it turned out to be an aortic dissection, which was diagnosed too late to save his life. He died in 2003 at the age of fifty-four.

Robert Ito and Larry Hama

Robert Ito appeared in only one episode of *MASH*—"The Korean Surgeon" from season five—but is instantly recognizable to fans of *Quincy, M.E.*, where he appeared as Sam Fujiyama, Quincy's lab assistant. Born in 1931, Ito first worked as a dancer for the National Ballet of Canada in the 1960s, and then moved on to television, including doing the voice of Henry Chan on *The Amazing Chan and the Chan Clan* animated series in 1972 (which has some stories written by Jamie Farr). He also appeared in "The Chinatown Murders" two-parter on *Kojak* in 1974, which featured Patrick (Ho-Jon) Adiarte. He also had prominent cameos in both *The Adventures of Buckaroo Banzai* (1984) and *Rollerball* (1975). He still does a number of television appearances, although he mainly does voice work on animated series now.

On *MASH*, Ito played one of two North Korean soldiers who end up kidnapping Frank Burns. The other soldier was played by Larry Hama, born in 1949, and mainly known as a writer of comics for both Marvel and

DC, and in particular helped for shaping the backstory for many characters in *G.I. Joe* through the years. In Ed Solomonson and Mark O'Neill's *TV's MASH: The Ultimate Guide Book*, Hama states that, as they were waiting to film, Robert Ito mentioned auditioning for a new television show about a coroner named Quincy, with Hama thinking that no one would watch a show about something like that.

Laurence Fishburne

Laurence Fishburne, born 1961, has had a career of big and small parts, appearing in *Apocalypse Now* (at the age of fourteen), as Ike Turner in *What's Love Got to Do with It* (1993), Morpheus in *The Matrix* series of films (1999–2003), and even Perry White in *Man of Steel* (2013). He also has been in a lot of television shows, from his first work in the soap opera *One Life to Live*; to the *MASH*-ish *The Six O'Clock Follies* (1980, and covered in chapter 12); *Trapper John, M.D.* (1981); *Pee Wee's Playhouse*, as Cowboy Curtis (with Lynn Marie Stewart, who is listed below); and *CSI: Crime Scene Investigation* (2008–2011).

He appeared in an episode of *MASH* during the tenth season, "The Tooth Shall Set You Free," as Larry Fishburne. His character was a soldier whose commanding officer is sending his African American troops out on dangerous missions in hopes of them being killed or wounded and leaving his command.

Ed Begley Jr.

Ed Begley Jr. had been a regular on *Roll Out*, the 1974 series that was to have been a companion piece to *MASH* and put together by Gene Reynolds and Larry Gelbart. It lasted only a handful of episodes, but Begley had obtained regular work in various shows by that point. Born in 1949, with his father being popular actor Ed Begley, Ed Begley Jr. would begin working in television and movies in the late 1960s, and popped up in a few episodes of *Room 222* while Gene Reynolds was involved with the show. He would later appear as a regular on *St. Elsewhere* (with Ed Flanders, listed below), amongst a variety of roles on television and in movies. He also appeared in a handful of episodes of *Providence*, the series with Mike Farrell, in 2000.

Begley appeared in the opening episode of season eight, "Too Many Cooks," as a clumsy soldier who is an amazing chef that the 4077th tries to keep for their mess tent.

Brian Dennehy

In an almost "blink and you'll miss him" moment, actor Brian Dennehy appears in an episode of *MASH* from season five, "Souvenirs," where he plays an M.P. looking for stolen Korean artifacts that Frank Burns bought but denies having.

Dennehy, born in 1938, popped up in television during 1977, including the *MASH* episode, and appeared in such films as *Semi-Tough* (1977), *Foul Play* 1978), and *10* (1980), before hitting it big in *First Blood* (1982). He also appeared in *Cocoon* (1985), *F/X* (1986), and *Tommy Boy* (1995), as well as on Broadway, winning two Tony Awards: one for *Death of a Salesman* (1999) and one *Long Day's Journey into Night* (2003).

Mary Kay Place and Linda Bloodworth-Thomason

Mary Kay Place has the distinction of having appeared in an episode of *MASH* she wrote without being a regular in the series (unlike Alda, Farrell, etc.). Born in 1974, Place got her first break as a writer for *The Tim Conway Comedy Hour* (which featured McLean Stevenson). In the early 1970s, she began writing scripts with Linda Bloodworth. The pair would be signed on to *MASH* in 1973 to help write scripts that would show Houlihan in a better light, and the first was "Hot Lips and Empty Arms" in season two, where Houlihan requests a transfer after feeling that she's wasting her life at the 4077th.

They would follow that up with "Springtime" in season three, which had the bonus of Place playing Lieutenant Louise Simmons, the nurse that Radar tries to impress but ends up being "slaked" by her. The pair would also write the third-season episode "Mad Dogs and Servicemen," and while the attempt to give Loretta Swit more to do by hiring the two female writers didn't quite pan out (they did more with Radar than Houlihan with the three episodes), they did at least give the cast more to do per episode than some of the other writers.

The pair would split off, with Bloodworth writing two more episodes, "Soldier of the Month" in season four and season five's "The Nurses" (which really was a breakthrough episode for Houlihan). Bloodworth would become better known as Linda Bloodworth-Thomason and as the creator of *Designing Women* and *Evening Shade*. Mary Kay Place would move on to write an episode each for *The Mary Tyler Moore Show* and *Phyllis* (with writer Valerie Curtin) before starring in her biggest role as country singer and next-door neighbor Loretta Haggers, in the nightly comedy soap opera *Mary Hartman, Mary Hartman* (1976–1977). In character, Place would record an album and get airplay with the song "Baby Boy" as well as a duet with Willie Nelson called "Something to Brag About."

She would appear on several television shows and in films, including *Private Benjamin* (1980), *The Big Chill* (1983), the cult series *My So-Called Life* (1994–1995), and *Big Love* (2006–2011).

Robert Alda and Anthony Alda

Alan Alda talks in both of his autobiographies of his love/hate relationship with his father, Robert Alda, who was born in 1914 and died in 1986. Robert Alda was a vaudevillian who worked in burlesque and eventually on Broadway in *Guys and Dolls* (1950–1953). He won a Tony Award for his role in *What Makes Sammy Run?* (1964–1965). He appeared in a number of movies, but never quite made the transition to stardom there that he did on the stage. He would later blame this on being contracted with Warner Brothers, who didn't know what to do with him. "I was Tiffany's, but they kept insisting on putting me in Woolworth's window," Robert Alda stated in an interview about his son, Alan, to *TV Guide* in 1977.

Robert Alda would appear twice on *MASH*, both times as the same character, Dr. Anthony Borelli. In "The Consultant," from season three, Hawkeye and Trapper meet Borelli while in Japan. After talking about the 4077th, Borelli comes to visit and offers up a new procedure that could save a wounded soldier's leg, but then gets drunk and can't operate, leaving Hawkeye to do it. Hawkeye still holds resentment about the incident when they meet up again in season eight for the episode "Lend a Hand." In that episode, they go to a battalion aid station and, due to injuries, have to work together during surgery. The episode also had Alan's half-brother Anthony Alda, with all three acting together during the scene at the battalion station.

George Lindsay

Lindsay played Goober on *The Andy Griffith Show* and *Mayberry, RFD*, as well as being a regular on *Hee Haw*. He also played a character much more like the surgeons of the novel in an episode of *MASH*.

Born in 1928, Lindsay is best known for playing Goober Pyle between 1964 and 1971. He then played essentially the same character on *Hee Haw* for a couple of decades, while periodically popping up in movies (mainly

Disney films of the late 1960s and early 1970s) until the time of his passing in 2012. In the season six episode "Temporary Duty," Hawkeye is sent to another MASH unit, the 8063rd, while Captain Roy Dupree (played by Lindsey) comes to the 4077th as a temporary trade. Dupree is vile, rude, inconsiderate to everyone, and a very good doctor, leading to Potter deciding to keep him. As both BJ and Charles can't stand him, they do their best to make sure Dupree doesn't stick around.

When Hawkeye comes back, he tells the others that the MASH unit he went to thought he was boring. Considering how Dupree seemed to slip in from an alternate dimension, maybe Hawkeye really ended up with people like Duke, Trapper, and Spearchucker from the novel and found himself in way over his head.

Patrick Swayze

A dancer and actor, Swayze had come off of playing Danny Zuko in a Broadway production of *Grease* when he appeared in the season nine episode "Blood Brothers." Swayze's role was that of a soldier who, when offering to give blood, finds out that he has leukemia and only a short time to live.

Swayze would gain popularity with roles in such films as *The Outsiders* (1983) and *Red Dawn* (1984), as well as appearing in the miniseries *North and South* (1985). The 1987 film *Dirty Dancing* and *Ghost* in 1990 would make him a superstar. In 2008, he discovered he had advanced pancreatic cancer, which he died from in 2009.

Edward Herrmann

Edward Herrmann (1943–2014) was an actor who seemed to spend a lot of time playing Franklin D. Roosevelt in *Eleanor and Franklin* (1976), *Eleanor and Franklin: The White House Years* (1977), and in *Annie* (1982). He appeared in a number of films, including *The Paper Chase* (1972), and portrayed William Randolph Hearst in *The Cat's Meow* in 2001. He also appeared in *The Aviator* (2004), which costarred Alan Alda.

On *MASH*, Herrmann played Steven Newsome, a surgeon who joins Hawkeye and BJ at the 4077th when Potter and Winchester both come down with the mumps in the season eight episode "Heal Thyself." The character starts off fitting in well, but soon the stress of the work gets to him, causing the doctor to have a breakdown and be shipped out.

Herrmann passed away in 2014 from brain cancer.

Stuart Margolin

Margolin (1940) was a staple of 1970s television, popping up in a variety of television shows, especially as Angel on *The Rockford Files* (1974–1980), for which he won two Emmy Awards in a row (1979 and 1980) for the role. He also appeared in James Garner's earlier series *Nichols*, which featured William Christopher as a semiregular. Margolin was also a regular in little blackout skits shown on *Love, American Style*. He also appeared in *S.O.B.*, which costarred Loretta Swit. Margolin directed many television series, including *Magnum, P.I.*, *Quantum Leap*, and *Northern Exposure*.

Margolin appeared in two early episodes of *MASH*, and both times as an officer who attacks Major Houlihan. The first was as psychologist Captain Philip Sherman in season one's "Bananas, Crackers and Nuts" (where he is tricked into attacking Houlihan, thinking she is infatuated with him) and "Operation Noselift" in season two as plastic surgeon Major Stanley Robbins (who is convinced to help when told a nurse will date him while he is there and he mistakenly thinks it is Margaret).

Ned Beatty

Ned Beatty, born in 1937, was already a very well-recognized actor by the time he turned up as the visiting chaplain, Colonel Hollister, who forces Father Mulcahy to write a letter to the family of a soldier before finding that the wounded man has taken a turn for the worse in the season four episode "Dear Peggy."

Beatty has never been afraid of going back and forth between television and films, appearing in such movies as *Network* (1976), *Deliverance* (1972), Robert Altman's *Nashville* (1975, with Timothy Brown), *Silver Streak* (1976), and as the dummy Otis in the first two *Superman* movies with Christopher Reeve. He also appeared in *The Big Bus* (1976) with Rene Auberjonois, Stuart Margolin, and Sally Kellerman.

Alex Karras

Alex Karras (1935- 2012) had already appeared with Alan Alda in the film *Paper Lion* (1968), but he's probably best remembered as Mongo in *Blazing Saddles* (1974). After a successful career in professional football, Karras did well in the field of acting, including playing a bodyguard who comes out of the closet in Blake Edwards' *Victor/Victoria* (1982). He also costarred in the sitcom *Webster* with his wife, Susan Clark. He played Corporal Wesson in the season three episode "Springtime," spinning Frank Burns around as Klinger gets married to his hometown sweetheart over the radio. Karras died in 2012 at the age of seventy-seven.

Rita Wilson

Born in 1956, Wilson appeared on *The Brady Bunch* at age sixteen. She would appear in several television shows and movies, such as *Volunteers* (with her future husband, Tom Hanks), *Sleepless in Seattle*, and *Barbarians at the Gate* (written by Larry Gelbart). She is also an alumnus of the improvisational group the Groundlings (like many others throughout this book).

She would appear in two late-season episodes as Nurse Lacey: "Blood and Guts" in season ten and "Hey, Look Me Over" in season eleven.

Pat Morita

Probably best remembered as Kesuke Miyagi in *The Karate Kid* series of films, Pat Morita (1932–2005) is also remembered for playing Arnold on *Happy Days* and for starring in the notorious sitcom bomb *Mr. T and Tina*. He started his entertainment career as a stand-up comic (and still performed as such even after achieving stardom in television) and had been a member of the Groundlings at one point.

Born in America to Japanese parents, Morita would play South Korean surgeon Captain Sam Pak in two episodes from the third season of *MASH* (and may have made more recurring appearances after that if the gig on *Happy Days* had not occurred). The episodes are "Deal Me Out" and "The Chosen People."

Jack Soo

Born on a ship while traveling to America from Japan, Jack So came into the world on October 28, 1917. During World War II, he found himself being placed in one of the Japanese American internment camps (when it was assumed that some Japanese Americans might attempt to sabotage American efforts in the war against Japan). While there, he became known for his singing ability and natural charm when working at events in the camp, and would eventually leave with a focus on a career in show business as a stand-up comedian.

A big break came when *Flower Drum Song* went to Broadway (the same production that featured Patrick Adiarte, who played Ho-Jon in season one), and he was hired to be in it and the film version that came later. It was here that he changed his name to Jack Soo (in order to make himself sound Chinese). He is best remembered for playing Detective Nick Yemana on *Barney Miller* in 1975. Due to a late diagnosis of cancer, he died during a season of the program and instead of writing his character out, the series did a retrospective episode with the actors reflecting on their time with Soo.

Jack Soo appeared in two episodes of *MASH* before moving on to *Barney Miller*: "To Market, to Market" in season one and "Payday" in season three.

Ed Flanders

Born in 1934, Ed Flanders appeared as the filmmaker who gives up on the documentary *Yankee Doodle Doctor* in the season one episode of the same name. Flanders had previously been married to Ellen Geer, who is the sister to Kate Geer. Kate Geer was married to Larry Linville at the time Flanders appeared on *MASH*.

A winner of a Tony Award for *A Moon for the Misbegotten* (1974), Flanders is probably best remembered as Dr. Donald Westphall on the NBC hospital series *St. Elsewhere* (1982–1988). He committed suicide in 1995.

Mariette Hartley

Hartley (born 1940) only appeared in one episode of *MASH*, the season seven episode "Inga," but she is fondly remembered for her work in shows such as *Star Trek* ("All Our Yesterdays" as a woman stuck in an ancient time who has a romance with Spock), *The Twilight Zone* ("The Long Morrow"), and in a two-hour episode for *The Incredible Hulk* ("Married") that won her an Emmy Award. She gained some odd fame in the late 1970s for a series of Polaroid camera commercials with James Garner that were received so well, people assumed they were husband and wife. She still acts today.

Gregory Harrison

Born in 1950, Gregory Harrison is probably best known for playing Dr. George Alonzo "Gonzo" Gates on the long-running series *Trapper John, M.D.* (covered in more detail in chapter 33). He also starred in the short-lived television version of *Logan's Run*.

He appears in one episode of *MASH*, season five's "The Nurses," where he plays the husband of one of the nurses (played by Linda Kelsey, who was on the television version of *The Paper Chase* and would go on to be a regular on *Lou Grant*). Harrison continues to work in movies, television, and on the Broadway stage. He served as a medic during the Vietnam War.

Lynne Marie Stewart

Born in 1946, Lynne Marie Stewart was a member of the Groundlings who also appeared on *MASH* five times, two of them as Nurse Baker. In the season five episode "Lt. Radar O'Reilly," Nurse Baker tries to seduce Radar, but instantly loses interest when he rises to the rank of lieutenant and is no longer "forbidden fruit" (she also shares a funny shower scene with Radar in "The Abduction of Margaret Houlihan").

She has appeared in a number of projects over the years, but due to her connections with the Groundlings, she would become better known as another seductive woman of mystery, Miss Yvonne of *Pee Wee's Playhouse*.

21

Here for the Duration

Fans' Favorite Periods of *MASH*

One of the biggest issues that fans discuss is "favorite eras" in the show. It can actually lead to heated arguments, especially between those who love the Frank Burns years and others that didn't really start watching until Winchester came along. But such eras are not based on when certain characters appeared—some have to do with when certain writers and producers were on the program, and others have to do with a general feel of the program in certain years that were not there in others.

The most interesting aspect of all the eras listed below is how many of them overlap with other periods. Not to mention that usually once the fighting is over, people can agree that there are a handful of episodes from even their least-liked eras that stand out as being watchable.

The Henry Blake Years

This is the basic model for fans who were there in the earlier years and especially those who watched the show as kids. The period goes from season one through Henry's last episode in season three. After that, Henry and Trapper would be gone, and the series would begin to shift in tone from the happy-go-lucky days of the first three years to the more serious, drama-filled years in season four through eleven.

There's no doubt about it, as mentioned in previous chapters, the first season is full of episodes that are very much joke-fests, with Gelbart himself admitting that he had a hard time stopping himself from writing material so it was consistently joke, joke, joke. It is also clear in that first season that writers were being brought in from other military-themed sitcoms to find material for the show that usually brought it down to a carbon copy of earlier shows. "To Market, To Market," the second episode of the series, may be a lot of fun, but ultimately it's an episode of *McHale's Navy* in Korea.

"Operation Noselift" in season two is relentlessly silly, to the point that you figure it has to have been a nightmare Burns had one night, as the payoff of everyone wearing bandages on their noses makes zero sense in reality. And there's, of course, the dreaded episode "Edwina" (where the nurses hold off from being affectionate with the men until they find a date for the clumsy nurse, Edwina) is just a flat-out episode of *Love, American Style* (and, thus, little wonder that the cast and crew tend to point to the episode as one of the worst of the series).

But the series was locking into place, and dramatic moments were coming. "Sometimes You Hear the Bullet" showed that the series could have its comedy cake and eat it too, with dramatic moments not throwing the show off its rhythm. Episodes like "Hot Lips and Empty Arms" and "Bulletin Board" could give advancement to characters like Houlihan and Blake. Even so, the show was still aiming for funny more than anything else. With Henry Blake's death in "Abyssinia, Henry" and the departure of Trapper, the dynamics would begin to change to more serious ideas, and it is at that point that some of the original fans began to bail. Fortunately for the show, many more would jump on at that point.

The Frank Burns Years/The Original Guards Years

Frank Burns would be there for seasons one through five. When he left, so did Gene Reynolds, with Larry Gelbart having left at the end of season four. The show's emphasis on an internal antagonist was shifting quickly after Margaret Houlihan began to change into a more likable character. It was impossible for this not to occur, as there had to be a voice there to speak for the female characters, and Houlihan was the logical choice to be it. To continue to make her the bad guy would lessen the chances to deal with storylines that looked at issues in the war from the angle of a nurse, from a woman. Yet, in doing so, Frank began the only target available. The writers—including Gelbart—would later regret going the easy route and turning Frank from what he was to simply a cartoon to be tortured over and over again.

There were still good moments. BJ's introduction in "Welcome to Korea" worked well to help expand the scope of the show past the camp, and both he and Potter were brought in without viewers having many problems. The premiere episode of season five, "Bug-Out," again allowed the series to shake things up a bit by forcing the characters outside of the camp, and Margaret would even be married that year.

Still, the show would shift gears in season six with the arrival of Winchester—a character that some fans never grew to appreciate, and who never experienced any real growth in the seasons to follow. Hawkeye too would be knocked down several pegs as he no longer was the shining hero of earlier seasons but one prone to question himself, make mistakes, and at times seem to be even hated by other people in the camp. For some viewers, Burns' departure meant the end of the fun. Seasons one through three were laughs; seasons four and five were a little rockier but still solid. After that, the gems became fewer as the emphasis moved to drama over comedy.

The Years of Potter, Hunnicutt, and Burns

This is a bit of an odd choice, but there are a few fans who feel that seasons four and five—with Potter and BJ, but before Burns left—were the pinnacle of the series. The show was getting away from the goofier antics of the early years and yet not stuck in what some saw as the depressing, maudlin years of season six onward. To them, an episode with these three characters would mean a nearly perfect mix of drama and comedy and the defining years of the show.

The Winchester Years

Perhaps the most radical split between fans is here. Maj. Charles Emerson Winchester III was brought in as a worthy opponent for Hawkeye (and to a lesser extent, BJ). There was also talk of him becoming a romantic interest of Margaret's as well (and most of the sixth season suggests that there were sparks of varying degrees between the two before it all fizzled out; that or scripts written with Frank in mind were rapidly changed to Winchester without much done to change the indication of intimacy between the two). To many fans, it was good to see Hawkeye have to try harder and not always being the one that got to leave the room in triumph when it came to the bickering between the characters. Besides, the early seasons were so silly, while the later ones were tougher and had more to say. To such fans, seeing David Ogden Stiers' name in the opening credits meant they were going to invest a half-hour in an episode that they were sure to enjoy.

To others, Winchester was an annoying, prissy overachiever who never truly became likable. Over time, such fans would amend their feelings somewhat—Charles became agreeable, but still not likable, and he fell into his own clichés of being the snobby opera lover who never quite adjusted

The main cast from seasons four and five of *MASH*, one of the most popular periods of the program.

(even a similar character in the novel eventually adjusted and became one of the team over time). Worse, the writers were not allowing Hawkeye and BJ to direct lethal jabs at Winchester because he had to win in their battles in order to prove he was not going to be another Frank Burns. To some fans, that meant Hawkeye and BJ let the blowhard get away with things they simply would not have in the past, but had to because the writers demanded that Winchester win. Earlier seasons, and certainly the movie, would have seen Winchester on a one-way trip to a stateside asylum within days of arrival, but Winchester had to stay because the writers needed him to stay. BJ and Potter worked and viewers adjusted; Charles was never an easy sell to some fans and left them feeling out in the cold.

The growing shift to more character-driven episodes also drove some viewers away. Some fans felt that the actors were driving the show, forcing writers to make the characters more likable because they had become too close to the characters themselves. Of course, on a series that had been on so long, characters tend to work better when they are closer to the personalities of the people playing them. To many viewers, that kept the show fresh and allowed the characters to grow. To others, the Hawkeye and Houlihan of the first few seasons were no longer the same, and it was time to go. Thus, with no intention of dismissing the actor who took a tough role like Winchester and did a great job in the role, when David Ogden Stiers' name pops up in the opening credits, there is a select number of fans who turn off the television set. Not because of him, but because they know the direction of the episode will not be to their liking.

The Radar Years

Even so, viewers adjusted to Winchester, and ratings were just as good as or better than some earlier seasons. Then Radar left in the eighth season. With him went a certain element of innocence that Radar brought into the program. The changes in other characters were more apparent as well. Hawkeye would begin a trek to being unsure of his abilities, Klinger would stop being the silly crossdresser that was there solely for gags, Houlihan would often be the voice of reason rather than military chaos, BJ was not the happy-go-lucky punster of his early years, and Winchester still annoyed. To some who watched, Radar was the last element of the old show, and even when they did attempt to change him, he always held on to a bit of the innocence he had before. With that gone, the show lost the sense of youth and began to wander, and some felt it was time to move on.

The Series

So the show went through periods where fans either came into or left the show. That said, it didn't mean that the show went through a crisis in general. Ratings were good, and the studio and network certainly were not having any issues with the way characters were going. Many fans never had a real problem with the series from beginning to end and don't look for anal-retentive signs in the opening credits that tell them to tune in or not. To them, *MASH* was a great series and one to be watched in any of the seasons. Over time, some fans who prefer one period of the show too have come back to readjust their opinions of other seasons.

Fans do have their favorite periods of the show, but more often than not, when it comes to watching old episodes of *MASH* in comparison to new or old shows, viewers know they're going to get some type of quality in *MASH* that they couldn't get elsewhere.

22

MASH Means Mobile!

The Various Time Slots

MASH goes as far as it can—within the uptight limits of television propriety—to re-create the tone (irreverent) and comedy (wild) of the movie it is based on. The language is more restrained and the lechery less explicit, and the blood flows less freely in the field-hospital operating room. But the gang's all here: Hawkeye Pierce (Alan Alda), Trapper John McIntyre (Wayne Rogers), Lt. Col. Henry Blake (McLean Stevenson), Hot Lips Houlihan (Loretta Swit), Maj. Frank Burns (Larry Linville), Radar O'Reilly (Gary Burghoff), Lieutenant Dish (Karen Phillip), Spearchucker Jones (Timothy Brown), Father Mulcahy (George Morgan), General Hammond (G. Wood) and the rest of the inmates of the 4077th Mobile Army Surgical Hospital compound in 'Korea, 1950 . . . a hundred years ago.' They can be found driving gold balls into mine fields, brewing 'Swampmen's Gin,' saving lives on operating tables, defying their superior officers, and plotting, plotting, plotting . . . Debut: CBS, Sep. 17.

—*TV Guide*, September 9, 1972.

For those who grew up on the series, *MASH* tends to be remembered as a Monday night ritual, where it ran from 9:00 to 9:30 EST. However, that was only in the final years. For a few seasons, CBS was not sure where they wanted to put the program, which led to some dicey time slots for the series, especially when other changes (such as characters leaving and coming) could have affected viewership. Still, the show remarkably held on to ratings, which led to CBS finally deciding it could be the centerpiece to the shows around it (and eventually to its move to Monday nights). But first, there were trying times.

Season One (1972–1973) Sundays at 8:00 p.m.

The first season aired on Sundays beginning September 17 at 8:00 p.m. EST in the CBS schedule. What some may forget is that network programming was tricky on Sundays before the late 1970s. By the early 1970s, evening network programming most days was much like it still is—starting at 8:00 p.m. and ending at 11:00 p.m. for local news, then followed by late-night programming. Sunday was different, however. Evening programming started at 6:00 p.m., with a break at 7:00 for local news (or whatever filler a station had if they didn't have news), then back to network programming from 7:30 p.m. until 10:30 p.m. After that, everyone had to go to bed, because it was a Sunday, you heathens. (Okay, actually, it was supposed to be more local news, but many stations aired game shows and syndicated half-hour shows in the slot instead.) Thus, *MASH* was airing midway through the evening programming at the time.

In September 1972, CBS kicked off its Sunday programming, after the half-hour break for local stations, with a new series from Gene Reynolds called . . . no, not *MASH*, but rather *Anna and the King*, starring Yul Brynner and Samantha Eggar, It was a nonmusical, serial version of *The King and I*, which lasted thirteen episodes and a lawsuit (the author of the original novel *Anna and the King of Siam*, Margaret Landon, sued 20th Century-Fox for copyright infringement, disliking the portrayal of the characters in the series). Rosalind Chao, who would go on to play Soon-Lee (Klinger's wife) on *MASH* and *After MASH*, played Princess Serena in the series and was remembered by Burt Metcalfe when it came time to find someone to play Soon-Lee.

Airing after *MASH* was *The Sandy Duncan Show*, which too only lasted thirteen episodes. With both it and *Anna and the King* disappearing at the end of 1972, CBS juggled their programming around a little for Sunday nights. *The New Dick Van Dyke Show* (1971–1974) was moved from 9:00 p.m. to 7:30 p.m., in front of *MASH*, and was followed by the detective series *Mannix* (1967–1975), starring Mike Connors, at 8:30 p.m. and *Barnaby Jones* (1973–1980), starring Buddy Ebsen, the series about an older detective, which premiered as a mid-season replacement.

The Sunday lineup for CBS ran in this order until September 1973 when CBS decided to move *MASH* to another night. As it was, with the CBS lineup going up against *The Wonderful World of Disney* on NBC and the Top Ten series *The F.B.I.* on ABC, CBS was getting clobbered in the early hours on Sundays. The series was also having problems with the network due to being a surgical war series at way too early in the evening on Sunday nights. "That was their position," Gene Reynolds remembered in *They'll Never Put That on the Air*. "They really felt that, oh, Jesus, you can't go in [the O.R.]. 'Cause they pictured wall-to-wall blood. We were much more discreet with blood than the feature." Still, it was a censorship issue that would continue to hit the show for years to come.

MASH would rank forty-sixth out of the network shows that season, only once getting in to the Top Twenty (with the season finale "Ceasefire"), then began to climb a bit in the ratings as summer repeats started in April 1973. One of the network executives' wives was also a fan and wanted to see it hang around another season, which can sometimes do more for a series than all the ratings in the world. CBS decided to give both it and *The New Dick Van Dyke Show* another chance for the following fall season, with the Dick Van Dyke series moving

HAWKEYE AND TRAPPER JOHN GO TO MARKET

A notorious black marketeer gets the business tonight. Alan Alda and Wayne Rogers star as a couple of army cut-ups.

M*A*S*H. NEW SHOW, 7PM. CBS◉8,10

An ad for the second episode of the series.

to Mondays, after *Here's Lucy* at 9:30 p.m. and *MASH* going to a dream time slot in September 1973. But only with thirteen episodes to film and, if CBS felt they were doing well enough, nine more after that. *MASH* was on the edge of being canceled, with just a thin lifeline to hold on.

Season Two (1973–1974) Saturday at 8:30 p.m.

Mash came back for a second season on September 15, 1973, which was a Saturday night. It was sandwiched at 8:30 p.m. between *All in the Family* at 8:00 p.m. and *The Mary Tyler Moore Show* at 9:00 p.m., with *The Bob Newhart Show* at 9:30 p.m. and *The Carol Burnett Show* at 10:00 p.m. It was a killer lineup, and while NBC was doing well with a younger audience with

Emergency! at 8:00 p.m., and ABC had *The Partridge Family* (in its last season) at 8:00 p.m., both had trouble keeping audiences with "movies of the week" after that, allowing the CBS schedule to dominate.

To help familiarize new viewers with the character, the first episode of the season, "Divided We Stand," had a psychiatrist visiting the camp to see if the 4077th needed some shaking up in personnel. This allowed the audience to get to know the characters' background and internal history, although in repeats it does tend to look as if we're watching the whole series start over again (which, in a sense, we were). The show would end up in the Top Ten, ending in fourth place out of all network shows in the season. It was a terrific year for *MASH* . . . and then CBS decided to move the program again.

Season Three (1974–1975) Tuesdays at 8:30 p.m.

Starting September 10, 1974, the series returned for a third season on Tuesdays at 8:30 p.m. Fortunately for the program, its lead-in was *Good Times*, the Norman Lear spin-off from *Maude* (which itself was a spin-off from *All in the Family*) that had been a mid-season replacement earlier in 1974 and was back, riding high in the ratings. *MASH* also had *Hawaii Five-O* after it, followed by *Barnaby Jones*, so CBS had a good run of hit shows for its Tuesday night lineup. Meanwhile, ABC had the first full season of *Happy Days* (which was struggling to get back after a strong mid-season start at the beginning of the year) at 8:00 p.m., a movie, and then *Marcus Welby, M.D.*; NBC had the final season of *Adam-12*, a movie, and then *Police Story*.

Before the season would begin, Gene Reynolds and Larry Gelbart realized that the well was running dry on ideas they could cobble together from the novel and other local sources. The pair went to the 8055th in Korea (the MASH unit that H. Richard Hornberger had been stationed in during the war) to talk to doctors, chopper pilots, nurses, and even an orderly who had been in the war. With this, the two came back with twenty-two hours of taped conversations and notebooks full of ideas.

The season would find *MASH* solidly performing in its new slot, although it skipped down to number five in the overall ratings of network shows for the season. The final two episodes, "White Gold" and "Abyssinia, Henry" (the farewell episode for McLean Stevenson), both reached #1 in the ratings.

And then CBS decided to move it again.

IF IT'S TUESDAY, IT MUST BE M*A*S*H!

The 4077th plays unexpected host to an enemy sniper who eats and runs. Just one of tonight's weird and wacky happenings. Alan Alda stars.

NEW NIGHT 8PM CBS◉10

Then stay tuned for a special replay of a favorite "All in the Family" episode: The Marriage of Mike and Gloria.

An ad promoting the series after its successful move to Tuesday nights. This would change once ABC began to experience success with its Tuesday night lineup, however.

Season Four (1975–1976)—Friday at 8:30 p.m.

CBS was getting hit hard on Fridays by NBC, which had a solid lineup of *Sanford and Son, Chico and the Man, The Rockford Files,* and *Police Woman* (a lineup held over from the previous season, with the two comedies in the Top Five and the two action series in the Top Fifteen). So they moved the surefire Tuesday lineup, minus *Good Times,* to Friday. The result? *Good Times* dropped out of the Top Twenty, and *MASH*—now following the rather limp sitcom *Big Eddie*—was seeing ratings like it did back in season one. Considering it was the first season to feature a major change in the program—Trapper and Henry replaced by BJ and Potter—the ratings could have made the network nervous. Instead, it was decided to test the show back in its old slot on Tuesdays, with the episode "Dear Peggy" on November 11, 1975. The ratings came back with *MASH* in the Top Ten at number eight. After two more episodes in the Friday slot, the show would move back to Tuesdays but at 9:00 p.m. for the rest of the season, finishing at number twelve, which isn't bad considering how lousy the season started.

And then . . . well, CBS finally decided to keep it on Tuesdays, actually.

Season Five (1976–1977) Tuesdays at 9:00 p.m.

Returning in the fall for the final season with Frank Burns, *MASH* would also have to do without one of the main forces of the first three years, developer and writer Larry Gelbart. It was also the year that Larry Linville decided to leave the series, stating that he wasn't tired of playing Frank Burns, but of "only playing Frank Burns" and wanted to move on. There were also minor issues due to William Christopher being out for eight weeks due to hepatitis, but they were able to work around it. Further, Gene Reynolds, who had helped set up the series in the first place, was getting ready to head out the door as well and move on to *Lou Grant*. Change was in the air on the set, but it would slowly build during the course of the filming.

On the scheduling front, *MASH* luckily avoided the one-two punch of *Happy Days* and *Laverne and Shirley* on ABC at 8:00 p.m. and 8:30 p.m. by staying at 9:00. Instead, *The Tony Orlando and Dawn Rainbow Hour* took the blows, while *MASH* would be number four for the season again, with its 9:30 p.m. partner *One Day at a Time* at number ten. *MASH* would also have two number one shows that season: "Lt. Radar O'Reilly" on October 12, 1976, and the finale, "Margaret's Wedding," on March 15, 1977.

But trouble was brewing thanks to ABC's lineup.

Season Six (1977–1978) Tuesdays at 9:00 p.m.

Gene Reynolds had made good on his promise to leave the series, and Burt Metcalfe became the new executive producer of the series. With that, and the introduction of Winchester to replace Burns, the series began to morph a bit as well. To Metcalfe's way of thinking, after five years of war stories, there was not much more to say about the conditions the characters were working in. There was, however, a lot of room to develop the characters, and the show began to build more storylines dealing with the main cast of characters going through troubles and changes, such as with "Fallen Idol" where Hawkeye shows true signs of not being able to perform as always in the O.R., and Radar realizing that his relationship with Hawkeye is about to change. It was also at this point that some viewers felt the show was starting on a path of navel-gazing that would get worse as the seasons went along. Alan Alda would also come on to do more with the creative direction as well, which was helpful to the show, but also led others to think the actors were running the ship—due to the changing emphasis on the characters instead of the war.

Network-wise, *The Tony Orlando and Dawn Rainbow Hour* was gone for Tuesdays at 8:00 p.m., and instead, there was a new short-lived drama series called *The Fitzpatricks* in its place. It lasted thirteen weeks against *Happy Days* and *Laverne and Shirley* on ABC. Worse for CBS, ABC added *Three's Company* (the series Larry Gelbart helped get started) and *Soap* to the Tuesday lineup, forcing *MASH* and *One Day at a Time* to struggle in the lower part of the Top Twenty. On January 30, 1978, CBS decided to stop the fight and moved both sitcoms to Mondays at the same times (forcing out the short-lived *The Betty White Show*, which ran fourteen episodes, and *Maude*, which was finishing its final season). *Good Times* and the amusing *Baby, I'm Back* aired from 8:00 to 9:00 p.m., followed by *Lou Grant* at 10:00 p.m. On ABC was the quickly canceled *The San Pedro Beach Bums*, followed by *NFL Monday Night Football* and movies and specials. On NBC was one of their few hits at the time, *Little House on the Prairie* at 8:00 p.m., and then a movie of the week at 9:00 p.m.

MASH would tie with *One Day at a Time* to hit number eight in the ratings, with the finale episode, "Major Topper," getting to number one for the week it aired. From here on out, CBS would keep *MASH* in the 9:00 p.m. time slot on Mondays. The only thing that would change was everything around it.

Season Seven (1978–1979) Mondays at 9:00 p.m.

The seventh season, which now found the show in a sturdy home on Mondays at 9:00 p.m., saw the production team wanting to shake things up a bit. Margaret would now divorce and find herself actively working to find a new way to live, and Klinger would begin to drift away from the dresses and start becoming more of the handy everyman that he would be in later seasons. The program also would move the show out of the camp a few times, such as with "C*A*V*E," to shake the look of the program up a little.

The series would return on Mondays with *One Day at a Time* and *Lou Grant* following it as in the previous half-season. With them at 8:00 p.m. was the first season of *WKRP in Cincinnati* and a magazine show called *People* (and based on the magazine, naturally enough) that quickly went away, and then a sitcom called *Flatbush* that lasted three episodes. On ABC was the final season of *Welcome Back, Kotter* (featuring Marcia Strassman from the first season of *MASH*) at 8:00 p.m., the only season of *Operation Petticoat* at 8:30 p.m. at the start of the season, and then a little more successful show, the Andy Griffith-led adventure series, *Salvage 1*. The 9:00 p.m. slot was then football or the miniseries *How the West Was Won*. NBC didn't want to risk messing with a good thing and still had *Little House on the Prairie* and a movie of the week for their lineup.

MASH was number six for the season—tying with *60 Minutes*—with episodes all in the Top Twenty, with the exception of a Wednesday night showing on February 14, 1979, that found the show at number twenty-four.

Season Eight (1979–1980) Mondays at 9:00 p.m.

Radar would make brief appearances at the start of the season before being written out in "Good-Bye Radar," leaving Klinger to take on the job that was Radar's and really solidify a good reason for Klinger to be spending all his time with the officers. Houlihan was becoming much more a new woman and being called on it, showing growth. There were more experimental episodes as well, such as "Dreams," which showcased the nightmares the cast were having about their own failings and troubles.

The dramatic series *The White Shadow* was tried at 8:00 p.m. for the first hour of network television on Mondays this season (it would be moved to Tuesdays at 8:00 p.m. later), with *MASH*, *WKRP*, and *Lou Grant* filling out the time slots. When *The White Shadow* got moved, *WKRP* and the series *The Stockard Channing Show* took its place, while Wayne Rogers' series *House Calls* would eventually move into the 9:30 slot. The season

A full-page ad for the best-remembered lineup for *MASH*—on Monday nights. The series will stay at the same time on Monday for the remainder of its run.

saw a lot of jumping around for the series, however, sometimes airing as early as 8:00 and other times at 9:30, but mainly it stayed in its proper slot of 9:00 p.m. The bouncing around didn't matter that much, however, as the series had by this time become a cornerstone of CBS's Monday night programming. It would end up at number three for the season, with the finale, "April Fools," tying for first the week it aired. NBC was still going with *Little House on the Prairie* and a movie, while ABC ran an adventures series called *240-Robert* in the fall and then found a hit with the stunt show *That's Incredible!* at 8:00, football in the fall and the shows *Family* and *Stone* after that.

Season Nine (1980–1981) Mondays at 9:00 p.m.

CBS wasn't sure what to do with the 8:00–9:00 schedule and attempted various sitcoms, such as *Flo* (a spin-off of *Alice*), *Private Benjamin* (an adaptation of the comedy film), *Ladies' Man*, and a variety show, *The Tim Conway Show*. *MASH* was still there at 9:00 p.m., but the season was cut to twenty episodes thanks to an actors' strike during the summer of 1980. Season ten would have a similar shorter season, thanks to a writers' strike in 1981.

House Calls still followed *MASH* at 9:30, followed by *Lou Grant*. NBC was still using *Little House on the Prairie* at 8:00 with a movie, while ABC had *That's Incredible* and football, although they would follow the football season with a new prime-time soap, *Dynasty*, at 9:00

The episode "The Life You Save," featuring a sniper's attack on the 4077th, was originally to air March 30, 1981, but got pushed back to be the finale of the season on May 4, 1981, due to the assassination attack on Ronald Reagan. This was the season where the cast and crew felt they were running out of steam, but still believed they had some stories left in them to tell. The series would end up number six for the season, with the March 2, 1981, episode, "Bottoms Up," reaching number one for the week.

Season Ten (1981–1982) Mondays at 9:00 p.m.

As mentioned above, a writers' strike pushed back the season until October 26, 1981. The 8:00–9:00 slot had pretty much become a place for CBS to throw sitcoms at a wall and hope something would stick, with *Private Benjamin* bouncing around between 8:00 and 8:30 there, along with shows like *The Two of Us* (featuring Peter Cook in an American version of the British series *Two's Company*); a show called *Report to Murphy*, starring Michael

Keaton; and the return of *WKRP* to Mondays. The slot after *MASH* found *House Calls* in its final season, followed by the sitcom *Making the Grade* and a series called *Filthy Rich*, created by Linda Bloodworth-Thomason (who had written a handful of *MASH* episodes in its first few years). *Lou Grant* still held at 10:00 p.m., but it was in its final season as well.

NBC didn't change anything, however, and ABC was happy with the schedule from the previous year as well. *MASH* would end up at number nine in the ratings, with the finale, "That Darn Kid," once again reaching number one for its week. Yet as things were rapidly changing around *MASH*, the cast and crew had gotten together to compare notes and decided that the series had a good run, but needed to end. Perhaps with a finale that would wrap everything up as the war comes to an end?

CBS didn't want to hear it. End the series with the war coming to an end? That was impossible. When the cast asked why, an executive mentioned that the network had problems selling *The Fugitive*—featuring David Janssen as an innocent man looking to find the real killer of his wife—for syndication after the final episode showed Janssen's character finding the killer. "Everyone knew how it would end, so they didn't turn it on. So you see, we can't do that here. It'll kill the syndication."

As everyone looked at the executive with blank stares, Mike Farrell finally spoke up. "It might surprise you to hear this, but most people already know the Korean War ended."

CBS finally reached a compromise with the cast and production team— there would be one final, short season of the program and then a movie to end the series. As Mike Farrell pointed out in his book *Call Me Mike*, the finale would never be made part of the syndicated package; thus allowing CBS to run the show in syndication with no ending. The main problem was that the production team had held back six scripts in hopes of doing a short season of six episodes and then the movie. Instead, CBS demanded nine more episodes for a total of fifteen. The production team scrambled to come up with nine more scripts for the final season at a point where coming up with the six was hard enough.

Season Eleven (1982–1983) Mondays at 9:00 p.m.

The final season had fifteen episodes, along with the movie, *Goodbye, Farwell and Amen*. CBS tried a show called *Square Pegs* at 8:00 that has become a cult classic since its one season aired. *Private Benjamin* was still around for the

8:30 slot, and then a new series from Bob Newhart called *Newhart* began airing after *MASH* at 9:30 p.m., followed by another new series called *Cagney & Lacey*, for which Loretta Swit had appeared in the original pilot movie back in October 1981. NBC tried to mix it up by creating *Little House: A New Beginning* at 8:00 p.m., follow by a movie, while ABC stuck with *That's Incredible!*, football, and movies.

The final season of *MASH* tied with *Magnum, P.I.* at the number three spot in the ratings for the season. The big news was the finale that aired on February 28, 1983. Originally set to run two hours, the program instead went for two and a half hours with commercials (that CBS sold time for at $450,000 for each thirty seconds). At 8:00 p.m. that night, an episode of *Alice* aired, followed by the finale. Many magazines gave coverage over to the show, along with plenty of television coverage and special events on television stations that were by this time airing the program two or more times a day in syndication, or even broadcasting the film as a way to bring it all back to the very beginning.

Alan Alda noted in the book *The Last Days of MASH* that the cast had gone to dinner together the night of the finale and left after dinner to find the streets deserted. Alda realized that it was because everyone was home watching the episode. It turns out that more than 121 million people watched the finale, making it the most-watched television event ever until the 2010 Superbowl, and still the most watched episode of a dramatic television series.

Other CBS Airings

For many years, CBS had a late-night program that was simply called *The CBS Late Movie*. The program was set up to show films, but sometimes they would show episodes of various programs available to them; from sitcoms, to horror shows (*Kolchak: The Night Stalker*), to detective shows (*Magnum, P.I.*, *The New Avengers*), to old episodes from the *NBC Sunday Mystery Movie*. When old episodes aired, CBS would not cut anything out, but merely run them with five additional minutes of commercials per half-hour. On the flip side of this, any movie aired usually was edited by ten to fifteen minutes in order to make it fit the "double feature" format of the program. Thus, a typical showing—which would be a Friday night up through March 24, 1978, then *MASH* was switched to Thursday night airings—would be an old episode of *MASH* at 11:30 p.m., followed by a shortened movie or a lengthened (by commercials) episode of another series at 12:05 a.m. This continued until September 6, 1979 (and thanks to the mash4077tv.com website for the dates there).

It was also not uncommon for networks to air old episodes of sitcoms during the day, especially when a half-hour spot would open up due to poor ratings for a game show or soap opera. What's interesting is that this usually occurred while the series was still running on the network, which was unusual to see happen with programs, as repeats of programming at various times of the day usually did not occur until a show was in syndication, and *that* didn't happen until the show was no longer on the networks. When it did happen, many shows would rename the series for the earlier day airings so as to "not confuse" viewers thinking they were new episodes, although commonly it just confused viewers into thinking that programs had different names at some point. Older half-hour episodes of *Gunsmoke* aired as *Marshal Dillon* on CBS after they had already begun showing the hour-long version of the series, for example. By the 1970s, such incidences avoided coming up with new names and simply aired older programs as they were, such as ABC airing *Three's Company* episodes during the weekdays in the summer during the early 1980s.

CBS did so with *MASH* as well, airing it from 3:30 to 4:00 p.m., Monday through Friday, from September 4, 1978, until September 14, 1979.

A comparison of the original DVD box set releases—which came in a bigger box and a booklet detailing information about the episodes—and the slimmer later DVD box set releases.

Stopping in September 1979 made sense, considering the program was going into general syndication at that point for stations around the country. Alan Alda would even do short advertisements for specific stations airing the program around the country to help promote it in syndication. The reruns were a success and continued for years, although with any show run so often on multiple channels (especially if one had cable), it was understandable that viewers eventually got into a rut about watching and ratings for the reruns begin to dive a bit. In 1992, Columbia House began releasing VHS tapes of three episodes each as part of a collection that was $4.95 for the first tape and then $19.95 for each additional tape. Seventy-one tapes were issued, for a total of 207 episodes, leaving most of the series past season eight unreleased when it ended in 1998 (although they did put out the finale on the final tape). Soon after, talks begin about releasing the show on DVD, which occurred, starting with the first season released in a DVD box set in January 2002, and for a much cheaper price than the earlier VHS run. Within two years, more than half a million copies of the first box set had been sold. The complete series finally was released by 2006, along with a special box set of all the seasons, plus the movie, and an extra disc with bloopers and documentaries under the title *The Martinis and Medicine Collection* released in November 2006. In 2008, the DVDs were reissued in slimmer cases without the inserts that served as episode guides in the original sets (instead, the episode titles were listed on the backside of the cover insert, which could be read through the clear plastic case once opened).

The show still airs in syndication today, while new technology allows for episodes to air on "channels" like Netflix (albeit in sometimes edited form for certain episodes) and on station channels such as ME-TV. The series continues to draw interest from new and old fans, especially when one happens to come across an episode on television while flipping channels. It is hard to pass by an old friend, and for those of us who grew up watching the program when it originally aired all over the place on CBS, it feels like a small slice of home.

23

You Certainly Came to the Right Place

Filming Locations

M oviemakers have always had to deal with filming scenes that take place outdoors. In the very early days, that wasn't a problem—natural light was the best way to get a good image on film anyway, so most scenes had to be in the sunlight, and even interior scenes were shot on sets that were essentially three walls with no fourth and no roof in order to get such light. Over time, brighter, hotter lights were developed for filmmaking, which allowed shooting inside an enclosed building on the studio lot, including scenes that took place "outside." This was great in many ways—indoors, under studio lights, you could control the weather conditions when filming a scene that took place in the great wide open and have no worry about rain, snow, or the wind as you would with outdoor filming. Nor was there the expense of transporting a crew to a nice location, and then have conditions not being ideal, hampering the chance to film.

On the other hand, filming nature scenes on the set does have the tendency to make everything look like you're shooting on a planet from *Star Trek*. There's a falseness to the look that—no matter how much of nature you bring into the set—announces to the audience, "Here's a fake sky, with fake trees, and about thirty feet of ground that we've masqueraded as dirt, rocks and grass." Yet, for most shows, it's not so much an either/or proposition as a question of "What's going to work and can we afford it?" Sometimes it just works better to shoot things outside and sometimes indoors, and every movie and television series has to consider what the best resolution to scenes and even episodes is.

But war isn't an indoor activity, and the logistics of filming a program dealing with a war necessitates shooting outside, at least at some points in the stories. Same with *MASH*. As mentioned in the chapter dealing with the making of the film, 20th Century-Fox was adamant that the Fox Ranch would be used for shooting (beyond some additional filming outside of a local golf course and the backlot for pretty much everything else). It was a natural decision—20th Century-Fox had owned the land since 1946, specifically to shoot westerns and other films that needed outdoor scenic locations. The land itself had been used in films since the early twentieth century, going back to Mary Pickford in 1917 (the romantic *Daddy Long Legs*) and a variety of films such as Elvis' *Love Me Tender* (1956), *Butch Cassidy and the Sundance Kid* (1969), and *Planet of the Apes* (1968—take a look at the scenery around Ape City in the film and notice how similar it looks to that used in *MASH* soon after).

Southern California was never going to look exactly like Korea, and this has been a minor contention of some viewers over the years. Korea tends to be rather lush, wet, and green, and those who go there today in peacetime won't find land that looks like it does in *MASH*. But the studio's number one reasoning was, "Who is really going to know?" Unless you were a veteran of the war, most people didn't really know what Korea looked like anyway. Further, war tends to turns even the most scenic places into craters, and the sparseness, with pockets of trees and brush of the Fox Ranch, struck some veterans of the war as being spot-on as some of the desolate areas they did see there.

Rather, the design of the 4077th in the movie, which was carried over to the series, was much more of a fantasy than the location itself. As mentioned in the beginning of the book, MASH units were built to hold hundreds of personnel and the wounded. They also needed to be mobile, so having a building for surgery and the wounded, as seen in *MASH*, was not a norm until very late in the war when the units pretty much could stay put. They were essentially tent cities. And looked it. And not just a series of little tents like the Swamp and Houlihan's as seen in the show, but rather long, circus-like tents as well as the smaller ones. Ironically, the movie *Battle Circus* from 1952 (discussed in chapter 12), which is a typical Hollywood glamorization of the war from the 1950s, shows a much more realistic representation of what such a unit looked like than the "grittier and more honest" *MASH* film and show, which was regulated to a dozen tents and a building.

To be fair, the movie never tried to really give us a good look at the place, as is the "magic of Hollywood." We can assume there's more to the unit than just the few passing tents seen and visited in the film. As well, the series could only hold up the illusion of something bigger for so long. The opening credits pretty much give the game away in showing how small the setting is, even though it cuts to and from the location in an attempt to make it look bigger (for example, the road leading from the choppers to the unit looks much longer than the short distance it actually is—what you see in the credits is pretty much the entire length of the road before you get to the mess tents). There are also camera pans in subsequent episodes that show how close together everything truly was (check out the first ten minutes of "The Consultant" in season three for a good look around, especially the landing of the helicopter Robert Alda is on, which shows just how close the landing area was to the rest of the camp).

Plus, one of the factors that got the series made in the first place was that they could use the standing sets from the movie already built on the Fox Ranch in order to cut costs, so they shot as best they could to hide things in order to make it look bigger. Even so, although the series would sometimes find characters discussing the motor pool, the library, and the laundry—all of which we briefly see at one point or another—it is obvious from the set itself that none of that is really there.

Filming occurred between the established set out on the Fox Ranch and Stage 9 back at the 20th Century-Fox studio (Stage 9 was also where the cast and production staff would meet to go over new scripts before shooting). It was one of the smaller soundstages at the studio—a point of contention Gene Reynolds regretted not being consulted about until they were already locked into using it. Most interior tent scenes, the mess tent, and night scenes (which could be shot during the day inside, and therefore cheaper than paying to film outside with a crew at night) were usually filmed at the studio using a partial re-creation of the ranch set. For fans, it is pretty easy to spot scenes that supposedly are "outside" but filmed in the studio, as Ranch scenes tended to be shot in bright sunlight, while studio scenes have a greyness to them, not to mention cleaner, flatter grounds, and a slight tininess to the sound recorded.

In most seasons, the filming would alternate between the two locations depending on the logistics of what needed to be done (for example, season three's episode "O.R." was all interiors, so no need to go out to the ranch, while "Rainbow Bridge" would need to be split between interiors and exteriors in order to show the Swamp men arriving in the bus to exchange wounded). Thus, scenes may be shot at the ranch for one episode, with some additional footage to fix camera goofs for an episode already completed, and perhaps one or two exterior shots for a later episode that only needed those outdoor scenes as per the script. Again, this was due to costs and convenience—the ranch wasn't next door to the studio; it meant a drive for the cast and crew to the outdoor set during the summer and early fall when filming would take place. The area would be freezing cold in the early hours, then temperatures would shoot up past 100 degrees by midday. For years, needing to use a telephone would mean a thirty- to forty-five-minute trek to get to a payphone at a gas station under supervision (Gary Burghoff in his autobiography states that they would have to be driven to and from the set by teamsters as they were forbidden to drive themselves to the location), and the dressing rooms on-site were known to have heating and cooling units that constantly broke down. Thus, location shooting was done when needed throughout the shooting weeks for the season, with an emphasis to get back to the small soundstage at 20th Century-Fox that at least was a little closer to certain comforts, even if it did mean having to walk over to the makeup building from Stage 9 just to use the bathroom.

Season five was a bit different from the other seasons, as William Christopher pointed out in *The Complete Book of MASH*. After filming had been ongoing for a while, Christopher contracted hepatitis and was unable to film for eight weeks. "But it was the year that Fox had a new deal out at the Ranch," Christopher noted. "The expectation was that we wouldn't have the Ranch, so we had done all the exteriors at one time, early on." Because of that, all exterior scenes with Father Mulcahy had already been filmed, allowing him to appear in more episodes than if they had been filming in the usual manner. As it was, the writers only had to rewrite the Stage 9 scenes to explain Father Mulcahy's disappearance, rather than write the character out completely, which Christopher believed to be a fortunate turn of events for him as it allowed him to appear in the episodes thanks to the forced outdoor shooting they needed to do.

Meanwhile, the ranch had been sold to the State of California in 1974 and became a public park in 1976, but filming for *MASH* and other films continued in the park for years. As the outdoor set was a "standing" one, in that it was left as is on the ranch, a security guard would be stationed at the location when not in use to make sure hikers and others didn't take off with anything. Even with a guard, however, it was not unusual for hikers to chance upon the standing set and be able to inspect it up close, under the close eyes of the guard present.

On October 9, 1982, just as the show was getting ready to film the finale to the series, the Gypsum Canyon brushfire broke out due to a downed power line, destroying the *MASH* set (leading to a fire being incorporated into the script). Because of this, there was not much remaining in the area when the show was finished, nor did anyone connected with the park or 20th Century-Fox think it was worth saving. For years the area was allowed to return to its natural state, but the consistent interest by visitors in seeing the area in the park where the show was filmed led to it being cleaned out and being turned into a tribute to *MASH* in the spot where the program and film were done.

On February 23, 2008, after the cleanup and some exhibits were established, a ceremony was held at the location in Malibu Creek State Park to commemorate the twenty-fifth anniversary of the show. Three hundred fans hiked to the location to see Gene Reynolds, Burt Metcalfe, director Charles Dubin, William Christopher, Jeff Maxwell (Igor on the show), Mike Farrell, and Loretta Swit talk about the program and the enduring interest in it.

Studio 9 at 20th Century-Fox is about smack-dab in the center of the lot, which is located at 10201 W. Pico Blvd in Los Angeles, but the studio is not open to the public for tours. Thus, if you want to get a little bit of insight into the filming location for *MASH*, the trek has to be made to the Malibu Creek State Park, which has a main entrance at 1925 Las Virgenes Road in Calabasas, California, northwest of the studio and about a twenty-nine mile drive (which in L.A. means that you'll get there sometime next year). There's

The location in 2013 at the Malibu Creek State Park (formerly the Fox Ranch) where *MASH* was filmed. This photo was taken from where the helicopter pads were at the time of filming.

a fee to enter, and there is no direct access by vehicle to the *MASH* site (yes, there used to be for filming purposes, but not anymore, so don't go expecting to simply drive right up to the location . . . as I stupidly did). The hike from the parking lot is close to five miles round-trip and takes you past very pleasant scenery and locations for shooting of other films, although not marked in any fashion—so don't expect signs stating "Here's where Ape City was." More adventurous (or cheaper) types can instead take the Cistern Trail, which is off Mulholland Highway, west of the park. The Cistern Trail knocks the distance down to three and a half miles, and it's a very scenic hike, but it is also directly in the sun and you're descending (and afterwards climbing) a very large hill, so keep that in mind.

The only sign along the trail to the *MASH* location in the Malibu Creek State Park that verifies you're on the right path.

Either hike will lead you to a smaller path that may make you wonder if you've gotten lost, but eventually you'll come across a small sign telling you you're heading toward the *MASH* site. The surroundings will also start to look somewhat familiar as well to fans, which will give some comfort. Eventually, you'll reach a clearing as the road widens back up, which will take you into the location. At the time, there were many discussions of all types of exciting things to do and see at the site, including the possibility of camping and of showing nightly outdoor screening of episodes, but the results seen today is rather modest. A couple of rusted-out vehicles, a signpost similar to the one used on the program, some camouflage netting up where the mess tent used to be, and some plaques to help give a general feel for the location to those who hike out there. The area where the helicopters would land along with the mess-tent area will be on the left, while other points of interest will be scattered around the site to the right. The mess-tent area has picnic tables set up under the netting, making for a good place to

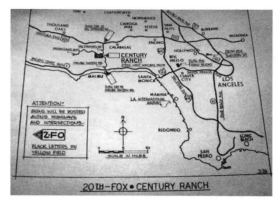

A map that was included in scripts for the actors and others in order to make sure they made it to the standing set at the Fox Ranch.

break for a snack or meal for those venturing out to the spot.

Fans who do visit the park should keep in mind that the area is not going to be set up as seen in the film or television show, nor are you going to find exhibits that are more than just ropes and plaques (nor bathrooms or concession stands selling mementos). Still, fans will certainly take in the scenery and get a better understanding of the logistics of the location and how filming must have been done there. And you can still look to the hills surrounding the location and know, for sure, that you're right where the MASH crew once was.

24

Now That Spring Is Here

I t was Korea . . . one hundred years ago.

Or, rather, the pilot of the series stated that the time was 1950 as we saw Trapper John hitting golf balls into the minefield in the pilot of the series. The thing was, there were common elements seen in episodes to come that obviously were not of the time period: Radar would be reading comics from the late 1960s, the Heat Wave pinball machine seen in the Officers' Club is from 1964, fictional characters mentioned—such as Godzilla, and Radar's impression of John Wayne—are sometimes from years in the future. Naturally, it was easy to see that the overtone was right and that we weren't really supposed to be looking at the small details. (Who knows enough about a pinball machine or a comic book to be able to tell what it is from the brief glimpses?) For the most part, the series would be trying to at least set the characters' story in a chronological order, though, right?

Not quite, and this had to do with the show going on for eleven seasons, which meant that the characters had to keep going back in time in order to reset where they are in the history of the three-year war, or else they would have been long-gone and into the next war by the time the series was over. It also came to a point where no one was quite sure where they were in the history of the war. Season one already saw it being 1951 by episode ten, while season eight would see references to it still being 1951, after BJ and Potter had been there for at least two Christmases. Season one also features a football game in "The Army-Navy Game" that would have made it 1952 already. One episode, "A War for All Seasons," takes place over a year's time, which would have been impossible for all the officers and enlisted to still be there in reality.

The cast filming the time capsule episode of the series in season eleven. By this point, the series had gone back and forth in time so often that it had pretty much given up trying to make sense of what year it was from episode to episode.

The fourth season opener, "Welcome to Korea," would establish that Potter joined the 4077th in September 1952. Radar was writing reports in season two with Henry there that were from October 1952 (and let's not forget that "A War for all Seasons" takes place through 1951, pretty much a full year before Potter and BJ are supposed to be there and with Radar and Blake sill supposedly around). In the fourth season, Potter mentions being married to his wife for twenty-seven years, making 1925 the year they got married. That later changed to 1916 as the year they got married. Potter also started the show claiming to be fifty-one years old in 1952, but then later sixty-two years old. In all, there were three distinct Christmas episodes over the years (season one's "Dear Dad," season seven's "Dear Sis," and season nine's "Death Takes a Holiday").

By the time we get into the later seasons, even the simplest things are starting to look as if there are time-shifts happening in this universe. In the season six two-parter "Comrades in Arms," Hawkeye and Margaret tell the doctors and nurses around them at the 8063rd about the new vascular clamp they invented at the 4077th recently. The episode featuring that invention being made comes three episodes later in "Patient 4077." Both Hawkeye and Klinger in later seasons mention being in Korea over two years each, something that would have been strongly fought by the military, as they rarely would allow personnel to stay even over a year in the field at that point.

In essence, the best thing to do for those of us who want to try to make sense of the time line is to not attempt to get it to work. There's simply no way to squish it into shape; no way to say that Blake was there until sometime in 1952, but Potter was actually there in 1950—it simply won't work. Canon was not something people worried about at the time, and since the perception was that most people would watch occasionally and not bother with repeats anyway, the producers and writers weren't worried about having someone double-check dates. (Which wouldn't have worked anyway, as who in 1972 would have expected the show to still be on in 1983?) Besides, the popularity of the series has lasted more than forty years with this discrepancy; it certainly isn't going to change for the nitpickers out there who feel a need to make it all work in one chronological order. Best to sit back and enjoy the show, which is what we really should be doing anyway.

25

Experimental Surgery

Ten Episodes Outside of the Norm

W ith people like Larry Gelbart and Gene Reynolds in charge, it is understandable that over time the series would try to expand beyond what was considered normal situational comedy fare for the networks. At first it was in minor ways, as seen below, but once that door was open, the production team began to take off into experimenting with the narrative, the characters, and even the structure of the show. After *MASH*, other shows would follow with experiments in what viewers got to see. Some of the episodes below were bigger successes than others, but for *MASH*, the attempts always clued viewers in that you never knew what to expect on the program.

"O.R." (Season three, airdate October 8, 1974)

The production team and the network had already run into issues pertaining to the use of the laugh track in the series (see chapter 26 for details), but everyone agreed that there should be no use of it in the O.R. when the surgeons are bloodied, trying to save lives. Yes, there was humor there, but it was just felt to be the wrong place for it. (There was one exception; in "Radar's Report" from season two, Henry ends up with a needle stuck in his hand that is a sedative. He begins counting backwards, waiting for it to take effect, and then falls to the floor unconscious. In that particular case—especially in light of the fact that the tension, of the scene ended with a sight gag—the scene called for a laugh, and thus the laugh track was used in the O.R.).

When it was decided to do an episode that took place completely in the O.R. (from the beginning of a run of wounded coming through the 4077th until the end) the idea was to save money by not having to shoot anywhere else but in the one set. However, this also opened up the opportunity to force the network to accept an episode without a laugh track. CBS knew they had been outfoxed, but accepted it and played it to the hilt in the advertising; even getting a "close up" box in the issue of *TV Guide* that week that promoted the show as being experimental thanks to the lack of the laugh track.

"Abyssinia, Henry" (Season three, airdate March 18, 1975)

Any reader here knows this episode. By that time, death had been introduced in the series on a number of occasions, most importantly in the first-season episode "Sometimes You Hear the Bullet," where Hawkeye cannot save the life of a childhood friend. In this case, the production team really threw the audience for a curve. Everyone tuning in knew by that point that McLean Stevenson was leaving the show, thus this final episode of season three would be his last. They also knew from that week's *TV Guide* that Henry would be sent home. Thus, viewers were expecting a sweet goodbye to the character and actor and perhaps a sense of what was in store for the following season.

Then came the ending. Radar comes into the O.R. in a daze to let everyone know that Henry's plane had been shot down over the Sea of Japan and there were no survivors. According to the usual way this story is told, the cast was unaware of what was to happen until they heard Burghoff read his lines, although some retellings of this have the cast being given the last page just before filming so they could digest it quickly before the scene was shot. Either way, there was a problem with the filming, and Burghoff had to redo the take. Even then, the take was almost ruined by someone dropping something in the middle of the take, causing a crash to be heard off-camera. Yet, as it fit in perfectly with the shock of the scene, it was left in.

Audiences were stunned when the episode aired. Furious letters went to Gelbart and Reynolds about killing off a beloved character on the show, but that was exactly the point—that war plays no favorites and good people sometimes do die. Gelbart kept his letters and donated them to the Smithsonian later on, noting that at the time the episode aired, a helicopter full of Vietnamese children that were leaving to start a new life in America crashed, killing all aboard. He wondered if any of the people who were so upset over the death of a fictional character cared as much about the real children that died in a similar fashion.

"Hawkeye" (Season four, airdate January 13, 1976)

This episode was, as Larry Gelbart put it, a "writing challenge." It involved Hawkeye receiving a head injury while driving in a jeep. He is able to rest at the home of a Korean family while help is sent for, but he worries that if he goes to sleep he'll never wake up. Thus, he spends the entire episode speaking to the family about his life and other things while waiting. With the rest of the cast being the family, who do not speak English, Alan Alda has to carry the episode on his own as a type of "monologue for television."

"The Interview" (Season four, airdate February 24, 1976)

Looking back at interviews famed news reporter Edward R. Murrow had done with soldiers in the fields of Korea during the war, Gene Reynolds and Larry Gelbart thought something similar could be done with the cast on *MASH*. To prepare them, questions and answers were devised, but when it came time for filming, additional questions were asked with the actors given a chance to improvise in character. Real-life news-reporter Clete Roberts appeared as the interviewer. The episode is most noted for William Christopher as Father Mulcahy responding to a question about the war affecting people by noting how the surgeons on cold days sometimes warm their hands over the patients after opening them up, and that it was a sight that would affect anyone. It's a strong line, but similar ones had been used before and after it in the series (Christopher's telling really sells it in the episode and is the strongest use of it, however).

The episode, filmed as if it were a television special about the surgeons at the 4077th, won a Humanitas Prize. It would also mark the end of Larry Gelbart's run on the program. The stunt would be repeated for the later episode "Our Finest Hour," but in that instance the interviews would set up a number of clips from earlier shows and not be quite as effective. Clete Roberts would also appear briefly in the pilot for Radar, *W*A*L*T*E*R*, in 1984 in a similar role.

"Point of View" (Season seven, airdate November 20, 1978)

This episode is told visually from the point of view (hence the title) of a soldier who is wounded in the throat and cannot talk. In silence he watches the doctors and nurses of the 4077th from his bed and gets involved in their stories.

Films and episodes of television shows shot from the point of view of the protagonist were not new at this point—the 1947 detective movie *Lady in the Lake*, starring Robert Montgomery, was shot from Philip Marlowe's point of view, while the first portion of *Dark Passage* (also from 1947), with Humphrey Bogart and Lauren Bacall, is told from Bogart's character's point of view. Still, it was not done often in serial television as in a program like *MASH* and makes for a good diversion from the norm in the season.

"Life Time" (Season eight, airdate November 26, 1979)

In this episode (which opens with the cast playing cards outside by where the choppers land—an oddity in the series itself), Hawkeye finds that he has twenty minutes to perform an aorta graft on a wounded man or else he'll be paralyzed. Upon announcing the time limit available, a clock appears on the screen and remains there for the rest of the episode (moving forward even during commercial breaks). BJ finds that a man who cannot be saved is a proper donor for the other wounded man, but has to wait for him to die first before he can operate to get the aorta needed. Thus, both surgeons have to deal with the minutes and seconds ticking away in hope of one man dying to save another man.

The experiment in this episode was in showing events in real-time, an element that rarely gets used in films and television (typically, productions want to squeeze time in order to get to the next important scene, which the audience accept as part of the narrative; forcing the audience to see the limitation of time available to the surgeons make the action tense).

"Dreams" (Season eight, airdate February 18, 1980)

Coming off a bruising time in O.R., everyone drifts off to their quarters to sleep, only to have dreams that become nightmares and allow the audience to see a little inside the heads of the individuals. Hawkeye is armless, adrift amongst the wounded he cannot save; Houlihan's romantic wedding is cut short by the wounded and her wedding dress covered in blood; BJ dances with his wife, but has to leave her to other men due to his duty; Klinger sees himself under the knife; Winchester finds that his tricks no longer produce results; and Potter—the only one whose sleep is pleasant—dreams of child-hood and home.

The series was beginning to dig deeper into the mind-sets of the char-acters by season eight, and this was a further extension of that idea. Dream

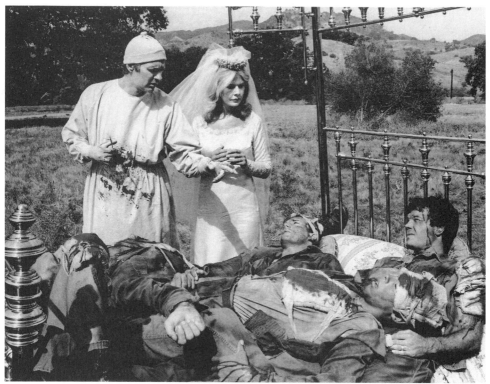

Hawkeye (Alan Alda) and Houlihan (Loretta Swit) confronting a bed full of injured soldiers within Houlihan's nightmare in the experimental episode "Dreams."

sequences were certainly nothing unusual in television and movies, but the episode finds several of the characters outside the world we know as *MASH*, assuming the audience will catch on and tag along to see where each dream leads them. It also continues to show elements of both Hawkeye's and Houlihan's psyches—both are compelled to help, even though they realize that it is leading them down roads that can be bad for them.

"A War for All Seasons" (Season nine, airdate December 29, 1980)

The episode starts at the beginning of 1951 and follows the characters through each season of the year. An interesting chance to see the changes the characters go through within a year's time, with their hopes rising and falling. Yet it is probably best remembered for a gag—Mulcahy grows corn so that everyone can have fresh corn on the cob for once in the mess tent. Igor then takes the corn and turns it into creamed corn, which is what they get

A promotional postcard of Klinger that from the time of filming of "A War for All Seasons."

all the time anyway, ruining the whole point of the exercise. Mulcahy is so angry that he calls Igor a ninny, and Igor tells them all that he was just trying to help out and next time everyone can have it on the cob for all he cares.

Well, it's a good enough joke to be a main reason to remember the episode.

"Follies of the Living, Concerns of the Dead" (Season ten, air-date January 4, 1982)

As Klinger ends up sick from a fever, a young soldier dies as a rush of wounded arrive. As a spirit, the man (Jeff Tyler) slowly concludes he is dead as he watches the regular cast go through the motions of what is a normal activity for them—dealing with the remnants of this dead man's life. As they wallow in self-important issues, Klinger briefly talks to the man while in a fever dream. The activities continue as normal at the 4077th in the end, but the man moves on with a group of other dead soldiers to whatever comes next.

An interesting episode that could have used a bit more of Klinger with the dead man talking (what is there is nice, but not quite fulfilling, especially as the episode was advertised with Klinger and this man going on a bit of a journey together . . . instead they say a total of six lines to each other before splitting off into their own worlds). It is interesting to note that the main cast comes off as rather callous and unfeeling, which is the point—the living momentarily can think of the dead, but the life, the love, and spirit of the dead can't stay with them and neither can he with them, thus making the ending with the group bickering while Klinger wonders what happened to him rather poignant.

"Goodbye, Farewell and Amen" (Season eleven, airdate February 28, 1983)

The finale of the series and a chance to wrap up the war and the character arcs for all of the main cast (and even the incidental ones that have been seen from time to time in the series). A normal series would have simply wrapped things up and sent everyone on their way, but the movie-length episode (which was financially broken down to the cast members as four episodes' worth of work, and then five when they got an extra half-hour from CBS) has many thing to do over a length of many days while everyone waits to see if there will be a cease-fire and they can go home.

Most alarming was to find the episode starting with Hawkeye in a mental hospital, suffering from a breakdown that the audience is slowly clued into. What first is remembered by him as a joyous day away from most of the camp turns into one about wounded soldiers and refugees, and then to a refugee who has a chicken that won't stop clucking. With enemy soldiers outside and the need for quiet, Hawkeye hisses at the refugee to shut the chicken up. It is then that he remembers that the chicken was actually a baby, and that the mother suffocates the baby to death in order to keep the child quiet. (This was based on an actual event that occurred during the war, and a plot that Alan Alda had been wanting to use on the program for some time, but which the production team felt was a step too far until it came time for the

TONIGHT! THE SPECTACULAR FINALE TO M*A*S*H

The war is ending! The 4077th is going home! Don't miss the laughs, tears, surprises and a celebration you'll never forget, as television's most honored series concludes.

Starring Alan Alda, Mike Farrell, Harry Morgan, Loretta Swit, David Ogden Stiers, Jamie Farr and William Christopher.

2½-HOUR SPECIAL **7:30PM CBS◉5**

An advertisement for the finale of the series, "Goodbye, Farewell, and Amen," probably the most experimental episode in the series.

finale.) The incident was enough to unhinge Hawkeye, but now that Sidney Freedman has helped him remember what occurred, he is on the road to recovering.

Back at the camp, there is confusion, with refugees and prisoners of war all around the camp. A tank driven by a wounded soldier ends up in the camp, leading to bombings that knock Mulcahy for a loop as he saves a number of the P.O.W.s from the shelling. He finds that he has nerve damage due to the bombing, however, and has to deal with his hearing slowly disappearing. BJ is given the okay to go home, but then the order is rescinded and he has to return, missing out on his daughter's second birthday. Margaret is torn between the right military move for her career, thanks to help from her father, or going back to America and working in a hospital. Klinger falls in love with a Korean woman who won't leave until she finds her family, and Winchester becomes friends with Chinese P.O.W.s who are musicians.

By the end of the episode, the war is over, and some find new hope for their lives, while others realize that they are forever changed by the events of the war. As Hawkeye leaves for a final time in the very type of helicopter that we always saw at the beginning of the show since the pilot, he sees the camp once more and sees that BJ has placed the word "Goodbye" in stones.

The finale was a huge success for CBS, 20th Century-Fox, and all involved. It would prove the story of the 4077th could be told and—most importantly—it did something that neither the novel nor the movie could do: it came up with a conclusive ending for the story about the surgeons at the 4077th.

Yet there's more to the oddness of this finale than length. Of course, Hawkeye being in a different location did and still does disarm viewers. Why is he there? What happened to him? But that's the mystery that is set up to be uncovered in the first hour (or ninety minutes if you were watching with commercials). We accept it because we have to; yet there's other, almost other-world-like moments in the episode:

- Hawkeye remembers everyone going to the beach for a party. Wait a minute—a beach? Where? When? How often did they do this? Weren't they always pretty much trapped at the 4077th, and now suddenly they're all playing in the surf? Sure, in reality, such units probably did do this, but we've never had a hint of it in the series before now.

- Klinger is frolicking with a young Korean woman at the beach. Since when? Who is she? This is the second episode she turns up in, and suddenly Klinger has known her long enough to want to marry her (yet, knowing Klinger, perhaps he has only known her for days . . . see chapter 28 for more details on that front).

- Prisoners of war in a guarded bunker area? How come this is the first we've really seen of such a thing? Yes, it helps set up Winchester's story-line, but it certainly does come out of left field in the show.

- The cameras film the camp in a manner much different from normal. There was a good reason for that—thanks to the fire (covered in chapter 23), the set was mostly burnt to the ground. The camera simply had to hide what it could until they could write in the fire that destroys the camp in the story and thus show more of it. Then again, there are episodes earlier in season eleven where sets back at the studio are shot from angles that seem odd. (Check out the way the Officers' Club is filmed in the episode "The Moon Is Not Blue"—from a bird's-eye view; a most unusual camera position for that set, and some of the standard set dressings are gone as well.)

- Why is the Swamp so close to the office all of a sudden? Winchester burst through the netting of the Swamp to the building within two seconds. (Actually, it is this close, but they always shot it in such a manner to suggest it was further away than five steps.)

Most of these things can be blamed on the timing of the filming and the fire that occurred. But at the same time it makes everything in the finale feel like it's not quite real. Perhaps that was intentional. After all, such moments of finally being released after so much tension and horror probably would feel slightly like a dream (or even a nightmare, as in Winchester's and Hawkeye's cases). And it all leads to something we'll get into in chapter 28.

26

Just Like the Actual Korean War

The Use of a Laugh Track

B lame Bing Crosby for the laugh track.

In the 1940s, Bing was getting tired of having to perform two live shows for his radio program every time—one for the East Coast and one for the West (as there are three hours' difference between the two, so a show at 8:00 p.m. would have to be done once at 8:00 on the East Coast and then again at 11:00 on the West Coast). Seeing the emerging technology of tape-recording, Bing got the network to agree to him recording the show at 8:00 and then they would just replay it for the West Coast. It would take time, but eventually others caught on to the idea and began using it as well.

Then someone had the bright idea that they could use some of the sounds already recorded again in other shows—in particular the laughs. This was beneficial in cases where guests on the program were given funny lines to say that didn't work with the audience (either because the audience didn't buy a particular famous guest star in saying such lines, or they weren't really that good). With laughs already recorded, the editors on the Crosby show could place tracks of laughter into the show where dead air existed and thus give audiences listening at home the idea that gags went off better than they did.

And why was this? Because, unless you were a king and could be an audience of one, humans had never been in a vacuum when watching entertainment. There were always others around, and the acknowledgment of others that something was funny helped raise the bar of the humor as well. How often is it that as kids we laughed along with others without knowing why we were laughing but happy to join in? Same as adults, and it was easy to see that the laugh track helped provide some members of the audience with the idea that a joke was funny and therefore they could laugh.

The laugh track would evolve over time, becoming more precise and versatile, leading to programs being able to be filmed without even an audience—such as single-camera shows like *MASH*—with no concerns as to laughs, as the production team knew they could add them later. Some shows, however, did fight the system, leading to CBS experimenting with an episode of *Hogan's Heroes* in 1965 to see if audience preferred the show with or without the laugh track. As it turned out, the laugh track version did better, thus proving to CBS that they were right to use it in this new show they were going to be airing called *MASH*.

The people behind the show hated it, though, especially Larry Gelbart. Gelbart saw a show that was set in Korea during a war and that had been a film that people had viewed without a laugh track and suddenly one was needed? Where were the laughs coming from in the middle of a war? Gelbart yelled and fussed until they network agreed to air an episode of the new series in a preview house, once with the laugh track and once without. The response was a fifty-fifty split between those who liked it with and those

The cast from the earlier years of the program. Although the production team fought against the laugh track, it would be used throughout the American run of the series (although aired without it in other countries).

who liked it without. To Gelbart that proved it could be done without, but to the network it proved that they needed it, as "why fix something that isn't broke?" Gelbart lost the battle, and the show aired in the U.S. with the laugh track. The only exception was for scenes in the O.R., where it was felt to be in bad taste to use it.

Gelbart also won in the rest of the world, where the show aired mainly without the laugh track. It is for this reason that when the series finally came out on DVD, viewers could decide for themselves if they wanted the laugh track in the episodes or not. In a final twist, however, for people who had grown up with the program, now watching the show without the laugh track feels somewhat awkward—as if the wind has been knocked out of the show at times. Thus, it isn't that uncommon to find older fans in America who end up watching it with the fake laughs.

Sorry, Larry.

27

The Collapsible Latrine

Ten Pranks of *MASH*

T he shower tent being lifted on Houlihan in the movie of *MASH* was just a start, as it would set up the pranks that would become the norm especially in the first few seasons of the television series. As time went on, BJ was introduced as a major practical joker (as listed below), leading to a number of pranks on various individuals through the remainder of the series.

Below are ten of the best pranks on the show. As one might suspect, most were with Frank as the pigeon.

The Guns of Five O'Clock Charlie ("Five O'Clock Charlie," season two)

In this episode, a North Korean pilot keeps trying to hit an ammunition dump on the outskirts of the 4077th. As we join the episode, it has been such a recurring failure that the members of the 4077th have turned it into a fun event each day and a pool has been raised to bet on how close Five O'Clock Charlie will get to the dump (even General Clayton takes part in the pool).

Frank Burns, however, is paranoid about the bombings and insists on carrying his gun with him. Throughout the episode he pulls it out to demonstrate being prepared, only to find that his gun has been replaced by a plunger, a prop gun, a water gun, and a stapler. When he finally gets a real artillery gun to use on the plane, Hawkeye and Trapper mess up the coordinates, and Frank ends up blowing up the dump himself, thus ending the need for Five O'Clock Charlie (although he will return in a later episode).

One thing the switching of the gun in Frank's holster does prove is that Frank is prone to pull the trigger, even when it's a stapler. (In later episodes he will continue to prove unable to not do so with real guns, shooting BJ in the leg in one episode.)

Boxed in ("As You Were," season two)

Frank wakes up one morning to find that Hawkeye and Trapper have put him and his cot inside a wooden crate. Frank is boxed in, but as Trapper states, "We all feel that way at times."

This seems to prove that Frank is a very sound sleeper, however.

Houlihan's Collapsible Tent ("Dear Dad," season one)

At a point where Frank and Houlihan were hiding their affair the most, Trapper and Hawkeye jury-rig Margaret's tent so everything goes wrong: the candle is a trick candle that refuses to go out; Margaret's cot has the legs sawed off; pudding is in the pillow; and, finally, the post holding the tent up is brittle, leading to it breaking and the whole tent collapsing on Frank and Margaret as Trapper and Hawkeye listen happily before going to bed.

The Fake Air Raid ("Dear Sigmund," season five)

In this episode, there's a practical joker on the loose who is hitting nearly everyone with a bunch of silly and harmless pranks. Elsewhere, Sidney Freedman is staying for a while in the camp and Frank is digging himself a foxhole. At the end of the episode, Freedman finds out that BJ is the culprit behind all the jokes, as Hunnicutt fills Frank's hole with water. In unison, the pair shout "Air raid!" This causes Frank to run out of the Swamp and dive face-first into the murky water. (Looking back on it, it's just as well—Frank stumbles before he gets to the hole, and if it had not been filled, he would have probably landed on his head.)

Radar Turns the Tables ("Deal Me Out," season two)

In this episode, a group of officers are getting together to play cards. Radar goes into the shower to tell Hawkeye and Trapper that everyone is there. When his glasses fog up, Radar takes them off, leading to Hawkeye making a crack about him not being completely offensive with them off. Trapper follows by saying to "leave the little guy alone." Radar casually states that he can take a joke, then turns around, grabs their robes, and leaves the shower with them, as Hawkeye and Trapper rapidly apologize.

Margaret, BJ, and Hawkeye Join Forces ("An Eye for a Tooth," season seven)

In this episode, Winchester pulls a series of practical jokes that aim to turn Hawkeye and BJ against Houlihan. When the trio figure out the situation, they stage one where Houlihan supposedly writes a letter to BJ's wife, saying that she and BJ are having an affair. BJ gets so upset that he begins to beat Margaret, leading to Winchester confessing to the pranks and how they had gotten out of hand. As it turns out, he had now been pranked as well, and the trio leave satisfied, as Winchester wallows in being set up.

The main joke here was actually based on one that occurred behind the scenes on the show. A bill for food had been charged to Gary Burghoff without his knowledge by Stiers, who made it look as if Farrell had done it. Burghoff and Farrell figured out the prank and staged a fistfight behind a curtain as Stiers stood nearby, aghast at what he had done.

April Fools ("April Fools," season eight)

The practical jokes are getting out of hand and even worse when Col. Daniel Webster Tucker arrives for a visit. The man puts everyone on edge, but treats Klinger as a man who needs to go home. Finally, the camp can't take it anymore, and they pull a prank on the colonel, dumping a bucket of beer on him. The colonel gets so angry that he falls to the ground from a heart attack. As Hawkeye feels remorse about the prank, the colonel whispers to him "April Fools!" It turns out the colonel is an old friend of Potter, and the whole thing was a gag to try something really stupid like the beer stunt. The final laughs come when Klinger arrives, ready to head back to the States with the colonel, although he obviously isn't in on the joke yet.

Fort Dix ("The Party," season seven)

Not so much a prank, but a sweet gesture. The camp is planning a party back home where all their families are to get together and have fun. Klinger, however, refuses to allow his family to be there, as he has faked letters to his mother to suggest he is at Fort Dix. To help him out, the others take a group photo for the part in front of a banner stating it is Fort Dix.

As it turns out, Klinger's mother already knows he is in Korea, but didn't want him worrying about her reaction to it. She considered what the others did a very nice thing and proves that he has friends with him, which makes her happy.

Captain Tuttle ("Tuttle," season one)

Sister Theresa wants to thank whoever is helping her orphanage with supplies, which Trapper and Hawkeye are actually stealing from the camp to give to her. Hawkeye tells her it is Captain Tuttle, with Tuttle being a childhood imaginary friend. The thing snowballs until finally General Clayton

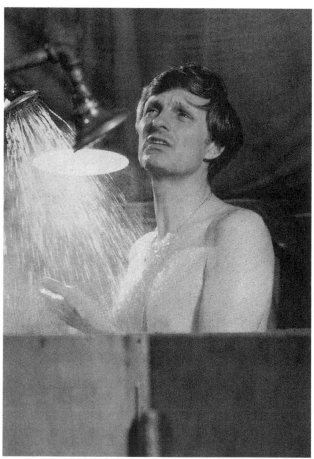

Hawkeye enjoying the shower. In a rare reversal, Frank Burns would turn the tables on Hawkeye in the shower with a complicated prank.

wants to give Tuttle a citation and Hawkeye has to admit that Tuttle no longer lives . . . faking a story about him jumping out of a helicopter to help a wounded man, only to forget his parachute.

Frank's Revenge ("Showtime," season one)

Frank was not always the victim, and sometimes the writers did allow him to get the better of Hawkeye. In the last episode of the first season, Hawkeye finds himself the victim of a series of practical jokes. Unable to get the still to work, Hawkeye holds the tubing up to his face, only to get blasted by gin. Entering the Swamp, a bucket of water is poured on his head. And, finally, in the shower, no matter what stall he uses, only the other stall will spray water from the nozzle.

The episode ends with Frank heading into the officers' latrine, a rope is cut, and the front of the latrine disappears to show everyone Frank sitting there, reading *Stars & Stripes*.

While Hawkeye does finally get the upper hand, in a gag that plays back to the original raising of the shower tent in the film, one does have to congratulate Frank on the sophistication of his gags, especially that of the shower nozzle only working when Hawkeye wasn't in the stalls. It makes one wonder what other things Frank could have done if he had bothered to put his devilish little mind to it.

28

In a Rubber Truck

The Character Arcs of the Major Characters

Most of the characters went through a type of arc during the course of the television series, although sometimes it wasn't quite easy to see. Of course, some of the characters were there so briefly, and during the early years "war stories" took precedence over personal stories, that there just wasn't a chance for it. This chapter covers not only those characters who were in the series for a short time like Spearchucker or Cutler—and it is easy to wonder how they would have been different over time if given a chance to grow—but also characters like Henry Blake and Trapper John (leading back to previously discussed comments by both Stevenson and Rogers that they may have stuck around if they had known the series would start emphasizing the characters more than in the three years they were there). Both left as pretty much Hawkeye and Duke did in the movie—none the worse for wear (not that it helped Henry in the end, of course).

Frank probably was helped a bit with being there in that tent with Hawkeye, Trapper, and BJ. Then again, he was helped by being on the show in the first place. Burns had to be changed to be a somewhat competent surgeon and one who occasionally would do the right thing, or else the audience would have turned on him in a few episodes instead of letting him into our homes for five years. Besides, if he was really that bad, why would Trapper, Hawkeye, and Henry allow him to kill the wounded? Burns had to occasionally be right and even sympathetic or else he logically could not exist there. Still, one couldn't pull for him too much. When Margaret heads off on her wedding and Frank is left behind, the audience can actually feel for Frank, because he could be human. No doubt, of course, he went back to being a snot once back in the world, but at least he'd probably give some things a second thought before doing the wrong ones.

Radar was the oddest change of all—he started off as a cigar-smoking, bourbon-drinking shyster and left as an innocent kid who gets sick smoking and one drink puts him under the table. Like the chronology of the series, you just have to accept the fact that his change doesn't make much sense, but it's there, and stop worrying about it. That, or suspect Radar got hit on the head and reverted to the age of fifteen at some point offscreen between season three and four. One could excuse some of the vices disappearing with Potter, as Blake was more of an older brother to Radar—tossing him the keys to go get laid at one point even; Potter was dad, and to be drinking in front of dad just seems weird. As for the cigars—he choked smoking one of Potter's, but it was implied that it was a really bad cigar anyway, so that's the answer there. If anything, one could say that Radar saw how he was shifting into this mousy, greasy guy and didn't like the look, thereby going back to how he used to be in Iowa before the war, and finally aggressively to the point where he became the kid. He liked being that way, and he stayed as such even during the toughest times he experienced there. Was it for the best? Things like W*A*L*T*E*R suggest otherwise, but at least it was his own decision.

Klinger also changed, although he came and left the war as a romantic. Think of it: he wanted to get out, but refused to take a gun to his foot or other desperate measure. Instead, he went elaborate, with schemes that were impossible but fun. He wanted to get out on his own terms or not at all. If he was that desperate, he surely would have taken Freedman's paperwork and signed it declaring himself a homosexual, but he just wanted to prove he could beat the system and then be left alone back in Toledo; nothing else. Better to be a big, red bird with fuzzy, pink feet than deemed something he wasn't.

This came through in his relationships as well. He married his child-hood sweetheart long-distance because what else says romance than doing it the hard way? When she left him, he was crushed; hurt even worse when no one would sympathize with him. When he had a chance to get a woman dating him after that, he backed out immediately upon discovering she was only in it for the fun and not anything long-term. Soon-Lee was someone who needed his help, and he was willing to sacrifice going home in order to help her find her family. Romance was and is all that mattered to him, even if he was Toledo in so many ways.

His main change is that he became serious. Before, everything was a gag, but as time went by, the more responsibilities he had to take on, the less he tried to laugh it off and instead actually did something about it. By the

Klinger would prove himself to be more than a one-joke player, eventually becoming the true romantic of the cast of characters—marrying twice and winning the girl in the end.

end of the series, he's wanting to do what is best for those around him instead of what is best for him, and he became a stronger person for it.

Same with Father Mulcahy, no matter if he was John, Francis, Patrick, or whatever. The priest became more determined and had a much better arc than in the novel or movie. The novel set him up as the cliché "Pat O'Brien" type of priest who was rough, tough, but easygoing when needed. The one in the film is a bit confused and struggling to do what was right. William Christopher, however, brought out the best in the character by showing him to be a man who strongly believes in his faith, but questions if he's measuring up to what is expected of him. He's not only good, but during the course of the series, he aims to make good, and becomes a much more determined person working for his faith (then again, he showed some of that spark early on in episodes like "Dear Dad" in season one). By the time Christopher had finished in the role, it was clear that he wiped away the thinking that Father Mulcahy was there to mock Christianity or Catholicism—at least by anyone who bothered watching the show.

Colonel Sherman T. Potter really didn't change much, with the exception that he was ready to mellow a bit when he first came into the picture and probably did more to shape up the other characters around him than they changed him. Winchester came into the show being hard to break and remained much the same, although he softened a bit with the others as time went on and realized that his upbringing was not always going to provide him with answers that kept him cocooned. No doubt, back in Boston, he will be a much more rounded individual and be able to handle people better than he was before arriving at the 4077th, although he was drinking so much by the end of the series that he may have ended up a chronic alcoholic upon his return to civilian life. BJ changed in more subtle ways, as he came in as someone who seemed to be so levelheaded that nothing would get to him, but he showed a violent side at times (look at the way he slapped at Hawkeye in a drunken rage in "Period of Adjustment" in season eight; the worst the seemingly more violent Trapper ever got was throwing a bag at Hawkeye and knocking him aside). And eventually he realized that he may have plenty of pat answers, but sometimes in reality they didn't work (as in his straying, although not intended).

Which leaves Hawkeye and Margaret, the two characters who stayed the duration and changed the most. Of all the characters, Margaret Houlihan went through the biggest arc in the show. She started off as pretty much a cliché, but even early on there were signs that she could not remain that way forever. Look at her reaction to Frank in "Sticky Wicket" where he begins tearing into Hawkeye for the problem patient he is dealing with; you can see her wince when Frank asks Hawkeye if he's killed anyone that day. Later in the episode she wants to help Hawkeye by suggesting that maybe he missed something—and in a manner that was soft-pedaled in order to hopefully avoid getting him angry about it (he does anyway, but she did try).

The bigger picture needs to be looked at as well. As the series goes along, we find that Margaret is an army brat. Yes, there's that bit about her father being dead and her mother being a klepto in "Bulletin Board" (season

Alan Alda, Wayne Rogers, and Loretta Swit, all smiles in the early days of the series. Although Rogers' character, Trapper John, would never get to experience a character arc, both Hawkeye and Houlihan would have major ones during the course of the series.

three), but look at the episode in which it occurs—Margaret already sees Frank in a somewhat lesser light by the third season and figures him a soft touch for a good sob story. In other words, she's lying. In later seasons, we discover that she wants to prove herself to her father, who has never quite given her the attention or love she needed—a reason she tends to lean toward being with generals and other higher-ranking officers (not to mention that they may be able to help her with her career)—they want her and can help her, which is something her father rarely did (no wonder for a time she may have played out the fantasy that he was dead and gone).

She loves the army because it really is her life, and anything outside of that norm doesn't feel right to her. She's attracted to Frank because he's the only one who acts the way she can understand; yet, quickly enough she begins to see his flaws and knows that she's saddling herself with a loser. Then again, he's at least a military type that perhaps she can whip into shape to be a better man. (Sure, she's dreaming, but at that point at the 4077th, what else has she got?)

But other things are not working out the way she expected either—the best surgeons there are Hawkeye and Trapper, and she's physically attracted to Trapper on top of that. They are even friendly with her at times when she's not being so set on being "military." Worse to her, in a way, is that they get results that the "proper method" does not. And keep in mind as well something we later learn in the series about Margaret—she had her rebellious streak at one time and was a party girl. An old friend comes to the 4077 and exposes to the others that Margaret used to party and would even cheat on tests. Also note every time we see Margaret away from the camp—she transforms into a party animal when in Tokyo, and gets along fine with Hawkeye and Klinger when sent to an aid station in an earlier episode. It is only when she has to be "Major Houlihan" that she becomes unlikable . . . perhaps even to herself. Where she has to be this thing called "Major Houlihan" instead of a person.

Yet who can really blame her? She, as with the other nurses, is treated as something for the men to laugh at. Rape is a joke (check out early season episodes like "House Arrest" to confirm this), and Hawkeye's innuendo with the nurses is considered cute, at least for several seasons. She feels obligated to rise to a higher level because it is the only way to get what she and the other nurses need. To do so, however, makes the men (and the women, as the season five episode "The Nurses" proved) treat her as other than human, leaving her torn between wanting to join in and wanting to fight them all.

The brief affair with Hawkeye is a turning point—the marriage that was supposed to be her Cinderella moment and whisk her away to being the wife of a dream had turned into a nightmare; instead, she is married to a man who avoids her and secretly goes back to the States to get away from her. Being with Hawkeye reveals to her that all the plans she probably had in her head since childhood may not only be wrong for her, but that something better could be found elsewhere. Not to say that being with Hawkeye was the answer, but rather none of what she had before was the answer either. Better yet, there was still time to change.

She begins to experiment more with getting to know the nurses, trying new ideas, and even bending the rules for the betterment of the camp. She also sees that the relationship with Hawkeye can be one of friendship and not of romance as she has done with other men in her life (and momentarily does with Hawkeye as well). In fact, men do not have to control her life at all. Once she realizes she can set her own goals, she even forsakes the advice

Thanks to Loretta Swit and the writers working with her character, Margaret Houlihan would end up going through one of the most expansive character arcs in the series, proving the one-time villain to be someone determined to become her own person.

of her father in the finale of the series and decides to go back to the States and work in a hospital—because although it is not "right" for her career, it is right for what she wants.

She becomes a full person thanks to her experience at the 4077th. A better person. In the novel, she was nothing more than a setup for jokes, and then forgotten. In the movie, Sally Kellerman managed to transform the character into a human being, although still a bit unclear due to the attention the movie had to give to other characters (we at least know she eventually learned to function within that society known as the 4077th besides being a "damn good nurse"). Loretta Swit in the series has enough time to really put the character into focus—as a career soldier who eventually learns that perfection is not always found through order. By the end of the series, she is her own person, and viewers can leave the show knowing that she'll be fine with whatever happens to her. Furthermore, she deserves it.

Hawkeye came in as he did with the novel and the movie—cocksure and trouble-free. He left troubled, but a better person for it, with his demons still present, but at least in check. It was obvious from the early seasons that Hawkeye was obsessive about what he could do with helping those in pain and was in danger of losing it (that may have been hidden in a way, as such moments of mental fatigue were done for laughs early on). He wanted to save everyone, and would drive himself to sleep deprivation in "Dr. Pierce and Mr. Hyde," and his sleepwalking ending in nightmares about childhood friends dying ("Hawkeye's Nightmare" from season five) were symptoms of that. His sneezing in season nine's "Bless You, Hawkeye" was a symptom of a suppressed memory of betrayal. It's no wonder the event on the bus in "Goodbye, Farewell, and Amen" put him into a mental hospital—to his mind he had helped kill this baby for his own self-interest. True, it was to save them all, and he had no idea that the mother would suffocate the baby in order to stop it from crying, but that didn't stop his mind from inflicting harm on himself for allowing it to occur. He should have seen it coming—he no doubt thought—didn't stop it, and needed to be punished for it. To him, he betrayed himself and everyone around him.

Yet there was a side of him that refused to give up, that kept cracking jokes, and kept the memories of what happened deep down in his mind until Freedman forced him to deal with them. Because he did face it, he was helped. No doubt he won't be trouble-free, but Hawkeye at least can continue doing his job and helping people. Only now not as the surgical god that the novel, movie, and even the early years of the show gave us, but as a compassionate man who just wants to do the best he can to help others instead of trying to save everyone.

Yet take a look at the finale once again. Besides some of the elements discussed already in chapter 26, there are other things that seem somewhat suspect:

- Hawkeye has his meltdown and rams a jeep into the Officers' Club, leading to everyone thinking he's insane. When he returns "cured," Hawkeye has his fill of the bombing, and he rams a tank into the garbage dump, leading to everyone thinking he's a hero. (He's turned his earlier act of insanity into one of bravery.)
- Thinking back to season four's episode "Hey Doc"—Frank gets into a tank (that was brought there to scare off snipers) and drives it through a shower tent, the Swamp, and finally out into a field outside of camp. He menaces both Margaret and Potter in the process and is cheered for a

moment when he is done. Hawkeye menaces both Margaret and Potter with a tank before driving over the latrine, then is cheered in the finale.

- BJ leaves, just as Trapper did (Hawkeye even points this out in the episode), but then is forced to come back and apologize to Hawkeye for leaving without a note. Hawkeye gets to relive the Trapper abandonment, only this time with the return of his friend and with his friend feeling sorry for what he did—something he never got with Trapper.

- Winchester ends up hating classical music thanks to his storyline with the Chinese musicians. What a fitting ending in Hawkeye's mind for a guy who tortured everyone with his love of classical music.

- Look at season nine's "Bless You, Hawkeye"—Hawkeye alters a memory in order to suppress a disturbing moment from his childhood, just as he does in "Goodbye, Farewell, and Amen."

- The entire bug-out sequence looks very familiar—it should, as they simply used footage from the season four opener, "Bug-Out," to save on having to restage tents being taken down, etc. (especially as most of the outdoor set was destroyed in the fire anyway). But it's the same soldiers, the same nurses, the same wounded, the same person bumping his head on the doorframe of the bus. All of which Hawkeye could have seen at least part of back during season four.

- Hawkeye comes back, but—thanks to the bug-out—he's soon in a new location for the camp, where there's trees, grass, little kids, a pond, and Freedman is there to help him talk. It's peaceful, and things are falling back into place all of a sudden. In this place that is as peaceful as the hospital Hawkeye just left.

- And it all ends with everyone going off to live their dreams. Klinger ends up with the girl and the irony of staying in Korea. Margaret breaks away from Daddy and becomes her own person. BJ is still the rock that is there for his friend. Potter quietly slips away into the sunset on his horse. Mulcahy is strong and true to a higher calling (although the whole hearing-loss element plays havoc with where we're going here). And then there's Hawkeye—leaving in a helicopter with no belongings, no transfer orders, just himself, as he takes a final look at the world he knew and leaves.

Was this Hawkeye after the cure or before? Yes, we have that whole messiness of Mulcahy losing his hearing and Klinger marrying Soon-Lee, which would suggest that everything in the finale actually occurred—but couldn't Hawkeye have heard about those things while in that nice little hospital away from the war? Everything points to a satisfactory ending for his friends and for himself—unsure, but crawling his way back to sanity once again. Yet so much feels unreal in the sense of what we had seen before in the series. Could his guilt at not being there until the end draw him to make this reality where they all live in the meadows with flowers and trees for a while—just as they went to the beach out of the blue in his memories of the chicken event—and then go home? That Winchester gets his final comeuppance? That Klinger gets the girl and BJ proves his loyalty? And all with Freedman there to hold Hawkeye's hand?

Further, if we can go that route, can we suggest that eleven years of adventures, blood, and horror could have all been elements of what Hawkeye has been inventing in his mind since season five's "Hawkeye's Nightmare"? (Heck, why stop there? Let's say season two's "Dr. Pierce and Mr. Hyde" where the first symptoms of Hawkeye's psychosis became evident.) Is everything after season four just a dream?

But then again, what is real here anyway? Let the heroes have their win and their sanity for once. After all, war may bring us horrors, but as Hawkeye reminded us back in season one, "no war is a movie." Or a television show.

29

Our Movie Tonight

Movies Shown in the Mess Tent

O ver the course of the series, one regular activity of the members of the camp was going to the mess tent to see movies. This usually involved one of the enlisted—often Klinger—at a broken-down projector showing scratched-up films on a screen at the other end of the tent. Often such showings would end with the film stopping either by project malfunction or due to a commotion inside or outside the mess tent.

Multiple times, titles of movies said to be playing in the mess tent were not real, so that a punch line could be set up. In other words, how bad are things for everyone? That the only movie they can get is *Ma & Pa Kettle Have a Baby*. In the *MASH* universe, this was a real film and it sounds terrible, but in our world, no such movie exists. (Not to mention sometimes getting movies that would have been impossible anyway, such as *Godzilla* sequels in 1952 when the original wasn't made until a year after the war in 1954.)

The emphasis of this chapter is not to discuss every movie mentioned in the series—Larry Gelbart wrote Hawkeye as such a movie-hound that he would sometimes blurt out several movie references in one scene alone—but rather the films that we as the audience got to see a bit of as well while the group sat in the dark in the mess tent. It should also be mentioned that several episodes, such as season six's "The MASH Olympics" and season ten's "Give 'em Hell, Hawkeye," surrounded the plots happening in the episodes with moments from *Fox Movietone News* newsreels. These short films aired in the theaters from the late 1920s to the early 1960s and gave audiences a chance to see events they may have only heard about on the radio or read about in the papers. Television's nightly news killed the need for such films in the 1960s, but they were still fresh enough in people's minds (and sometimes such reels would turn up as filler on television stations even into the 1970s) that they were recognizable to viewers of *MASH*.

One thing that's for sure about the films that were seen in episodes: most of the ones listed below were made at 20th Century-Fox. Certainly makes sense, considering that was the studio making *MASH*, not to mention that Hawkeye could mention *Casablanca* from here until the sun goes down in season four's "The More I See You," but there was no way 20th Century-Fox was going to pony up the money for us to see any of that Warner Brothers classic in the show, even if it was supposedly playing in the mess tent at the time.

Blood and Sand (1941)

The film, which was in color but probably would be shown in the mess tent in a black-and-white print, stars Tyrone Power and Rita Hayworth. Power plays a bullfighter who lets fame and fortune go to his head, with Rita Hayworth is the woman who helps herself to that money and power.

In the third-season episode "O.R.," the doctors are tied up in the operating room, so it is decided to pipe in the movie's soundtrack through the P.A. system for people to enjoy while stuck there. Eventually, Henry gets sick of hearing it and demands that it be turned off, with Radar obliging. (Well, it's certainly not an "up" picture to listen to while working away on wounded soldiers.)

Tin Pan Alley (1940)

A musical with Alice Faye and Betty Grable as sisters who sing in vaudeville. It won an Oscar for Alfred Newman's music. The film appears at the very beginning of the season three episode "Alcoholics Unanimous," and ends abruptly when the rain rips through the roof of the tent and pours down on the projector, shorting it out.

The Littlest Rebel (1935)

Although you would think otherwise from what is seen in the third-season episode "Bulletin Board," this is not a musical, but rather a dramatic film about a family that owns a plantation in the South during the Civil War. Shirley Temple stars and dances with Bill Robinson, who plays their slave, in the scene featured in the episode.

Leave Her to Heaven (1945)

In the third-season episode "House Arrest," Hawkeye finds out that the mess tent is going to be running *Leave Her to Heaven* while he is stuck in the Swamp under house arrest for slugging Major Burns. To help him out, and because everyone is happy to see someone punch Major Burns, the film is moved instead to the Swamp (with the projector outside the tent in order to get back far enough to fill the screen within the tent).

The film stars Gene Tierney as Ellen, a woman so fixated on Richard (played by Cornel Wilde) that she will stop at nothing to keep him to herself, including killing his brother and framing her adopted sister, Ruth, whom she suspects of being sweet on Richard.

Hawkeye wanted to see the film because he loved Tierney's overbite, and when Tierney kisses Wilde in the film, Hawkeye threatens to kill him if "he straightens out that overbite." Meanwhile, when Henry is not pawing the woman sitting next to Hawkeye, he's "very deep" into the movie and cries.

My Darling Clementine (1946)

One of the most famous examples of movies used in the series, not only because it is a classic, but because it is the setup for everything that happens in the final portion of the episode.

The film was directed by John Ford and features Henry Fonda as Wyatt Earp in a dramatization of the "Gunfight at the OK Corral." In the season five episode "Movie Night," Colonel Potter notes that everyone in the camp is on edge. To help remedy this, he managed to get a copy of *My Darling Clementine* to show in the mess tent. Things go well at first, but the projector keeps acting up. To help pass the time, everyone pitches in by singing songs and doing impressions (including Radar doing an impression of John Wayne from *McLintock!*, a movie released in 1963). By the time the film is ready to play again, everyone is feeling better, having shared camaraderie, even if the film did keep breaking down (or, rather, because of it).

History Is Made at Night (1937)

Charles Boyer and Jean Arthur star in this movie about a woman who falls in love with a headwaiter, enraging her homicidal husband, played by Colin Clive.

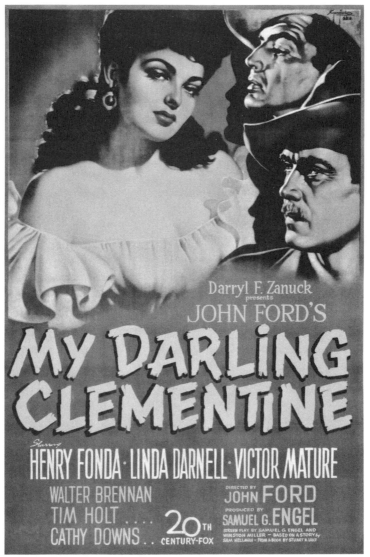

My Darling Clementine (1946): a classic film that Potter will try to plan in the mess tent in one of the more memorable episodes of the series, "Movie Night."

Colonel Potter has the movie playing multiple times in the mess tent in the season eight episode "Morale Victory," due to it being a favorite of his and his wife. However, the camp nearly riots over having to see it again. The film is a rarity for *MASH* as it was made by United Artists rather than 20th Century-Fox.

Sahara (1943), *State Fair* (1945), and *The Moon Is Blue* (1953)

These films are listed together as all three play important parts in the eleventh-season episode "The Moon Is Not Blue." Although it seems unlikely any MASH unit would do it, they've been running a film every night. A bigger concern, however, is that the film is the classic Humphrey Bogart film *Sahara*, where he plays a tank commander during World War II. That wouldn't be a big deal except that a film set in the desert has been the only film the camp has seen for a month. (Although we actually don't get to see any of the movie in the episode, only hear it.)

Hawkeye and BJ read about a new movie called *The Moon Is Blue*, starring William Holden, David Niven, and Maggie McNamara and directed by Otto Preminger. The movie deals with a young woman who attracts the attention of both a younger and older man. They each try to bed her, but she seems more interested in talking about issues dealing with sex than sex itself. Although the subject matter is handled in a delicate way that would not shock anyone today, the film ended up being censored by certain states due to supposed immoral content. It is for this reason that Hawkeye and BJ think getting a copy would be a good morale booster for the camp.

In trying to obtain it, they end up with a copy of *State Fair* instead. *State Fair* is one of two musical remakes of a film from 1933, with Jeanne Crain, Dana Andrews, and Vivian Blaine. After much effort, the camp finally gets *The Moon Is Blue*, only to discover that it really is nothing like the scandalous movie everyone thought it would be, to their disappointment.

As mentioned in other sources as well, the movie was not released until July 1953, meaning that when Klinger must have arranged a pretty sweet piece of blackmail to get it, since the war ended the month before the movie was released. But such nitpicking would have messed up the whole plot of the episode, so best to let it go. After all, that's Hollywood for you.

30

After W*A*L*T*E*R

The Spin-offs

T he old HBO comedy series *Not Necessarily the News* once did a short skit that was supposed to be a promo for a new series called *Before MASH*. The promo showed two Koreans—a man and a woman—in a field working. The man stops to reminisce about the days ahead where Hawkeye and BJ come to their land to do hysterical things. The woman agrees, stating she can't wait to see Klinger in his funny dresses and mocking the military.

Within one short skit, *Not Necessarily the News* wrapped up an issue with the sequels to the show. If you're no longer in the original series, what was the purpose of anything afterwards for the characters but to reminisce about all the things that happened in the past? And if that's the case, then why is reminding the viewers of better times worth the trouble in establishing a new series anyway?

There would be three attempts to break out of *MASH* with characters from the series. Only the first managed to do so, and it did it in a way that worked, but would have been nearly impossible for the other two. One of those two would struggle for more than a season to find its bearings, while the other wouldn't even get off the ground.

Trapper John, M.D. (1979–1986)

It was an odd thing to do in many ways. CBS was set to start airing a new series from 20th Century-Fox that dealt with a character from a top-rated program made by the same studio and network; only to move that character twenty-eight years into the future, jettison the past of that character, and build a new show around him. Odder still, it was a ratings success.

When Wayne Rogers left *MASH*, he found new vehicles to do, like *City of Angels* and *House Calls*. True, both had their own built-in derivatives—*City of Angels* was a *Chinatown* clone, and *House Calls* was another television adaptation of a movie—but they also attempted to step beyond those shadows and create something new and distinctive. In some ways that worked—*City of Angels* may have died quickly, but today it's a cult favorite; meanwhile, *House Calls* lasted three seasons. After that, Rogers had other new projects to deal with, so there was no need to go backwards to this character from another show.

Even so, when word broke that CBS was thinking of doing a new series with the Trapper John character, it was only natural for fans to wonder if Rogers would be back. Instead, it was announced that Pernell Roberts was taking on the role, and that the series would be set not just after Trapper returned home, but in the present, with an older, gentler John McIntyre as chief surgeon at a hospital in San Francisco. Which looks surprisingly similar to something else.

As it was, the creators of the series had just finished with another medical series for CBS called *Medical Center* (1970–1976). The series had been developed by Al C. Ward and Frank Glicksman, with a writer by the name of Don Brinkley writing nearly thirty episodes. In 1978, Don Brinkley and Frank Glicksman decided to do another medical show that also took place in a hospital, but with a slight twist. *Medical Center* dealt with a number of doctors—in particular Chad Everett as Dr. Joe Gannon—and the lives of the patients at a hospital in Los Angeles. The new show would deal with a number of doctors and the lives of the patients at a hospital, only this time in San Francisco. Better yet, the show would be edgier, more relevant, and feature a character already known to the public, Trapper John McIntyre.

Conceptually it wasn't that bad an idea. The plot would be that this rebel had mellowed and become part of the system (although still working outside of it when it came to patient care). Then a young doctor, Dr. George Alonzo "Gonzo" Gates, who even has his own nickname and had served in a MASH unit in the then-recent Vietnam War, enters the hospital and the life of the older doctor, who reminds him of how he used to be. The series would center on their conflicts of young/old and establishment/outsider, but—there's no other way to really look at it—it had all the trappings of *Medical Center* with a new set and new characters.

The star of the series was Pernell Roberts, a rebel in his own right, who was never one to hide his feelings about political and professional wrongdoings. He had left *Bonanza* and a boatload of money back in the mid-1960s because he felt the production team was not giving him and the other actors anything to do with their characters. He instead did theater and made appearances in various television shows and movies, forsaking a regular series. It had been over ten years away from serial television work when the offer for the new medical series came his way, and Roberts took it, not only because the show looked promising, but because it offered financial security at a time he knew the end of his career was closer than the beginning.

Yet beyond the aspect of luring Pernell Roberts back to television was also the idea of using this established character that the viewers had gotten to know from a still-running series, Trapper John from *MASH*. With Wayne Rogers leaving the series in 1975, the character was sitting there unused by the program. So now there was this rebellious, but now calmer, character being played by this rebellious, but now calmer, actor in a setting that had already been established as working for CBS in the previous *Medical Center*. Everything looked good to go, for the creators of the series, 20th Century-Fox, and CBS.

But not to the developers and producers of *MASH*. They had worked to shape Trapper John into the character that viewers knew, and now this other production team was taking their character away and doing whatever they wanted with it. Even worse, they weren't going to see a dime off of those years of molding the character. There were protests, but ultimately those working on *Trapper John, M.D.* had a trump card: Trapper John wasn't their character to begin with; it had been created by "Richard Hooker" in the novel *MASH*, which 20th Century-Fox had the rights to use. (And, no doubt, with H. Richard Hornberger's permission—anything to stir the pot with the people over at *MASH* that he didn't like.) In doing so, however, the

The cast from the series *Trapper John M.D.* Although using the same character from the series, movie, and novel, it was never considered to be a spin-off from the television series.

new show had to play down the references to the past. Hawkeye was briefly mentioned in the pilot, brief glimpses were seen of photos of the war that looked suspiciously like early promotional photos from the *MASH* series, and Gonzo would bring up the reputation Trapper had back in the Korean War, but that would be it. From there on, it was as if the character was brand new, with a past that viewers just happened to know and didn't need to have spelled out for them.

In the sixth season, Gonzo would leave while Trapper's son would arrive to start work at the hospital as a doctor. The series would go one more season for a total of seven before ending in 1986. Over 150 episodes were filmed, and the series would do well in the ratings, but it rarely is seen these days due to being an hour-long medical drama series, which usually does not do well in syndication. Nevertheless, the series did last for a good length of time for a television series, but the question will remain: did the series attract viewers because of the story it wanted to tell, or because the character was one that viewers already knew and wanted to see again?

After MASH (1983–1985)

Eleven years is a long time for any series, and although only a few of the regular actors from the show had been there for most of the duration, even the ones that came later had been there longer than most actors get to stay in a series (Farrell and Morgan had both been there eight years; Stiers, seven years). Many in the cast and crew were ready to move on, but there was one hitch. Okay, two hitches. The first was that some of those involved loved doing these characters (in front or behind the cameras), and the other was that the studio and the network were both making a boatload of money from the program. Was there any way to keep it going?

As the series entered its tenth season, with the cast ready to move on, it became known that Harry Morgan, Jamie Farr, and William Christopher were also tepid about the announcement. Yes, the series had run its course, and Morgan would even admit that the cracks had started showing by that season, but they still thought there was life in the characters. It was then suggested that perhaps they were right—maybe there was something still to say here with these characters, and about the life of soldiers after the war.

Larry Gelbart, who had developed the show for television back in the early 1970s, was asked if he would be interested in coming back and doing something new with the show. The idea intrigued him—what could be done with the characters at that point? Gelbart decided to sign on, stating that

The main cast from *After MASH* with a turkey. No, that joke is way too easy.

he would stick around for the pilot and the first few scripts. He would end up staying for much longer, however.

Also returning were Burt Metcalfe as executive producer (the same role he had in the last several seasons of *MASH*), as well as writers David Isaacs, Dennis Koenig and Ken Levine as producers and writers for the program. Between them, they would produce most of the work of the new series, which would bring back Colonel Potter as the new chief of staff at a veterans' hospital in Missouri, the General Pershing (also known as General-General), in September 1953, just a couple of months after the end of the war). Needing an assistant in his new role, Potter writes to Klinger, who had returned to the States with his wife, Soon-Lee; which means they must have immediately found her family in Korea, since that is where we left them at the end of the *MASH* series. Meanwhile, Father Mulcahy had ended the series teetering on what will happen to him—he had found himself slowly going deaf in the final episode, but had hopes of turning things around by coming back to the States and working with deaf children. In the opening for the new series, Potter would find that Mulcahy was in a downward spiral due to his deafness. Yet, although this plot element from the *MASH* finale is dealt with, the resolution is quickly nailed with Mulcahy getting an operation that heals his hearing and he is all better again—a rather flimsy out for a major character arc there.

Mulcahy comes to join Potter and Klinger at the veterans' hospital, thus giving us three characters from the original series in one place. The new series would be called *After MASH* and deals with their lives working at the hospital that was full of soldiers returning from the war and trying to put their lives back together. Rosalind Chao would also come back as Soon-Lee, while newcomers would be Barbara Townsend as Mildred Potter; Jay O. Sanders as Dr. Gene Pfeiffer; Wendy Schaal as secretary Bonnie Hornbeck; John Chappel as hospital administrator Mike D'Angelo; Brandis Kemp as his secretary (and Klinger's nemesis), Alma Cox; and Patrick Cranshaw as long-time patient Bob Scannell.

The series would start out strongly in the old Monday night, 9:00 p.m. slot on CBS that had housed *MASH* for several seasons before it, but things began to taper a bit in the coming weeks, and it was decided that the character of Dr. Pfeiffer was not working out. Instead David Ackroyd came in as a new character, Dr. Boyer, who was struggling to adjust to life after losing a leg in the war. Even so, the season ended strongly, in the Top Twenty shows for the season.

There were plenty of references to the former series, as could be expected in the lives of men who were now working with veterans of the same war, and Gary Burghoff returned as Radar for a two-parter, "It Had to Be You," later in the season. The finale episode, "Fall Out," which dealt with solders who had been exposed to atomic testing, had even won the series and Larry Gelbart a Peabody Award. But CBS didn't seem to have learned from past mistakes and decided that changes had to come.

The first season had ended on a cliff-hanger: Soon-Lee had gone into labor just as Klinger was being arrested for assaulting a crooked real estate agent who had ruined what Klinger had hoped to be a home for him and his family. The second season would find Klinger back in a dress and on the run from the authorities, while other things had been changed in the hospital due to the influence of . . . well, the network, actually.

Klinger (Jamie Farr) and Potter (Harry Morgan) in a publicity photo for the spin-off series, *After MASH*. The series would run for a year and a half, and with numerous changes made, before finally being cancelled.

D'Angelo has been removed, with a new administrator, Wally Wainwright (played by Michael Goetz), coming in. D'Angelo secretary, Alma Cox, was moved to being Potter's assistant, as Klinger was in trouble. Meanwhile, a psychiatrist was brought in, Dr. Lenore Dudziak (Wendy Girard), to study Klinger, who was hoping to go with an insanity plea for the assault at the end of the first season. Klinger would also be put back into a dress for this reason (a decision that Farr was vocal in saying was not in the best interest of the character), but mainly in order to invoke wackier times on the original series, while the actress playing Mildred Potter was replaced by Annie Pitoniak in order to make the character more of an airhead instead of the sensible Mildred already addressed to in the original series and seen in season one of *After MASH*.

The worst thing to happen for the series, however, was that CBS decided to move it to Tuesday at 8:00 against the juggernaut that was NBC's *The A Team* in hopes of getting viewers who were tired of the cartoon violence of the action series. Instead, it spelled the doom of *After MASH*. Only nine episodes would be produced for the second season, and of those, only eight would ever air on the network (the final episode, "Wet Feet," had been scheduled twice, but was pulled both times and only ran in foreign markets). The series would end with Klinger out of trouble and his and Soon-Lee's baby finally being named Cy Young Klinger. There were still things to do for the characters and situations, but not from the viewpoint of CBS, who canceled the series, airing the next-to-last episode in May 1985.

In retrospect, the series wasn't a bad idea. The problem was that the network got cold feet and tried to imagine it as a version of the previous show that hadn't been there since the early days. *MASH* had changed, and more than half of its run found it dealing with dramatic topic and a few gags here and there, not the other way around. *After MASH* was continuing that tradition, and it would be one that would run through other programs after it that fashioned themselves as comedies with dramatic moments. It was ahead of its time in a way, yet for CBS it was a Frankenstein monster that had been built out of parts of the former body and other pieces.

Instead of trying to shape the show as it went along—which CBS had allowed the original series to do—the network forced changes that hurt its integrity. In doing so, *After MASH* is remembered as one of the worst programs ever, a reputation based solely on the fact that it didn't perform up to the standards of *MASH*. It is a reputation not really deserved, but still stands. Even those who worked on the series would have little to say about it afterwards. Larry Gelbart in his autobiography, *Laughing Matters*, and Jamie Farr in his book *Just Farr Fun*, both ignored the series (Gelbart could talk about the horrors of working on *Neighbors* and *Tootsie*, but not the disappointments of *After MASH*). After the glow of *MASH*, which ended as a television triumph, it was painful to admit that the gloss had been somewhat dimmed by what occurred in *After MASH*.

W*A*L*T*E*R (1984)

Let's face it: writers really seem to hate Radar O'Reilly.

In the original series, Radar was shown as a character who had managed to hold onto his innocence even in the middle of a war. Yet for that very reason, he became an easy character to do terrible things to. In his swan song from season eight, Radar misses out on meeting the girl of his dreams because he has a plane to catch, finds his job a mess because Klinger couldn't do it, and learns that his uncle has died, forcing him to return to the States to take care of his family. His time on *MASH* ends with him leaving his teddy bear behind, looking ahead to a new life as an independent adult.

But when we meet him again in *After MASH*, he is back to being indecisive and with bad luck following him. He suspects the woman he is about to marry has been cheating on him. He is talked into the marriage and going forward and—once again—it appears that Radar has turned a corner and is about to start fresh and in control.

Then there's the pilot, *W*A*L*T*E*R*, which was filmed in early 1984 as a possible series for Gary Burghoff. The pilot, written by Bob Weiskopf, Bob Schiller, and Everett Greenbaum, and directed by Bill Bixby, followed what happened to Radar after the events in *After MASH*. As it turns out, he was right about his wife, who leaves him for another man after their honeymoon. He also fails at running his Iowa family farm, and has to sell it. Sending his mother away to live with relatives, Radar is at the end of his rope and goes to a drug store to buy sleeping pills in order to commit suicide.

So it's hard as a viewer to not think that the writing gods really looked down on Radar.

But it is all a setup to bring the character down to his lowest level in order to—if the series got picked up—let him rise again to find himself in a new and happy life. At the drug store he meets a worker named Victoria (played by Victoria Jackson, who would go on to fame on *Saturday Night Live* a couple of years after the pilot), and it is clear that a relationship would be developed between the two in the series. He also meets up with his cousin Wendell (Ray Buktenica) in St. Louis, who helps him get a job on the police force. Thus, the thrust of the series would be Radar as a police officer and working to rebuild his life.

But timing is everything. Yes, CBS had seen *After MASH* do fine its first year, but the network was still worried about the future of the program. *W*A*L*T*E*R* (a title that really doesn't make much sense trying to play off the *M*A*S*H* logo; his name is Walter, after all, not an abbreviation of anything) was not picked up by CBS as a series. Instead, as is common with unsold pilots, CBS aired it as a summer replacement special on July 17, 1984. Because the Democratic National Convention was also happening that night, CBS preempted the pilot on the West Coast, thus leaving half the country without having even seen what supposedly happened to Radar after *MASH*.

It was the end of the run for Radar, and with *After MASH* soon to disappear as well, the phenomenon that was *MASH* was about to come to a halt. In a final irony, the show that featured one of the *MASH* characters—but "not the one from the television show"—*Trapper John, M.D.* would last into 1986, more than a year past the real sequel series that followed *MASH*.

31

A Lunch Pail for Munchkins

The Merchandising of *MASH*

S ince the series took some time to come to a boil as an American pastime, there was little in the way of merchandise in the early years of the program. It was not until the show was already in its final years that the merchandising really began to take off—just when the show was to end and there wouldn't be that free advertising for the products being produced.

Still, there certainly were a lot of things for collectors to buy who wanted them, from calendars to playing cards to toys. Below are ten of the better-known pieces of merchandise that were released over the years.

Promotional Glasses

Four six-inch promotion glasses released through Libby, although no one seems to be sure where they were sold. Typically, such glasses would be given out at fast-food restaurants, but thirty years' time has pushed that evidence out into the ether. Each glass featured two characters from the show: Radar and Father Mulcahy, Klinger and Winchester, Hawkeye and BJ, and Houlihan and Potter. These seem to pop up individually as often as the Vodka dispenser seen below in this list, but getting all four together is a bit harder to do.

Action Figures

Action figures had been the rage for years but really picked up after *Star Wars* with the Kenner line of smaller toys that allowed for easy playing and a desire of collectors to get them all. One of the other companies releasing action figures besides Kenner was TriStar International Ltd. out of New

The back of the packaging for the *MASH* action figures, which shows all the figures as well as some other accessories available.

York City, who released a set of eight action figures based on characters from *MASH* in 1982. Each was three and three-quarter inches high, with ten points of articulation and—oddly—fit in perfectly with *G.I. Joe* figures from the time period.

Each figure came on its own card with a plastic bubble where the figure went on the card. The card featured the logo and a helicopter at the top, a picture of the cast to the right and a drawing of a name tag showing the name of the figure on the card. The back of the card showed all the figures, plus vehicles to buy that could be used with the figures: a helicopter, a jeep, and an ambulance. The Kenner *Star Wars* sets had special offers that involved cutting out reward tokens from the packages to send in for special prizes, and the TriStar packaging did the same: offering to send a *MASH* fabric patch to put on your clothes if you sent in four of the "offer circles" from the front of the package.

The figures were of Hawkeye, BJ, Houlihan, Winchester (yes, what kid didn't long to have a Winchester action figure), Potter, Father Mulcahy, and two version of Klinger—one of him in army clothing and the other in a pink

A number of action figures were created based on the series in the latter days of its run. There were two versions of the Klinger doll available—one with him in army fatigues and the other in a dress, as seen here.

dress. TriStar also released a *MASH 4077th Military Base* set that included a sixteen-square-foot vinyl play mat, and tents, benches, and other pieces to make the Swamp, the mess tent, the post-op building, and more for the action figures, although much harder to find than the action figures these days.

MASH Sit 'N' Play Inflatable Jeep

This oddball toy came out in 1981 from the Hong Kong toy company Arco. The yellow box shows a toddler happily sitting on what is an inflatable jeep that measured fourteen inches by thirty inches and could support up to eighty-five pounds once inflated (not inflated, it probably could support a lot more). A repair-patch kit was included in case your three-year-old takes on sniper fire from the North Koreans while playing with it. It doesn't bounce, it doesn't move, and that's about it. Imagine the hours of play children would have with it.

Which is why you so rarely hear about it today.

First Aid Kit

Not really that bad an idea—the *MASH First Aid Kit* was a simple variation of a standard first aid kit sold in auto stores to put in the glove compartment of your car in case you needed it. It contained bandages, road flares, tape wraps, some cream, and cotton balls, as well as a plastic piece and tubing to do mouth-to-mouth resuscitation without having to lip-lock someone. The only difference was that the *MASH* version came with the show's logo and was in green instead of white. The kits were sold through Akron Novelty Manufacturing and sold in cartons of twelve for $4.50 each (the regulars were $4); the idea being for kids to go door-to-door and sell these in order to raise money for their clubs or schools.

Board Games

There were two board games that involved advancing pieces around a board in order to win. The first was one from Transogram in 1975. The game came in a box that shows what is supposed to be Hawkeye, Houlihan, Blake, and Radar in a jeep, but looks more like Joe Namath, Carol Burnett, a guy wearing Henry's hat, and Peter Falk. Whoever they are, they're driving to get to the wounded, although that's not the objective of the game. Pieces inside the box are a board with a path, four player pieces, cards to help move your piece, a plastic helicopter, a plastic jeep, and a plastic tent in order to make the game "fun" but really just gets in the way of playing the game.

The objective, as per boardgamegeek.com, is to use the cards to advance around the board in order to obtain either the jeep, the helicopter, or both so that you can get a transfer order in order to go home and win the game. Or, if you're Henry, get shot down over the Sea of Japan. Okay, actually they don't do that part. Still, for a show about helping wounded, it seems odd that the game is all about getting away from them.

The second game, from 1981, shows figures waving to a helicopter, and to the left there are pictures of Hawkeye, Houlihan, BJ, and Klinger. Each player gets a plastic jeep to use as his or her piece, and the objective is to move from the helicopter pad to each player's home base.

The *MASH* Atari game, which had users doing things that never would have been the norm in the series. Even so, some Atari fans remember it as being a rather fun game to play.

There was also a trivia game released by Western Publisher called the *Golden Trivia Game—MASH Edition* in 1984. There were two editions of the game—one that came only with the trivia questions and answers in a green box, and one with the same cards in a larger box with a photo of the cast members on the front. The larger box came with a plastic holder for the cards and die in order to play the game with a fancy frame.

The Video Game

In 1983, we got a home video-game version of *MASH* that was released on Atari 2600, Atari 800, Colecovision, and for the Texas Instruments home computer (the Colecovision version is the rarest of the bunch). There are three games and a bonus round between them that can be played, either as one-player or against another person in two-player mode.

Game 1 has you as Hawkeye flying your helicopter against Frank Burns in his in order to pick up wounded in the forest. You must avoid the trees and missiles being fired by North Korean tanks on the ground. No doubt by this point, you've abandoned the game and returned it for your money. But if you've decided to stick it out, once thirty wounded men have been picked up, you move to the bonus round where you perform surgery and attempt to remove as much shrapnel as you can within fifteen seconds. Like the game Operation, if you touch the sides of the patient, the bonus round is over. In challenger mode, Frank gets additional points against you if you've touched the patient.

Game 2 has Colonel Potter and "his skydiving medics" jumping out of a plane without parachutes. Just like him to do that. Your job is to maneuver your helicopter so you save them before they hit the ground (yes, it is difficult to figure out how you save dropping men with a helicopter without involving the blades, but there you go). Then another bonus round of shrapnel digging.

Game 3 involves picking up wounded again, only this time it is during a cease-fire, so you don't have to worry about missiles, while the helicopter is smaller.

The game came with an illustrated cover showing people running from the camp with the post showing the destination of cities around the world and a helicopter in the background. It certainly looks much more action-packed than the game itself, but it was the early days of home video games and there were limits on what could be done in them at that point.

Donruss Bubblegum Cards

Donruss, along with Topps and Fleer, had produced trading cards for television shows since the early 1960s, including for *The Monkees*, the band KISS, and *Dukes of Hazzard*. In 1982, they released a set for *MASH*, which came with six cards and a hard piece of bubblegum (that, by god, you ate because it was there) in a green wrapper with the *MASH* logo on the front, underneath a helicopter carrying wounded (probably from the bubblegum . . . okay, okay, enough about the bubblegum).

There were sixty-six cards in the series, and it usually took several packages to get to a complete set (unless you could get your hands on a full box, which usually allowed a buyer to put together a few sets). All the photos were from the final years of the program, bypassing any photos of Trapper, Henry, Frank, and Radar. As usual for such sets, many of the photos were publicity pictures of the actors instead of scenes from particular episodes, some of which were used for the basis of the promotional glasses listed above.

View-Master Slides

If one could get bubblegum cards, then there was always the next step—View-Master slides. In the days before video-cassette players and DVDs, kids had limited choices to look back on events and shows that they loved. View-Master helped out by not only giving kids a chance to see pictures of their favorite movies, shows, and stars (the rock band KISS, for example, had a set released in the 1970s), they also were printed in a system that, when viewed with the View-Master, made the images 3-D.

In 1978, a set was released for *MASH*. The cover shows the cast from season six and included three discs in the packaging (which was either an envelope or plastic with a cardboard backing showing all three discs). With the framework of showing action scenes in 3-D, it was decided to use photos from "Major Topper," an episode that is nearly all talk and little action. (Plot: Winchester's stories annoy Hawkeye and BJ due to always topping their own, and they plan to force him to admit he's lying; meanwhile, Klinger meets a new enlisted man who actually may be crazy, and the doctors have to convince the wounded that sugar pills they're giving them are really strong pain medication.)

To help kids follow the story in the pictures, a little book is included with additional black-and-white photos from the episode and the plot written in story form with letters and numbers to help cue up the pictures on the View-Master slides. There's also a hidden word puzzle for kids to play that has the names of the characters in it.

Nothing really wrong with what you get here, but you do wish they could have picked an episode with a little more zip in the visuals.

4077th MASH Vodka with Complete Dispensing System

There's little background on this piece of merchandise that seemingly is

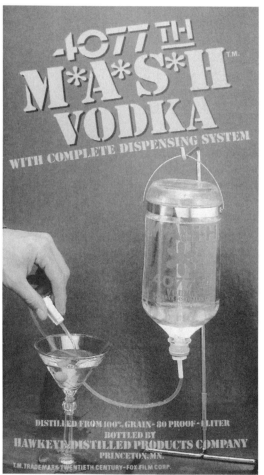

The infamous *MASH* vodka dispenser that could be set up like an IV. One of the more popular pieces of merchandise available, it instantly lost a lot of its value once someone drank the vodka enclosed in the packaging.

rare enough that everyone is selling it on eBay. The concept is not bad—there's an episode in the early years of the show where Trapper and Hawkeye share some gin from an IV drip while they shower, so why not something like that for *MASH* fans to use at parties?

The set came with a full liter bottle of "100% Grain–80 Proof" vodka, along with the stand and tubing to set up the bottle upside-down and then have vodka pouring out of the tube and making a mess. Okay, actually, if you hook it up right, it doesn't pour out until you release the valve on the tubing.

As stated, it's a neat and logical tie-in with the show. The thing is that it appears everyone in the universe bought one when it came out. The complete set with a full bottle of vodka can get a bit of cash, but otherwise the set is so common that it usually sells for rather cheap.

MASH 4077th Supply Train

Released in 1983 by Bach-mann, who has produced model train sets since 1966, the "89 Piece Electric Train set with Realistic *MASH* Compound Platform" is a completely illogical toy to connect with the series. (Yes, how often we watched Hawkeye and Trapper bumming a ride on the supply train out of the camp.) Still, the set is cool for offering fans a diorama of the 4077th. It doesn't make any sense (Look! There's the water tower that the 4077th never had!), but it's still a fascinating idea to show tents and the hospital (okay, it looks more like a barn), as well as a helicopter, a tank, and little figures of people (men, women, and children). The train is in camouflage green and brown, with the *MASH* logo slapped on the side ("No, comrade! Don't shoot at the train! It is going to the 4077th to help our wounded brothers in arms!") On the other hand, it does show the efficiency of the military, in that it goes around the camp . . . and nowhere else.

This is such a unique and odd item that it goes for a good amount of money online these days. For some, that's what matters, more than the logic of the merchandise itself.

32

Captain Tuttle

Parodies, Rip-offs, and Homages

As expected, *MASH*'s popularity automatically meant that there would be parodies and homages of the show over the years. Mostly the homages have been quick references in dialogue—such as someone referring to someone else as Radar or Hawkeye. Many shows have also done gags that refer to *MASH* episodes, such as in *The Simpsons* February 10, 2002, episode, "Half-Decent Proposal," where Marge leaves in a helicopter to see an old boyfriend and Homer has rocks in the front yard spelling out "Keep Your Clothes On." But most of these types of references to *MASH* are so quick that it would be hard to cover them all. Instead, listed below are some of the more interesting of the parodies and homages over the years.

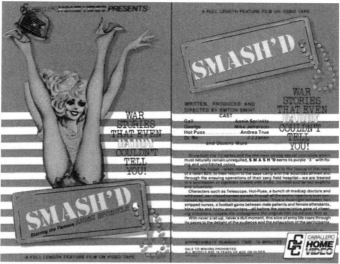

SMASH'D: The first parody film based on the movie/series was one in name only, as the film itself had little to suggest a parody of *MASH*.

Mad Magazine

For a time in the 1960s through the 1980s, one way to know you've truly made it in Hollywood is when *MAD* magazine would get around to parodying you. Such was the case with *MASH* in the October 1982 issue (No. 234), where most of the cast of *MASH* (including Trapper and Henry) are seen on the cover, drawn by famous artist Mort Drucker, around *MAD* mascot Alfred E. Neuman dressed as Radar. While there would be earlier *MASH* parodies in *MAD*, this issue was the first and only one to get a cover.

The story, entitled "M*U*S*H," written by Arnie Kogen and drawn by the amazing Jack Davis, sledgehammers the show (which was just about to air its final season) for the tendency to let "messages" override plots, and comedy in the final seasons, as well as the concerns of the series starting to repeat itself. Arnie Kogen also wrote the first parody of *MASH* in *MAD*. Back in the October 1970 issue (No. 138), Kogen and artist Angelo Torres took on the movie in a five-page strip called "M*I*S*H*M*O*S*H." Three issues later, Stan Hart would write a parody of *Catch-22* that ends with Alan Arkin's character on an operating table. Hawkeye (drawn as Donald Sutherland) and Trapper (drawn as Elliott Gould) are about to get to work but mention that the whole "War is crazy hell" plot of *Catch-22* had already been covered in the film *MASH*, "and we got here first." There was also the first parody of the series, "M*A*S*Huga" by Stan Hart and drawn by Angelo Torres in the April 1974 issue (No. 166), which concentrated on the "bad taste" aspect of comedy in war, as well as the show's growing ratings thanks to being on Saturday nights at the time (see chapter 22 for more details).

Cracked magazine, an inoffensive comic book-style parody magazine in the spirit of *MAD* also did a few *MASH* parodies over the years. Most, if not all, were collected in the September 1983 "Collector's Edition" issue called *MASH Fun Book*. This special edition featured all the previous story-length parodies—all drawn by John Severin—along with a picture game where drawings of the various characters from the show could be cut so that different images could be made.

M-U-S-H

In 1975, ABC began airing a new Saturday morning series called *Uncle Croc's Block*. The show featured Charles Nelson Reilly as Uncle Croc, a man forced to dress in a crocodile outfit as host of a kid's Saturday morning cartoon show. In other words, it was a parody of what most television stations had done since the '50s: have someone at the station put on a silly costume and

FILMATION
Presents
Children's
CARTOON FESTIVAL
M·U·S·H

U

A short-lived cartoon that parodied some elements of the series in rather vague ways. Even so, it is one of the more fondly remembered parodies by fans who remembered watching it back when it originally aired.

introduce cartoons. The show also featured Jonathan Harris (Dr. Smith from *Lost in Space*) as the director of the show trying to whip Reilly into shape, as well as various other actors appearing as parodies of similar-style television hosts.

Between all the meta of the live-action bits, there were three cartoons shown, all three of which were created by Filmation (who also produced the live-action material): *Fraidy Cat* (about a cat who is down to his last life and has the ghosts of his previous lives causing life-threatening problems), *Wacky and Packy* (a caveman and pachyderm who wind up in the present), and *M-U-S-H*.

M-U-S-H stood for "Mangy Unwanted Shabby Hounds" and involved a group of dogs, dressed like Canadian Mounties, who live and work at an outpost in "Upper Sibonia," which was a snow-covered land (hence, mush as in what is said to sled dogs). Most of the characters have names similar to their counterparts on *MASH*—Bullseye, Trooper Yoe, Major Sideburns, Cold Lips, Sonar, and Colonel Flake—and the emphasis was on storylines where Major Sideburns tried to get Bullseye and Trooper Yoe sent away, but that's about where the comparison ends. The fort was not a medical unit (or much of anything else, actually), although there was a big female dog named Hilda who was also a nurse.

Uncle Croc's Block started out as an hour show and did so poorly that it was reduced to a half-hour midway through its run before finally being canceled in February 1976. There were only sixteen episodes of the series made, but the cartoons produced were only six minutes long, and *M-U-S-H* had the most produced out of the three, with thirty episodes.

In 1978, Filmation packaged a number of short-lived series made for Saturday mornings together into 104 half-hour episodes for five-days-a-week broadcast by stations around the country. The shows, which included

M-U-S-H, along with *Lassie's Rescue Rangers* and *The New Adventures of Gilligan*, used openings that mainly featured Filmation's Groovie Goolies, and the show was called *The Groovie Goolies and Friends*. Only five of the *M-U-S-H* cartoons made it to the syndicated package.

Nine *M-U-S-H* shorts were later released on VHS by Intervision Video in 1988.

Porn

Pornographic movies had become in vogue by the early 1970s, to the point where they were considered in some ways respectable. Not by much, but there seems to be a general sense that, as long as everyone involved filming and watching the movies were not causing anyone problems, where was the harm? And with that acceptance came an opportunity to do more than just show various sex acts. They could structure stories around them, perhaps something even of intellectual value.

But in most cases, comedy was the route taken, which was understandable as most people attending such films really were not there to learn anything about themselves or see how people actually could act when not "acting." To many, porn movies were a gag—a laugh—and so many of the films of the 1970s, if plot was included, stuck with taking it far less than seriously. And parodies of television shows and movies were easy targets for such films. *MASH* became an easy target for such parodies, although rarely even approaching a successful result.

The simplest method was to parody the title of the show, such as the sketch "T*R*A*S*H" in the film *Naughty Network* (1981). The sketch itself had nothing really to do with the show, but just the twist on the name was supposed to supply all the guffaws there. This is somewhat true of the first parody as well, *SMASH'D* (1976), which starred famed porn actress Annie Sprinkle as Gail, a nurse who meets up with some old comrades, and they reminisce about their times fighting and doing other things in the jungle. It features Andrea True as "Hot Puss," and that and the title are pretty much the only connections you'll find with *MASH*. The poster art did try to sucker people into the "art theaters" with the promise of a full-on parody of the series, with blurbs stating that "It's *MASH* with an X" and exclaiming that it contains "War Stories that even *MASH* couldn't Tell You!" The poster art is also a vague attempt at capturing a bit of the *MASH* spirit by showing a woman's legs up in the air with a helmet on top of the right leg, just as the

The poster for the X-rated parody of *MASH*, *Nurses of the 407th*. The pornographic film had surprising amounts of production value, which raised it over that of other pornographic parodies done over the years.

helmet sits on the "peace sign on legs" image used for the film. Everything else about the movie itself, however, is strictly standard sex acts in military dressing (or out of it) with the parody title slapped on it.

At the other extreme of parody is *Not MASH XXX*, which was released in 2010. The video is one of a number released over the past few years that feature a growing trend of taking classic films, cartoons, movies, and anything else from our youth and turning it into porn as a form of "parody."

Such videos have titles that use the real names of the various subjects being parodied with either "Not" or "This Ain't" added at the beginning, and character names are, surprisingly, the same as in the originals—for example, *Not MASH XXX* features a Hawkeye, Trapper, Houlihan, etc. ("Hot Puss" in *MASH'D* is high-comedy thinking in comparison with what you get in *Not MASH XXX*.) Costuming and sets are along the lines of a junior high school production, and the comedy is grade school at best. Of course, no one bothering to watch these things cares about all that, but for a *MASH* fan who may be curious, such aspects may be more important than the sex.

It did have a plot at least—Hawkeye and Trapper try to get Radar laid—which is more than can be said for the others listed here, even the best of the bunch, *N*u*r*s*e*s of the 407th* (1983). While it lacks in plot, *N*u*r*s*e*s of the 407th* is like Stanley Kubrick compared to the other porn films on the level of production value alone. Establishing shots of the camp looks amazingly close to the Fox Ranch set (in fact, one could wonder if maybe . . . nah). Costumes and interior sets (save the O.R.) look close to those of *MASH* as well, and there's even a scene with bombs going off and a truck turning over into a ditch—things that leave you wondering if you've wandered into a regular film . . . until the sex starts, of course.

The film stars Jessie St. James (a popular porn star) as Captain Janet "Hot Hips" Henderson (well, that's still better than "Hot Puss"), and Paul Thomas as Captain Jack "Jaybird" Anderson. There isn't much plot, but the emphasis is on comedy even more than the porn, making it probably the best of the porn parodies listed here, as it does what such films do best—yes, there's sex, but there's also the underlying acknowledgment that it's all rather stupid.

Family Guy, "Fifteen Minutes of Shame"

In this April 25, 2000, episode of the animated comedy series, the Griffins agree to appear on a reality show, which eventually decides to kill off Meg in order to boost ratings. This is done in a parody of the famous ending scene in "Abyssinia, Henry" from season three of *MASH*, with the family in the *MASH* O.R. performing surgery as their dog, Brian (dressed as Radar), arrives to tell them that Meg's plane was shot down over the Sea of Japan and there were no survivors.

Futurama, "War Is the H Word"

In an episode of this futuristic animated series, which aired November 25, 2000, Fry, his robot friend Bender, and (the much smarter) Leela go to a planet as part of the Earth Army to battle aliens that look like bouncing balls. Bender is hurt in battle and sent to a field hospital, which is where the *MASH* parody comes into play. As Bender arrives, an announcement is made over the P.A. system, using the same actor, Todd Sussman, from the *MASH* series. The robotic surgeon, iHawk, talks and acts like Hawkeye Pierce (and comes with a switch that allows him to move instantly from being irreverent to maudlin).

30 Rock, "Kidney Now!"

This series, which is based around the making of a comedy show, featured Alan Alda in several episodes as a character named Milton Greene, who is an outsider to the show. In the episode "Kidney Now!" another character, Tracy Jordan (played by Tracy Morgan), has a breakdown in front of Greene about an incident in high school where he was too scared to dissect a frog and backed out of it with a story about a baby. As Jordan exclaims that "there was not baby! I was chicken!" Greene responds by saying, "A guy crying about a chicken and a baby? I thought this was a comedy show."

Of course, having Alan Alda being the one to question the use of a baby and a chicken in a comedy show immediately recalls Hawkeye's storyline in the *MASH* finale, "Goodbye, Farewell and Amen," and demonstrates that Alda could joke about such the storyline that has been a basis of contention with fans ever since.

TV Guide with *Scrubs* Homage

The January 24, 1976, edition of *TV Guide* featured a cover for *MASH* that shows Hawkeye sitting in a chair, with BJ behind him and Potter standing stage right. All are wearing bathrobes, and the famous sign showing directions to various spots on the globe is behind Potter. In October 2006, three members of the medical comedy show *Scrubs* would reenact the cover for *TV Guide*. Zach Braff (who played J. D. on the program) took Hawkeye's seat, Donald Faison (Turk) in BJ's position, and John C. McGinley (authority figure Perry Cox) in Potter's position. *Scrubs*, incidentally, was a comedy program that had dramatic moments much like *MASH*, and featured no laugh track.

Community, "Investigative Journalism"

In the January 14, 2010, episode of this comedy series set at a community college, one of the character, Abed (Danny Pudi), compares another, Jeff (Joel McHale), to Hawkeye. The comparison leads to Jeff starting to dress and act like Hawkeye while Abed takes on the look of Radar. The episode ends with a parody of the common late-season freeze-frame shot, along with (fake) credits in the typeface used by *MASH* and a bit of the closing theme song from the series.

IBM Ads

For years, IBM had used the image of Charlie Chaplin as their mascot in ads for their computer systems, but in 1987 the company decided it needed a fresher image to help promote their line of personal computers (with a rumored $47 million being spent on the ad campaign). In the magazine ad and series of commercials, the cast of *MASH* appear in modern-day dress as characters working at an office where concerns about personal computers are addressed. Gary Burghoff, who had been doing ads for BP (British Petroleum), was typically a major figure in these ads, while others played more supportive roles, always as fellow workers in the office. Of the main cast, only McLean Stevenson, Mike Farrell, and David Ogden Stiers did not appear, with Alan Alda having to hold out until 1988 due to a contract as a spokesperson for Atari that didn't end until that year.

Fans and others both noticed one thing in particular about these ads for IBM: none of the actors appeared as their *MASH* characters, although some had characteristics similar to those of their television roles (Burghoff being the anticipating, smart one, Linville as the somewhat prissy upper-management type, Morgan as the cantankerous leader). The show had become so ingrained into the thinking of American culture that the actors didn't have to appear in green, or in a camp, or specifically make reference to the program—simply placing them together (one by one or all in a group) was enough to let the audience make the connection. These ads, and the homages listed above, trade in on what had become common knowledge in popular culture—everyone everywhere knew *MASH*.

33

Gentlemen, Take My Advice

In 1972, *MASH* went on the air for CBS. By the time it was off the air in 1983, it had been involved in radical changes within television programming in America. *MASH*, along with series like *All in the Family* and *The Mary Tyler Moore Show*, had shown that adult topics like violence, sex, politics, and war could be featured in shows geared toward adults. Better yet, they could say more about the human condition than the shows that came before them. Such shows also credited audiences with not being as easily distracted or needing to be led by the nose as the networks thought they did. Viewers could figure things out for themselves, and while once in a while such programming would not do what was assumed, in the long run people appreciated the creativity of the people working on such shows to do the unpredictable. (People may have been mad about Henry Blake dying, but there's no denying that it is one of the defining moments in television comedy history.)

MASH would also break out of the mode that said comedies needed to have laugh tracks, which are not as common today. And, moreover, that dramatic series could be funny as much as comedy series could be dramatic, and moments of lightness can sometimes drive a heavier message home than always pressing the "drama" button in a program. Shows like *Hill Street Blues* and *ER* and *The West Wing* could do the deep dramatic stuff, but they also picked up on the comedic possibilities that *MASH* proved could work when mixed with drama.

In fact, in today's market it is hard to say whether some programs are comedies or dramas. Nor is there a need to have to prove to be one or the other anymore. Gene Reynolds and Larry Gelbart wanted to do a dramatic comedy series, and they got results that changed the way we as viewers accept shows today.

The cast in serious discussion at a press conference during the final days of filming on the series. *MASH* had proven itself to be a success at the time, but could it be so today?

But could it work today? If their creators had not come along, could someone take *MASH* and make it work? In all probability, any attempt today would turn to cable, or such as on Netflix or Amazon, where there is more freedom to show the blood and other less family-oriented aspects that the novel had demonstrated. In today's climate, someone could readily do "Shaking Sammy" and get away with it. On the other side of that, however, we could have just as easily gotten the Hawkeye and Trapper of the novel who could come off as mean-spirited and with no arc to fulfill, rather than the men from the television version who were not perfect and had to be a little more down-to-earth.

Today, you could make *MASH* like the novel (and perhaps someday someone will try to do so), but in a way that would lessen what we got from all the individuals who worked on the series. H. Richard Hornberger gave us the genesis, but many others tinkered with the material and the characters and made it something even better. There's really is a good reason that the series is better remembered than the novel and even the movie, no matter how great those are—*MASH* as a series was right for its time and is still watchable today. Perhaps it wasn't always perfect, and everyone has their favorite periods of the show, but it really was a crowning achievement on television.

Will there ever be another *MASH*? Perhaps the question should be, will there ever be a program that changes television and the public's perception of what we can have in a program as much as *MASH* did?

One can only hope.

34

Earning That Purple Heart

Awards

hile those working on the program as well as the series would be nominated for a number of awards, below only the winners are listed:

1973

- American Cinema Editors, The Eddie for Best Edited Episode from a Television Series—Fred W. Berger for "Bananas, Crackers, and Nuts"
- Directors Guild of America Award for Outstanding Directorial Achievement in Comedy Series—Gene Reynolds, Wesley J. McAfee, Ronald J. Schwary for pilot episode.
- Writers Guild of America Award for Best Episodic Comedy—Larry Gelbart for "Chief Surgeon Who?"

1974

- American Cinema Editors, The Eddie for Best Edited Episode from a Television Series—Fred W. Berger and Stanford Tischler for "The Trial of Henry Blake"
- Directors Guild of America Award for Outstanding Directorial Achievement in Comedy Series—Gene Reynolds, Red Butcher, Leonard S. Smith Jr., and George R. Batcheller Jr. for "Deal Me Out"
- Emmy Award for Outstanding Comedy Series
- Emmy Award for Best Lead Actor in a Comedy Series—Alan Alda
- Emmy Award for Best Directing in Comedy—Jackie Cooper for "Carry on Hawkeye"

- Emmy Award for Best Actor of the Year in a Series—Alan Alda
- Golden Globe for Best Supporting Actor—Television—McLean Stevenson

1975

- American Cinema Editors, The Eddie for Best Edited Episode from a Television Series—Fred W. Berger and Stanford Tischler for "A Full, Rich Day"
- Directors Guild of America Award for Outstanding Directorial Achievement in Comedy Series—Hy Averback, Red Butcher, Leonard S. Smith Jr., and George R. Batcheller Jr. for "Alcoholics Unanimous"
- Emmy Award for Outstanding Directing in a Comedy Series—Gene Reynolds for "O.R." (all nominations in this category were for *MASH* this year)
- Golden Globe for Best Actor in a Leading Role—Musical or Comedy—Alan Alda
- Peabody Award for series
- People's Choice Award for Favorite Male Television Performer—Alan Alda
- WGA Award for Best Episodic Comedy—Larry Gelbart and Laurence Marks for "O.R."

1976

- Directors Guild of America Award for Outstanding Directorial Achievement in Comedy Series—Hy Averback, Red Butcher, Leonard S. Smith Jr., and George R. Batcheller Jr. for "Bombed"
- Emmy Award for Outstanding Directing in a Comedy Series—Gene Reynolds for "Welcome to Korea"
- Golden Globe for Best Actor in a Leading Role—Musical or Comedy—Alan Alda
- Humanitas Prize for 30 Minute Network or Syndicated Television—Larry Gelbart for "The Interview"
- WGA Award for Best Episodic Comedy—Everett Greenbaum, Jim Fritzell, and Larry Gelbart for "Welcome to Korea"

Trapper (Wayne Rogers) and Hawkeye (Alan Alda) investigate a bomb in the camp. Fortunately for the series, bombing was never a thing the production team and cast had to worry much about.

1977

- Directors Guild of America Award for Outstanding Directorial Achievement in Comedy Series—Alan Alda, Ted Butcher, David Hawks, and Lisa Hallas-Gottlieb for "Dear Sigmund"

- Emmy Award for Outstanding Continuing Performance by a Supporting Actor in a Comedy Series—Gary Burghoff
- Emmy Award for Outstanding Directing in a Comedy Series—Alan Alda for "Dear Sigmund"
- WGA Award for Best Episodic Comedy—Alan Alda for "Dear Sigmund"

1978

- American Cinema Editors, The Eddie for Best Edited Episode from a Television Series—Larry L. Mills and Stanford Tischler for "Fade Out, Fade In"
- People's Choice Award for Favorite Television Comedy Series

1979

- Emmy Award for Outstanding Writing in a Comedy or Comedy-Variety or Music Series—Alan Alda for "Inga"
- People's Choice Award for Favorite Television Comedy Series
- WGA Award for Best Episodic Comedy—Gary David Goldberg for "Baby, It's Cold Outside"

1980

- American Cinema Editors, The Eddie for Best Edited Episode from a Television Series—Larry L. Mills and Stanford Tischler for "The Yalu Brick Road"
- Emmy Award for Outstanding Supporting Actor in a Comedy or Variety or Music Series—Harry Morgan
- Emmy Award for Outstanding Supporting Actress in a Comedy or Variety or Music Series—Loretta Swit
- Golden Globe for Best Actor in a Leading Role—Musical or Comedy—Alan Alda
- Humanitas Prize for 30 Minute Network or Syndicated Television—Alan Alda (teleplay and story) and James Jay Rubinfier (story) for "Dreams"
- People's Choice Award for Favorite Television Comedy Series
- WGA Award for Best Episodic Comedy—Thad Mumford and Dan Wilcox for "Are You Now, Margaret?" (tied with *Taxi*)

Cast photo from the last years of the program.

1981

- Golden Globe for Best Actor in a Leading Role—Musical or Comedy—Alan Alda
- People's Choice Award for Favorite Television Comedy Series
- WGA Award for Best Episodic Comedy—Dennis Koenig (teleplay and story) and Gene Reynolds (story) for "Heal Thyself"

1982

- Directors Guild of America Award for Outstanding Directorial Achievement in Comedy Series—Alan Alda, David Hawks, and Cathy Kinsock for "The Life You Save"
- Emmy Award for Outstanding Lead Actor in a Comedy Series—Alan Alda

- Emmy Award for Outstanding Supporting Actress in a Comedy or Variety or Music Series—Loretta Swit
- Golden Globe for Best Actor in a Leading Role—Musical or Comedy—Alan Alda
- Golden Globe for Best Television Series—Musical or Comedy
- Humanitas Prize for 30 Minute Network or Syndicated Television—David Pollock and Elias Davis for "Where There's a Will, There's a War"
- People's Choice Award for Favorite Television Comedy Series

1983

- Directors Guild of America Award for Outstanding Directorial Achievement in Comedy Series—Alan Alda, David Hawks, and Cathy Kinsock for "Where There's a Will, There's a War"
- Golden Globe for Best Actor in a Leading Role—Musical or Comedy—Alan Alda
- Humanitas Prize for 30 Minute Network or Syndicated Television—David Pollock and Elias Davis for "Who Knew?"
- People's Choice Award for Favorite Television Comedy Series

1998

- Online Film & Television Association—for OFTA TV Hall of Fame for series

2003

- TV Land Awards for Classic TV Doctor of the Year—Alan Alda
- TV Land Awards for Drama Theme Song You Can't Get Out of Your Head

2006

- TV Land Awards for Favorite Series Finale

2007

- TV Land Awards for Series Finale You Had a Party to Watch

2009

- TV Land Awards—Impact Award to cast and crew of *MASH*

2010

- Television Critics Association Awards—Heritage Award—for series

Appendix

For Your Dining and Dancing Pleasure

MASH Websites

A s can be expected, a lot of details about *MASH* and especially episode guides can be found on the Internet. Besides details on such sites as Wikipedia and the Internet Movie Database (IMDB), the following are popular pages for *MASH* fans:

https://boardgamegeek.com/boardgame/16521/mash-game
http://www.jazzwax.com/2008/10/interview-joh-5.html
http://www.mash4077tv.com/features/nurses_opening/
http://www.thedailybeast.com/articles/2014/03/13/ robert-duvall-discusses-his-storied-career-a-night-in-old-mexico-and-why-he-s-ditching-the-gop .html)
http://thisisinfamous.com/interview-fred-hammer-williamson : "Interview: Fred 'The Hammer' Williamson," September 19, 2013.
http://www.whitewolfzone.co.uk/pflug1.htm

Fan Pages

MASH4077TV.com—http://www.mash4077tv.com
The *Monster MASH* Wiki—http://mash.wikia.com/wiki/Main_Page
After *MASH* Blog—http://aftermash.blogspot.com
Best Care Anywhere—http://www.bestcareanywhere.net

Official Pages

Alan Alda—http://www.alanalda.com

Wayne Rogers—http://waynerogers.webs.com

Loretta Swit—http://www.switheart.com

Mike Farrell—http://www.mikefarrell.org

Kellye Nakahara—http://www.kellyesart.com/bio.html

Malibu Creek State Park (Fox Ranch)—http://www.malibucreekstatepark.org/
  MASH.html

Ken Levine (writer/producer)—http://kenlevine.blogspot.com

Selected Bibliography

Alda, Alan. "On the Front Lines with Larry Gelbart." September 14, 2009. http://articles.latimes.com/2009/sep/14/entertainment/et-alda-gelbart14.

Alda, Alan. *Never Have Your Dog Stuffed.* New York: Random House, 2005.

Alda, Alan, and Arlene Alda. *The Last Days of MASH.* Morris Plains, NJ: Unicorn Publishing House, 1983.

Apel, Otto F. M.D., and Pat Apel. *MASH: An Army Surgeon in Korea.* The University Press of Kentucky, 1998.

Armstrong, Charles K. "Korean History and Political Geography." http://asiasociety.org/korean-history-and-political-geography.

Burghoff, Gary. *To MASH and Back: My Life in Poems and Songs (That Nobody Ever Wanted to Publish).* Albany, GA: BearManor Media, 2009.

"Catch-All-22." *Mad* magazine, March 1971, No. 14.

Christopher, William, and Barbara Christopher. *Mixed Blessings.* Nashville, TN. Abingdon Press, 1989.

Cowdrey, Albert E. "*MASH* v. MASH: The Mobile Army Surgical Hospital." *Medical Heritage,* Volume 1, Issue 1, 1985.

Davidson, Bill. "C*L*A*S*H." *TV Guide,* Volume 24 No. 4.

Davidson, Bill. "Vintage Year for Wayne." *TV Guide,* Volume 22 No. 44, 1974.

Farr, Jamie. *Just Farr Fun.* Clearwater, FL: Eubanks/Donizetti, 1994.

Farrell, Mike. *Just Call Me Mike: A Journey to Actor and Activist.* New York: Akashic Books, 2007.

Farrell, Mike. *Of Mule and Man.* New York: Akashic Books, 2009.

Fehrenbach, T. R. *This Kind of War.* Dulles, VA: Brassey's, 1963.

Gelbart, Larry. *Laughing Matters.* New York: Random House, 1998.

Halberstam, David. *The Coldest Winter.* New York: Hyperion, 2007.

Hano, Arnold. "Nobody Ever Calls Him Dave." *TV Guide,* Volume 26, No. 8.

Hastings, Max. *The Korean War.* New York: Simon & Schuster, 1987.

Heinz, W. C. "The Man with a Life in His Hands: in the Drama of an Operating Room a Great Surgeon Pits His Skill Against Cancer and Makes the Ultimate Decision." *LIFE* magazine, January 20, 1961.

Kalter, Suzy. *The Complete Book of MASH.* New York: Harry N. Abrams, 1984.

Karp, Alan. *The Films of Robert Altman.* London: Scarecrow Press, 1981.

King, Booker and Ismail Jatoi. "The Mobile Army Surgical Hospital (MASH): A Military and Surgical Legacy." *Journal of the National Medical Association*, Vol. 97, No. 6, May 2005.

Lardner, Ring Jr. *I'd Hate Myself in the Morning: A Memoir*. New York: Thunder's Mouth Press/Nation Books, 2000.

Marble, Sanders. "Forward Surgery and Combat Hospitals: The Origins of the MASH." *Journal of the History of Medicine*, Vol. 69, January 2014.

Maxwell, Jeff. *Secrets of the MASH Mess: The Lost Recipes of Private Igor*. Nashville, TN: Cumberland House Publishing, 1997.

Medved, Harry, and Michael Medved. *The Golden Turkey Awards*. New York: Warner Books, 1980.

Neuwirth, Allan. *They'll Never Put That on the Air: An Oral History of Taboo-Breaking TV Comedy*. New York: Allworth Press, 2006.

Reiss, David. *MASH: The Exclusive, Inside Story of T.V.'s Most Popular Show*. Indianapolis: Bobbs-Merrill, 1980.

Rogers, Wayne. *Make Your Own Rules: A Renegade Guide to Unconventional Success*. With Josh Young. New York: AMACOM, 2011.

Sandler, Stanley. *The Korean War: an Encyclopedia*. New York: Garland Publishing, Inc., 1995.

Solomonson, Ed, and Mark O'Neill. *TV's MASH: The Ultimate Guide Book*. Albany, GA: BearManor Media, 2009.

Stein, Linda. "Altman Is Determined to Make Pix Own Way." *Film/TV Daily*, March 3, 1970.

Sung-ok Kim. *The Unending Korean War: A Social History*. Larkspur, CA: Tamal Vista Publications, 2000.

Swit, Loretta. *A Needlepoint Scrapbook*. New York: Doubleday, 1986.

Ward, Nathan. "A Life in the Loser's Dressing Room." *American Heritage*, August/September 2004, Vol. 55, Issue 4.

Wexman, Virginia Wright, and Gretchen Bisplinghoff. *Robert Altman: A Guide to References and Resources*. Boston: G. K. Hall, 1984.

Whitney, Dwight. "Being a Star Is a Nuisance." *TV Guide*, Volume 25, No. 23, 1977.

Zuckoff, Mitchell. *Robert Altman: The Oral Biography*. New York: Borzoi Books, 2009.

Wilson, John M. "No Time to Think About the Future." *TV Guide*, Volume 24, No. 35, 1976.

Index

THE FAQ SERIES

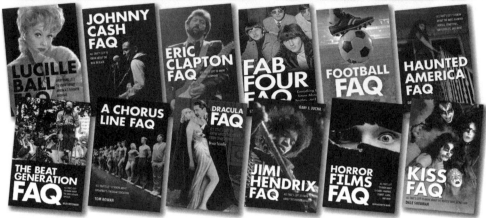

Prices, contents, and availability
subject to change without notice.

Morrissey FAQ
by D. McKinney
Backbeat Books
978-1-4803-9448-3............ $24.99

Nirvana FAQ
by John D. Luerssen
Backbeat Books
978-1-61713-450-0............. $24.99

Pink Floyd FAQ
by Stuart Shea
Backbeat Books
978-0-87930-950-3............$19.99

Elvis Films FAQ
by Paul Simpson
Applause Books
978-1-55783-858-2............. $24.99

Elvis Music FAQ
by Mike Eder
Backbeat Books
978-1-61713-049-6............. $24.99

Prog Rock FAQ
by Will Romano
Backbeat Books
978-1-61713-587-3............... $24.99

Pro Wrestling FAQ
by Brian Solomon
Backbeat Books
978-1-61713-599-6............... $29.99

Rush FAQ
by Max Mobley
Backbeat Books
978-1-61713-451-7................. $24.99

Saturday Night Live FAQ
by Stephen Tropiano
Applause Books
978-1-55783-951-0............. $24.99

Prices, contents, and availability
subject to change without notice.

Seinfeld FAQ
by Nicholas Nigro
Applause Books
978-1-55783-857-5............... $24.99

Sherlock Holmes FAQ
by Dave Thompson
Applause Books
978-1-4803-3149-5............. $24.99

The Smiths FAQ
by John D. Luerssen
Backbeat Books
978-1-4803-9449-0........... $24.99

Soccer FAQ
by Dave Thompson
Backbeat Books
978-1-61713-598-9............... $24.99

The Sound of Music FAQ
by Barry Monush
Applause Books
978-1-4803-6043-3............ $27.99

South Park FAQ
by Dave Thompson
Applause Books
978-1-4803-5064-9........... $24.99

Bruce Springsteen FAQ
by John D. Luerssen
Backbeat Books
978-1-61713-093-9...............$22.99

Star Trek FAQ
(Unofficial and Unauthorized)
by Mark Clark
Applause Books
978-1-55783-792-9...............$19.99

Star Trek FAQ 2.0
(Unofficial and Unauthorized)
by Mark Clark
Applause Books
978-1-55783-793-6................$22.99

Star Wars FAQ
by Mark Clark
Applause Books
978-1-4803-6018-1............. $24.99

Quentin Tarantino FAQ
by Dale Sherman
Applause Books
978-1-4803-5588-0........... $24.99

Three Stooges FAQ
by David J. Hogan
Applause Books
978-1-55783-788-2...............$22.99

The Who FAQ
by Mike Segretto
Backbeat Books
978-1-4803-6103-4........... $24.99

The Wizard of Oz FAQ
by David J. Hogan
Applause Books
978-1-4803-5062-5............ $24.99

The X-Files FAQ
by John Kenneth Muir
Applause Books
978-1-4803-6974-0............ $24.99

Neil Young FAQ
by Glen Boyd
Backbeat Books
978-1-61713-037-3.................$19.99

HAL•LEONARD®
PERFORMING ARTS
PUBLISHING GROUP

FAQ.halleonardbooks.com

0815